Lecture Notes in Computer Science 7991

Commenced Publication in 1973
Founding and Former Series Editors:
Gerhard Goos, Juris Hartmanis, and Jan van Leeuwen

For further volumes:
http://www.springer.com/series/7408

Antonio Cerone · Donatella Persico
Sara Fernandes · Alexeis Garcia-Perez
Panagiotis Katsaros · Siraj Ahmed Shaikh
Ioannis Stamelos (Eds.)

Information Technology and Open Source: Applications for Education, Innovation, and Sustainability

SEFM 2012 Satellite Events,
InSuEdu, MoKMaSD, and OpenCert
Thessaloniki, Greece, October 1–2, 2012
Revised Selected Papers

 Springer

Editors

Antonio Cerone
Sara Fernandes
United Nations University
Macau SAR
China

Alexeis Garcia-Perez
Siraj Ahmed Shaikh
Coventry University
Coventry
UK

Donatella Persico
Consiglio Nazionale delle Ricerche
Genoa
Italy

Panagiotis Katsaros
Ioannis Stamelos
Aristotle University of Thessaloniki
Thessaloniki
Greece

ISSN 0302-9743
ISSN 1611-3349 (electronic)
ISBN 978-3-642-54337-1
ISBN 978-3-642-54338-8 (eBook)
DOI 10.1007/978-3-642-54338-8
Springer Heidelberg New York Dordrecht London

Library of Congress Control Number: 2014932690

LNCS Sublibrary: SL2 – Programming and Software Engineering

Printed on acid-free paper

Springer is part of Springer Science+Business Media (www.springer.com)

Preface

This volume contains the proceedings of the three satellite events of the 10th International Conference on Software Engineering and Formal Methods (SEFM 2012), which was held during October 1–5, 2012, in Thessaloniki, Greece:

InSuEdu 2012

First International Symposium on Innovation and Sustainability in Education, held on October 1, 2012;

MoKMaSD 2012

First International Symposium on Modelling and Knowledge Management for Sustainable Development, held on October 2, 2012;

OpenCert 2012

6th International Workshop on Foundations and Techniques for Open Source Software Certification, held on October 2, 2012;

The SEFM Conference and its three satellite events were hosted by the University of Sheffield International Faculty, CITY College, and the South East Research Centre (SEERC), under the auspices of the Macedonia Thrace Chapter of the Greek Computer Society.

The title of this volume, *Information Technology and Open Source: Applications for Education, Innovation, and Sustainability,* reflects the theme shared by the three events: the use of information and communication technology (ICT) and open source software (OSS) as tools to foster and support education, innovation, and sustainability.

The First International Symposium on Innovation and Sustainability in Education aimed to bring together educators, researchers, and policy-makers who are interested in investigating innovative and sustainable models, methodologies, and tools for any level of education. This proceedings volume includes a paper co-authored by the InSuEdu 2012 Program Co-chairs, which provides a *founding manifesto* for the symposium. Among the 16 papers submitted to the symposium, the InSuEdu 2012 Program Committee selected eight regular papers and two short papers, which were presented at the symposium and are included in this proceedings volume. All papers were reviewed by at least three Program Committee members. The program also included a keynote talk by Grainne Conole, University of Leicester, UK, titled "New Ecologies and Trajectories of Learning." The keynote talk provided an overview of new technologies and how they can be used to promote different pedagogical approaches. It considered the implications of these for learning, teaching, and research. The talk argued that we are seeing the emergence of a new dynamic learning ecology, with learners and teachers interacting in increasingly sophisticated ways with technologies. It provided examples of new emergent patterns of user behavior and new business models, which blur the boundaries between formal and informal learning. Finally, it presented a new learning design methodology that aims to help practitioners make better design decisions that are pedagogically effective and harness the affordances of new technologies.

The First International Symposium on Modelling and Knowledge Management for Sustainable Development aimed to bring together practitioners and researchers from academia, industry, governmental and nongovernmental organizations to present research results and exchange experience, ideas, and solutions for modelling and analyzing complex systems and using knowledge management strategies, technology, and systems in various domain areas, including economy, governance, health, biology, ecology, climate and poverty reduction, that address problems of sustainable development. This proceedings volume includes a short paper co-authored by the MoK-MaSD 2012 Program Co-chairs, which provides a brief introduction to the motivations and aim of the symposium. Among the five papers submitted to the symposium, the MoKMaSD 2012 Program Committee selected one regular paper and three short papers, which were presented at the symposium and are included in this proceedings volume. All papers have been reviewed by at least three Program Committee members. The program also included a keynote talk by Corrado Priami, COSBI, Italy, titled "Algorithmic Systems Ecology". In the keynote talk, a novel computing approach to model and simulate complex ecological systems was presented that can help unravel the fragility of food webs in natural ecosystems. New insights were given by adopting modelling technologies that take concurrent interactions (e.g., plant-pollinator; predator-prey; host-parasite) between species into account, using COSBI language for stochastic dynamics. The modelling and simulation framework were presented by relying on real case studies. This proceedings volume includes an invited paper titled "Algorithmic Systems Ecology: Experiments on Multiple Interaction Types and Patches", co-authored by the keynote speaker and based on the content of the keynote talk.

The 6th International Workshop on Foundations and Techniques for Open Source Software Certification was the 2012 edition of a well-established event whose previous five editions since 2007 have been successfully held in Braga (Portugal), Milan (Italy), York (UK), Pisa (Italy), and Montevideo (Uruguay). This workshop provides a unique venue for advancing the state of the art in the analysis and assurance of open source software with an ultimate aim of achieving certification and standards. The dramatic growth in open source software over recent years has provided for a fertile ground for fundamental research and demonstrative case studies. Over the years, OpenCert has attracted papers from a range of domains including certification to security and safety analysis, in areas as diverse as railways, aviation, and the open source developers community. The current edition of the workshop equally attracted a diverse set of papers tackling themes ranging from migration of legacy Web applications to using open source software for electronic health records to certifying Android applications. A total of seven papers, five regular papers and two short papers, were submitted to the current edition of the workshop, all of which were found worthy of publication.

We are grateful to the International Institute for Software Technology of the United Nations University (UNU-IIST), Macau, SAR China, for sponsoring the two keynote speakers of InSuEdu 2012 and MoKMaSD 2012. We are also grateful to all members of the Program Committees of the three satellite events, to the Organizing and Steering Committees of SEFM, and to all referees for their timely hard work. Our special thanks go to George Eleftherakis, who worked very hard to coordinate the conference and the satellite events, and to Stefan Gruner, who actively contributed to setting up the satellite events and their publication policy. Finally, we would like to thank all authors and all participants of the three satellite events.

August 2013

Antonio Cerone
Donatella Persico
Sara Fernandes
Alexeis Garcia-Perez
Panagiotis Katsaros
Siraj Ahmed Shaikh
Ioannis Stamelos

Organization

SEFM 2012 Workshop Co-chairs

Sara Fernandes   United Nations University, UNU-IIST, Macau SAR, UN/China
Panagiotis Katsaros Aristotle University of Thessaloniki, Greece

InSuEdu 2012 Program Co-chairs

Antonio Cerone   United Nations University, UNU-IIST, Macau SAR, UN/China
Donatella Persico   Istituto per le Tecnologie Didattiche, Consiglio Nazionale delle
                    Ricerche, Italy

InSuEdu 2012 Program Committee

Luis Barbosa	Universidade do Minho, Portugal
Leonor Barroca	The Open University, UK
Marco Bettoni	FFHS - Fernfachhochschule Schweiz, Switzerland
Stefania Bocconi	EC-JRC Institute for Prospective Technological Studies (IPTS), EU/Spain
Jonathan P. Bowen	Museophile Limited, Macau SAR, UN/China
Daniel Burgos	International University of La Rioja, Spain
Antonio Cerone	United Nations University, UNU-IIST, Macau SAR, UN/China
Brock Craft	London Knowledge Lab, UK
Fred De Vries	Open Universiteit, Netherlands
Carlos Delgado Kloos	Universidad Carlos III de Madrid, Spain
Stavros Demetriadis	Aristotle University of Thessaloniki, Greece
Yannis Dimitriadis	University of Valladolid, Spain
Gabriella Dodero	Free University of Bolzano, Italy
Claudio Dondi	SCIENTER, Italy
George Eleftherakis	CITY International Faculty, University of Sheffield, Greece
Elsa Estevez	United Nations University, UNU-IIST, Macau SAR, UN/China
Simon Fong	University of Macau, Macau SAR, China
Patrizia Ghislandi	University of Trento, Italy
Dimitris Gouscos	University of Athens, Greece
Stylianos Hatzipanagos	King's College London, UK
Lynne Hunt	University of Southern Queensland, Australia

Panagiotis Kampylis	EC-JRC Institute for Prospective Technological Studies (IPTS), EU/Spain
Ioannis Kazanidis	TEIKAV, Greece
Maria Beatrice Ligorio	University of Bari, Italy
Allison Littlejohn	Glasgow Caledonian University, UK
Stefania Manca	Istituto per le Tecnologie Didattiche, Consiglio Nazionale delle Ricerche, Italy
Andreas Meiszner	United Nations University, UNU-MERIT, UN/The Netherlands
Yishay Mor	Open University, UK
Paul Birevu Muyinda	Makerere University, Uganda
Pantelis M. Papadopoulos	Aristotle University of Thessaloniki, Greece
Carlo Perrotta	FutureLab and London Knowledge Lab, UK
Donatella Persico	Istituto per le Tecnologie Didattiche, Consiglio Nazionale delle Ricerche, Italy
Francesca Pozzi	Istituto per le Tecnologie Didattiche, Consiglio Nazionale delle Ricerche, Italy
Maria Ranieri	University of Florence, Italy
Lucia Rapanotti	The Open University, UK
Steve Reeves	University of Waikato, New Zealand
Symeon Retalis	University of Piraeus, Greece
Claudia Roda	American University of Paris, France
Neil Rubens	University of Electro-Communications, Japan
Santi Scimeca	EUN - European SchoolNet, EU/Belgium
Siraj A. Shaikh	Coventry University, UK
Sulayman K. Sowe	United Nations University, /UNU-IAS, UN/Japan
Marcus Specht	Open University of The Nethderlands, The Netherlands
Julita Vassileva	University of Saskatchewan, Canada
Win Veen	Delft University of Technology, The Netherlands

MoKMaSD 2012 Program Co-chairs

Antonio Cerone	United Nations University, UNU-IIST, Macau SAR, UN/China
Alexeis Garcia	Coventry University, UK

MoKMaSD 2012 Program Committee

Rajeev Bali	Coventry University, UK
Roberto Barbuti	University of Pisa, Italy
Thomas Anung Basuki	Parahyangan Catholic University, Indonesia
Ettore Bolisani	University of Padua, Italy
Antonio Cerone	United Nations University, UNU-IIST, Macau SAR, UN/China
Steve Culley	University of Bath, UK

Simone D'Alessandro	University of Pisa, Italy
Francesco De Angelis	UNICAM - University of Camerino, Italy
Rocco De Nicola	University of Florence, Italy
Alexeis Garcia-Perez	Coventry University, UK
Tatiana Gavrilova	St. Petersburg University, Russia
David Gurteen	Gurteen Knowledge
Meliha Handzic	International Burch University, Bosnia and Herzegovina
Mark Hooper	Coventry University, UK
Marijn Janssen	Delft University of Technology, The Netherlands
Erik Johnston	Arizona State University, USA
Ozan Kahramanogullari	COSBI, Italy
Nicos Komninos	Aristotle University of Thessaloniki, Greece
Franz Lehner	University of Passau, Germany
Siu-Wai Leung	University of Macau, Macau SAR, China
Chris McMahon	University of Bath, UK
Paolo Milazzo	University of Pisa, Italy
Jeremy Millard	Danish Technological Institute, Denmark
Sandra Moffett	University of Ulster, UK
Adegboyega Ojo	United Nations University, UNU-IIST, Macau SAR, UN/China
Matteo Pedercini	Millennium Institute, USA
Ion Petre	Department of IT, Åbo Akademi University, Finland
Barbara Re	University of Camerino, Italy
Siraj A. Shaikh	Coventry University, UK
Michael Sonnenschein	University of Oldenburg, Germany
Massimo Tavoni	FEEM — Fondazione Eni Enrico Mattei, Italy
Hefeng Tong	Institute of Scientific and Technical Information of China, China
José M. Viedma Martí	Polytechnic University of Catalonia, Spain
Shaofa Yang	Shenzhen Institutes of Advanced Technology, Chinese Academy of Sciences, China

Opencert 2012 Program Co-chairs

Siraj A. Shaikh	Coventry University, UK
Ioannis Stamelos	Aristotle University of Thessaloniki, Greece

OpenCert 2012 Program Committee

Luis Barbosa	Universidade do Minho, Portugal
Jaap Boender	University of Bologna, Italy
Alexander Chatzigeorgiou	University of Macedonia, Greece
Andreas Griesmayer	Imperial College London, UK
Rene Rydhof Hansen	Aalborg University, Denmark

George Kakarontzas   Aristotle University of Thessaloniki, Greece
Panagiotis Katsaros   Aristotle University of Thessaloniki, Greece
Siraj A. Shaikh   Coventry University, UK
Diomidis Spinellis   Athens University of Economics and Business, Greece
Ioannis Stamelos   Aristotle University of Thessaloniki, Greece

Additional Reviewers

Bouyias, Yannis
Bush, Vicky
Demmans Epp, Carrie
Karakoidas, Vassilios
Karakostas, Anastasios
Krishnan, Paddy

Orji, Rita O.
Passas, Isidoros
Peach, Neil
Stroggylos, Kostas
Tabuenca, Bernardo

Contents

OpenCert 2012 — 6th International Workshop on Foundations and Techniques for Open Source Software Certification

InSuEdu 2012 —
1st International Symposium
on Innovation and Sustainability
in Education

Innovation and Sustainability in Education

Antonio Cerone[1]([✉]) and Donatella Persico[2]([✉])

[1] UNU-IIST — International Institute for Software Technology,
United Nations University, Macau SAR, China
ceroneantonio@gmail.com
[2] CNR-ITD — Istituto per le Tecnologie Didattiche,
Consiglio Nazionale delle Ricerche, Genova, Italy
persico@itd.cnr.it

Abstract. This paper aims at proposing a *founding manifesto* for the *International Symposia on Innovation and Sustainability in Education (InSuEdu)*. We analyze two possible interpretations of *Innovation and Sustainability in Education:* (1) sustainability of methodological and technological innovation processes in education, and (2) creation and implementation of innovation processes that can make education a key driver in sustainable development. After a discussion of these two interpretations we briefly visit the ten contributions to the *1st International Symposium on Innovation and Sustainability in Education* and show how the solutions they propose address one or both of these interpretations.

1 Introduction

Innovation and Sustainability in Education can be interpreted and investigated in a range of different ways. This contribution focuses on two key interpretations that were addressed at the *1st International Symposium on Innovation and Sustainability in Education (InSuEdu 2012)*, which was held on 1 October 2012 in Thessaloniki, Greece.[1]

The first interpretation is the sustainability of the innovation processes that Technology Enhanced Learning (TEL) research is striving to support in education. Following this interpretation, in Sect. 2 we analyse some desirable processes of innovative change in education and we identify challenges in the diffusion and sustainability of such innovations. We consider Rogers model of diffusion of technological innovation [22] and observe that it does not fully apply to most educational innovations. We then highlight the deep contrast between the current proliferation of learning technologies and the great opportunities that social networks and associated tools are giving us in terms of informal learning on one side and the slowly evolving world of formal learning on the other side. Such a contrast reveals a challenge to the innovation of education and its sustainability. In this context we identify important aspects that must be understood and explicitly addressed in order to support innovation in formal learning and make sure it is sustainable.

---

[1] http://sites.itd.cnr.it/insuedu/

A. Cerone et al. (Eds.): SEFM 2012 Satellite Events, LNCS 7991, pp. 3–16, 2014.
DOI: 10.1007/978-3-642-54338-8_1, © Springer-Verlag Berlin Heidelberg 2014

The second interpretation is the creation and implementation of innovation processes that can make education a key driver in sustainable development. Following this interpretation, in Sect. 3 we highlight the importance of education in sustainable development and we discuss how innovative technologies may effectively contribute to the *EFA (Education For All) goals* [8,9].

In Sect. 4, we close the loop by proposing how to work towards innovation and sustainability in education by critically analysing the ten contributions to the *1st International Symposium on Innovation and Sustainability in Education*, which are included in this volume. Finally, in Sect. 5, we discuss how such contributions address the two Rogers factors, simplicity and trialability, that are seldom present in an education context.

2   Sustainable Innovation in Education

Innovation in education can be seen as a process of change, whereby something new happens in educational systems, in the way people learn, or in the environments where learning takes place [13,14]. This process of change may be driven by external, not controllable factors, but it may also be endogenous, that is, it may be led, or at least influenced, by the entities that are involved in the learning process, such as learners and teachers. Although innovation, as well as change, are not intrinsically positive concepts (innovation can indeed be for the better or the worse), the actions of teachers and learners (as well as researchers) are generally meant to drive innovation in education towards some kind of desirable change, that is, for example, making the learning process more effective or more efficient.

Making the learning process more effective means, in very basic terms, trying to obtain better learning results: deeper understanding, longer retainment, more solid or otherwise valuable learning. Making it more efficient means trying to obtain the same results with a smaller effort, either on the side of the teacher or on the side of the learners. This is what we do, for example, when we build tools that support teachers in their work, unless these tools aim to change teachers' teaching styles. If we make use of industrial terminology, we can characterise these two kinds of innovation as *product innovation*, whereby the product is the outcome of the learning process, and *process innovation*, that is, innovation of methodological and support aspects of the learning process. However, in education, the border between the two concepts is rather blurred, because it is difficult to change the process without changing the product and vice-versa. It often happens that, if we change the process, what we obtain in terms of learning outcomes is quite different. Thus, what we usually aim at when we try to introduce innovation in education is a different balance, a lower cost/benefit ratio between the effort invested and the learning outcomes obtained, where costs are controlled and benefits maximised, and both are operationalised in qualitative, not just quantitative terms.

To sum up, in this view, innovation in education is a change process, hopefully driven by external and internal factors, that aims at improving the conditions for learning and/or the results of the learning process but also finding ways to move on from small scale, experimental approaches, to larger scale, sustainable innovation.

In the last decade, research in the field of TEL has devoted considerable efforts to the endeavor of better understanding the costs and benefits in those innovation processes that have been made possible by technology and its almost ubiquitous availability [15]. In many cases, however, more attention has been devoted to the benefits made possible by the affordances of technology, than to the costs in terms of the effort needed on the side of the teachers, the institutions and the learners to sustain the new processes [30]. This is fair enough, given that we all know that bootstrapping an innovation process usually pays off only in the long run.

However, it is now time to start thinking about sustainability of innovation processes. Once an innovative process is started, it doesn't necessarily proceed on its own. While Rogers' model of diffusion of technological innovation [22] may lead to believe that powerful innovations, once ignited, can spread spontaneously, this doesn't apply to most educational innovations, even if it is technology based. Actually many researchers [6,17] claim that there is a gap between the promises of TEL research and the practice in educational institutions and that educational institutions today do not seem to meet the needs of society.

In the context of the crisis [29] that has been affecting education during the last 20 years, the great impetus that the theories of *social constructivism* and *connectivism* have given to innovative educational practices is now resulting in a proliferation of attempts to take advantage of learning technologies to enhance the learning process, especially in the areas of collaborative learning, problem based learning and inquiry learning. In line with such theories and approaches, the integration of technology in education should be driven by the following principles: *education should be learner-centred* and *learning should be social and fun* [26]. The new generations of learners, on the one hand, are no longer comfortable with traditional modes of education, in which information is presented linearly, mostly in a text-based way, with almost no activities aiming to put acquired knowledge into real-life practice. On the one hand, living in a technology rich environment, they learn very quickly how to handle new technological tools, on the other hand, their competence in using technology is often rather superficial, thus preventing them from taking advantage of the affordances of technology and sometimes even leading them to underestimate the risks inherent in its use, as the diffusion of cyber-bulling and personal data dealing seems to demonstrate.

Although web technologies, social networks and associated tools are more and more widespread and give us great opportunities in terms of informal learning, learning technologies are often in strong contrast with the conservative style of educational institutions. This creates a mismatch between

- a rapidly evolving world of **informal learning**, in which:
    information is *offered* to the public in daily life throughout multiple streams and multiple modalities simultaneously that allow the learner to

quickly *navigate* through tree-like or even graph-like structures towards the targeted information;

knowledge is built by *sharing* and *discussing* collected information through social networks and other virtual environments, which have the potential to overcome barriers that in face-to-face learning prevent learners from externalisations and from transforming tacit knowledge into explicit knowledge; and

– a slowly evolving world of **formal learning** [23], which struggles in integrating new technologies within traditional curricula whose objective is more focused on rote learning rather than knowledge acquisition and often misses proper connection with real-life practice.

Given the above premises, we do not maintain here that learning technologies are a panacea and their integration in formal educational processes will bridge the above gap. On the contrary, learning technologies only work effectively if their integration in education is pedagogically sound, that is, if they are used in the right context and in the right way; otherwise they may even hinder the learning process. In informal learning this is not a major problem, since self-regulated learners will be able to test alternatives and choose the most appropriate technological solution for their learning objectives. However, in formal learning, effective integration of technology often needs to overcome resistances and barriers on the side of the teachers, of the students and even of the institutions themselves [16,31]. In order to make innovation in formal learning sustainable, removing such obstacles is necessary but not sufficient. The gap between the promise of research in TEL and practice in educational institutions will not be bridged unless a participatory culture of learning design is disseminated among teachers and decision makers at institutional level. The dissemination of such a culture requires, first of all, the development of learning design principles, methods and tools to support decision making in learning design, so that an optimal match can be reached between learning objectives, on one side, and students' needs, teachers' preferences and contextual requirements on the other side. This would make learning design more systematic and evidence-based [20]. Secondly, it requires approaches and tools that facilitate sharing and reuse of successful pedagogical plans, best practice examples and effective resources. In particular, the movement of Open Educational Resources [28] seems to

1. hold a promise for sustainability of high-quality education, capable of integrating formal and informal learning;
2. sustain learners' motivation and improve outcomes;
3. address critical target users such as students/practitioners with limited background, aged or unwilling learners, and people with temporary or permanent disabilities;
4. promote deep learning strategies in complex domains, such as mathematical/formal principles, methodologies and techniques;

5. encourage teachers to experiment and try new methods and tools, thus becoming action researchers [15].

The *International Symposia on Innovation and Sustainability in Education* aim to focus on the above-mentioned aspect of Sustainable Innovation in Education by fostering the discussion and deep understanding of sustainability of methodological and technological innovation processes in education.

3   Education Innovation for Sustainable Development

The 2012 Report to the UN Secretary-General "Realizing the Future We Want for All" by the UN System Task Team on the POST-2015 UN Development Agenda [27] characterises the contribution of education to the core dimension of *Environmental Sustainability* as follows:

> Education for sustainable development provides the values, skills and knowledge needed for shaping new attitudes, and consumption and production patterns conducive to sustainable development. Appropriate technical and vocational education and training will be essential for preparing people, including youth, for jobs enhancing environmental sustainability.

This implies that education may effectively contribute to sustainable development only if learners are provided with an education context that aims at shaping the required new attitudes and patterns. Providing such a context requires large innovation efforts in the development of education strategies, methodologies and tools that address the challenges of our rapidly changing world as well as the deployment of education systems and capacity building efforts that integrate disciplines from social sciences, humanities, natural sciences and computer science, and address the globality of the industrialised and developing countries. Major changes in living environments and human societies such as dramatic climate changes and unprecedented, pervasive world population aging require education approaches primarily aiming at instilling adaptability to change in learners. The outcomes of these new education approaches can no longer be limited to the development of skills that are strictly dependent on current contexts, regulations and technologies, but must enable learners to acquire by themselves the skills they may happen to need at any stage of their lives.

UNESCO's international agenda involves a numbers of leading themes aiming at the development of coherent policies and plans and the definition and effective implementation of strategies to bring about real and sustainable change in education systems worldwide. Here we focus on those themes that are most relevant for our symposia:

- *Education for All;*
- *Education for Sustainable Development;*
- *ICT in Education.*

The 2012 EFA Global Monitoring Report [9] examines how skills development programmes can be improved to boost young people's opportunities for decent jobs and better lives. The 2010 EFA Global Monitoring Report [8] highlights that the impact of the recent financial crisis, especially through rising malnutrition and deteriorating prospects for poverty reduction, has strongly worsened the crisis of education and especially penalised developing countries as well as deprived social systems that are present in industrialised countries. The EFA Global Monitoring Reports also analyse the EFA goals to address the issues of how to enable individuals to realize their right to learn and to fulfill their responsibility to contribute to the development of their society. The development of innovative educational technologies potentially provides important measures to contribute to the achievement of the EFA goals[2]:

EFA goal 1 Expanding and improving comprehensive *early childhood care and education.*
EFA goal 2 Ensuring that by 2015 all children have access to and complete free and compulsory *primary education* of good quality.
EFA goal 3 Ensuring that the learning needs of all young people and adults are met through equitable access to appropriate *learning and life skills* programmes.
EFA goal 4 Achieving a 50 per cent improvement in levels of adult *literacy* by 2015.
EFA goal 5 Eliminating *gender* disparities in primary and secondary education by 2005, and achieving gender equality in education by 2015[3],
EFA goal 6 Improving all aspects of the *quality of education.*

The usage of innovative technologies is an effective way to improve education from childhood to adulthood and create a life-long learning environment, to reduce the cost and improve the quality of education, to reduce gender disparities by removing cultural barriers to gender equal opportunities in education. Such technologies have therefore the potential to effectively contribute to all EFA goals as well as to address youth and adult skills required by the expanding opportunities in the new global economy.

In order to introduce in learning systems innovations that are sustainable and can support sustainable development it is important to allow learners:

---

[2] The EFA goals are here shortened; full text is available at http://www.unescobkk. org/education/efa/efa-goals/
[3] Although "convergence in enrollment between boys and girls has been one of the successes of the EFA movement since 2000", in 2012 there is still "more to be done to ensure that education opportunities and outcomes are equitable": sixty-eight countries have not achieved gender parity in primary education and girls are disadvantaged in sixty of them; ninety-seven countries have not achieved gender parity in secondary education and girls are disadvantaged in forty-three of them. "In much of the Arab States, South and West Asia, and sub-Saharan Africa gender disparities are at the expense of girls, while in many countries in Latin America and the Caribbean, and in East Asia and the Pacific, disparities are at the expense of boys." [9].

1. to develop skills and competences that are essential to work towards a sustainable future;
2. to develop at an early stage skills that are essential for effective learning at later stages as well as adaptivity to change;
3. to experience a smooth transition between formal learning and work environment;
4. to access life-long informal learning opportunities as a follow-up of their formal learning paths.

The *International Symposia on Innovation and Sustainability in Education* aim to focus on these aspects of Education Innovation for Sustainable Development.

4   Working Towards Innovation and Sustainability in Education

The aim of the *International Symposia on Innovation and Sustainability in Education* is to close the loop between *sustainable education* and *education for sustainable development* and propose approaches

1. to introduce and sustain innovation in educational systems (see Sect. 2);
2. to make effective use of education for sustainable development (see Sect. 3).

In this section we illustrate how the research works presented at the *1st International Symposium on Innovation and Sustainability in Eduction* contribute to this aim. The 10 contributions presented at the Symposium can be regarded as pertaining four different strands, which are discussed in Sects. 4.1–4.4.

4.1   ICT-Enabled Innovation for Learning and Innovative Pedagogies

Bocconi, Kampylis and Punie [3] define the term "ICT-enabled innovation for learning" as "the profoundly new ways of using and creating information and knowledge made possible by the use of ICT" provided that "this ICT potential for innovation" is "realized and accompanied by the necessary pedagogical and institutional change".

In this context Bocconi, Kampylis and Punie propose a multi-dimensional concept for *Creative Classrooms (CCR)* that consists of eight encompassing and interconnected key dimensions: Infrastructure, Content & Curricula, Assessment, Learning practices, Teaching practices, Organisation, Leadership & Values and Connectedness. Their work is part of the Europe 2020 strategy, which emphasises the need for new skills and competences to allow Europe to remain competitive, overcome the current economic crisis and trigger new opportunities (see item 1 in Sect. 3 above). The aim is to capture the significant changes in *what, how, where, when* and *with whom* we learn in order to achieve a sustainable and systemic change of education and training in Europe and effectively meet the needs of the 21st century learners.

4.2   The Key Roles of Collaboration and Peer-Based Approaches in Innovation and Sustainability

Bittel and Bettoni [2] present a practical model in which fairytales are used to promote the persistence of learning and working groups both at organisational and individual level. The developed model defines and links the aspects of Knowledge Management, storytelling and fairytales with the community as a core element.

Papadopoulos and Cerone [19] present three studies on the *peer-review method* aiming to show that its implementation in a TEL Environment (TELE) enhances the learning experience of the students with a consequent positive impact on the learning environment itself, in terms of its capability to maintain an active group of engaged students.

In general, social networks allow individuals geographically distributed and with different cultural backgrounds to become friends, participate in online activities and games and join discussion fora. Individuals feel less inhibitions in socialising through a social network than by direct relationship. This has positive effects in overcoming individual socialisation problems as well as cultural attitudes that tend to limit social life. Therefore, social networks offer affordances enabling socio-costructivist approaches to learning including those that take place in communities of practice. Geographically distributed collaborative learning is essential for developing countries to overcome the lack of qualified local teachers and to widen the horizon of learners. Communities of practice allow learners to be exposed to approaches that are different from the one normally used in their cultures and countries and offer a more global form of learning that fosters adaptability to heterogeneous contexts. This happens in many specialized professional communities. For example, *Free/Libre Open Source Software (FLOSS)* communities engage in peer-production activities having as final goals the production, review, testing and modification of software, but also involving to a large extent collaborative learning and the implicit production of explicit knowledge [4,5,24].

Fernandes, Cerone and Barbosa [10] present the preliminary results of a questionnaire addressed to *FLOSS contributors* to investigate their awareness of *learning processes* occurring and *learning patterns* emerging throughout their participation in FLOSS projects. Aim of their work is to integrate the informal learning that "naturally" occurs within a FLOSS community in the formal learning context given by a software engineering course at undergraduate level (see item 1 in Sect. 2 above). Moreover, participation in real-world projects is expected to facilitate the transition between formal learning and work environment (see item 3 in Sect. 3 above), while creating an engagement that persists beyond the formal learning context with students' long-term involvement in the FLOSS community (see item 4 in Sect. 3 above).

4.3 Tools and Environments for Fostering Innovation and Sustainability in Education

Learning Management Systems (LMS) are software applications for the administration, documentation, tracking, reporting and delivery of courses or training programs. LMSs become essential tools when education is delivered through e-learning modalities where a platform for information storage and retrieval, as well as knowledge sharing a collaboration, supports the learning process and ensures sustainability.

Fernandes et al. [11] present a comparative analysis of *FLOSS LMS* that focuses on the availability of tools for communication and assistance, such as forum, email, calendar, portfolio, etc. The analysis shows that appropriateness of a specific LMS can be greatly affected by the specific needs of students, instructors and institutions.

Well established tools such as DokuWiki, a Wiki application aimed at the needs of small companies, and Apache Subversion (SVN), a software versioning and revision control system, can be used as effective supporting technologies in teaching and learning.

Franke and Kowalewski [12] present an approach based on the use of DokuWiki and SVN to create and manage software-related seminar papers. They also present experiences on applying such an approach to a student seminar and illustrate its practical advantages as well as drawbacks, based on student and advisor evaluations.

Virtual reality allows the definition of educational environments in which learners are enabled to quickly "navigate" towards the targeted information and put it "virtually" into practice; all this using modalities and activities that appeal to learners much more than typical academic work. In addition, in the context of EFA, virtual reality can be seen as a learner's window on a technologically advanced reality, which may not be experienced in the local physical world due to the absence of adequate infrastructure.

Augmented reality is a live, direct or indirect, view of a physical, real-world environment whose elements and contents are augmented by computer-generated sensory input and content information, such as sound, video, graphics or GPS data, with a resultant enhanced perception of reality.

Ternier et al. [25] present a tool for *augmented reality*, ARLearn, that uses multimedia capabilities and location based services on smartphones to adapt learning to a variety of contexts. The use of the tool in two pilot studies for fieldwork of Cultural Sciences students has supported students with systematical collection of data for their essays.

Finally, Persico et al. [21] present a case study of a small Italian virtual university were a number of actions were carried out to make technological and methodological innovation proceed hand in hand and to drive innovation towards a higher quality of the teaching and learning experience.

4.4   Building Basic Skills for Learning in Complex Domains and for Long-Term Effects

In order to develop at an early stage skills that are essential for effective learning at later stages as well as adaptivity to change (item 2 in Sect. 3) it is important that high school curricula and learning strategies fully address the basic skills and the ability to think and reason that are essential to acquire more advanced skills and knowledge at the tertiary level of education. Mathematics and logical basis for reasoning are basic pre-requisites for learning in several complex domains, which range from engineering and computer science to economics and biology. Such pre-requisites must be addressed at an early stage to make formal learning in complex domains possible and innovation effective in the long-term at tertiary level (see item 4 in Sect. 2 above).

Barbosa and Martinho [1] contribute to the debate on strategies for achieving a higher degree of *mathematical fluency* and overcome the widespread perception of mathematics as difficult or boring. They focus on argumentation and proof as the main ingredients in strategies for developing mathematical skills and structured reasoning.

Nikolova and Stefanova [18] present an application of the *inquiry-based science education (IBSE)* approach to teach programming in high school. Two variations of the approach, open inquiry and guided inquiry, are analysed from the point of view of long-term effect of education.

5   Conclusion and Final Remarks

According to Rogers [22] the five factors influencing the spread of technological innovations are:

- *relative advantage*, that is, the relative improvement over the previous generation;
- *compatibility*, in terms of assimilation into an individual's life;
- *simplicity*, perceived by the individual who is a potential user;
- *trialability*, that is, possibility to be experimented before adoption;
- *observability*, in terms of visibility to the potential users.

Some of these factors, however, do not seem to apply to educational innovations, even when such innovations are technology driven. Notably, *simplicity* and *trialability* are seldom present in an education context, in which innovations are often perceived as very complex to implement, due to the perceived resistances and actual barriers [7], and difficult to be experimented with, mostly because failing an experiment involving real students may have negative effects on their learning and their lives.

In this section we briefly discuss how these issues emerge in or are addressed by the contributions illustrated in Sects. 4.1–4.4 and what would be important to focus on in future work.

We can identify several parameters that contribute to the perception of complexity. One of Roger's elements, the *social system*, is intrinsically complex due to the large number and interrelation of the units that define it and drive the complexity of the diffusion process through bottom-up problem solving activities that may result in the accomplishment of the common goal with the unpredictable emergence of a stable system state. Thus, the outcome of the diffusion process is hard to predict and is inevitably perceived by individuals as complex. Innovations based on collaboration and peer-based concepts and approaches [2,3,10,19,21] are also quite complex. Collaboration emerges from the interaction of several individuals and can never be fully controlled, hence the unpredictability of the final result. In peer-based approaches, such as peer-review and peer-production, it is possible to apply control only to some extent. For example, scripts or other kinds of structured approaches may be used in peer-review to provide support and scaffolding to students [19]. Papadopoulos and Cerone present a study in which highly structured approaches fostered better collaboration patterns and allowed students to outperform those who worked with weaker constraints in acquiring the same domain conceptual knowledge [19]. However, in two other case studies Papadopoulos and Cerone replace the assigned-pair protocol, in which students work together in instructor-defined dyads, with a free-selection protocol, in which students freely browse and select by themselves peer work to review, and find that the new protocol enhances the degree of students' engagement and involvement: students choose to study and review more answers than mandatory, most likely due to the freedom in selecting peer work to review [19].

Although in some contexts the right balance between freedom and control may be successfully experimented and show in the end both simplicity and trialability, in other contexts imposing a structure to interaction is not applicable at all; it can actually be counter productive if the development of self-regulating learning skills is among the aims. This is the case of FLOSS communities, in which peer-production and peer-review are usually governed by a philosophy of freedom and equality [5,10]. Here the intrinsic interrelations among the units of the social system (contributors of the FLOSS community) are mostly free and, in general, leave little space to leadership intervention and control.

An additional problem for trialability in an education setting is given by ethical reasons. In education great caution should be taken in experimenting innovations in order to assess their effects before adoption. Although the use of pilot studies and projects restricts adoption to the experimental context, in the end the subjects of experiments are students and instructors, who may be negatively affected by the introduced innovations. There is no obvious solution to this problem. A way to reduce a possible negative impact of the experimentation phase is to make such a phase more effective by adopting a systemic approach. In this perspective, Bocconi, Kampylis and Punie [3] consider a set of 28 reference parameters/building blocks derived from the literature in the field to support large-scale experimentation and implementation of 8 key dimension of their multi-dimensional concept for Creative Classrooms. For example, "engaging teachers through social networks" has a main interrelation with the Connectedness key dimension and ancillary interrelations with the Teaching practices and Organisation key dimensions.

Another problem arises from the large variety of attitudes and natural skills in instructors and learners. A new technology may be appropriate for some instructors/students and be inappropriate for others (see items 2 and 5 in Sect. 2). For example, it has been sometimes observed that e-learning technologies that appear to be positively accepted by average instructors and/or learners are actually rejected by both least skilled instructors/learners and most brilliant instructors/students, the former being unable to use them, the latter finding them inadequate or hindering their highly developed approach to teach/learn. This has ethical implications in formal learning, since enforcing new technologies on instructors/learners who are unable to effectively exploit them or unwilling to adopt them may have disastrous consequences. In such a context, approaches based on freedom [10,19] and graduality [21] present clear advantages. Finally, it is essential to address critical target users of education "products" (see item 3 in Sect. 2), not only for the ethical need to overcome the problem of reaching people with limited background, aged or unwilling learners, and people with temporary or permanent disabilities, but also, from a pragmatic point of view, because in our rapidly developing and, at the same time, aging world such users are increasingly playing essential roles.

Acknowledgments. We would like to thank Stefania Bocconi and Elsa Estevez, who read and informally reviewed a draft of this paper, providing us with valuable comments and suggestions. This work has been partly supported by Macao Science and Technology Development Fund, File No. 019/2011/A1, in the context of the PPAeL project.

References

1. Barbosa, L.S., Martinho, M.H.: Mathematical literacy as a condition for sustainable development. In: Cerone, A., Persico, D., Fernandes, S., Garcia-Perez, A., Katsaros, P., Shaikh, S.A., Stamelos, I. (eds.) InSuEdu 2012. LNCS, vol. 7991. Springer, Heidelberg (2014)
2. Bittel, N., Bettoni, M.: Learning CSCW through fairytales: a practical model. In: Cerone, A., Persico, D., Fernandes, S., Garcia-Perez, A., Katsaros, P., Shaikh, S.A., Stamelos, I. (eds.) InSuEdu 2012. LNCS, vol. 7991. Springer, Heidelberg (2014)
3. Bocconi, S., Kampylis, P., Punie, Y.: Creative classrooms: A systemic approach for mainstreaming ICT-enabled innovation for learning in Europe. In: Cerone, A., Persico, D., Fernandes, S., Garcia-Perez, A., Katsaros, P., Shaikh, S.A., Stamelos, I. (eds.) InSuEdu 2012. LNCS, vol. 7991. Springer, Heidelberg (2014)
4. Cerone, A.: Learning and activity patterns in oss communities and their impact on software quality. In: Proceedings of OpenCert 2011, vol. 48 of Electronic Communications of the EASST (2012)
5. Cerone, A., Sowe, S.K.: Using free/libre open source software projects as e-learning tools. In: Proceedings of OpenCert 2010, vol. 33 of Electronic Communications of the EASST (2010)
6. Conole, G.: Designing for Learning in an Open World. Springer, New York (2013)

7. Delfino, M., Manca, S., Persico, D., Sarti, L.: Online learning: attitudes, expectations and prejudices of adult novices. In: Proceedings of the the IASTED International Conference on Web Based Education (WBE 2004), 16–18 Feb 2004, Innsbruck, Austria, pp. 31–36, ACTA Press, Anheim (2004)
8. EFA. EFA Global Monitoring Report – Reaching the marginalized. Technical report, UNESCO. http://www.uis.unesco.org/Library/Documents/gmr10-en.pdf (2010)
9. EFA. EFA Global Monitoring Report – Youth and skills: Putting education to work. Technical report, UNESCO. http://unesdoc.unesco.org/images/0021/ 002180/218003e.pdf (2012)
10. Fernandes, S., Cerone, A., Barbosa, L.S.: A preliminary analysis of learning awareness in FLOSS projects. In: Cerone, A., Persico, D., Fernandes, S., Garcia-Perez, A., Katsaros, P., Shaikh, S.A., Stamelos, I. (eds.) InSuEdu 2012. LNCS, vol. 7991. Springer, Heidelberg (2014)
11. Fernandes, S., Cerone, A., Barbosa, L.S., Papadopoulos, P.M.: FLOSS in technology-enhanced learning. In: Cerone, A., Persico, D., Fernandes, S., Garcia-Perez, A., Katsaros, P., Shaikh, S.A., Stamelos, I. (eds.) InSuEdu 2012. LNCS, vol. 7991. Springer, Heidelberg (2014)
12. Franke, D., Kowalewski, S.: Concept and experiences on using a wiki-based system for software-related seminar papers. In: Cerone, A., Persico, D., Fernandes, S., Garcia-Perez, A., Katsaros, P., Shaikh, S.A., Stamelos, I. (eds.) InSuEdu 2012. LNCS, vol. 7991. Springer, Heidelberg (2014)
13. Hage, J., Meeus, M.: Innovation, Science, and Institutional Change: A Research Handbook. Oxford University Press, New York (2009)
14. Hannon, V., Patton, A., Temperley, J.: Developing an innovation ecosystem for education. http://www.cisco.com/web/strategy/docs/education/ecosystem_for_edu.pdf, December 2011
15. Laurillard, D.: The teacher as action researcher. Stud. High. Educ. **33**(2), 139–154 (2008)
16. Lloyd, M., Albion, P.R.: A new angle on teacher technophobia. J. Technol. Teacher Educ. **17**(1), 65–84 (2009)
17. Mor, Y., Craft, B.: Learning design: reflections upon the current landscape. Research in Learning Technology - Supplement: ALT-C 2012 Conference Proceedings, 20:85–94, 2012. http://www.researchinlearningtechnology.net/index.php/rlt/ article/view/19196
18. Nikolova, N., Stefanova, E.: Inquiry-based science education in secondary school informatics - challenges and rewards. In: Cerone, A., Persico, D., Fernandes, S., Garcia-Perez, A., Katsaros, P., Shaikh, S.A., Stamelos, I. (eds.) InSuEdu 2012. LNCS, vol. 7991. Springer, Heidelberg (2014)
19. Papadopoulos, P.M., Cerone, A.: The role of peer review in supporting the sustainability of Technology-Enhanced Learning environments. In: Cerone, A., Persico, D., Fernandes, S., Garcia-Perez, A., Katsaros, P., Shaikh, S.A., Stamelos, I. (eds.) InSuEdu 2012. LNCS, vol. 7991. Springer, Heidelberg (2014)
20. Persico, D., Manca, S., Pozzi, F.: Adapting the technology acceptance model to evaluate the innovative potential of e-learning systems. Comput. Hum. Behav. (CHB) **30**, 614–622 (2013)
21. Persico, D., Manca, S., Pozzi, F.: Innovation and sustainability in higher education: lessons learnt from the case study of an online university. In: Cerone, A., Persico, D., Fernandes, S., Garcia-Perez, A., Katsaros, P., Shaikh, S.A., Stamelos, I. (eds.) InSuEdu 2012. LNCS, vol. 7991. Springer, Heidelberg (2014)

22. Rogers, E.M.: Diffusion of Innovation. Free Press, New York (1962)
23. Salmon, G.: http://mooc.efquel.org/week-11-mooocs-massive-opportunities-to-overcome-organisational-catastrophes-by-gilly-salmon/ (2013)
24. Sowe, S.K., Stamelos, I.: Reflection on knowledge sharing in f/oss projects. In: Russo, B., Damiani, E., Hissam, S., Lundell, B., Succi, G. (eds.) Open Source Development, Communities and Quality. IFIP, vol. 275, pp. 351–358. Springer, Heidelberg (2008)
25. Ternier, S., de Vries, F., Börner, D., Specht, M.: Mobile augmented reality with audio; supporting fieldwork of cultural sciences students in florence. In: Cerone, A., Persico, D., Fernandes, S., Garcia-Perez, A., Katsaros, P., Shaikh, S.A., Stamelos, I. (eds.) InSuEdu 2012. LNCS, vol. 7991. Springer, Heidelberg (2014)
26. Tokoro, M., Steels, L.: The Future of Learning. IOS Press, Amsterdam (2003)
27. UN System Task Team on the POST-2015 UN Development Agenda. Realizing the future we want for all – report to the secretary-general. Technical report, United Nations, New York, June 2012
28. UNESCO and COL. Guidelines for Open Educational Resources (OER) in higher education. http://www.col.org/PublicationDocuments/Guidelines_OER_HE.pdf, (2011)
29. Wain, K.: The Learning Society in a Postmodern World: The Education Crisis, vol. 260. Peter Lang, New York (2004)
30. Wang, F., Hannafin, M.J.: Design-based research and technology-enhanced learning environments. Educ. Tech. Res. Dev. **53**(4), 5–23 (2005)
31. Wood, E., Mueller, J., Willoughby, T., Specht, J., Deyoung, T.: Teachers' perceptions: barriers and supports to using technology in the classroom. Educ. Commun. Inf. **5**(2), 183–206 (2005)

Inquiry-Based Science Education in Secondary School Informatics – Challenges and Rewards

Nikolina Nikolova[✉] and Eliza Stefanova

Faculty of Mathematics and Informatics, Sofia University St. Kl. Ohridski,
Sofia, Bulgaria
{nnikolova, eliza}@fmi.uni-sofia.bg

Abstract. The paper presents an application of the inquiry-based science education (IBSE) approach in the context of informatics, specialized classes, in the process of studying Java language by 11 graders. The experiment under consideration presents classes, performed in parallel in two mathematics high schools in Sofia, Bulgaria, in two consequence years.

The levels of IBSE as well as meta-levels of inquiry skills developed by students in process of learning are described. Next, the context of the experiment is presented.

Two different variations of the approach application are shown – *open inquiry* and *guided inquiry*. The products, developed by student as results of the education, are presented.

The analysis of the challenges, staying in front of the students and the teachers, in process of application of the inquiry-based science education takes special place in the paper.

In conclusion, the application of IBSE is analysed from the point of view of long-term effect of education.

Keywords: Inquiry-based science education (IBSE) · Design of education · ICT enchanced skills

1 Introduction

The *specialized classes in informatics* are real challenge for the teachers. There are approximately 30 schools having such classes in Bulgaria, three of them – located in Sofia. These classes deal with advanced object-oriented programming. The curriculum is similar to the curriculum applied during the first two years at the university. This means the learning process is quite heavy in terms of content.

The main efforts of the teacher in these classes usually are focused on acquiring some basic knowledge and skills in programming and data structures, as well as in algorithmic thinking development.

In practice, the training is often reduced to teaching the very language constructions, usually by lectures and uniform examples, which are not meaningful for the students. Our personal experience and the experience shared by other teachers in informatics strengthens our conviction that applying this widely used approach leads to a lack of motivation and to superficial skills.

A. Cerone et al. (Eds.): SEFM 2012 Satellite Events, LNCS 7991, pp. 17–34, 2014.
DOI: 10.1007/978-3-642-54338-8_2, © Springer-Verlag Berlin Heidelberg 2014

In harmony with the constructionist's spirit, we have been applying in our practice the credo: *learning by programming is more important than learning to program* [1].

Toward the elimination of the deficiencies of the traditional approach of teaching programming, we tried to apply project- and inquiry-based science education in the specialised classes of informatics [2]. Effectiveness of such type of education encouraged us, but in the same time placed in front of us new challenges. The main one was how to design the process of education, so that to cover state educational goals – the curriculum-related requirements (as defined by the state standards), and in the same time to increase the motivation of the learners.

In response to that challenge we decided to design the learning process, applying *I*Teach* methodology [3]. It is developed in the frame of the *Innovative teacher project* (*I*Teach*) [4], implemented under the Leonardo da Vinci program. Its characteristics are:

- The learning process is driven by students' interests.
- The students are faced with a challenge, which motivates them to participate actively in the process of learning.
- The students work in teams on a project, whose goals they formulate themselves.
- The *road to the goal* is a metaphor behind a specific educational scenario with *milestones* of intermediate objectives. The teacher guides the students to the ultimate project goal by interweaving his/her own pedagogical goals concerning the learning content with the building of ICT-enhanced soft skills (working-in-a-team skills, working-on-a-project skills, and information and presentation skills).

When we speak about the synergy between the I*Teach methodology and the Inquiry Based Science Education, we think about *fishing* – we just put the appropriate challenge in front of students and let them research, try, ask, and find their own solutions, getting better and better in the learning /discovered material (Fig. 1).

We already have provided an evidence of the effectiveness of the I*Teach methodology in series of trainings in ICT with teachers [5, 6] and students [7], but we had not applied it in the informatics education at school so far. In addition, it was

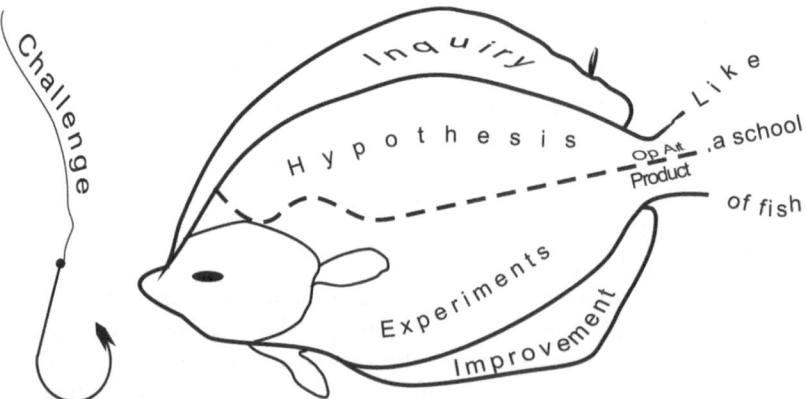

Fig. 1. Metaphor of the I*Teach methodology in the context of IBSE

necessary to think about the choice of the right level of the IBSE, depending of aiming students skills.

2 Levels and Skills, Developed Through Inquiry-Based Science Education

2.1 Inquiry-Based Science Education

The original idea for IBSE belongs to John Dewey [8] and includes concepts related to construction of the subject knowledge by student-centred learning based on student presented inquiries. It comes in contrast of the traditional approaches based on memorising contents, achieving basic problem solving skills in laboratory courses, where experiments mostly include not inquiry but verification of known principles.

The idea has been developed during the further years and the IBSE has been more precisely defined according to the specific needs and goals. According to a definition by Linn, Davis and Bell, inquiry is the intentional process of diagnosing problems, critiquing experiments, and distinguishing alternatives, planning investigations, researching conjectures, searching for information, constructing models, debating with peers, and forming coherent arguments [9]. As a consequence, Inquiry Based Science Education is *an approach to learning that involves a process of exploring the natural or material world, and that leads to asking questions, making discoveries, and rigorously testing those discoveries in the search for new understanding* [10].

Although this approach is rather difficult and time-consuming for the teachers, it pays off in terms of effectiveness, and it is therefore worth applying, if not for the whole curriculum, at least to achieve in-depth understanding of critical, core concepts that are the cornerstones of scientific disciplines.

2.2 Levels of Inquiry-Based Science Education

According Tafoya [11], the following levels of inquiry-based science education could be defined (Fig. 2):

Five inquiry skills areas, which could be developed at the meta-level, could be defined, depending on the level of the inquiry-based science education (Table 2) [12].

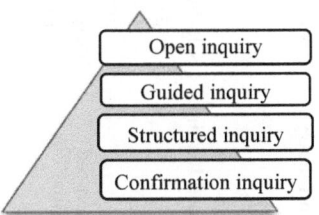

Fig. 2. Tafoya's classification of levels of inquiry

Table 1. Meta-levels of inquiry skills (table adapted by Okada, 2008)

Level of inquiry	Inquiry skill area				
	1. Scientifically orientated questions	2. Priority to evidence	3. Explanations from evidence	4. Explanation connected to knowledge	5. Communicate and justify
4 Open inquiry	Posing a scientific question	Determining what constitutes evidence, and collecting evidence	Formulating explanations after summarizing evidence	Examining independently other resources and forming the links to explanations	Forming reasonable and logical argument to communicate explanations
3 Guided inquiry	Selecting among given questions and posing new scientific questions with guided support	Collecting certain data with guided support for what constitutes evidence	Formulating explanations from evidence with guided support	Linking areas and sources of scientific knowledge to clarify explanations	Communicating explanations based on scientific reasoning with guided support
2 Structured inquiry	Sharpening or clarifying question provided by teacher, materials, or other source	Analyzing given data to select evidence	Selecting ways to use evidence with directed support to formulate explanation	Selecting possible connections to clarify explanations	Selecting broad guidelines to use sharpen communication
1 Confirmation/ verification	Engaging in questioning provided by teacher, materials, or other source	Analyzing given data to select evidence with directed support	Applying provided evidence to formulate explanation with directed support	Selecting possible connections to clarify explanations with directed support	Applying given steps and procedures for scientific communication

Table 2. Responsibilities depending on the level of inquiry

Level of inquiry	Problem	Procedure	Solution
Level 4 Open inquiry	**Student**	**Student**	**Student**
Level 3 Guided inquiry	Teacher	**Student**	**Student**
Level 2 Structured inquiry	Teacher	Teacher	**Student**
Level 1 Confirmation/verification	Teacher	Teacher	Teacher

As it is visible in Table 2 above, the higher inquiry level requires bigger responsibility to be taken by the students. This presumes that, in order to go from one level to another, they should have already developed enough cognitive and social skills, as well as previous meta-level inquiry skills. The teacher responsibility is to estimate the maturity of his students in advance and then – to make a choice of the level and to design the IBSE project (Table 1).

3   The Context of the Application of IBSE Approach in Informatics Education

3.1   Background and Methodology

In the described experiments the methodology I*Teach combined with IBSE approach were applied in two consequence years – 2010/2011 and 2011/2012, in four *specialized informatics classes* of 11th grade students from two mathematical high schools.

The main goals of the 11th grade specialized classes in informatics in the Bulgarian high schools as defined by the state standards, are: *mastering skills and knowledge about the syntax and the semantics of programming language, algorithms and basic data structures.*

The time determined for this is 108 academic hours (40 min each). The classes were taught in the context of the Java programing language. The students are expected to move from the procedure-oriented to the object-oriented programming paradigm and to acquire the concepts of classes and objects, data encapsulation, composition and inheritance.

The teacher diary, together with some observations and conclusions, were used to collect data, on the basis of which the phases of the experiment are described below. Unstructured interviews have been used for getting feedback from the students.

3.2   IBSE Assignment

Both pilots of the experiment were based on working on an inquiry project, related to the stream in the modern art named *Op Art*. The students had not only to examine carefully the art and its well-known representatives, but also to study technologies, through which such works are created: How the optical illusions are achieved? What are the types of optical illusions? – questions, related to physics, biology, psychology and other sciences.

After the study they were grouped in teams of 2 (in the National High School of Mathematics and Science - NHSMS) or 3 (in the First Private Mathematical Gymnasium - FPMG) members and had a programming assignment under the topic *It's a kind of Magic!*: to develop a simple Java application presenting Op Art graphics. Some of the requirements were:

- To show *Op* Art pictures – really based on the optical illusions;
- To create Op *Art* products – the resulting images should have aesthetic value. For validation of this requirement public final presentations were organized and visitors (other students) used evaluation cards to share their feelings.
- To develop Java *application* – the result should not be just a static drawing, but an application which allow users interaction.

The assignment was challenging for the students and required very well organized learning design in terms of milestones definitions, conducting students work, selecting additional learning resources and time management.

As a result, the main stages of the IBSE project were defined:

- Preliminary study about the Op Art, famous representatives, and technics and technologies for optical illusions creation. This stage finished with the class presentations and discussions. Duration: 1 week (3 academic hours).
- Forming teams. Students were grouped by themselves. Result: each group informed the teacher. Duration: 1 week out of the class doors.
- Choosing/creating a model and development an idea for further development, possible derivatives, opportunities for parameterization and interaction. At the end of the stage all teams reported and received feedback and ideas by other students and the teacher. Duration: 1 week in the class for preparation and presentation, and the last week out of the classroom to respond to the class requirements.
- Application development and improvement. At this stage the students should develop their plans and timesheets, to distribute the roles and responsibilities in the team, to design classes and their relationships, to determine desired functionality. They were asked to work mainly out of the class, and to use the face to face meetings to present intermediate results and problems to the teacher, to discuss their TODO list, to ask for assistance or additional sources of information. Duration: 3 weeks.
- Presentation of final products and evaluation. Duration: 1 week.

Requirements for the final presentation were closely related to the evaluation criteria. The teams should present the idea and the mathematical model behind it, to demonstrate the application, what problems they had met and how they solve them, and, the most important, to share what new knowledge and skills they had been acquired during the work on the IBSE project. They were appreciated to present all aspects of the evolution – new mathematical knowledge discovered and used, new programming concepts and algorithms learned and implemented, new Java-integrated classes familiarized with, new information from other sciences – biology, psychology, physics, etc., new skills in workflow management and control, new attitudes to the team members.

The evaluation process combined teacher's assessment as well as peer assessment. The evaluation criteria covered four rubrics:

– The initial model and related mathematical model assessment – does it provide opportunities for flexibility and reuse, does the appropriate mathematical lows were applied and how they were used, does the class design is appropriate and does in provides opportunity for implementation and further enlargement of the project.
– Project implementation – the use of appropriate programming structures, style of coding, effectiveness of algorithms, etc.
– Final presentation – covering the initial requirements, verbal and non-verbal communication with audience, presentation structure and design.
– Team work –the role of each member of the team, are tasks well balanced, how the team solved internal problems, are there "gaps" in the project because of the lack of communication among the team.

The detailed evaluation criteria were shared among all students. Each team was evaluated by all other students and the teacher using quantitative scale from 2 to 7 where the 6 presented the maximum expected achievement but 7 was a bonus – only if the team show much more. The students were asked to provide argumentation for each offered score.

In addition, the teacher assessed student arguments in the peer evaluation and if they correspond to the provided scores.

Finally, each team received five scores – for each rubric, and a feedback presented by diagrams of summarized results by rubrics and a list of the students and teacher argumentations, presented anonymously.

3.3   Pilots

The first experiment [2] was designed as an **open inquiry**. It was conducted in 2010/2011 school year in the two schools: NHMS and FPMG. Two teachers and three classes of totally 62 students – 52 from the NHSMS and 9 from the FPMG, participated in the pilots. There were two classes from the NHSMS which were separated in two groups by 13 students and taught in parallel by both teachers. The students from the FPMG were taught by one teacher.

Before stating the assignment the students were able to draw by means of Java only simple geometrical figures: circle, square, and rectangle. They have been introduced with the classes and object concept and they have been realized simple classes as a common group work.

Working on the project challenged them to discover, explore, analyse and apply additional learning materials, related to mathematical model and dependences as well as to object-oriented programming concepts (overload and override concepts, class composition, controlling access to the class members, etc.) and different programming technics – right parameterization of the functions, finding repetitive patterns, top-down and bottom-up approaches, through which to realize their ideas.

Fig. 3. Products of students, presented after the open inquiry

During the process of their studies on the project the students learnt and discovered themselves also a variety of Java language possibilities, especially the methods of the Graphics2D integrated class, and they were very proud to present developed by them as a result of their work on a project products (Fig. 3.).

The trend to follow the models of the founder of the Op Art stream – Bridget Riley, was visible in the students' products: use of well-known simple geometrical figures, work in black-white tonality or just with plain colours.

Although the students created very attractive products and they achieved exiting results, there were observed also some difficulties:

- Team work – in both schools there were teams which members were not able to work together. Some of these teams were destroyed (2 of 29) and members continued individually, other were reformed (3 of 29) but met a lack of time to finish the project because new teams started later than others.
- Project work – there was a clearly manifested difference between students in both school. While the managers (principal, head teachers) of the FPMG promote the inquiry-based science education and the project-based learning (PBL) and required their application in almost all disciplines – chemistry, physics, biology, philosophy, etc., in the NHSMS the individual competitive style on working on a specific simple problems /tasks dominated. As a result the students from FPMG felt in *their own water*, while for the students from the NHSMS it was completely new situation. The most of them expect the teacher to organize their work, to prepare a plan, to say what and when should be done. When the time become shorter and they should present intermediate results, they started to panic and tried in chaotic way to catch up the lost time and missing results.
- Time management – all the teams met difficulties to finish their tasks in time and the deadline was prolonged with two weeks.
- Academic maturity –the students from the NHSMS were very well trained to search for, select, process and apply the needed new information and knowledge (they write science essays frequently in other disciplines), while the skills of students from the FPMG were limited to search for given keywords and to transfer the found information in their work without even any adaptation– the technique that usually does not work in programming.

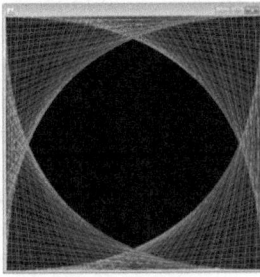

Fig. 4. Students products, presented after guided inquiry

The second pilot held a year later, in 2011/2012 school year. Only one class (8 students) from the FPMG continued the participation in the experiment. Considering the problems after the first application of the IBSE approach and having in mind the lower lever of the meta-inquiry skills of the new group, it was concluded that the **second application** of the IBSE approach - **the guided inquiry**, will be more convenient and it was chosen. The goal was: the students to be guided during the process of *discovery* of some mathematical models and methods of class *Graphics2D*, and in such a way to be well-grounded with regard to the programming concepts.

The results (Fig. 4) give evidence that this time the students really felt more self-confident. In that case, besides of use of set of simple geometrical figures with which they were already familiar, the students tried to experiment more with different settings and metric dependences, related to colours. Even more, some of them made a successful attempt to model through the use of affine transformation in the plane (*Java AffineTransform class*), developing by their own decision and their own hard work and experiments new mathematical knowledge and skills!

4 Challenges of IBSE in the School Practice

As it is visible by the provided examples, the IBSE implementation conceals a lot of challenges for both – students and teachers.

4.1 IBSE Challenges for the Students

For the students of one of the schools, the main challenge was to implement the IBSE approach for the first time. At the second school it was visible that, working on IBSE projects in other school disciplines, the students had been started already to develop inquiry-based science skills. So the work with them progresses far more easily. But for them the main challenge was to learn how to work efficiently with new information.

A serious challenge in front of all students occurred in combining together series of new *soft* competences: selection of reliable sources of information, organization of the tasks of the project, role distribution, time management, taking responsibilities, as well as in integration of knowledge from other school subjects, mainly from mathematics.

To learn how to learn – this was the biggest challenge for the students. It is true that they have enriched their knowledge and developed skills related to mathematical modelling and various concepts of object-oriented programming – became aware of notion on *Class*, *Object* and *Inheritance*. But they did not relay fully on teachers to receive it. They realized that they just should start and go through analysis of the sources and their evaluation, next to read *thick* (although some of them in electronic format) books, and become a part of professional forums. During the process of their work, the students felt natural need to respect the programming style standards (because without them it was not possible to program in a team) as well as to seek for the optimization of the programming code. In natural way they discovered *Top-down* and *Bottom-up* programming approaches. Last but not least – they got to know additional interesting and useful for them information, like Op Art for example.

4.2 IBSE Challenges for the Teachers

Most teachers do not dare to apply the IBSE and PBL approaches because they feel that the situation *spirals out* of control. They fear that there is no guarantee that they would ensure equal absorption of the learning material, that there will be students who will participate or not correctly interpret an experiments.

We can find reasons for such a view in some scientific papers [13], where inquiry based science education and project-based learning are associated with minimal guidance during instruction. Most educators still underestimate the fact that really effective IBSE and PBL approaches need careful design to be successful and that the role of the teachers remains one of paramount importance, even if it isn't any more that of the knowledge source. The teacher role becomes even more difficult with these approaches, because the aim is no longer that of transferring content knowledge, but rather that of facilitating its appropriation, development of confidence with epistemic practices and mastery of soft skills such as collaboration and self-regulation [14]. Especially the more learner centred types of IBSE, where the students gain the ownership on the research question, the research process and the outcome demand an often unfamiliar and challenging role from the teachers [15]. To do this, teachers also need to consider differences between pupils and, at the same time, promote cooperation among them.

However, the motivation to learn and the success of inductive learning processes depend on the gap between the challenge and the knowledge needed to address it.

In addition, the design and organization of an interdisciplinary inquiry-based science education project requires wide general culture and knowledge in different areas of science, art, social life, etc. However, is there such a teacher, who is an expert in everything?! With what quantity of additional information should he be familiarized prior to design such a project? How much time should he sacrifice for his preparation? Is there anyone whom to ask for help? Moreover, the teacher usually is the elder than his students and he is not able to adopt process and memorize new information as quickly as the students can.

The crucial points are the selection of the problem and the guidance that teachers give their students when they are inquiring a problem; such guidance helps students to elaborate proper concepts, and to meet troubles and difficulties arising during the inquiry process. Planning for an inquiry learning process is a challenge for the teacher's ability to understand students' unanticipated questions, and his reasoning ability to handle them.

Regardless how well designed the inquiry-based science education project is, the challenges related to its implementation remain:

- What questions will arise by the students? Will he find the answers?
- How to manage in the same time several teams, working in parallel on different projects? What will happen if they fail to complete their projects in time? Shall he give them additional time? Is it acceptable to grand them such time?
- Is it possible he do not be able to react on time, because of rising of great number of many-sided questions, for some of which he can be completely unprepared?
- How **to guide the process** instead of **to teach**, as he used to do?
- How to organize differentiated education, so to reach the maximum with each student, regardless of the complexity of the project he/she undertook and his/her current capabilities, knowledge and skills?
- What approaches and tools for assessment to be used in order to stimulate the students to continue their development, instead just to do *an autopsy* of them.

The challenge, the teacher is most unfamiliar with, is **how to design the inquiry-based science education project**. It requires the teacher firstly to select attractive for the students topic, then – to perform preliminary study, including selection of sources of information, resources and activities, to define a clear formulation of the project and assessment criteria, to define the key milestones, and to intervene during the implementation only if it is necessary (during the experiment the next question often appeared: *To help or not to impede?!*).

5   Prerequisites for National-Wide Spread of IBSE

On the base of our practical experience and observations we try to summarize the prerequisites for wide spread in teachers' practice of the inquiry-based science project education.

The necessary conditions for national-wide spread of IBSE could be divided at three levels: micro level (teachers), mezzo level (schools), macro level (national education system). There is close relation between them: the prerequisites at national level are condition for flexibility and opportunity of the schools and the teachers to apply IBSE effectively and efficiently.

Existing experience in some European countries – we focused especially on Ireland, Northern Ireland and Finland, seams also to prove summarised below prerequisites as *necessary and sufficient* condition for national-wide spread of IBSE and the other innovative approaches.

5.1   Prerequisites at Micro Level (People – Teachers, Parents)

The change in the *teacher's attitude toward the IBSE* is the first important prerequisite at micro level. In most of the cases teachers are trained to teach how to use traditional (deductive) methods of math and science teaching, and lecturing is widely spread in teacher education courses. As teachers tend to teach as they were taught, it is likely that they also teach through lectures even if it doesn't lead to appropriate understanding. McDermott et al. [16] point out that instructional strategy is content specific. "If it is not learned in the context in which it is to be implemented, teachers may be unable to identify the critical elements". The results, as they have been reported by High Level Group [17], are that science subjects are often taught in a much too abstract way: "It is abstract because it is trying to put forward fundamental ideas, most of which were developed in the 19th century, without sufficient experimental, observational and interpretational background and without showing sufficient understanding of their implication."

The practice shows that teacher's attitude is related to teacher's self-confidence. That is why next prerequisite is to change the *teacher's self-confidence* with respect to his abilities.

For some teachers an obstacle to introduce IBSE is their vision that students are not capable to face challenges of such complex project. Because of that, it is important *to change the teachers' mind* – the teacher should be ready *to give the credit to his students*.

The *support and understanding* of *parents* for the importance of inquiry-based science education is last but not least prerequisite. That prerequisite is crucial especially in countries, like Bulgaria, where parents are taught in traditional (lecturing) style and expect teacher to use the same style.

5.2   Prerequisites at Mezzo Level (School Level)

The *strong support at the school level* is really important for wide application of new approaches in the daily school practice. To facilitate the change in teacher's work, it is needed to build a *team* which *to manage and support the IBSE implementation* at each school. A good practice, shared by schools in Northern Ireland during the Peer Learning Activity (PLA) *Thematic Working Group for Mathematics Science & Technology*, shows that such team has very positive effect on teachers willingness through its regular discussions with teachers on the ways of introducing and applying the new approaches and improvements of established practices.

In addition, *team work of teachers* and *sharing developed resources and experiences* among the same subject area teachers and between inter-subject teams is enabling IBSE implementation factor. As it was shared by Irene Stone, Maths coordinator at St Marks Community School, Ireland, *collective intelligence makes easier to overcome challenges and to develop better materials*.

Without *information and communication technologies* it is very difficult even to imagine that the IBSE implementation can be successful. They are needed to support spreading and sharing of resources, experiences, and so on. Moreover, they enlarge the space, the time and the possibilities in front of the students, teachers, schools and educational systems, providing flexibility, communication, permanent support, etc.

The last condition is related to accessing sustainability in the IBSE approach application. In order to ensure long lasting systematic use of these new approaches, they should be *built in* and become *integral part of the whole school practice*.

The school principal is responsible for the development of constructive environment, in which IBSE could be applied.

5.3   Prerequisites at Macro Level (National Level)

One of the most imperative prerequisite for wide spread of inquiry-based project education is a *reform of curriculum and assessment*. The curriculum itself should give enough freedom to teachers to have flexibility in time and distribution of the learning content. In the same time the assessments approaches and tools should consider new knowledge and skills, aiming to develop in process of learning. A good practice is presented by the project Maths [18] implemented in Ireland, where the new teaching approaches correspond with new assessment system.

In addition, the *consensus building* is important for successful application of the IBSE.

In North Ireland the idea is realized during the development of new national educational standards (2010), the North Ireland Educational Department worked extensively with teachers, school leaders, unions, inspectors, and policy makers to understand what they would expect young people to be able to do. It has also worked to build parents', business leaders' and politicians' confidence in the quality and appropriateness of the standards.

We saw the other way to implement the idea for consensus and cooperation at national level in Finland, where the government, research institutions, teacher training institutions and business organizations established together the national LUMA centre [19]. The aim of the LUMA Centre is to promote the learning, studying and teaching of natural science, mathematics, computer science and technology on all levels. The LUMA Centre works together with schools, teachers, students of education and several other cooperation partners in order to achieve its goals (Fig. 5).

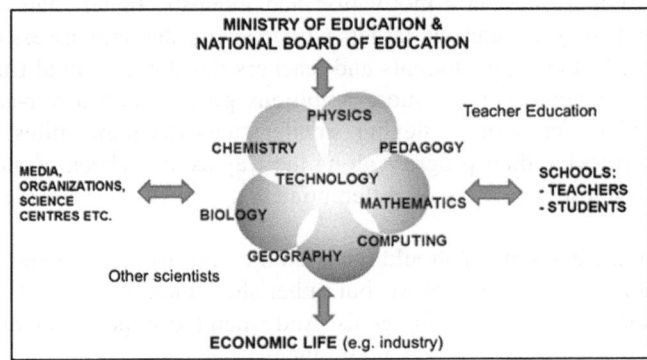

Fig. 5. LUMA is an umbrella organisation coordinated by the Faculty of Science of the University of Helsinki to bring schools, universities and industries together

But just a reform in standards, curriculum and assessment system is not enough if the teachers do not feel well prepared. That is why the *professional development of teachers* and *wide teachers' trainings* should take place in parallel with the educational system reform. Although there have been some successful but sporadic experiences with IBSE, today's teachers, in most European countries, do not have a consolidated and extensive experience in implementing it at all school levels. The uneven distribution of experience in the use of IBSE suggests that massive teacher training activities at European level are needed, and can take advantage of experience transfer from more advanced and successful contexts to others where uptake should be fostered. In addition, IBSE should become a school culture.

A good example of how to build IBSE culture in school could be found again in North Ireland experience in introducing new standards and spreading widely systematic application of formative assessments: North Ireland apply in-service training for the school staff on the place, building the school capacity in common and forming the school culture. Such trainings give positive results and support the spreading of new approaches in the school.

The training of teachers is not enough if there is no *continues teachers support*. *Support by experts* (face-to-face, online) as well as by *the resources* developed by teachers' trainers and by teachers themselves, available and shared online, increases the chance for application of the new approaches in the school practice.

5.4 Assessment for Learning

In order to apply widely inquiry-based science education, special attention should be paid to the assessment.

Traditionally, schools and teachers emphasize student assessment through final exams, rather than through on-going assessments. In recent years the focus moved to the assessment for learning.

The assessment should guarantee that students are well informed about their current achievements and next steps to the goals, as well as to identify these next steps and needs of new knowledge.

The student's engagement in the assessment process is also important. Assessments should support student's motivation and interests, rather than to discourage learners. Students may set learning targets with teachers, and may assess the quality of their own work. In this way, students and teachers develop a mutual trust.

High-flying students may set more ambitious goals, while lower-achieving students may need to focus on achieving smaller steps (frequent milestones) toward learning goals, tracking their progress along the way as they check off items on a *can do* list. This is closely related to differentiated approach to each student and his progress.

In addition, the assessment should focus on the improvements, which the students could make, not just to do an *autopsy*, but rather show them what and how to change, so to become closer to their learning goals. And when the students *comes to their pick* (final goal), it is important to congratulate them.

The teachers should understand very well their responsibilities for the students' results.

All these statements are known in pedagogical science, but unfortunately they are not widely spread in the practice.

The school practice in Northern Ireland and Ireland practices show an evidence for a national-wide effectiveness.

For example, the Northern Ireland strategy supports teachers and students in taking ownership of learning and assessment. Teachers already pay much closer attention to learner motivation and progress.

The importance of identifying small successes through providing regular feedback on how to improve, and of celebrating students achievements is an accent in Ireland Project Maths [18].

5.5   The Sufficient Condition

The conducted and described experiment proves that *the teacher* really is a *sufficient condition*: when he has willingness, the teacher could manage to apply the IBSE regardless of the *lack of necessary conditions*. But is it necessary he to be jaded?

Even if the teacher is so self-motivated to make efforts to do everything along, at some point he becomes exhausted, with no energy for more. Moreover, he has no time and strength all-the-time to prepare along for the IBSE classes. In such circumstances the most of the teachers set the IBSE idea aside. If they begin using IBSE at all! Is it necessary to bring them in such conditions?! Because, as Neda Gerginova (teacher) says: *The truth is that students like to have hard time and challenges, while the teachers prefer the easy way.*

So, if there is no *necessary and sufficient conditions* for IBSE, as a result the natural students' motivation and desire *to have hard time* is not used, and with passing time students lose their enthusiasm, and finally, they take the *easy way*.

6   It is so Difficult! Is It Worth?

Below we would like to share what it is observed by us and what could happen even only *sufficient conditions* are available. Then just to open the door for the imagination what the results could be if all *necessary and sufficient conditions* for IBSE are available.

The attempts to implement the IBSE approach, not only in described experiments, but also in small groups of students and individual work with students during the last 15 years convincingly prove sustainability of the results over the time.

Only one year after the first experiment we observe that the students, who participated in the pilot, are more responsible, take independently initiative for new projects, show maturity in organization and management. For example, last year's eleven graders of First Private Mathematical Gymnasium, today already twelve graders, themselves proposed they to analyse and improve the school web site, defined their own assignment, distribute roles among the class, control the process, and finally, completed the tasks they put themselves.

When the next project in informatics classes was laid, they desired to take part in formulation of the assignments. As a result several projects were defined, provoked by students' interests and motivation:

- A project, serving the process of price-formation in the small private company owned by a student's father;
- A project, enhancing the Op Art ideas of the one of the previous teams by new interface and functionalities;
- An application of combinatorial games, based on early studied algorithms;
- An application, supporting his developers to train for other subjects (in that case - physics).

Two of the National High School of Mathematics and Science students, already admitted students at University of Cambridge, with self-confidence shared that during the entrance interview, telling the interviewers about the inquiry-based project they took part in, the students were delight to the special attitude: *They accepted us as real researchers!*

The evidence for sustainability of the results of the approach is given also by students, graduated National High School of Mathematics more than 5 years ago, and trained in the same style. For example, Kaloyan Slavov, already graduated Massachusetts Institute of Technology (MIT) shares: *I remember almost nothing of what I learned in school, but you taught us to learn and know how to prove own self ideas!*

But most touching award was the proposal of Ruslan Russev (graduated National High School of Mathematics 11 years ago, nowadays owner of a software company): *I would like to develop for you such a learning programming environment, so to be able to teach students in the best way you would like to!*

Looking from the distance in time, we could summarize: the results of the application of the approach give us reasons to conclude: **the efforts are deserved and many times rewarded – as for the student, so for the teacher**!

7 Let's Do It Together!

Keeping in mind the observation and conclusions of experiments as described above and other research results [2, 10], Bulgarian Ministry of Education, Young and Science (MEYS) started the reform, aiming to make the changes evidence and research driven.

The Bulgarian MEYS started a procedure of development of new national standards, curriculum and assessment. Through them the MEYS endeavours to put the accent on development of key competences. In order to consolidate as much as possible experience, research and different point of views, the MEYS involves into the developments researchers, university professors, and teachers. The authors of the paper contribute to the work of the MEYS experts' commissions for the development of national standards, curriculum and assessment for Informatics and Information Technologies. The authors bring to the commissions results their long-standing international research observations and conclusions as well as rich school and university experience. As consequence they search for approaches to build in IBSE in the nature of the curriculum, to stimulate and to integrate it as deep as possible, as well as to use it potential for synergy among disciplines. In addition, as members of stated examination boards for Informatics and Information Technologies, reflecting on international research, the authors work in direction to change the evaluation criteria and work towards putting the accent on the assessment for learning.

All these make us to believe that the change is started and IBSE national-wide is possible, when all work in one direction together. It is a challenge, but the reward worth it!

References

1. Sendova, E. (2011) Assisting the art of discovery at school age – a Bulgarian experience, in *Talent Development Around the World,* http://www.cpti.com.mx/publicaciones/LIBRO.pdf
2. Nikolova, N., Stefanova, E., Sendova, E.: Op Art or the art of object-oriented programming (plenary talk). In: Bezakova, D., Kalas, I. (eds.) Proceeding of Selected Papers, 5th International Conference on Informatics in Schools: Situation, Evolution and Perspectives ISSEP2011, 26–29 October 2011, Bratislava, Slovakia, pp. 28, ISBN: 978-80-89186-90-7 (2011)
3. Stefanova, E., Sendova, E., v. Diepen, N., Forcheri, P., Dodero, G., Miranowicz, M., Brut, M., et al.: Innovative Teacher - Methodological Handbook on ICT-Enhanced Skills. Faleza-Office 2000, Sofia (2007)
4. Innovative Teacher (I*Teach) project. http://i-teach.fmi.uni-sofia.bg Accessed 12 June 2012
5. Stefanova E., Sendova E., Nikolova I., Nikolova N.: When I*Teach means I*Learn: developing and implementing an innovative methodology for building ICT-enhanced skills. In: Benzie, D., Iding, M. (eds.) Abstracts and Proceedings of the Joint IFIP Conference: WG3.1 Secondary Education, WG3.5 Primary Education: Informatics, Mathematics, and ICT: a 'golden triangle' IMICT 2007, CCIS, Northeastern University, Boston, MA, ISBN-13:978-0-615-14623-2 (2007)
6. Sendova, E., Stefanova, E., Nikolova, N., Kovatcheva, E.: Like a (school of) fish in water (or *ICT-enhanced skills* in action). In: Mittermeir, R.T., Sysło, M.M. (eds.) ISSEP 2008. LNCS, vol. 5090, pp. 99–109. Springer, Heidelberg (2008)
7. Stefanova E., Nikolova N., Kovatcheva E., Sendova E., Peltekova E., Hubenova N., Miladinova M., Katrandjieva E.: From a "Flap of a Butterfly Wing" to the "Wind of Change". In: Proceeding of Constructionism 2010, Paris, France, 16-20 August 2010, CD ISBN: 987-80-89186-66-2 (2010)
8. Dewey, J.: Science as subject matter and as method. In: Archambault, R.D. (ed.) John Dewey on Education: Selected Writings, pp. 182–195. University of Chicago Press, Chicago (1964)
9. Linn, M.C., Davis, E.A., Bell, P.: Internet Environments for Science Education. Lawrence Erlbaum Associates, Mahwah (2004)
10. National Science Foundation: Foundations. Volume 2: a monograph for professionals in science, mathematics, and technology education: Inquiry: Thoughts, Views, and Strategies for the K-5 Classroom. Variation National Science Foundation US NSF 02084. http://www.nsf.gov/pubs/2000/nsf99148/pdf/nsf99148.pdf (2000) Accessed 29 July 2012
11. Tafoya, E., Sunal, D., Knecht, P.: Assessing inquiry potential: a tool for curriculum decision makers. Sch. Sci. Math. **80**(1), 43–48 (1980)

12. Okada, A.: Scaffolding school pupils' scientific argumentation with evidence-based dialogue maps. In: Okada, A.; Buckingham Shum, S.J., Sherborne, T. (eds.) Knowledge Cartography: Software Tools and Mapping Techniques. Springer, London (2008)
13. Kirschner, P.A., Sweller, J., Clark, R.E.: Why minimal guidance during instruction does not work: an analysis of the failure of constructivist, discovery, problem-based, experiential, and inquiry-based teaching. Educ. Psychol. **41**(2), 75–86 (2006). doi:10.1207/s15326985ep4102_1. Lawrence Erlbaum Associates, Inc. 10 Industrial Avenue Mahwah, NJ 07430-2262 USA
14. Hmelo-Silver, C.E., Duncan, R.G., Chinn, C.A.: Scaffolding and achievement in problem-based and inquiry learning: a response to Kirschner, Sweller, and Clark (2006). Educ. Psychol. **42**(2), 99–107 (2007). doi:10.1080/00461520701263368. Routledge
15. Furtak, E.M.: The Dilemma of Guidance. An Exploration of Scientific Inquiry Teaching. VDM Verlag Dr. Müller, Saarbrücken (2008)
16. McDermott, L., Shaffer, P., Constantinou, C.: Preparing teachers to teach physics and physical science by inquiry. Phys. Educ. **35**(6), 411–416 (2000)
17. High Level Group on Science Education: Michel Rocard (Chair), Peter Csermely, Doris Jorde, Dieter Lenzen, Harriet Walberg-Henriksson, Valerie Hemmo, (2007), Science Education now: A renewed pedagogy for the future of Europe, Directorate-General for Research Science, Economy and Society, European Commission
18. Project Math. http://www.projectmaths.ie/. Accessed 12 June 2012
19. University of Helsinki. (n.d.). About the LUMA centre. From Finland's Science Education Centre LUMA: http://www.helsinki.fi/luma/english/. Accessed 3 Sep 2012

Innovation and Sustainability in Higher Education: Lessons Learnt from the Case Study of an Online University

Donatella Persico$^{(\boxtimes)}$, Stefania Manca, and Francesca Pozzi

Istituto per le Tecnologie Didattiche, Consiglio Nazionale delle Ricerche, Genova, Italy
{persico,manca,pozzi}@itd.cnr.it

Abstract. The need for higher educational systems to undergo a radical process of innovation is recognized worldwide, but how such a process has to be triggered, managed and sustained is far from being fixed. The paper illustrates the case study of a small Italian online university where a number of actions (i.e. a preliminary analysis of the existing system, the development of a new platform, a training course addressed to teachers and staff, a pilot test of the new system) were carried out to make technological and methodological innovation proceed hand in hand and to drive innovation towards a higher quality of teaching and learning experience. The paper describes context, method and outcomes of the approach adopted and then discusses its strengths and weaknesses.

Keywords: Innovation · Sustainability · Higher education · Online university · Technology Acceptance Model

1 Introduction

Currently, in Europe and elsewhere, universities are undergoing a process of transformation often associated with technological development and featuring strong differences across the various countries and institutions [1]. Such differences concern the aims and drivers of the innovation process, the role and impact of technology, and the effects in terms of organizational, educational and cultural change. This process is definitely complex and difficult to manage, because it includes actions which are deliberately started and promoted by the individual universities, and it is also intertwined with technological and social developments that may not be under the institution's control.

This paper assumes that innovation is not necessarily, by definition, a positive phenomenon, especially if technology is its only driver. Educational institutions and universities in particular should try to define the aims of any innovation process and control such process at least to the extent that its aims are not forgotten or overridden. Of course, technology can play an important role in the innovation process because it can act as a trigger and help improve both the quality and the efficiency of the system, but it should not be the only driver of transformation. Rather, academic institutions and their staff should have a clear idea of what they want to innovate - the educational

A. Cerone et al. (Eds.): SEFM 2012 Satellite Events, LNCS 7991, pp. 35–52, 2014.
DOI: 10.1007/978-3-642-54338-8_3, © Springer-Verlag Berlin Heidelberg 2014

process? the learning outcomes? the organizational aspects? - and why - to make them more effective? more efficient? in what way? from whose point of view?.

In the following, a case study is presented where the introduction of a new technological platform into a small Italian online university was accompanied by a number of actions aimed at supporting the innovation and driving it towards a higher quality of the teaching and learning experience. This work was carried out through the STEEL (Sistemi, Tecnologie abilitanti E mEtodi per la formazione a distanza) Project, aimed at supporting a gradual introduction of technological and methodological innovations in the online university. The paper describes the approach adopted in terms of its context, method and outcomes and later discusses its strengths and weaknesses.

2 Theoretical Background

The literature concerning technological innovation in higher education is exceptionally rich [2–8]. It shows how a better understanding of social needs, pedagogical theories and technological developments can all contribute to and inform educational innovation. Educational institutions of all kinds are adopting and integrating technological systems so that online and blended learning can take place, educational resources are becoming increasingly available and new pedagogies can be implemented.

Research has proved that under the impulse of these changes both the teachers' and the students' roles can change: the teachers are no longer the "sage on the stage" delivering instruction, but rather designers, managers and facilitators of learning processes that are becoming more and more personalized, self-regulated, collaborative and flexible [9]. The learners, on the other hand, will need to become much more responsible, active, engaged and ever more in control of their learning, both inside and outside educational institutions [10, 11]. This determines a shift towards a participatory culture of learning whereby all actors contribute according to their competence, dispositions, aims and beliefs [12].

However, these changes are far from being guaranteed or easy to achieve, neither is their sustainability. For them to become reality they should be planned, fostered and accompanied, and results need to be consolidated and capitalized on. Innovation does not take place overnight, neither can it be fully controlled; rather, it can be supported and driven on the basis of a gradual process of concerted actions of all the actors involved: decision makers, who can promote innovation in a top-down manner, educators and learners, who can implement its uptake though a bottom-up approach [13].

According to Rogers' [14] theory on diffusion of innovation, innovation spreads gradually: a small percentage of innovators trigger the process; a slightly larger percentage of early adopters follow; then, the early majority takes up the new method and/or technology thus achieving a critical mass; thereafter, the process is likely to self-sustain and proceed involving the late majority and, finally, the laggards, until the innovation has reached its saturation point. Educational innovation, in particular, needs to be nurtured and monitored because the aims and understandings of the actors involved are not always aligned with one-another and, hence, the outcomes may turn out not to be coherent with the intended aims.

Focusing on higher education, the uptake and success of innovation is heavily influenced by several conditions: the need of society and institutions to reach a low cost/benefit ratio where costs and benefits are not necessarily evaluated in quantifiable terms, but also in terms of effort and quality of the educational system; the needs of students, comprising their learning aims and expectations but also their desire to cope with social and family life as well as work commitments; the objectives and attitudes of university staff, including their beliefs and possible resistance towards the innovation.

A recently published survey [15] involving learners from around the world following distance education degree courses highlighted how the promise of Technology Enhanced Learning (TEL) research does not match reality. For most of the interviewees, in fact (i) the main approach adopted is a systematic, sequential and individual study of paper documents; (ii) web access is considered marginal with respect to the objective of passing the exam and is often considered a waste of time; (iii) flexibility is not perceived as an attribute of the formative system but rather as the ability to integrate learning into one's own daily routine. These results confirm the hypothesis according to which the introduction of technology alone does not guarantee a significant change in the learning approach, let alone the development of an attitude towards personalized learning.

In Italy, a national survey carried out by the Italian Society for E-Learning in 2007 [16] highlighted a remarkable level of dissatisfaction as to the quality of e-learning services and stressed that in most cases (63 %) the low quality of e-learning is due to poor instructional design as well as lack of adequate theoretical background. As a matter of fact, even in online universities e-learning often consists of making learning materials available to students on some Learning Management Systems (LMS). Typically, these materials include lecture notes, lesson slides, video or audio lessons. This transmissive approach differs from the traditional face-to face approach merely by the medium used and does not take full advantage of the potential offered by technology to improve and enhance the learning experience.

According to the studies above, the diffusion of a pedagogically sound approach in higher education and specifically in online universities is still at a rather early stage, whereby technological innovation is perhaps leading the way while pedagogical innovation lags behind, with a risk that technology becomes the driver of an unbalanced process where educational quality does not move forward fast enough.

3   A Case Study of Innovation in an Online University

As mentioned above, this article reports on a study carried out through the STEEL (Sistemi, Tecnologie abilitanti E mEtodi per la formazione a distanza) project, funded by the Italian Ministry of Education, University and Research under the FIRB Programme.

Within this project, an innovative e-learning system was developed for an Italian virtual university, called UNISANRAFFAELE, partner of the project.

UNISANRAFFAELE is a small, private online university offering, at the beginning of the project, only three study programmes. As such, this university is not a typical example of an Italian public higher education institution, but rather one out of a dozen Italian virtual universities, all established following a Ministerial Decree of April 17th, 2003. Despite bitter controversy and doubts as to the ways in which they developed and the actual purposes pursued by their management [17, 18], these universities are growing along with expectations as to the quality of their educational offer.

The aim of STEEL was to support the introduction of technological and methodological innovations in this online university, thus establishing a model transferable to similar contexts. The project lasted 4 years, during which the project partners designed, developed and tested an innovative educational platform, which intended to serve: (a) static users who normally access the Internet from their desktops; (b) nomadic users that do not have preferred access points and therefore need to be able to connect randomly from various places, possibly with their laptops; (c) mobile users who normally need a Wi-Fi connection and prefer light, mobile devices such as smart phones, tablets, etc. Sustainability of these changes of approach and technological introduction was also addressed in the STEEL project, by providing mid-term support to the teachers involved in the project. However, longer-term support could not be provided after the end of the project. To ensure long-term sustainability, efforts were made to favour the creation of a teacher community able to self-sustain after the end of the project.

3.1 Phases of the Approach to Innovation

While little more than half of the project time was devoted to the development of the technological platform and communication infrastructure of the STEEL system, during the remaining part actions were taken to support the introduction of both the technological component and the desired methodological innovation.

These actions consisted of (Table 1 provides an overview of the project timing, with particular focus on the process of innovation promoted by the STEEL project):

- A preliminary analysis of the existing platform, as well as approaches adopted within the online university before the introduction of the STEEL system.
- The STEEL platform development (i.e. implementation and testing of the hardware and software components).
- A blended course called DID@STEEL, addressing those teachers that inside UNISANRAFFAELE had been identified as the first kernel of innovators and were meant to use the STEEL approach and platform during the pilot test. This course included a follow-up, partially overlapping with the pilot test of the system, during which DID@STEEL staff were available for counselling for the online university teachers.
- A one-year pilot test of the STEEL system during which the teachers of eight courses of UNISANRAFFAELE tested both the technology and the methodologies introduced.

Table 1. The timing of the STEEL project (started in mid 2007 and ended in mid 2011), where each year is divided into 4 terms

	2007	2008		2009		2010		2011
	YEAR 1		YEAR 2		YEAR 3		YEAR 4	
Analysis of existing approach								
Platform development								
DID@STEEL course								
STEEL pilot test								
Monitoring & data analysis								

The phases are described in the following. Data were collected throughout all of these phases and analyzed to monitor and assess the effects of the innovation process. The data collection method and the results of data analysis, described in the subsequent sections, provided a picture ensuring formative evaluation of the STEEL project.

Preliminary Analysis. The preliminary analysis of the courses delivered by UNISANRAFFAELE university revealed a context quite coherent with those described by Selwyn [15] and in the Sie-l report [16]. The analysis was limited to the three-year Sports Science Programme that had been chosen for the STEEL field test.

The general information on courses (title, program and objectives) was publicly available on the website of the Programme, while access to course content was restricted to teachers and students only. The e-learning platform (a customized version of Moodle) plunged students directly into the courses with no support or guidance material as a common denominator. The instructional model was quite homogeneous for all courses, with little adaptation to discipline differences. All courses consisted of a sequence of lessons, mostly delivered through video-lectures (the talking-head teacher presenting content synchronized with slides) or audio-lectures synchronized to a text. Intermediate self-assessment (tests or questions in a forum) was available only in a minority of the courses. In few cases, educational software external to the platform proposed drills and/or tutorials. Forums were used by few teachers and generally hosted question-and-answer sessions between students and lecturers, mostly concerning logistic and organizational information. A registry log was available to all students to see a report of their online sessions within each course.

The most evident weaknesses of the modus operandi at UNISANRAFFAELE were:

- a general lack of material providing information on how to move about the course or describing the objectives, the contents, the type of activities and the examination modalities or guidelines for course or material use;
- a reductive use of the platform, which was mostly used to host learning material consisting of lectures and exercises. Collaboration between students was not encouraged and student-teacher interaction was rather marginal; hence, the proposed instructional approach was mostly transmissive and the main pedagogical model was self-instruction;

- the university organization did not consider the possibility of lecturers autonomously editing their courses: whenever they wanted to upload a new piece of material or create a new module, teachers had to ask technical staff to do it for them, therefore limiting course flexibility;
- hardly ever did students have options on how to study or what to study: personalization was rather poor and therefore student self-regulation was limited to decisions about time rather than method and topics.

Platform Development. Based on the preliminary analysis and on the weaknesses that emerged [19], a new platform was designed and then developed, whose features were meant to overcome the existing drawbacks. The new platform was an extension of the pre-existing one. So, during the project, the courses were carried out with the old infrastructure until the new one was ready and available to be tested. At this point in time, the courses involved in the pilot test were moved to the new platform with virtually no inconvenience for teachers and students.

The new technological infrastructure was based on a satellite-terrestrial network and integrated different media and communication modes. The implemented system was designed in such a way as to comply with national and international guidelines for virtual universities through the latest generation technologies, with a focus on open source ones [19].

As a result, the platform is based on a modular structure integrating the different components for access to the service. The underlying network architecture guarantees information transport services of a higher quality than that usually offered by the Internet. Also the interface of the platform features a modular structure, where the instructional design of each course is based on choices concerning media, technological tools and instructional approaches and allows for personalised learning paths according to users' needs and preferences.

The platform consists of two integrated and tightly interconnected macro-components - an asynchronous open source LMS (Moodle)[1] and a Virtual Synchronous Classroom based on Elluminate Live![2], allowing audio-video-textual videoconferencing enhanced with some collaboration functions (sharing of applications, guided tours of the Web, etc.) particularly useful in online learning. The new environment allows teachers to devise and make online/offline tasks, simulations, tools for e-portfolio management, formative evaluation and assessment tests available. Teachers can also release learning material and structure educational contents into learning units; as to tutoring, they can use several tools to monitor students' online work and to manage evaluation activities. Besides, the system features both asynchronous tools such as forums and wikis, and synchronous tools such as textual chats, instantaneous messaging and audio-visual communication (mainly via Elluminate Live!).

---

[1] Moodle is a well-known LMS featuring various functions, among which storage and use of multimedia material and the possibility for users to communicate in an asynchronous way, http://moodle.org/.

[2] http://www.elluminate.com/

From an instructional point of view, the system allows the implementation of different e-learning approaches, from mere individual and self-instructional solutions (through the fruition of audio or video lessons, individual exercises, etc.) to collaborative activities (group discussion, collective tasks, etc.), both synchronous (brainstorming, group problem solving, etc.) and asynchronous (e.g. collective writing).

Besides, the system was designed to allow students to benefit from the courses in different modalities (static or mobile).

DID@STEEL Course. This course was aimed at laying the base to experiment with the STEEL system and make sure that the teachers involved were well prepared to try it out and adopt the relevant methodological innovations. Participants were selected from UNISANRAFFAELE teaching staff and preference was given to eight teachers who were also meant to pilot test the STEEL system within the project. It should be noted that, although they appeared to be quite motivated to learn about instructional design and TEL, they had been chosen by the university management and were not 'volunteers'. This information will be relevant to the discussion of the whole experience, since much of the literature concerning innovation in higher education points out that commitment of both the staff involved and of the higher levels of the institution's management is an essential factor for success [2].

The DID@STEEL course focused on those methods and practices that were under-used or impossible before the introduction of the STEEL system. Among these, student-teacher interaction and collaborative learning were deemed particularly important.

The course learning objectives were (for more detail on this course see [20]):

- understand the different types of e-learning and the basic principles of instructional design;
- learn how to use the technological tools made available by the STEEL platform and become autonomous in using them and setting them up, thus improving learning flexibility;
- become aware of a range of instructional strategies and learn how to use the relevant platform functionalities;
- (re)design the courses and choose tools and methods suitable for the training context.

The course was a blend of face-to-face and online activities. The latter were based on those very strategies and tools whose use needed to be encouraged among the teachers. The platform used was very similar to that of the STEEL system. In this environment, each lecturer could simulate the set up of the tools and the launch of course activities, receiving feedback from the tutors.

The last activity of the DID@STEEL course was for participants to try to put into practice what they had learnt by designing or re-designing their courses (only one was a new course and was thus designed from scratch, the others were re-designed starting from previous editions). The main objective of this activity was the integration of the newly acquired methods and tools. The plans of the new courses were thoroughly analyzed by tutors who provided detailed feedback on them.

Of course, both the design and the implementation of these innovations fostered practice-based reflection that needed a longer term perspective than the DID@STEEL course. For this reason, at the end of the course, the tutors remained available online to give support to participants while they implemented their plans.

During this follow-up several requests were brought forward concerning practical use of the system, including, for example, assistance during the use of synchronous communication tools, especially audio-visual. Less frequent, instead, were requests concerning methodological aspects, perhaps due to the pressure of implementing the courses and supporting the students. However, a number of small adjustments and additions of new activities were made to the original design of the courses, which testifies for second thoughts about some decisions and increased self-assurance of the teachers with the new functionalities.

The Pilot Test. The pilot test of the STEEL system took place from April 2010 to March 2011, while the remaining months to the end of the project were devoted to the analysis of the data collected during the pilot run. This phase of work consisted in using the system to deliver eight courses, selected from those of the Sports Science Programme of UNISANRAFFAELE. These courses involved about 100 "active" students each (active meaning who accessed the course at least once). The field test was aimed at verifying the impact of the new system from both the standpoint of methodological effectiveness and that of the technological quality. The methodological aspects mostly concern soundness and effectiveness of the instructional design of the courses, while the technological aspects primarily regard the suitability of the platform architecture and the reliability of its software functionalities.

The eight teachers of the courses were in different positions: only one of them had already designed and delivered various editions of her course; the others were newly hired and their courses had been taught by others, or never taught. At the end of the DID@STEEL course, all of teachers (re)designed their courses to include, where appropriate, the new methods and tools dealt with in the training course.

As a result, the pilot test was focused on use of the platform to run the (re)designed courses enhanced with STEEL methods and tools.

3.2   Data Collection Method

As mentioned above, data concerning all the phases described in the previous sections were collected and analyzed. In particular, the preliminary analysis yielded information allowing us to obtain a picture of the modus operandi at UNISANRAFFAELE, including what the dominant approach was, what tools were available on the platform used by the online university before the introduction of the STEEL system, which of these tools were commonly used and which were not.

At the end of the DID@STEEL course, data were collected thorough a questionnaire filled in by course participants to obtain a picture of course acceptance and impact.

At the end of the follow up phase the newly designed courses were analyzed and the data gathered were compared to those that emerged from the preliminary analysis, thus obtaining a matrix describing the planned innovation.

Finally, the data collected during and after the pilot test allowed the evaluators to get a picture of what was actually implemented in the new courses, how much each new feature was used by the teachers and the students and what the perceived ease-of-use and usefulness of the implemented methodological and technological innovations were.

More specifically, the approach adopted to evaluate the impact of the STEEL system was based on an adaptation of the Technology Acceptance Model (TAM), originally proposed by Davis [21] as a theory to model how users of a new technology accept it and take it on, based on two main acceptance factors: perceived usefulness and perceived ease-of-use. Although the TAM model was not developed specifically for educational contexts, several authors have subsequently proposed and demonstrated how adaptations of the TAM theory can also be used to evaluate the impact of technology in these contexts [22–24]. The TAM was thus adapted to the purpose of the STEEL evaluation in order to gather data about all the phases of use of the system (course design, running and evaluation), all the users of the system (students, teachers and e-learning management), and all the components of the system (the e-learning platform, the learning resources and, last but not least, the pedagogical approach underlying the e-learning system).

In addition, data concerning actual use of the system and its effectiveness were also considered. The former were obtained through the tracking facilities of the e-learning platform, while the latter were provided by the teachers through a structured form and comprised both teachers' judgment and the results of students' assessment. Further detail about the approach adopted to evaluate the STEEL system can be found in [25]. In the following section a selection of data is provided, focusing on aspects that shed light on the dynamics of the innovation process ignited by the STEEL project.

3.3   Outcomes

DID@STEEL Outcomes. Table 2 highlights the main changes planned after the course (re)design by the UNISANRAFFAELE teachers as an effect of the DID@ STEEL course and its follow up. Only one course (course 8) was designed from scratch and it is striking to see that it was the one that best accommodated the new ideas introduced with STEEL, though it is not possible to say for sure whether this is due to a teacher more open to change or to the fact that she did not start with consolidated practices. In any case, most of the teachers modified their course objectives at least partially while the contents did not undergo major changes. Despite this, a great effort was devoted to restructuring the sequence and re-arranging blocks of contents.

The learning materials were enriched (rather than radically changed) mostly introducing material that puts learners in more active roles. All the teachers tried to

Table 2. Methodological changes after the course (re)design

Course	Objectives	Contents	Organization	Communication	Materials	Meta-material
Course 1	Re-phrased, to make them clearer	Shift of focus	Organization in blocks of con-tents allowing for flexibility	Mainly asynchronous (some attempts with synchronous)	Unchanged	Created
Course 2	Unchanged	Unchanged	Unchanged	Mainly asynchronous	Introduction of new exercises	Created
Course 3	The spectrum of competence was widened	Unchanged	Reorganization in blocks of contents	Mainly asynchronous	Same video-lectures and slides; new exercises	Created
Course 4	Slightly modified, to operationalize them	Unchanged	A path was suggested but not imposed	Both asynchronous and synchronous; but without collaboration	Revised; new resources integrated	Revised
Course 5	Slightly revised, to include acquisition of practical skills	Unchanged	Reorganization in modules, there is no pre-determined sequence	Stress on individual work	Revised to support learning of practical competencies	Revised
Course 6	Unchanged	Slightly changed to integrate new contents	Reorganization to have the same structure in each module	Mainly asynchronous	Introduction of exercise and lecture notes	Created
Course 7	Modified to stress that human movement is an evolving event	Content was reduced	Unchanged	Introduction of synchronous communication	Unchanged	Created
Course 8	Designed from scratch	Designed from scratch	Designed from scratch	Collaborative activities, asynchronous and synchronous	Designed from scratch	Created

put emphasis on student-teacher interactions, especially through the use of asynchronous tools, while few of them planned collaborative activities (justifying this weakness is the fact that the university allows enrolment at any time during the year and, as a consequence, students are often at different stages of the course study).

Finally, among the innovations proposed by DID@STEEL, the suggestion to create meta−material to support and guide students throughout the course was recognised as important and all teachers changed their courses accordingly.

Table 3 shows the choices made by the teachers as to the use of the technological tools. In particular the table specifies:

- the use of tools offered by the STEEL system and not available before ("++" in the table);
- the repurposing of tools which were already available in the previous platform, but whose use was empowered as a consequence of STEEL ("+" in the table);
- tools already available and in use before STEEL ("=" in the table). Grey cells in stand for "not used" tools.

Outcomes of Pilot Test. This section provides a brief overview of the data concerning the pilot test of the eight courses (for a complete coverage of the data collection method and results see [26]). As mentioned before, the core of the data obtained concern perceived ease-of-use and usefulness from the point of view of the system users (teachers, students and e-learning managers) and, for each of them, they focus on the design, delivery and evaluation of the courses. This information was complemented with data from the automatic tracking system on the actual use by users and from the students' final learning assessment. For the sake of this paper, the data are summarized and the focus is on the educational and technological innovations determined by the STEEL project.

From the educational point of view, data from tracking and from the TAM model analysis as adapted to the STEEL system suggest that the introduction of the system determined important changes in the approach adopted within each subject − most teachers consciously paid the necessary attention to subject matter presentation, to objectives and contents as they had redesigned them. Some also featured the possibility of making the courses more flexible, mainly from the point of view of time, sequence of fruition and learning assessment (both in progress and final). The use of tools facilitating communication among actors of the formative process increased remarkably, mostly under the form of asynchronous communication and one-to-many support, while the promotion of interaction among students and group work based on many-to-many communication was still not extensively adopted.

Consistently with the data on educational aspects, the acceptance degree of the platform by students, in general quite high, is lower only for those tools supporting real time communication (chat and videoconference). In this case, on the one hand, difficulties of use determined a sort of distrust on the usefulness of this tool and, on the other hand, the lack of confidence on their usefulness determined limited use. As a matter of fact, the opinion of the e-learning managers and teachers is that the use of synchronous tools presents organizational difficulties especially when a large group needs to be synchronously online. In addition, the tool used for synchronous

Table 3. Technological changes after course (re)design.

Course	File upload	Forum	Web-pages	Chat, video conferencing	Quiz	Glossary	Assignment	Wiki	Database
Course 1	=	+	++		++	++		++	
Course 2	=	+	++	++	++				
Course 3	=	+		++	++				
Course 4	=	+	++	++	++		++		
Course 5	=	+	++	++	++		++		
Course 6	=	+	++		++				
Course 7	=	+		++					
Course 8	++	++	++	++	++	++	++	++	++

The tools in question are the standard Moodle tools.

communication (Elluminate Live!) is rather professional and advanced but also too complex for the needs of UNISANRAFFAELE users. Similarly, the limited use of Moodle functions more oriented to collaborative learning, such as wiki, database and glossary, clearly shows that the maturity of the STEEL users, both teachers and students, towards the educational use of this type of functions is still rather low. It should be noted that this type of collective "maturity" cannot be attained in a short time. In this sense, the DID@STEEL course was certainly useful, and a long term counselling service to teachers would further promote the uptake of innovation. Similarly, ad hoc initiatives for students, oriented to the use of complex tools could foster their wider use.

4   Discussion

In her literature survey on the diffusion of innovative practices in higher education, Smith [2] lists six lessons learnt from the studies analyzed:

1. The need for senior staff to support an innovation for it to spread effectively.
2. The need for a sound and robust infrastructural set-up to iron out technological issues.
3. The need for adequate skills on the side of both teachers and students.
4. The crucial role of contextual relevance in the adoption of innovation.
5. The importance of supportive networks that can facilitate the adoption diffusion of innovation.
6. The importance of the time factor- innovation is time consuming and it needs a long term perspective to consolidate, let alone to evaluate its impact.

The above are a useful guideline to discuss the data that emerged from our case study.

4.1   The Need for Senior Staff to Support an Innovation for It to Spread Effectively

This statement, applied to the STEEL project, is almost an understatement. Given that the online university was involved in the project, the institutional support to the innovation introduced by the project could be taken for granted. However, institutional commitment does not guarantee teachers' commitment. As already mentioned, in STEEL, the teachers selected by the management for participation in the pilot study were not volunteers; besides, most of them were newly hired staff taking on the courses for the first time, except for one teacher, who was 'senior'. The DID@STEEL course was aimed to sensitize the teachers and motivate them and – to confirm the saying that sometimes consolidated habits are more difficult to eradicate than younger traditions - the senior teacher showed less motivation and commitment than the others who, being quite young and technology savvy, were willing to start their new jobs in the best possible way, thus proving more open to innovation.

Despite this, we also have to acknowledge that in UNISANRAFFAELE, which is a small and relatively new private institution, the influence of the senior staff was less important than what seems to be the case in Smith's study, while what played an essential role was the commitment of the new teachers and the university management to the project.

4.2   The Need for a Sound and Robust Infrastructural Set-up

According to the STEEL project plans, not only the communication infrastructure, but also the technological platform developed during the first part of the project needed to be tested and smoothly working before the beginning of the pilot test, involving teachers and students. Smith's principle that technical problems need to be ironed out as much as possible to avoid falls in motivation of the users involved was crystal clear to the project partners. For this reason, for example, the criteria for choosing the synchronous component of the STEEL system led the project partners to prefer a reliable commercial tool, Elluminate Live!, to other possible open source options, which did not guarantee the same degree of reliability. For the same reason, some of the system components which were not fully tested and validated (e.g. those for mobile access) were left out of the platform for the pilot test.

4.3   The Need for Adequate Skills on the Side of Both Teachers   and Students

This "lesson learnt" from Smith's study was fully shared by the STEEL partners and led to the decision to organize the DID@STEEL course, aiming to develop the needed skills among UNISANRAFFAELE teachers, with particular reference to those who were to participate in the pilot test. This course (and the coherent changes to the platform) definitely provided them with a higher degree of autonomy in making changes to their course structure or producing new learning material with little external support. As for the students, the very fact that they had enrolled in an online university gave reasons to believe that they were likely to possess the necessary basic skills. However, it is well known that basic operational skills with technology are not all that is needed to take full advantage of an online programme: a set of important transversal skills, such as negotiation, collaboration and self-regulation are also needed. To support students in the development of these skills in relation to the specific courses involved in the STEEL pilot test, all the teachers were encouraged to develop what can be termed 'meta-material': a course presentation, containing information about what students are expected to do and how, with clear instructions as to how to proceed and organize one's own study. Each teacher chose different media to implement this course introduction, applying the DID@STEEL considerations concerning media choice.

4.4   The Crucial Role of Contextual Relevance in the Adoption of Innovation

"Innovations that sit well within a specific context spread better" is the formulation of this lesson learnt in Smith's paper [2: 176]. In view of this principle, the (re)design of the courses for the pilot test started from context specific problems, that is the teachers addressed the main learning issues of their students and the main pedagogical problems of their discipline and adopted those functionalities of the platform that seemed to address their needs. Needless to say, practice based reflection is also essential for sustainability of innovation. Together with the next two lessons learnt, this is perhaps one of the main weaknesses of the STEEL project, as well as that of many other innovation processes that were made possible by ad-hoc funding with a short-term agenda.

4.5   The Importance of Supportive Networks that Can Facilitate the Adoption and Diffusion of Innovation

Innovation can be championed by practitioners within a discipline and/or by central university departments devoted to staff educational development. This is also a precondition for sustainability that the STEEL partners intended to put in place before the end of the project, in order to make sure that the whole system did not collapse as soon as the project support ended. As a consequence, the creation of communities, supported by social networking tools or also by one or more dedicated forums within the university platform, often played a determining role. In the STEEL project, the pilot study involved only a small group of teachers and so it was not possible to have disciplinary groups; nonetheless, one of the aims of the DID@STEEL course was to favour the birth of a trans-disciplinary community comprising all the people involved in the pilot test, with some of the STEEL partners surrogating the role of a staff development department (not all universities have such a department, and UNI-SANRAFFAELE is one of these, although STEEL put forward the proposal to create it to increase sustainability). As a matter of fact, some of the practices proposed during the DID@STEEL course were recognized as effective by all the teachers and became part of the common repertoire of the new community.

4.6   The Importance of the Time Factor: Innovation Is Time Consuming and It Needs a Long Term Perspective to Consolidate, Let Alone Evaluate Its Impact

Last but not least, time is recognized as a major barrier to the adoption of innovative practices [27]. The production of new resources, the introduction of new methods and tools cannot happen overnight and they are usually the result of a gradual process requiring a substantial investment, both in depth (in terms of more time dedicated at least to bootstrap the process) and longitudinally (in terms of elapsed time needed). The teachers involved in the STEEL pilot test were confronted with both of these time related issues: the former was evident when they had to implement the new designs of their courses: making the plans required time and for this reason some of their plans were not realized in the new courses but postponed to subsequent versions. The latter was related to the need for a longer term perspective: although persistence and sustainability of the innovation is often mentioned in many projects nationally or internationally funded, the time span of their lifetime is often almost incompatible with the long term approach that is needed to ensure sustainability. STEEL is no exception: the four years of work were just enough to bootstrap a positive process, but at the end of it new investments are needed to nourish and strengthen the initial team of innovators, as well as favour its expansion to a more solid set of early adopters.

5   Conclusions

This paper illustrates a project where a small Italian online university was supported to innovate both the educational methods and the technology used. The project also laid the basis for the sustainability of these innovations. The innovation approach adopted entails a preliminary analysis of the existing system, the development of a new platform, a training course addressed to teachers and staff, and a pilot test of the new system. The sustainability of the whole innovation process was bootstrapped by making the creation of a teacher community possible and by putting forward the proposal to create a staff development department of the university. The paper provides context, method and outcomes of the approach adopted and discusses its strengths and weaknesses.

In the following some concluding remarks are provided concerning how to bring about innovation in a STEEL-like context, and recommendations on future developments in investigation and research.

As already mentioned, the study was based on the assumption that making technology available in an educational system does not guarantee that its potential is fully exploited, let alone that a sound methodological innovation takes place.

A first indication that emerged from the study refers to the ways processes of introduction of innovation in educational contexts can be activated, especially at university level. As Laurillard and colleagues [13] state, experience proves that innovation cannot be imposed on an existing system from above – a mixture of top-down and bottom-up approach should be preferred instead. Commitment and propelling force should come from all the actors involved: the institution, the staff involved, and the students, that need to be sensitized and made aware of the advantages of the innovation. In particular, the institution should provide management and coordination, resources and funds, while teachers should actively participate, believe in the innovation's importance and share its aims, which can only be obtained if they are involved from the planning stages of its implementation and suitably trained. A golden rule of this training is that it should be based on the same approaches the teachers are supposed to adopt; in this way they can try out benefits and drawbacks of innovation before they themselves take it up. E-learning managers and other university staff should also be involved as early as possible and share the same aims. Graduality of change is also essential to prevent the time barrier from hindering the whole process.

In the STEEL project, the contextual requirements led to some important decisions. In spite of the fact that TEL research of the last twenty years points out that social constructivist approaches are a major added value of technology in education [28], it was recognized that a virtual university where student workers are the majority, a constant presence on the platform and approaches heavily based on peer-interaction and collaboration is not advisable, since individual study of materials is the preferred approach of most students. Flexibility and personalization are the most pressing requirements. Hence, collaborative approaches were limited to small groups and the emphasis was placed on the need to provide alternative and tailorable learning paths. However, the social component of learning was recovered by supporting the creation of informal communities and networks of peers.

To conclude, it stands to reason that introducing technology, per se, is not sufficient to produce changes, at least in educational settings. A larger investment is needed, encompassing not only the provision of new tools and platforms, but also investments in terms of human resources (through training and guided, contextual reflective practice) and time (recognition of time commitment of the innovators, long-term investments for gradual change). Another important point is that neither change nor innovation are intrinsically positive: assessing the cost-benefit ratio is necessary, and this evaluation should involve all the stakeholders and all the phases of the innovation process.

References

1. Mayes, T., Morrison, D., Mellar, H., Oliver, M.: Transforming Higher Education Through Technology Enhanced Learning. The Higher Education Academy, York (2009)
2. Smith, K.: Lessons learnt from literature on the diffusion of innovative learning and teaching practices in higher education. IETI **49**(2), 173–182 (2012)
3. Ehlers, U.-D., Schneckenberg, D. (eds.): Changing Cultures in Higher Education. Springer, Heidelberg (2010)
4. Garrison, R., Anderson, T.: E-learning in the 21st Century A Framework for Research and Practice. Routledge, London (2003)
5. Curran, C.: The phenomenon of on-line learning. Eur. J. Educ. **36**(2), 113–132 (2001)
6. Salmon, G.: Flying not flapping: a strategic framework for e-learning and pedagogical innovation in higher education institutions. ALT-J. Res. Learn. Technol. **13**(3), 201–218 (2005)
7. Perrotta, C.: Innovation in Technology-Enhanced Assessment in the UK and the US: future scenarios and critical consideration. Technol. Pedag. Educ. (in print)
8. Karamouzis, S.T.: Networked Universities in the United States. In: Proceedings of the IASTED International Conference Web-Based Education, Innsbruck, Austria, 16–18 February 2004, pp. 414–416 (2004)
9. Collins, A., Halverson, R.: The second educational revolution: rethinking education in the age of technology. J. Comput. Assist. Learn. **26**, 18–27 (2010)

10. Goodyear, P., Ellis, R.A.: University students' approaches to learning: rethinking the place of technology. Distance Educ. **29**(2), 141–152 (2008)
11. Bartolomé, A., Bergamin, P., Persico, D., Steffens, K., Underwood, J. (eds.): Self-regulated learning in technology enhanced learning environments: problems and promises. In: Proceedings of the STELLAR-TACONET Conference, pp. 180. Shaker Verlag (2011)
12. Jenkins, H., Clinton, K, Purushotma, R Robison, A.J., Weigel, M.: Confronting the Challenges of Participatory Culture: Media Education for the 21st Century. MIT Press, Cambridge (2006). http://digitallearning.macfound.org/atf/cf/%7B7E45C7E0-A3E0-4B89-AC9C-E807E1B0AE4E%7D/JENKINS_WHITE_PAPER.PDF
13. Laurillard, D., Oliver, M., Wasson, B., Hoppe, U.: Implementing technology-enhanced learning. In: Balacheff, N., Ludvigsen, S., de Jong, T., Lazonder, A., Barnes, S. (eds.) Technology-Enhanced Learning: Principles and Products, pp. 289–306. Springer, Dordrecht (2009)
14. Rogers, E.M.: Diffusion of Innovations, 5th edn. Free Press, New York (2003)
15. Selwyn, N.: Digitally distanced learning: a study of international distance learners'(non)use of technology. Distance Educ. **32**(1), 85–99 (2011)
16. Eletti, V., Sponsiello, M: Osservatorio SIe-L 2007. I Risultati dell'Indagine. In: Colorni, A., Pegoraro, M. Rossi, P.G. (eds.) eLearning tra formale ed informale - Atti del IV congresso della Società Italiana di eLearning, Macerata 3-6 luglio (2007)
17. Ferri, P.: Atenei virtuali in Italia un'altra occasione mancata? Molti mercanti ed alcune iniziative serie: indicazioni per rimanere al passo con l'Europa http://www.scribd.com/doc/3470323/Atenei-virtuali-in-Italia-unaltra-occasione-mancata (2008)
18. Rizzo, S., Stella, G. A.: Le mille stravaganze degli atenei privati. Corriere della Sera, 29 dicembre. http://www.corriere.it/Primo_Piano/Cronache/2006/12_Dicembre/29/stella.html (2006)
19. Del Re, E., Delfino, M., Limongiello, G., Persico, D., Scancarello, I., Suffritti, R.: Systems, enabling technologies and methods for distance learning: the STEEL project. ISDM – Information, Savoirs, Décisions & Médiations - Information Sciences for Decision Making, vol. 39, article n. 657 (2010) http://isdm.univ-tln.fr/PDF/isdm39
20. Bozzini, S., Delfino, M., Limongiello, G., Manca, S., Persico, D., Pozzi, F., Sarti, L., Scancarello, I.: Innovazione tecnologica e metodologica in una università telematica. Research on Education and Media (REM) (in press)
21. Davis, F.D.: Perceived usefulness, perceived ease-of-use, and user acceptance of information technology. MIS Q. **13**(3), 319–340 (1989)
22. Edmunds, R., Thorpe, M., Conole, G.: Student attitudes towards and use of ICT in course study, work and social activity: a technology acceptance model approach. Br. J. Educ. Technol. **43**(1), 71–84 (2012)
23. Park, S.Y.: An analysis of the technology acceptance model in understanding university students' behavioral intention to use e-Learning. Educ. Technol. Soc. **12**(3), 150–162 (2009)
24. Teo, T.: Modelling technology acceptance in education: a study of pre-service teachers. Comput. Educ. **52**(1), 302–312 (2009)
25. Persico, D., Manca, S., Pozzi, F.: Three by three by three: a model for e-learning evaluation. In: Proceedings of the ECEL 2012 Conference, Groningen, The Netherlands, 26-27 October 2012 (2012)
26. Delfino, M., Manca, S., Persico, D., Pozzi, F., Sarti L.: Rapporto sulla qualità didattica del corso pilota. STEEL Technical Report RT-2.4.1 (2011)
27. Kahler, T.: Some time to play: individual technology adoption decisions and a diffusion strategy. Distance Learn. **6**(1), 59–66 (2009)

28. Dillenbourg, P., Järvelä, S., Fischer, F.: The evolution of research on computer-supported collaborative learning: from design to orchestration. In: Balacheff, N., Ludvigsen, S., de Jong, T., Lazonder, A., Barnes, S. (eds.) Technology-Enhanced Learning: Principles and Products, pp. 3–19. Springer, Dordrecht (2009)

Mobile Augmented Reality with Audio
Supporting Fieldwork of Cultural Sciences Students in Florence

Stefaan Ternier, Fred de Vries$^{(\boxtimes)}$, Dirk Börner, and Marcus Specht

Centre for Learning Sciences and Technologies, Open Universiteit, Heerlen, The Netherlands
{stefaan.ternier,fred.devries,dirk.boerner,marcus.specht}@ou.nl

Abstract. In this article the use of augmented reality with a smartphone for fieldwork of Cultural Sciences students is discussed based on two pilots in Florence. A tool named ARLearn developed to support different learning in different contexts using the multimedia capabilities and location based service on smartphones. In the pilots assignments were given in spoken messages and students collected notes by recording their own voice and taking pictures of artifacts in Florence. The use of the tool for fieldwork helped students with systematical collection of data for their essay. The educational design and ARLearn toolkit is developed further to enable individual fieldwork students and other educational scenarios.

1 Introduction: Augmented Reality

Today, smart-phones, iPods, PDAs and other mobile devices account for a swiftly growing market. In this article, mobile learning is used broadly and points at situations where these devices are engaged to support learning. Mobile learning can support learning while being on the road. For instance accessing learning resources while traveling. Often mobile devices are found equipped with camera, GPS, gyroscope, accelerometer, digital compass and other sensors that frame the mobile context. This makes them compelling to support location based learning, a sub-domain of mobile learning that zooms in on situations where a user's particular location is important to support the learning process in an authentic context. Augmented Reality is one technique to realize location-based learning. It can be considered a physical real-world environment in which elements are augmented by virtual computer-based sensory input such as images or sound. Although Augmented Reality is often perceived as a technique to project a virtual reality on a video feed, it should more properly refer to any media that is specific to the location and the context of what you are doing [1]. Milgram and Kishino [2] define a Reality - Virtuality Continuum that spans from the real environment to a purely virtual environment. Augmented reality is positioned here as a real environment that is augmented with virtual elements.

In this article, ARLearn augments a location by means of audio. In some situations it is better not to rely on particular sensory inputs. For instance while driving a car, relying on sight for giving a driver extra information is not a good a idea. New cars

A. Cerone et al. (Eds.): SEFM 2012 Satellite Events, LNCS 7991, pp. 53–63, 2014.
DOI: 10.1007/978-3-642-54338-8_4, © Springer-Verlag Berlin Heidelberg 2014

sometimes come with the ability to indicate accidentally driving over a white line. Vibrating the chair to indicate this builds on touch as a sense to indicate crossing a line. In location based learning, sight is an important sense. Supporting location based learning with smart-phone applications risks that sight is consumed to interact with the application. Just like a user should - while driving a car - use sight as much as possible to drive, we believe that with location based learning, a learner's eyes must be primarily used to examine the environment. ARLearn therefore builds on hearing to support location-based learning through mobile phones.

Secondly, a great deal of location based applications for smart-phones focus on location-based access to content. Mobile apps such as Layar, AroundMe, Aloqa[1] present information through layers or channels and are without doubt useful to support just in time location based access to content. In a way they can be compared to what GPS based car-navigation does in supporting drivers to navigate. Both help users to fulfill tasks more efficiently. However the question remains whether these kind of tools also lead to deep learning and insight in the matter. Will consistent use of car navigation systems lead to similar geographic insight compared to with not using these systems? ARLearn, therefore does not focus merely at providing location based information but also enables users to digest information and contribute insights through the notion of annotations.

In this article, ARLearn is presented together with the results of a pilot study. Every year, students of the School of Cultural Sciences take part in a field-trip to Florence, where they study the available visual arts in its original context. During this trip, students train skills such as collecting data in the field, conducting a literature study, developing their own research questions and oral presentation skills.

Part of the group, that visited Florence, on their study visit in the autumn of 2010 and 2011, was equipped with a smartphone. Via the smartphone, students received audio recordings containing either information or assignments relative to their location. The goal of this pilot was threefold. Firstly, we were interested whether the students appreciated a personalized learning experience. Secondly, with this toolset paperless mobile fieldwork should be supported. Finally, an online portfolio should be transparently made available, enabling the learners to revisit their trip, but also to extend and further process the notes they made.

2   ARLearn

Information in context can be filtered according to location, direction, focused object, time period or learner's personal interests. Augmented reality browsers like Layar and Wikitude[2] support filtering dependent on the sensors available on the mobile device. These browsers have implemented a Point Of Interest (POI) browsing interaction pattern, delivering the same experience for every user. That is, on arrival on a new

---

[1] Apps can be found a at www.layar.com, www.aroundmeapp.com and www.aloqa.com

[2] www.wikitude.com

location a user can select a channel and retrieve information about their surroundings. ARLearn contrasts with this one-fit-all approach in two ways:

- Rather than only presenting information to a learner, authors are invited to create location based assignments that trigger reflection on an artifact.
- Authors can submit information that is only presented automatically to a selection of students in a group.

Layar and Wikitude build on GPS, Compass and accelerometer data to augment the life camera feed on a smartphone. As the software is aware of user's location and can determine in which direction the device is held, it can annotate artifacts with a relative high precision.

In one of our preliminary experiments with Augmented Reality, a game was built that uses the technology. The goal of the experiment was to introduce interaction with elements of Augmented Reality and verify how users perceive these. The game named Locatory was played twice at the campus of the Open Universiteit. Each time, four teams played the game. Although there is no quantitative data on these pilots [3], reports some interesting findings:

- Participants were all very enthusiastic about the tool. Most of them had never worked with Augmented Reality tools before. Even so, the use of the tools was rather intuitive.
- The Locatory app absorbed all of the attention of the users, which might lead to dangerous situations. While playing the game, observers had to highlight the danger of cars entering and leaving the campus.
- We found that the way users perceived the game environment relates to tunnel vision. The players were discovering their surroundings by means of the smartphone camera. Holding the smartphone in front of their eyes like spectacles they could gaze at the virtual artifacts. In a location based learning setting, for example a city trip, this might make the technique less suitable as eventually we want users to use their vision to explore their environment.

Our findings with Locatory triggered reflection on AR usability patterns. Therefore, in the Florence fieldwork we decided to explore the effects of an alternative interaction pattern, by rendering an audio augmentation layer with the smartphone, so students can use their eyes to explore artifacts around them. This is particularly useful for students on a fieldtrip as their objective is to study and report on the actual treasures in Florence. Beside this note taking facilities were to complement the augmented reality experience to support the students in their fieldwork.

The ARLearn platform is designed for university tutors that organize fieldwork, but can support other scenarios as well. For example, professionals could use the app when inspecting a site a make notes that are synchronized with their current location. Alternatively a serious game can be created in which trainees are to respond to each other based on augmented or virtual information played by smartphones [4]. With a desktop based authoring tool, authors can add assignments or information to the map and define the conditions for the audio to be played. As we wanted to lower the threshold for the use of the application, we decided to build it on a cloud computing infrastructure in combination with open standards. As a result, authors do not need to set up a server for using the tool; neither do they need to rely on the infrastructure of the Open Universiteit. ARLearn originally builds on two Google products:

- 'Google maps' offers an API through which client applications like ARLearn can view, store and update data on a map.
- 'Google sites' is a kind of Wiki where people can work together. Like Google maps, this site offers an API through which client applications can create, view and update both pages and attachments.

As Google APIs build on the atom publishing protocol porting ARLearn to another platform is possible given that it supports AtomPub.

2.1   Authoring Environment

A simple authoring environment facilitates collaboration through shared Google Maps, prior or after the excursion. This tool lets tutors create and upload assignments or information to a map and define when and how they will be played. Unlike usual authoring environments the tool uses the shared map as the direct mean of interaction. Technically based on the Google Maps API and in line with the well-known interaction patterns of Google Maps the author can pan and zoom the map as well as change the form of rendering to elaborate geographical details.

Using one's own Google account the author can work with an arbitrary number of maps. The author can position map features accurately to a meter anywhere on the map. The features are used as narrator objects that store the spatial assignment or information. The objects can be adjusted to the author needs and are characterized by the following properties:

- A name identifying the object and the spatial range in which the respective audio notification gets played. The range is defined by a maximum and a minimum value depicting the object's activity radius in meters and thus the playback volume. When a user enters the perimeter defined by the maximum value, the audio will start playing automatically. The minimum value must be further away than the maximum value. When a user moves in between this span, the volume will adjust automatically. As a result, the playback volume will fade out, as the user walks away from the object and fade in, as the user gets closer to the object.
- An optional audio file, image file, and/or textual description. The audio file is the central entity of ARLearn system, augmenting the user experience. Using the authoring environment the author can simply upload an audio file, ideally a self-recorded sample, which will then be played automatically when a user enters the defined spatial range around the object and alternatively can be played manually. Furthermore the author can also upload an image file that represents the object and will be shown if a user inspects an object. Similarly to the image, the author can add a textual description that will also be shown when the user inspects an object.
- An optional comma-separated list of assignees for whom the object is reserved. Other users will also be able to see the respective object on the map, but they will not receive the automatic audio notification.

For each narrator object that is created, a feature is added to Google Maps using the Google Maps Data API and a page is created on Google Sites using the Google Sites Data API. This page contains both the audio and/or the image as an attachment as well as the textual description as content. Additionally the specific properties (spatial range, audio and/or image url, textual description, assignee list) are submitted with the feature and stored as custom attributes that are not visible using the default Google Maps interface, but can be queried using the respective Data API based on AtomPUB. The API also allows submitting geospatial queries as well as a filtering using single. After the submission the created features are instantly visible on the map and can also be updated or deleted.

2.2 ARLearn Client Application

The ARLearn smartphone client is a Google Android application. Android's multi-tasking infrastructure and the ability to register location-based events made this operating system a good candidate for this product.

The Android client is intended for students and features multiple views. During the excursion, students can switch between list view and map view. The map view (a) renders ARLearn objects relative to user's position, while the list view (b) sorts the objects ordered by distance. Green icons indicate that the narrator object is not assigned to anyone particular, while purple objects are assigned to a list of students. Although these views help a user, ARLearn was intended to use in standby mode. In this mode, ARLearn will vibrate when a students approximates an object and plays the associated audio stream automatically through the earphones. The auto-play mode (d) functions in standby mode, but also operates when a user has another application open. An Android notification, that is similar to receiving an SMS message, is then displayed at the top. When a user responds to this notification, he is taken to (c) where further information is available on the audio stream that is playing. Purple (assigned) narrator objects will only play automatically if they are assigned to the student that is currently logged in. These objects are indicated by icons with the label "me" (Fig. 1).

Fig. 1. (a) map view (b) list view (c) open object (d) auto-play

Fig. 2. (a) Create an annotation (b) record audio (c) review and/or publish annotation

As interacting with the artifact studied by the student triggers reflection, ARLearn features note taking functionality. A note can be randomly taken by a student or can be a response to an open question. Figure 2 illustrates how a student can navigate from the map view (a) to the annotate view (b). Here a user can take a picture, record audio and provide a title for the annotation. When at least one media item has been provided, the publish button appears (c), allowing the student to publish the annotation to Google maps and Google sites. Next an icon labelled "me" will appear on the map. Annotations made by others are presented by icons without a label.

After the excursion, students have access to their notes via Google Sites pages that groups all ARLearn objects by account and date in a portfolio. Here, students can revisit and replay there notes (Fig. 3). Furthermore, the Wiki functionality of this application enables them to further process and extend their portfolio with additional knowledge.

3 Pilot During Cultural Sciences Fieldwork

The context of fieldwork has potential in re-arranging its educational set-up, abandoning the guided tour principle where students and tutor explore as a group the treasures of Florence, making it a more individual exploration endeavor. In the two pilots, six and nine students from the faculty of Cultural Sciences of the Open Universiteit volunteered to use ARLearn for one afternoon ARLearn in the context of a personal study-theme.

The pilots were conducted during the regular one week Cultural Sciences study visit in Florence, Italy in November 2010 (pilot A) and November 2011 (pilot B). The day before a group instruction was given on the use of a smartphone in general and the

Fig. 3. Student notes are available through Google Sites.

ARLearn application specifically, supporting their fieldwork. Afterwards all students were given a smartphone with ARLearn and were tasked to use and to get acquainted with the device during the course of the next day.

In the course of the pilot, students worked on their own in the center of Florence on the individual study-tasks that their tutor prepared with the authoring environment. The tasks of the students were not overlapping. Each student was given a series of 2-5 small tasks by the tutor. The tasks were presented as a series of spoken messages by the tutor. The same tasks could also be re-read using the screen of the smartphone. In some cases graphics were used to clarify the task given. The tasks presented by the tutor are designed as guides for the students in working out their fieldwork. After the completion of their fieldwork students filled out a questionnaire followed by an interview in which clarification and explanation on the questionnaires was obtained together with observations that were not captured in the questionnaire. An overall view on the use of the ARLearn application was obtained by using product reaction cards [5].

The students were all positive on the use of ARLearn as a study-tool (first entry in Table 1). All participants marked 4 or 5, only in pilot B one person marked 1, which explains the lower average. Most participants added that the personal assignments explained by their tutor, helped them to focus on specific aspects of the cultural treasures in a rich environment. A student expressed "this tool makes it easy to do my fieldwork on my own. I am not depending on the pace of the rest of the group, and it makes me focus on the treasures that I want to examine".

The ARLearn app makes the smartphone in pilot A vibrate and starts playing audio clips automatically when a student comes close to study-object. Only two students appreciated this, the other three perceived it as irritating and preferred to start the audio clip manually and one was indifferent. It was suggested to give only haptic feedback (e.g. audio signal, vibration) when an object is approached, after which the audio-fragment can be started manually. When artifacts to be studied were within close range of each other, audio clips often started playing while the student was still focused on

Table 1. Summarized data from questionnaire and portfolio

Questionnaire (5 point Likertscale)	Pilot A (n = 6)	Pilot B (n = 8)
"The support of ARlearn in performing my fieldwork on artifacts in different locations in Florence is useful?"	4.56	4.24
"Creating notes by typing text is useful"	2.00	Not available
"Creating notes by taking pictures is useful"	4.83	4.75
"Creating notes by recording my voice is useful"	3.50	3.11
Number of notes collected in portfolio of students		
Average number of notes with typed text	2.17	Not available
Average number of notes with pictures	4.83	4.86
Average number of notes with voice recordings	3.50	3.50

another task. This caused irritation. In the second pilot B the assignments were for this reason listed on the student's smartphone but not played automatically. The phone consequently plays a signal and vibrates if a new assignment comes available.

The audio fade out feature, that starts when walking away from an object, was not noticed by five out of six students in pilot A. Probably the street-noise made them not notice this. Besides, the fading out only works when a users' position can be accurately determined, which was often not the case. In Florence, a city with narrow streets and high buildings, the GPS signal is often very poor. This feature was for this reason not used in the second pilot B and replaced by the haptic feedback mentioned above.

Students were encouraged to gather their data for their fieldwork by using the annotation function in which their voice could be recorded using the microphone, photos could taken using the built-in camera and short texts could be typed using the touchscreen. All students made notes, where taking pictures was the most popular with on the average almost 5 pictures taken by each student (Table 1). This was supported by the feedback acquired in the questionnaire students showed most positive about taking pictures of the artifacts examined. They expressed it as an easy and fast way to collect their data.

Besides taking pictures students could take notes by either typing them on the smartphone or by recording their own voice. In pilot A the typing of notes turned out to be complicated for the students, who explained that the virtual keyboard on the touchscreen was rather small and that it was difficult to see in the bright sunlight. This explains the low number of notes taken and the low appreciation. In pilot B the use of typed notes was, although technical possible not mentioned and not used. In both pilots students recorded their own voice to take notes. Although it was considered a suitable option, most students felt somewhat uncomfortable to speak out their observations loud and to listen to their own voice. This explains the lower score in the Questionnaire compared to taking pictures. Still each student created on an average 3.5 voice recordings in both pilots. This can be considered substantial given the fact that it was for all students the first time they took notes by recording their own voice. Students expressed in the interviews: "It is very awkward to speak to myself and then listen to my own voice" and "superfast to simply think aloud, makes it much easier to work-out my observations afterwards".

After the study visit in Florence students worked out an essay in order to complete their coursework. They were to use the collected data accessible in their portfolio (Fig. 3). The tutor in both pilots confirmed the statements of the students that in the reports sent, more systematically the observations of the Florence fieldwork were covered and explained by the students.

3.1 Discussion

In the two pilots conducted students showed critical positive towards the use of the ARlearn in their fieldwork. The original design with automatically playing the audio fragments and the change of volume showed not applicable and was abandoned in pilot B. Note taking turned out to be quite easy using the audio recording and camera functions of the smartphone, but students have to get used to do this orally, as most of them are not used to record and play their own voice. Given the feedback of the tutor, the students in the pilots collected systematically date for their essay.

4 Conclusion

This article contributes to a broader vision on augmented reality. Rather than relying on sight to augment, auditory senses can be used to augment what a students observe around them. For this purpose, a complete open source toolkit has been built including an authoring environment and a smartphone application. Furthermore this toolkit synchronizes content through open standards such as Atom and AtomPub content to Google Maps and Google Sites. This realizes a tool that is free to download, free to modify and relies on the free of charge usage of Google services. The integration of these Google services realizes a cloud based approach.

From the two pilots it can be concluded that the ARLearn tool installed on an Android smartphone was appreciated by the students as a useful learning tool, taking into consideration the difficulties in positioning and the automatic playing of audio-fragments. Moreover the students indicated that the Audio Augmented Reality function was only one of the valuable learning tools. The possibility to record their spoken notes and take pictures was as important for them. The principle to play and record in a visual rich environment audio-fragments using ones auditory sense for questions and notes was supported in the pilots.

The value of an individual study visit with fieldwork of the students as such depends mainly on the assignments the tutor designs, taking into consideration the previous work of a student and details of the historical treasures to be observed. If over time more students visit the same locations, it is interesting to have students build upon the observations and conclusions of those who worked on the same artifact before. By this the nature of the student's essay on the field trip will change. If individual field-trips are to be implemented on a larger scale it is advised to reconsider all procedural, procedural and technical aspects.

In future implementations of the ARLearn toolset, it is considered to make a distinction between notes and answers to assignments. Furthermore, some students solicited for the ability to making notes private and hide for the tutor and peers. Improvements will be made to the user-interface and the play-stop function of the audio-fragments. The technical difficulties in determining the exact location using GPS cannot be solved. Admittedly, in Florence - due to the narrow streets and high facades - car navigation systems deliver poor results too. In the current version of the toolset there is no worked out module for the tutor. During the pilots, we noticed that the tutor had to refrain himself in giving feedback to the students. In a new version, a tutor backchannel will be build-in that enables the tutor to be available at a distance, following and guiding them as needed.

The ARLearn toolkit can make the organization of fieldwork for Cultural Sciences students more sustainable as it enables students to visit Florence alone and not depend on an organized study-trip by the university. If planned in advance the tutor can be available at a distance for immediate feedback while checking the portfolio of the student. In this way a study trip can be combined with a holiday, saving a second visit to Florence. As there are some vulnerable artifacts in Florence access can be limited to their locations. By collecting annotated data in the portfolios of different students examining these artifacts, visits can be limited and focused in order to protect the treasures.

5 Future Work

The current version of ARLearn supports narrator and annotator objects. We are implementing other functionalities based on the interviews with both the tutor and the students.

In ARLearn, there is no distinction between an answer to a particular question or a random annotation. In next versions, the set of ARLearn objects are extended with rich media such as multiple choice questions, polls, location based forums or questions that involve finding a location or bringing an artifact to another location. Furthermore answers will be modeled as separate entities linked to the original question. This makes it possible to extend the use of ARlearn to other learning scenarios like serious games.

All objects are currently represented within a Google map. This has as a consequence that when an excursion starts, the map (and thus the entire excursion) is altered by the students. In order to enable reuse of an excursion, a distinction will be made between the design of an excursion, including the media a teacher uploads and the excursion itself that is linked to design and that represents the advancements of a student.

During the pilots, we noticed that the tutor had to refrain himself from giving feedback to the students. In a new version we will provide a tutor messaging facility, which enables live support by the tutor. Through this facility, the tutor will not only be able to track a student's progress, he will also be able to intervene and guide the students through new questions and messages.

As indicated in this article the ARlearn set of applications is developed further and deployed in different educational settings. Practitioners are encouraged to use ARlearn to design their own learning scenarios including specific assignments. Information on this can be found on the website of the Centre for Learning Sciences and Technologies[3] of the Open Universiteit.

References

1. Shute, T.: Is it 'OMG Finally' for augmented reality? Interview with Robert Rice. UgoTrade: Virtual Realities in "World 2.0." Retrieved 30 May 2012 (2009)
2. Milgram, P., Kishino, A.F.: Taxonomy of mixed reality visual displays. IEICE Trans. Inf. Syst. **E77-D**(12), 1321–1329 (1994)
3. Specht, M., Ternier, S., Greller, W.: Dimensions of mobile augmented reality for learning: a first inventory. J. Res. Cent. Educ. Technol. **7**(1). http://www.rcetj.org/index.php/rcetj/article/view/151/241 (2011). Accessed 30 May 2012
4. Gonsalves, A., Ternier, S., De Vries, F., Specht, M.: Serious games at the UNHCR with ARlearn, a toolkit for mobile and virtual reality applications. In: Specht, M., Sharples, M., Multisilta, J. (eds.), Proceedings of the 11th World Conference on Mobile and Contextual Learning (mLearn 2012), 16–18 October 2012, Helsinki, Finland, pp. 244–247. http://ceur-ws.org/Vol-955/ (2012)
5. Benedek, J., Miner, T.: Measuring desirability: new methods for evaluating desirability in a usability lab setting. Paper presented at the UPA 2002 Conference, Orlando, FL, 8–12 July 2002 (2002)

---

[3] http://portal.ou.nl/en/web/topic-mobile-learning/home/-/wiki/Main/ARLearn

Mathematical Literacy as a Condition for Sustainable Development

Luís Soares Barbosa[1]($\boxtimes$) and Maria Helena Martinho[2]

[1] HASLab - INESC TEC & Informatics Department,
Universidade do Minho, Braga, Portugal
lsb@di.uminho.pt
[2] Cied - Institute of Education, Universidade do Minho, Braga, Portugal

Abstract. Argumentation and proof are two main ingredients in strategies for developing mathematical skills and structured reasoning. This paper reports on a research project aimed at 'refactoring' school Mathematics in other to achieve a higher degree of mathematical literacy. In a sense this builds on a number of 'lessons' learnt from the practice of Computing Science. We further argue that mathematical fluency, broadly understood as the ability to reason in terms of abstract models and the effective use of logical arguments and mathematical calculation, became a condition for democratic citizenship and sustainable development.

1 Introduction

> *We must give industry not what it wants, but what it needs*
> — E. W. DIJKSTRA, quoted in the program of his birthday symposium,
> Austin, Texas, 2000

Critical infrastructures in modern societies, including those related to finances, health services, education, energy and water supply, are critically based on information systems. Moreover, our way of living depends on software whose reliability is crucial for our own work, security, privacy, and quality of life. This places the quest for software whose correctness could be established by mathematical reasoning, which has been around for a long time as a research agenda, at the centre of a debate which is no longer a technical one. Actually, for IT industry correctness is not only emerging as a key concern: it is simply becoming part of the business.

Collaboration with João Ferreira, at Teeside University, and Roland Backhouse, at Nottingham University, in the context of the MATHIS project, is greatly acknowledged. The authors express their gratitude to Paulo Silva who developed the teaching scenario on logarithms from which some examples discussed in the paper were taken. This work is partially funded by ERDF - European Regional Development Fund through the COMPETE Programme (operational programme for competitiveness) and by National Funds through the FCT (Portuguese Foundation for Science and Technology) within projects MATHIS, FCOMP-01--0124-FEDER-007254, and Professional Practices of Teachers of Mathematics, PTDC/CPECED/098931/2008.

A. Cerone et al. (Eds.): SEFM 2012 Satellite Events, LNCS 7991, pp. 64–77, 2014.
DOI: 10.1007/978-3-642-54338-8_5, © Springer-Verlag Berlin Heidelberg 2014

Companies are becoming aware of the essential role played by proofs and formal reasoning in this process. At present, at least in what concerns safety-critical systems, *proofs pay the rent*: they are no more an academic activity or an exotic detail.

This places serious challenges to higher education and training programmes for future software engineers and IT-professionals. On the one hand, there is a growing demand for highly skilled professionals who can successfully design complex systems at ever-increasing levels of reliability and security. On the other, and in general, IT-driven societies also require from people a higher degree of *mathematical literacy*, i.e., the ability to resort to logic to build models of problems and reason effectively within them. Such an ability is at the heart of what it means *to understand* and it may be considered a fundamental condition for democratic citizenship. Either directly, by supporting the implementation of high-assurance information infrastructures, or indirectly, by empowering citizenship, mathematical literacy became, in a broader perspective, a main ingredient for promoting sustainable development.

Actually, skills as basic as the ability to think and reason in terms of abstract models and the effective use of logical arguments and mathematical calculation in normal, daily business practice are on demand. This concerns not only highly skilled IT professionals, who are expected to successfully design complex systems at ever-increasing levels of reliability and security, but also specialised workers monitoring, for example, automated plants and computer aided manufacturing processes.

Even more it concerns, in general, everyone, who, surrounded by ubiquitous and interacting computing devices, has an unprecedented computational power at her fingers' tips to turn on effective power and self-control of her own life and work. Neologism *info-excluded* is often used to denote fundamental difficulties in the use of IT technologies. More fundamentally, from our perspective, it should encompass mathematical illiteracy and lack of precise reasoning skills rooted in formal logic.

Irrespective of its foundational role in all the technology on which modern life depends, Mathematics seems absent, or invisible, from the dominant cultural practices. Regarded as *difficult* or *boring*, its clear and ordered mental discipline seems to conflict with the superposition of images and multiple *rationales* of the post-modern way of living. Maybe just a minor symptom of this state of affairs, but *mathphobia*, which seems to be spreading everywhere, has become a hot spot for the media. Our societies, as noticed by E. W. Dijkstra a decade ago, are through an *ongoing process of becoming more and more "amathematical"* [12]. On the surface, at least.

Under it, however, Mathematics is playing the dominant role, and failing to recognize this and training oneself in its discipline, will most probably result in people impoverished in their interaction with the global *polis* and diminished citizenship.

In such a context, this paper aims at contributing to the debate on strategies for achieving a higher degree of *mathematical fluency*, which the authors strongly think to be a condition for sustainable development in the years to come. By this we do not have in mind the exclusive development of numerical, operative competences, but the ability to resort to the mathematical language and method to build models of problems, and reason effectively within them. Our claim is that such strategies should be directed towards *unveiling* Mathematics by rediscovering the relevance of both

- *argumentation* skills, understood as the ability to formulate and structure relationships, justifications and explanations to support an argument;
- and *proof*, as the formal certification of an argument, which encompasses the effective development of proof design and manipulation skills.

Although both aspects are often emphasized separately, the development of educational strategies to bind them together in learning contexts may have an impact in empowering people reasoning skills and, therefore, their ability to survive in a complex world.

Section 2 frames the paper in the context of the MATHIS project [9,10], a Portuguese research initiative on reinvigorating mathematical education, coordinated by the first author. A main component of this project is concerned with refactoring school mathematics, which is illustrated in Sect. 4 through an example on the development of calculational proofs. Before that, however, Sect. 3 characterises our conceptual framework on argumentation and proof. Finally, Sect. 5 concludes and enumerates some current research concerns.

2 The MathIS Project

The need for policies capable of reinvigorating Mathematics education and its effective application at all problem-solving levels was the starting point of a research project lead by Universidade do Minho in Portugal: the MATHIS project.

The project was launched in 2009, aiming at exploiting the dynamics of algorithmic problem solving and calculational reasoning in both maths education and the practice of software engineering in an integrated way. The project's overall approach stems from two decades of research on correct-by-construction program design which brought to scene a whole discipline of problem-solving and shed light on the underlying mathematical structures, modelling and reasoning principles. A most relevant consequence has been the systematization of a calculational style of reasoning which, proceeding in a formal, essentially syntactic way, can greatly improve on the traditional verbose proofs presented in natural language.

A main contribution of MATHIS, at the educational level, was an effort to reframe a collection of themes in pre-university mathematics along these lines and assess its merits not only on the development of general calculational and algorithmic skills, but also as a tool for discovery (see [9,10] as well as João Ferreira's Ph.D dissertation [8]). Recall, for example, that it was the formal manipulation of Maxwell's equations that led to conjecturing the existence of electromagnetic waves, confirmed experimentally shortly afterwards.

On the technology side, MATHIS capitalizes on recent developments and increased flexibility in Human-computer interaction technology, to provide an infra-structure for the envisaged methodological shift. In this context, a second axis in MathIS concerned the development of innovative computer-based tools exploiting Tablet PC technologies in order to provide learning environments oriented to calculational reasoning and algorithmic problem solving [18]. These principles, although consistent with traditional blackboard-style teaching, can benefit from the enhanced facilities provided by computers.

3   Argumentation and Proof

Argumentation

Mathematical learning requires a stepwise construction of a reference framework through which students build their own personal account of mathematics in a dynamic tension between previous and newly acquired knowledge. This is achieved along the countless interaction processes taking place in the classroom. In particular, the nature of the questions posed by the teacher may facilitate, or inhibit, the development of argumentation and reasoning skills [4]. A student who is given the opportunity to share her intuitions, conjectures and previous knowledge, as well as to explain the way she thought about a problem, will develop higher levels of mathematical literacy in the broad sense proposed in Sect. 1. Team work, which entails the need for each participant to expose his views, argue and try to convince the others, is an excellent strategy to achieve this goal.

Strategies which call students to analyze their arguments and identify its strengths and weaknesses are also instrumental to this aim [15]. Reference [17] singles out a number of basic issues in the development of what is called a *reflexive* mathematical discourse: the ability to go back (either to recover previous arguments in a discussion or to introduce new view points) and the ability to share different sorts of images supporting argumentation (e.g., sketches, tables, etc.).

Training argumentation skills is not easy, but certainly an essential task if one cares about mathematical literacy in modern societies. The teacher's role can not be neglected. She/he is responsible for stimulating a friendly, open discussion environment [1], avoiding rejection and helping students to recognize implications and eventual contradictions in their arguments to go ahead [11,21]. Her role is also to make explicit what is implicit in the students' formulations [6], helping them to build up intuitions, asking for generalizations or confronting them with specific particular cases.

The following opening statement of Paul Halmos' autobiography [14] is particularly elucidative, written as it was by a mathematician, who in the 1950's, at the University of Chicago, was director of doctoral studies in what was then one of the top Mathematics Departments of the world: *I like words more than numbers, and I always did (...) This implies, for instance that in Mathematics I like the conceptual more than the computational. To me the definition of a group is far clearer and more important and more beautiful than the Cauchy integral formula.*

Often in school practice conceptual disagreements are avoided (let alone encouraged!), with negative effects in the development of suitable argumentation skills. On the contrary, such skills benefit from exposition to diverse arguments, their attentive consideration and elicitation, as empirically documented in, e.g., [23]. Actually, classroom interactions can shape the mathematical universe of students. School mathematics is an iceberg, of which students often only sees what emerges at surface (typically, definitions and procedures). Rendering explicit what is hidden under the water is the role of effective mathematical training in argumentation.

Proof

If the development of suitable *argumentation skills* is a first step to a Mathematics-aware citizenship, mastering *proof technology* is essential in a context where, as explained above, *proofs pay the rent*. Such is the context of software industry and the increasing demand for quality certified software, namely in safety-critical applications. But what contributions may Computing Science bring to such a discipline? And how could they improve current standards in mathematical education?

As a contribution to a wider debate, we would like to single out in this paper the emphasis on the central role of *formal logic* and the development of a *calculational* style of reasoning.

Clearly, Computer Science fostered a wider interest in applied logic. A simple indicator is the almost universal presence of a course on formal logic in every computing undergraduate curriculum. Proficiency in mathematics, however, would benefit from an earlier introduction and explicit use of logic in middle and high school. Note this is usually not the case in most European countries; the justification for such an omission is that *logic is implicit in Mathematics and therefore does not need to be taught as an independent issue*. Such an argument was used in Portugal to eliminate logic from the high-school curriculum in the nineties. The damage it caused is still to be assessed, but it is certainly not alien to the appalling indicators in what concerns the country overall ranking in mathematics education [20].

High-valued programmers are heavy users of logic. At another scale, this is also true of whoever tries to use and master information in modern IT societies: the explicit use of logic enables critical and secure reasoning and decision making. On the other hand, a heavy use of logic entails the need for more concise ways of expression and notations amenable to formal, systematic manipulation.

The so-called *calculational style* [3,22] for structuring mathematical reasoning and proof emerged from two decades of research on *correct-by-construction* program design, starting with the pioneering work of Dijkstra and Gries [7,13], and in particular, through the development of the so-called *algebra of programming* [5]. This style emphasizes the use of systematic mathematical calculation in the design of algorithms. This was not new, but routinely done in algebra and analysis, albeit subconsciously and not always in a systematic way. The realization that such a style is equally applicable to logical arguments [7,13] and that it can greatly improve on traditional verbose proofs in natural language has led to a systematization that can, in return, also improve exposition in the more classical branches of Mathematics. In particular, lengthy and verbose proofs (full of *dot-dot* notation, case analyses, and natural language explanations for "obvious" steps) are replaced by easy-to-follow calculations presented in a standard layout which replaces classical implication-first logic by variable-free algebraic reasoning [12, 22].

Let us illustrate with a very simple example what we mean by a *calculational* proof. Suppose we are given the task to find out *whether* $\log_a(2) + \log_a(7)$ *is greater than, or lesser than* $\log_a(3) + \log_a(5)$. The 'classical' response consists of first formulating the hypothesis $\log_a(2) + \log_a(7) \leq \log_a(3) + \log_a(5)$ and then verifying it as follows:

(1)   function $\log_a$ is strictly increasing
(2) $\log_a(x \times y) = \log_a(x) + \log_a(y)$
(3) $14 < 15$
(4) $14 = 2 \times 7$ and $15 = 3 \times 5$
(5) $\log_a(14) < \log_a 15)$ by (1) e (3)
(6) $\log_a(2) + \log_a(7) < \log_a(3) + \log_a(5)$ by (2), (4) e (5)

The proof is easy to follow, but, in the end, the intuition it provides on the problem is quite poor. Moreover, it is hard memorize or reproduce. Most probably it was not made, originally, by the order in which it is presented. This may explain why, in general, this sort of proofs, although dominant in the current mathematical discourse, fails to attract students' enthusiasm.

Consider, now, a *calculational* approach to the same problem. The main, initial difference is easy to spot and has an enormous impact: its starting point is not an hypothesis to verify, formulated in a more or less diligent way, but the original problem itself. The proof starts by identifying an unknown $\square$ which stands, not for a number as students are used to in school mathematics, but for an order relation. Then it proceeds by the identification and application of whatever known properties are useful in its determination. The whole proof, being essentially syntax driven, builds intuition and meaning.

$$\log_a(2) + \log_a(7) \;\square\; \log_a(3) + \log_a(5)$$
$$= \quad \{ \text{ function } \log_a \text{ distributes over multiplication. } \}$$
$$\log_a(2 \times 7) \;\square\; \log_a(3 \times 5)$$
$$= \quad \{ \text{ routine arithmetic. } \}$$
$$\log_a(14) \;\square\; \log_a(15)$$
$$= \quad \{ \; 14 < 15 \text{ and function } \log_a \text{ is strictly increasing. } \}$$
$$\square \quad \text{is} \quad <$$

Empirical evidence gathered within MATHIS suggests the systematization of such a calculational style of reasoning can greatly improve on the way proofs are presented. In particular, it may help to overcome the typical justification for omitting proofs in school mathematics: that they are difficult to follow for all but exceptional students.

4 Refactoring School Mathematics

A main objective set for the MATHIS project was the 'refactoring' of several pieces of school mathematics, systematically introducing the sort of *proofs by calculation* illustrated in the previous section. Although it is too early to draw general conclusions (preliminary results, however, appeared in [8,10]), this effort shows how the formalization of topics arising in different contexts results in formulae with the same *flavour*, which can be manipulated thereafter by the same rules of the predicate calculus, without reference to a 'domain specific' interpretation in their original area of discourse. This is the essence of formal manipulation, and yields proofs that are shorter, explicit, independent of hidden assumptions, easy to re-construct, check and generalize.

An Illustration

To illustrate the direction of such a 'refactoring' let us consider a few examples related to the use in school mathematics of definitions by universal properties, as one is used to in program calculus (see, for example, [5]).

We begin with the simple definition of the pairing function. Its *explicit* definition looks rather obvious

$$\langle f, g \rangle (c) = (f\,c, g\,c)$$

but is not so easy to handle in calculations. Suppose students are asked to show that a function which builds a pair is a pairing function, i.e.

$$\langle \pi_1 \cdot h, \pi_2 \cdot h \rangle = h$$

where π_1, π_2 are, respectively, the first and second projection associated to the Cartesian product. A typical proof is as follows. Suppose $ha = \langle b, c \rangle$. Then,

$$\langle \pi_1 \cdot h, \pi_2 \cdot h \rangle a$$
$$= \quad \{ \text{ pairing definition, composition } \}$$
$$\langle \pi_1(ha), \pi_2(ha) \rangle$$
$$= \quad \{ \text{ definition of } h\}$$
$$\langle \pi_1 \langle b, c \rangle, \pi_2 \langle b, c \rangle \rangle$$
$$= \quad \{ \text{ definition of projection functions } \pi_1 \text{ and } \pi_2\}$$
$$\langle b, c \rangle$$
$$= \quad \{ \text{ definition of } h \text{ again } \}$$
$$ha$$

Refactoring this proof involves replacing the explicit definition of a pairing function given above, by a *property* which characterises its behaviour completely. Therefore, define

$$k = \langle f, g \rangle \; \equiv \; \pi_1 \cdot k = f \;\wedge\; \pi_2 \cdot k = g$$

Notice that in this property $\Rightarrow$ gives *existence* and $\Leftarrow$ ensures *uniqueness*[1].

With this definition the envisaged proof becomes trivial:

$$h = \langle \pi_1 \cdot h, \pi_2 \cdot h \rangle$$
$$\equiv \quad \{ \text{ universal property with } f := \pi_1 \cdot h, \; g := \pi_1 \cdot h \; \}$$
$$\pi_1 \cdot h = \pi_1 \cdot h \;\wedge\; \pi_2 \cdot h = \pi_2 \cdot h$$

This shift from *explicit* to *implicit* definitions lead, usually, to simpler and smaller proofs, rid of unnecessary variables and more general, in the sense that they can be replicated in different situations and corners of the mathematical experience.

Let us now come back to logarithms and investigate what can be proved directly from the very basic property which records the primitive fact that the logarithm is the inverse of the exponential function. Formally,

$$\log_a(x) = c \; \equiv \; a^c = x \tag{1}$$

To prove *cancellation*, i.e. that $a^{\log_a(x)} = x$, it is enough to instantiate variable c with $\log_a(x)$, therefore making the left side of equivalence (1) trivially true. Note the similarity with the pairing proof above. Formally,

$$\log_a(x) = c \; \equiv \; a^c = x$$
$$\equiv \quad \{ \text{ instantiate } c := \log_a(x) \}$$
$$\log_a(x) = \log_a(x) \; \equiv \; a^{\log_a(x)} = x$$
$$\equiv \quad \{ \text{ reflexivity} \}$$
$$\text{True} \; \equiv \; a^{\log_a(x)} = x$$

---

[1] The attentive reader will recognise this property as the categorial definition of the universal arrow associated to a product construction [2], but such a formal setting is unnecessary for our purposes here. Reference [16] provides, however, an introduction to categorial arguments most suitable for didactical practice and research.

Consider now a slightly more difficult result, which students learn (often by heart) as the *product rule* for logarithms:

$$c = \log_a(x \times y)$$
$$\equiv \quad \{\text{ logarithm definition}\}$$
$$a^c = x \times y$$
$$\equiv \quad \{\text{ cancellation (proved above)}\}$$
$$a^c = a^{\log_a(x)} \times a^{\log_a(y)}$$
$$\equiv \quad \{\text{ product of exponentials}\}$$
$$a^c = a^{\log_a(x)+\log_a(y)}$$
$$\equiv \quad \{\ (\Rightarrow)\ \text{the exponential function is injective; } (\Leftarrow)\ \text{Leibniz rule}\}$$
$$c = \log_a(x) + \log_a(y)$$
$$\therefore \quad \{\text{ indirect equality}\}$$
$$\log_a(x \times y) = \log_a(x) + \log_a(y)$$

The *same* proof structure, i.e.,

$$\cdots$$
$$\equiv \quad \{\text{ logarithm definition}\}$$
$$\cdots$$
$$\equiv \quad \{\text{ cancellation}\}$$
$$\cdots$$
$$\equiv \quad \{\text{ property of the dual structure}\}$$
$$\cdots$$
$$\equiv \quad \{\ (\Rightarrow)\ \text{the dual function is injective; } (\Leftarrow)\ \text{Leibniz rule}\}$$
$$\cdots$$
$$\therefore \quad \{\text{ indirect equality}\}$$
$$\cdots$$

applies to find out (or to compute the prove of) the power logarithm rule:

$$c = \log_a(x^p)$$
$$\equiv \quad \{\text{ logarithm definition}\}$$
$$a^c = x^p$$
$$\equiv \quad \{\text{ cancellation}\}$$
$$a^c = (a^{\log_a(x)})^p$$

$\equiv$ { product of exponentials}

$$a^c = a^{p \times \log_a(x)}$$

$\equiv$ { ($\Rightarrow$) the exponential function is injective; ($\Leftarrow$) Leibniz rule}

$$c = p \times \log_a(x)$$

$\therefore$ { indirect equality}

$$\log_a(x^p) = p \times \log_a(x)$$

The reader may check that the same proof structure is still valid for computing the rule for the logarithm of a quotient. Actually, the common pattern underlying the three proofs comes from the adoption in all cases of the same proof strategy: *the introduction of the corresponding property of the dual function.*

Identifying this strategy, and the proof pattern it leads to, enriches students' reasoning skills: as a rule one may attempt to establish properties of a structure (the logarithm, in this case) by resorting to properties of its dual (the exponential). Moreover, in the long term, this process helps students to build and dynamically enrich a personal *classification* of proofs, which is a basic ability to master Mathematics.

At this point the teacher may challenge students with more complex properties: for example the ones involving change of basis,

$$\log_a(x) \ = \ \frac{\log_b(x)}{\log_b(a)}$$

Discovering that again a very similar proof structure applies, a conclusion students arrive quite quickly, builds insight on the subject and empowers their mathematical skills. Actually,

$$\log_a(x) = y$$

$\equiv$ { logarithm definition}

$$a^y = x$$

$\equiv$ { ($\Rightarrow$) the exponential function is injective; ($\Leftarrow$) Leibniz rule}

$$\log_b(a^y) = \log_b(x)$$

$\equiv$ { power logarithm rule (proved above)}

$$y \times \log_b(a) = \log_b(x)$$

$\equiv$ { routine arithmetic}

$$y = \frac{\log_b(x)}{\log_b(a)}$$

$$\therefore \quad \{ \text{ indirect equality} \}$$

$$\log_a(x) = \frac{\log_b(x)}{\log_b(a)}$$

Note, finally, that this calculational approach allows students to be more constructive because the requirements emerge from the calculations themselves.

Teaching Scenarios

The examples above are part of what we call in the MATHIS project a *teaching scenario* [9]. Actually, a main component of this refactoring programme is the development of specific educational material supporting the use of a calculational approach and algorithmic problem solving strategies in the *practice of mathematics*. This material, in the form of example-driven *teaching scenarios* is designed for use with teams of up to 20 volunteer high school students in the context of extra-curricular "Maths' Clubs". The latter are aimed at students between 15 and 17 years old and do not require any extra-curricular prerequisite knowledge.

A scenario is a fully worked out solution to a problem in a domain integrated in school curricular topics, together with a "method sheet" [9]. The latter provides detailed guidelines on the principles embodied in the problem, on how it can be tackled and solved. Although they can be used directly by the student, they are primarily written for the teacher. In general, each scenario is divided into the following sections:

- **Brief description and goals:** This section provides a summary of the scenario, allowing the teacher to determine if it is adequate for the students.
- **Problem statement:** This section states the problem (or problems) discussed in the scenario.
- **Students should know:** This section lists pre-requisites that should be met by the students. The teacher can use it to determine if the scenario is adequate for the students.
- **Resolution:** This section presents a possible solution for the problem in the style advocated here.
- **Notes for the teacher:** In this section the solution presented above is decomposed into its main parts and each part is discussed in detail. To maintain the balance mentioned in the first paragraph, we also recommend how the teacher should present the material, including questions that the teacher should or should not ask and important concepts that should be introduced.
- **Extensions and exercises:** This section can be used for homework or project assignments. All the exercises are accompanied by their solutions.
- **Further reading:** Recommended reading for the teacher and the students. It may include discussions and comparisons between conventional solutions and the one presented in the scenario.

The success of teaching depends on the amount of discovery that is left to students: if the teacher discloses all the information needed to solve a problem, students act only as spectators and become discouraged; if the teacher leaves all the work to the students, they may find the problem too difficult and become discouraged too. It is thus important to find a balance between these two extremes. Self-discovery is also promoted by the sections *Extensions and exercises* and *Further reading*, which are both designed to encourage further work by the students.

Finally, a word on the role of the 'teacher'. Our experience, however limited it is, suggests she/he is more likely to be expected to act as *coacher* than as repository of pre-framed knowledge. The adoption of new educational practices, would not be effective without an assessment of how teachers feel about that and how this interacts with their own images of their profession. Also at this level, further research is certainly needed.

5   Conclusions and Future Work

Understood, more and more, as a condition for democratic citizenship in modern Information Societies, mathematical literacy has to be taken as a serious concern for the years to come. From our perspective this entails the need for a systematic (and, given *l'esprit du temps*, courageous) *unveiling* of Mathematics. That is, to make mathematical reasoning explicit at all levels of human argumentation and develop, through adequate teaching strategies, the skills suitable to promote correct reasoning in all sorts of social, cultural or professional contexts.

This paper focused on two main issues in this process: empowering *mathematical argumentation*, by developing adequate teaching strategies, and *proof*, made simpler, easier to produce and more systematic through a new calculation style which has proved successful in reasoning about complex software. The study of *mathematical arguments* is still an issue in Mathematics Education (see, e.g., [1,19]). On the other hand, the rediscovery of the essential role played by *proofs* (and the associated relevance given to formal logic), has been raised, for the last 3 decades, in a very particular context: that of Computing Science. It may be, so we believe, a contribution of Computing Science to reinvigorating mathematical education.

A final word is in order on the above mentioned relationship of Mathematics and Computing. Actually, the latter is probably the paradigm of an area of knowledge from which a popular and effective technology emerged long before a solid, specific, scientific methodology, let alone formal foundations, has been put forward. Often, as our readers may notice, in software industry the whole software production seems to be totally biased to specific technologies, encircling, as a long term effect, the company's culture in quite strict limits. For example, mastering of particular, often ephemeral, technologies appears as a decisive requirement for recruitment policies.

This state of affairs is, however, only the surface of the iceberg. Companies involved in the development of safety-critical or mission-critical software have already recognized that mathematical rigorous reasoning is, not only the key to success in market, but also the warrantee of their own survival. With a long experience in training software engineers and collaborating with software industry, the authors can only claim the need for a double change:

- in the Mathematics *middle school curriculum*, in which the notion of *proof* and the development of argumentation skills are virtually absent;
- in a popular, but pernicious, technology-driven computing education which fails to provide effective training in tackling rigorously the overwhelming complex problems software is supposed to solve.

Future research goes exactly in this direction. In particular, we are currently working on strategies for developing argumentation and calculational proof skills in probabilistic reasoning. As researchers in Computing Science and Education, respectively, the authors see their job as E. W. Dijkstra once put it, *We must give industry not what it wants, but what it needs*. Mathematics should, definitively, be in the package.

References

1. Alro, H., Skovsmose, O.: Dialogue and Learning in Mathematics Education: Intention, Reflection, Critique. Kluwer Academic Publishers, Dordrecht (2002)
2. Awodey, S.: Category Theory. Oxford Logic Guides. Oxford University Press, Oxford (2006)
3. Backhouse, R.C.: Mathematics and programming. A revolution in the art of effective reasoning. Inaugural Lecture, School of Computer Science and IT, University of Nottingham (2001)
4. Barrody, A.: Problem Solving, Reasoning, and Communicating, k-8: Helping Children Think Mathematically. Macmillan, New York (1993)
5. Bird, R., Moor, O.: The Algebra of Programming. Series in Computer Science. Prentice-Hall International, Englewood Cliffs (1997)
6. Buschman, L.: Communicating in the language of mathematics. Teach. Child. Math. **1**(6), 324–329 (1995)
7. Dijkstra, E.W., Scholten, C.S.: Predicate Calculus and Program Semantics. Springer, New York (1990)
8. Ferreira, J.F.: Principles and applications of algorithmic problem solving. Ph.D. thesis, University of Nottingham (2010)
9. Ferreira, J.F., Mendes, A., Backhouse, R., Barbosa, L.S.: Which mathematics for the information society? In: Gibbons, J., Oliveira, J.N. (eds.) TFM 2009. LNCS, vol. 5846, pp. 39–56. Springer, Heidelberg (2009)
10. Ferreira, J.F., Mendes, A., Cunha, A., Baquero, C., Silva, P., Barbosa, L.S., Oliveira, J.N.: Logic training through algorithmic problem solving. In: Blackburn, P., van Ditmarsch, H., Manzano, M., Soler-Toscano, F. (eds.) TICTTL 2011. LNCS(LNAI), vol. 6680, pp. 62–69. Springer, Heidelberg (2011)
11. Forman, E., Ansell, E.: The multiple voices of a mathematics classroom community. In: Kieran, C., Forman, E., Sfard, A. (eds.) Learning Discourse: Discursive Approaches to Research in Mathematics Education, pp. 115–142. Kluwer Academic Publishers, Dordrecht (2002)

12. Gries, D., Feijen, W.H.J., van Gasteren, A.J.M., Misra, J.: Beauty is our Business. Springer, New York (1990)
13. Gries, D., Schneider, F.: A Logical Approach to Discrete Mathematics. Springer, New York (1993)
14. Halmos, P.R.: I Want to Be a Mathematician. Springer, Berlin (1985)
15. Hiebert, J.: Reflection and communication: cognitive considerations in school mathematics reform. Int. J. Educ. Res. **17**, 439–456 (1992)
16. Lawvere, F.W., Schanuel, S.H.: Conceptual Mathematics. Cambridge University Press, Cambridge (1997)
17. McClain, K., Cobb, P.: The role of imagery and discourse in supporting students' mathematical development. In: Lampert, M., Blunk, M.L. (eds.) Talking Mathematics in School: Studies of Teaching and Learning, pp. 17–55. Cambridge University Press, Cambridge (1998)
18. Mendes, A.: Structured editing of handwritten mathematics. Ph.D. thesis, University of Nottingham (2011)
19. O'Connor, M.C.: Can any fraction be turned into a decimal?: a case study of a mathematical group discussion. In: Kieran, C., Forman, E., Sfard, A. (eds.) Learning Discourse: Discursive Approaches to Research in Mathematics Education, pp. 143–185. Kluwer Academic Publishers, Dordrecht (2002)
20. OCDE Report: Education at a clance: OCDE indicators 2006. OCDE Publishing, Paris (2006)
21. Rittenhouse, P.S.: The teacher's role in mathematical conversation: stepping in and stepping out. In: Lampert, M., Blunk, M.L. (eds.) Talking Mathematics in School: Studies of Teaching and Learning, pp. 163–189. Cambridge University Press, Cambridge (1998)
22. van Gasteren, A.J.M. (ed.): On the Shape of Mathematical Arguments. LNCS, vol. 445. Springer, Heidelberg (1990)
23. Wood, T.: Creating a context for argument in mathematics class. J. Res. Math. Educ. **30**(2), 171–191 (1999)

Learning CSCW Through Fairytales:
A Practical Model

Nicole Bittel[✉] and Marco Bettoni

Research Management Unit, Swiss Distance University of Applied Sciences (FFHS),
Brig, Switzerland
{nicole.bittel,marco.bettoni}@ffhs.ch

Abstract. This paper focuses on the claim that the development and persistence of learning and working groups, which are key to managing knowledge and experience-based content, both at an organisational and individual level, can be promoted via the relatedness inherent within fairy tales.

In the first section of this paper, a brief overview of the current research situation is provided (Sect. 2). In Sect. 3, a collaborative storytelling model is developed, explaining that learning and working in line with Knowledge Cooperation requires social exchange and collaboration (Sect. 3.1), that (digital) storytelling is an appropriate method for promoting social interaction by bringing people and their (tacit) experiences together (Sect. 3.2) and finally, that fairytales can do much more in terms of *holding* learners in a community together (Sect. 3.3). In Sect. 4, a concrete project idea is presented based on the theoretical considerations outlined in Sect. 3, before the most significant results are finally summarised (Sect. 4).

Keywords: Learning and working communities · Knowledge Management · Knowledge Cooperation · Storytelling · Tacit knowledge · Fairytales · Relatedness · Transfer · Metaphor

1 Introduction: Starting with a Story of Experience

When people learn, they learn within and through the experiences that they assemble daily. An infinite treasure trove of knowledge can arise from sharing these experiences with others. As will be shown below on the basis of an anecdote from the educational domain, the path to this treasure trove of knowledge can lead through fairytales, because they bring and keep learners and their experiences together within a community. This core message can also be transferred to a work setting.

How do you explain to 17-year old vocational school students that human development is not just influenced by the social environment but also by one's own will and self-determination? And ideally in such a way that they understand it, remember it after a week and have fun with it?

Following several less successful attempts at helping students understand the difference between exogenous and autogenic factors, the teacher then started the next lesson by entering the classroom, darkening the room and playing a DVD. It was not long before there was a reaction: 'Hey Harry Potter... Cool!!!' The brief was clear:

A. Cerone et al. (Eds.): SEFM 2012 Satellite Events, LNCS 7991, pp. 78–88, 2014.
DOI: 10.1007/978-3-642-54338-8_6, © Springer-Verlag Berlin Heidelberg 2014

find all the possible examples of factors influencing the lives of the characters and organise them according to social and self-determined factors. It was hardly surprising that the students appreciated their teacher giving them a bit of variety but the results of the research were certainly surprising too. The students spent double the time originally planned compiling the relevant factors. Everyone had something to contribute; something which he or she felt should not be omitted under any circumstances. Discussion naturally turned to the Sorting Hat – the hat which allocates the apprentice sorcerers to the different houses at the school. The teacher's conclusion was clear: a social factor helps determine from the outside the direction taken by the hat wearer. However, half of the class did not agree. The hat would not tell Harry which school house he would be in; instead the hat would adapt to Harry's wishes. And therefore the hat would be autogenic. Even more interesting than these human development factors was the clear motivation of the students and teachers as they exchanged ideas about what they believed. This fact alone makes the lesson one of the best.

Fairytales encourage people to exchange ideas with others – and Harry Potter is a fairytale in a modern form. In this way, fairytales create a sense of community – a community where experiences are shared with others and which give rise to new experiences by revolving around people using images and metaphors. This means that stories and fairytales in particular, given their links to everyone's experiences, are suitable for implementing learning and working in a cooperative and collaborative understanding. This paper explores this hypothesis.

In Sect. 2, we will review the research situation and try to identify what is the predominant established view and what is the key missing aspect in relation to the aforementioned hypothesis. This missing aspect or gap will be addressed in Sect. 3, the main part of this paper, where we present our proposal for filling the gap by means of an innovative Model of Collaborative Storytelling based on a radical constructivist approach to Knowledge Management and on a social theory of learning [16]. The following Sect. 4 will outline why and how we plan to apply our model within the context of our university and finally in Sect. 5 we will conclude with reflections which evaluate our proposal and summarise its main messages.

2 State of the Art

The cultivation of knowledge at an individual and organizational level reflects the requirements and demands of modern institutions. Over the last few years, numerous approaches have sought to go beyond a traditional understanding of Knowledge Management. Bettoni [2] introduced the Knowledge Cooperation model, for example. Based on a radical constructivist approach, he assumed learning and working to be social processes within which knowledge is communicated, shared, negotiated and (re)created. Moskaliuk et al. and Ozmen, among others, also follow this approach when they refer to the significance of tacit knowledge for the creation of new knowledge [6, 7]. According to the authors, knowledge gained from experience is dynamic knowledge which can only unfold its potential for (further) development (of both the organization and individual) through (social) exchange. The bottom line in research literature is that stories are suitable for cooperative Knowledge Management because they embody interaction and collaboration. Storytelling is discussed at various points as a means of interactive access to the silent wealth of experience of its owners by serving the two purposes of dissemination of information and conveying meaning at a high level of understanding [7], according to Ozmen. Erlach et al. see the storytelling method as a new method of Knowledge Management that provides access to the experiences of employees, initiates change processes, promotes learning and raises awareness about the internal values of an enterprise [18]. Reissner comes to a similar conclusion when she indicates the potential of stories as an evaluation and reflecting method for learning processes in the workplace [19]. Stories (according to her conclusion) are a powerful tool for making worked-based learning processes and experiences visible and therefore manageable [19].

While there is a broad range of literature already addressing the issue of storytelling in the context of learning and working, few works investigate the issue of fairytales as a special form of story. One exception is Thissen [12]. Using his D.E.S. method, he applies existing stories to (problem-focused) learning in the virtual domain. The basic dramaturgical structure of the story enables the learner to acquire knowledge by exchanging information with others and to transfer this knowledge to a problem and its solution [12]. In this way, Thissen shows how the example of Mother Hulda and her two daughters can be used as a model for hygiene and hygienic behaviour. Through the dramaturgical presentation and the images and analogies of this fairytale, employees learn about what needs to be addressed in hygiene terms [12].

If we summarise the research situation according to the hypothesis that fairytales are particularly suited to creating relatedness through openness, optimism and symbolic power as part of a cooperative Knowledge Management, the following image emerges: learning and working as social processes require a dynamic understanding of Knowledge Management. Learners need opportunities to exchange experiences and build up new knowledge in this way. Stories embody these opportunities thanks to their potential for conveying a sense of common understanding by providing access to the wealth of tacit experiences of the users. What is missing in the current state of research is the contribution of fairytales to learning and working as a means of collaboration and cooperation, a gap which is particularly unfortunate if we consider the relevance of the function fairytales could fulfil.

In this sense, the model presented in this paper fills a relevant research gap because it brings fairytales back into the spotlight as a special form of storytelling and investigates them systematically in their role as means of promoting a collaborative and socialised Knowledge Management [15].

3 The Model: Theoretical Considerations

A system-theoretical collaborative storytelling model is developed in this chapter. To this end, the following sections demonstrate that Knowledge Management, understood as a dynamic Knowledge Cooperation, takes place through social interactions (Sect. 3.1), that stories and their application support this social interaction because they bring learners and their tacit knowledge (Sect. 3.2) together and that fairytales perform even better, as they hold these learners together in a community (Sect. 3.3).

3.1 Knowledge Management as Interactive Knowledge Cooperation[1]

Communities and networks of all kinds are gaining in significance in modern everyday business, including firms which have a decentralised organization in geographical or thematic terms. Employees at various national and international sites and with different professional backgrounds are bringing their knowledge to the organization in question and enriching it with new experiences each and every day. Given the ever shortening half-life of knowledge, these experiences will gain in significance too. Companies today face the challenge of making learning processes for their employees visible and accessible as well as supporting and promoting these processes to benefit from this dynamic wealth of experience and knowledge.

If we adopt a radical constructivist understanding and assume that reality is only accessible to the individual through his/her experience of the environment, then reality per se cannot exist for the individual [1]. In other words: whatever is experienced as reality depends on the experiences the individual has acquired in relation to his/her environment [1]. As such, learning (seen as an ongoing digesting of experiences) primarily becomes a social process [2, 12].

Based on a radical constructivist approach of this nature, Bettoni formulates his Knowledge Cooperation model, extending the traditional understanding of Knowledge Management [2]. When knowledge is constructed within a social process as an on-going and unending exchange of experiences, it is not sufficient to simply gather and manage knowledge. Modern companies instead face the challenge of perceiving the knowledge of their employees as dynamic. By investigating this radical constructivist model of Knowledge Cooperation, communities and networks become a fundamental instrument of Knowledge Management whereby learning and working are seen as social processes within which knowledge and experience are shared with others, re-designed and expanded. Participation and sharing therefore become key criteria for successful Knowledge Cooperation where professional and/or geographical distances are involved.

Web technologies designed to foster participation and creation correspond to this understanding. Learning platforms (such as Moodle, Olat etc.), Web 2.0 and social media tap into the dynamic principle of Knowledge Cooperation and implement this within teams for virtual learning and working: with their assistance, the individual is transformed from a consumer into an active designer [4]. "We are creating a new and profound mechanism of democratic communication," says Lambert about the development of digital media [11]. Tools make it possible to contact others quickly, easily and regardless of the time and place as well as to create a shared understanding through the exchanging of experiences and to acquire new knowledge on this basis. Learning and working as social interaction and collaboration processes are developing to become eLearning and eCollaboration with the aid of web technologies [9]. Nevertheless, tools alone are not sufficient for achieving collaboration and cooperation [2, 9]. As a form of knowledge and experience exchange, the latter are first and foremost social and not technical, meaning that equating team work with web technologies falls short of the mark. The result of this is less surprising: learning and working

---

[1] Early versions of parts of this and of other sections have been used in a short sketch of our approach which was published as a blog post [17].

communities are only as successful as the socially motivated goals and the objects, meanings, motivations, needs and competences accomplished within them [9]. In other words: it is only possible to actively participate in a group by promising yourself positive things; by feeling settled, by being valued and respected, by not needing to be afraid etc. Social skills and a culture of communication, mistakes and criticism are just some examples of the genuine social being of communities.

In summary, it can be established that learning and working take place within and via social exchange – through sharing, devising and gaining (new) experiences together. Web technologies such as blogs, wikis, forums and social platforms support this collaborative learning and working, even beyond geographical and temporal boundaries and thereby meet the needs of modern companies to manage the knowledge and expertise of their employees and handle them in an active and dynamic manner. The application of technology alone is not sufficient to ensure the success of learning and working in communities. The latter are always (also) socially motivated. The question which remains to be answered is therefore which methodological processes (can) correspond to this.

(Digital) storytelling is presented as an appropriate method for socialised learning and working in the next chapter. After all, stories bring people and their (silent) experiences together. They call for the exchanging of experiences and create access to the meaning, providing tacit knowledge which holds together all knowledge like glue [7].

3.2   (Digital) Storytelling as a Method for Promoting Interactive Exchange

The method of (digital) storytelling has been observed and rediscovered for many decades by researchers, practitioners and experts in various fields and from various perspectives [14]. But what are stories? When is it correct to call something a story? And how can this be distinguished from other narrative forms? Aristotle defined a story as a plot with a beginning, middle and end [10]. While many authors still adhere to this interpretation today (albeit sometimes in an adapted form[2]), it was Boje in particular who proposed a differentiated view of stories in an organizational context [3].

According to Boje, everyday stories as are found in every company, institution and inter-human relationship do not (always) follow Aristotle's principle of having a beginning, middle and end [3]. Instead, these stories are often unfinished, undefined, inconclusive, unstructured, unconscious, unorganised or unfamiliar [3]. In his view, traditional narrative access routes are insufficient and cannot do justice to the complex character of stories in organisations and in society. Instead, the concept of the 'improper story' needs to be added [3]. One difficulty which emerges from such a broad interpretation of stories, as presented by Boje, is the fact that everything ultimately becomes a story. There are no clues in the literature as to how to react to this fact. A middle path between the two positions presented here is adopted by Erlach and

---

[2] See Sharda et al. [10].

Thier in their definition of organisational stories either as 'complete stories with a plot, flow and characters or only in fragments [sic, N. B.]' [5].

Despite this wide range of views concerning what constitutes a story, there is consensus in one matter: the telling of stories as an educational or general social principle is not new [4]. Humans have been telling one another stories ever since communication began in order to explain the world, make the incomprehensible comprehensible, bring sense and direction to life and actions, learn from mistakes and pass on knowledge to help shape one's own future [17]. Stories correspond to fundamental requirements – including those of modern man. Stories are therefore gradually finding their way back into a dynamic and digitalised society; a society which requires communication and interaction, like all societies which have gone before[3]. In this sense, it comes as no surprise to hear of a 'narrative turn' [14] or that digital storytelling is not much more than just the packaging of a traditional principle in the robes of new digital technology [11]. Given these circumstances, it is no coincidence that the storytelling principle is featuring ever more frequently in learning and working contexts too[4]. Among others, Standley addresses the potential of bringing the method of digital storytelling to schools and making stories part of everyday learning and teaching [11]. On the other hand, Reissner focuses on the narrative approach in general for learning processes within work settings [19]. She concludes that stories are a powerful tool to evaluate and reflect upon learning processes in the workplace.

The idea of learning and working with stories reflects a cooperative understanding of knowledge [2]: social interaction is always implicit in storytelling [8]. Stories bring people and their individual experiences together. Storytellers as well as listeners participate in stories as individuals with a biography – a biography which manifests itself in terms of experiences without being fully aware of this range of experiences. Erlach et al. likewise started to apply stories to Knowledge Management contexts at the beginning of the new millennium in order to visualise these *'soft' experiences* of employees [18]. Researchers have concluded that the method of storytelling may have different benefits in enterprise settings such as: sharing experiences with colleagues or getting familiar with the internal values of the company. But first of all, the use of stories promotes learning as well as change processes on the basis of tacit knowledge [18]. And it is here that the special potential of stories lies – as the literature[5] confirms. Stories enable the communication of what often remains unexploited as tacit knowledge[6]. They make experiences tangible which helps determine human thoughts and actions without having full accessibility as an individual [7]. In this sense, it

---

[3] An increased need for such social interaction and communication is suggested by the key phrase of the communication society.

[4] Studies document the positive effects of the storytelling method on the learning process in different ways. Yang and Wu state that the use of storytelling in foreign language lessons has a positive impact on academic achievement, critical thinking and learning motivation [13].

[5] See Moskaliuk; Ozmen among others [6, 7].

[6] Ozmen describes tacit knowledge as knowledge which may not be codified. Therefore the core element of tacit knowledge is that it is not tangible [7].

becomes clear why Ozmen describes tacit knowledge as the glue "that holds all knowledge together and makes sense of it" [7] and that "the greatest benefit of using storytelling in K[nowledge] M[anagement] [N. B.] is seen from its ability to capture tacit knowledge" [7]. Stories bring together the (tacit) experiences of participants, link them together and expand on them to create new knowledge.

Thus, based on these considerations, we are convinced that there is good reason to look at digital storytelling as a suitable method for learning the skills needed in Computer Supported Cooperative Working. The following chapter shows that fairytales can do much more in terms of holding learners together, not just bringing them together. As such, they make a special contribution to developing and shaping communities where learning and working are perceived as social processes within the knowledge exchange.

3.3   Fairytales and Their Specific Potential in Building Communities via Relatedness

This section investigates the contribution of fairytales to interactive learning and working. It will be demonstrated how fairytales create communities, one of which forms the basis for dynamic and cooperative Knowledge Management.

Fairytales differ from other stories due to their metaphorical expressive powers which promote social exchange. Interdisciplinary research literature is united in the view that the telling of fairytales and stories in general represents a key component of inter-human communications and interaction. Stories bring people together. Stories have long been used to explain the world, to create meaning, understanding and structure, to trade and pass on values and to create the past, present and future [4]. Stories thrive on the fact that standards, relationships, wishes, fears, experiences and expectations are shared through them. In this way, stories create a sense of commonality. Fairytales achieve much more than this too in the sense that they hold people together as well as bringing them together. And this represents their special potential for collaborative learning and working. This potential is described according to the three aspects of **optimism**, **openness** and **symbolic power**.

Unlike other stories, fairytales are stories which always have a positive and optimistic message and ending. No fairytale ends before the King has found his Queen or the hero has successfully completed his task. The happy ending is an integral feature of every fairytale. Thanks to this optimism, fairytales have a motivating effect because they signal to learners that everything is possible and that anything can be achieved. The overriding message is the same for all fairytales: you can create what you are dreaming of if you are prepared to fight for it. Fairytales therefore motivate people to take action themselves – without setting the direction.

A second aspect of fairytales is that they have an open message – and this makes them a suitable subject for discussion. It is up to the listener to decide if Cinderella is about envy and jealousy, justice and reward, complicated family relations or the contrast between dreams and reality [17]. In other words: everything is possible in (and with) fairytales. By expecting the listener to disregard the strict boundaries of rationality and feasibility for a time, fairytales open themselves up to interpretation. As a result of this openness, fairytales invite an exchange of individual perceptions and are suitable for the shared learning of new perspectives [17].

After all, fairytales have a strong symbolic power expressed through images and metaphors with which they create a sense of community among readers and storytellers. They build bridges with the biography of the individual via analogies. What happens in fairytales concerns everyone because they address fundamental questions and answers in human life. Since we all know what it is like to lose something valuable due to not paying enough attention, we are touched and moved by the unlucky fairytale characters because everyone suffers misfortune from time to time – and Hans in Luck is no exception. In this way fairytales create an emotional link between the protagonists of the story and the listener. Turning a blind eye would reflect ignorance about one's own living situation. In this way, fairytales create the impossible: they represent an analogy for human actions – and this fact brings and holds people together. Thus fairytales create community – a community of participants which thrives on the experiences, perspectives and knowledge of each individual involved.

It appears that fairytales motivate the listener to share individual experiences with others through their optimism, openness and symbolism– and as such they create (emotional) ties among learners. Fairytales create an environment which is motivating, tolerant, inspiring, open and error and criticism-friendly as well as being appreciative and trusting. Fairytales therefore promote a kind of learning which is understood as a social process of interaction and collaboration.

The following systemic-theoretical model summarizes the thoughts presented in this chapter in graphical form (Fig. 1).

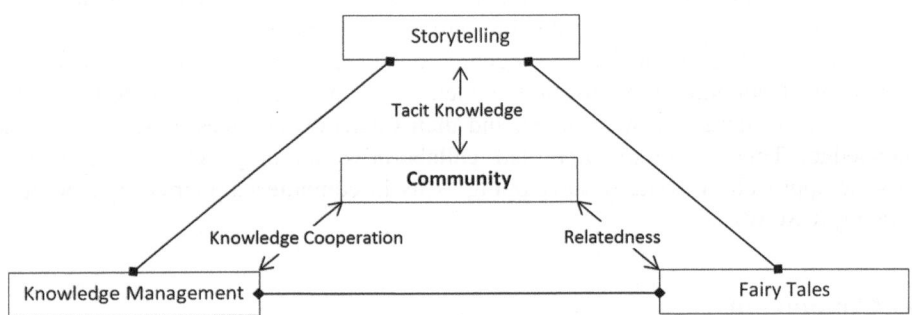

Fig. 1. Model of Collaborative Storytelling.

The model shows that communities form a link between modern companies and their Knowledge Management and the newly identified method of storytelling through dynamic Knowledge Cooperation which is about bringing and holding together employees and their (tacit) knowledge in order to learn and work. And fairytales are a motivating approach to this with their relevance to everyone's life and experience.

4   The Model at Work

This section helps the reader to gain an idea of the implementation of the model within the practical setting of a Distance University of Applied Sciences. As part of the Story@eTeam project at FFHS, the model presented in this paper is applied to concrete learning and working settings within the virtual domain.

Starting with the theoretical considerations outlined in Sect. 3, FFHS is launching an online course which conveys the social aspects of successful virtual teamwork. Since working together with others means following a common goal, sharing becomes an essential part of (e)Collaboration. In order to encourage people to share their knowledge, ideas, experiences etc., the implementation of technical tools is not sufficient. In addition to an appreciating environment and a flat hierarchy, virtual teamwork is enabled by other social and more personal criteria like constructive communication, trust, openness and autonomy.

The online course focuses on these human values of a knowledge-friendly and dynamic enterprise culture. With the support of fairytales, the learners experience what it means to share, shape and develop experiences with others as part of a dynamic process of Knowledge Cooperation.

The following activities are included in the course design in order to devise a (social) basis for successful virtual teamwork both online and collaboratively: (1) getting familiar with the virtual course platform; (2) setting up an individual profile; (3) meeting the other participants in a virtual greeting room; (4) receiving an introduction to the course contents and procedures; (5) collaboratively solving different tasks relating to the topics of *communication, trust, openness* and *autonomy*. This main part of the course is based on the fairytale *The Devil with the Three Golden Hairs* and all its activities are enabled by different eCollaboration tools such as wikis, forums and social media platforms like Twitter etc. (6) finally, the participants finish the course by exchanging and reflecting on their personal learning experience.

The course offers a practical introduction to the social topics of eCollaboration and Knowledge Cooperation by using the method of storytelling – promoting social exchange and interaction with others and their (tacit) experiences, wishes, fears and knowledge. Thus computer-supported collaborative learning (CSCL) becomes a possible approach en route to developing skills in computer-supported collaborative working (CSCW).

5   Conclusion

This paper argues that learning and working through social exchange are fundamental to a cooperative Knowledge Management in companies today and that fairytales are particularly suited to the creation and existence of social communities because they bring and hold together individuals and their (tacit) experiences through references, metaphors and analogies. A model has therefore been developed for this purpose which defines and links the aspects of Knowledge Management, storytelling and fairytales with the community as a core element.

When knowledge is seen as the socially constructed sharing of experiences and managing knowledge from this radical constructivist viewpoint is therefore no longer sufficient (any more), Bettoni's Knowledge Cooperation model raises the question of how sharing, constructing and negotiating experiences can be promoted, supported and structured as a social experience [2].

The (digital) storytelling method has proven itself to be a means of tried-and-trusted access here because stories bring people and their (tacit) experiences together as a form of inter-human interaction. Even those experiences which are of limited availability to the learner as a form of tacit knowledge but which are nevertheless involved in the development of knowledge are liberated by stories as a means of social interaction: anyone who participates in stories does so as an individual with his/her own biography and always with the (necessary) readiness to open up the content of this biography to others.

After all, fairytales have been discussed as a form of story which brings learners together and *keeps* them together by creating emotional ties through **optimism**, **openness** and **metaphors**. In other words: although nobody was actually here in this long-forgotten age at this unknown location, fairytales appeal to everyone because they can be adapted to the life and learning of each individual. In this sense, fairytales create a simple and promising pathway of supporting learning and working as a collaborative and interactive process within a community by motivating participants to share their individual perspectives, experiences, wishes and knowledge. Demonstrating this is the aim of the 2011 FFHS Story@eTeam project.

References

1. Bettoni, M.: Success Factors for Community Learning. A constructivist Perspective, pp. 105–112. Shaker, Aachen (2011)
2. Bettoni, M.: Wissenskooperation. Die Zukunft des Wissensmanagement. Lernende Organisation. Zeitschrift für systemisches Management und Organisation. 25, 7–25 (2005)
3. Boje, D.M.: Breaking out of narrative's prison. Improper story in storytelling organization. Storytelling. Self. Soc. 2, 28–49 (2006)
4. Brown, P.: The Psychological Power of Storytelling, Positively Media, 16 Jan 2011. http://www.psychologytoday.com/blog/positively-media/201101/the-psychological-power-storytelling
5. Erlach, C., Thier, K.: Mit Geschichten implizites Wissen in Organisationen heben. In: Wyssusek, B. (ed.) Wissensmanagement komplex: Perspektiven und soziale Praxis, pp. 207–226. Schmidt, Berlin (2004)
6. Moskaliuk, J., Knipfer, K., Cress, U.: Das 'stille' Wissen der Mitarbeiter nutzen. Wissensmanagement. Das Magazin für Führungskräfte. 3, 44–46 (2012)
7. Ozmen, F.: The capabilities of the educational organizations in making use of tacit knowledge. Procedia Soc. Bus. Behav. Sci. 9, 1860–1865 (2010)
8. Parboosingh, J., Reed, V.A., Caldwell Palmer, J., Bernstein, H.H.: Enhancing practice improvement by facilitating practitioner interactivity. New roles for providers of continuing medical education. J. Continuing Educ. Health Prof. 31(2), 122–127 (2011)
9. Patel, H., Pettitt, M., Wilson, J.R.: Factors of collaborative working. A framework for a collaboration model. Appl. Ergon. 43, 1–26 (2012)

10. Sharda, N.: Using storytelling as the pedagogical model for web-based learning in communities of practice. In: Karacapilidis, N. (ed.) Web-Based Learning Solutions for Communities of Practice. Developing Virtual Environments for Social and Pedagogical Advancement, pp. 67–82. Information Science Reference, Hershey (2010)
11. Standley, M.: Digital Storytelling. Using new technology and the power of stories to help our students learn and teach. Cable in the Classroom, http://mstandley.com/digital_storytelling.pdf16–18 (2003)
12. Thissen, F.: Lohnt sich eLearning? Neue Wege in der virtuellen Aus-und Weiterbildung. http://www.competence-site.de/weiterbildung-fremdsprachen/ Lohnt-sich-eLearning-Neue-Wege-in-der-virtuellen-Aus-und-Weiterbildung (2003)
13. Yang, Y.-T.C., Wu, W.-C.I.: Digital storytelling for enhancing student academic achievement, critical thinking, and learning motivation. A year-long experimental study. Comput. Educ. **59**, 339–352 (2012)
14. ZHAW: Storytelling in management research. In: Thorpe, R., Holt, R. (eds.) The SAGE Dictionary of Qualitative Management Research, pp. 1–5. Sage, London (2008)
15. Bettoni, M., Eggs, C.: User-centred knowledge management: a constructivist and socialized view. Constructivist Found. **5**(3), 130–143 (2010)
16. Wenger, E.: Communities of Practice. Learning, Meaning and Identity. Cambridge University Press, Cambridge (1998)
17. Bittel, N.: Learning CSCW by Fairytales. Linex Blog. http://www.linexsystems.com/linex-blog/itemlist/date/2012/6?catid=1 Accessed 22 June 2012
18. Erlach, C., Their, K., Neubauer, A.: Story Telling – mit Geschichten Organisationen bewegen. Narrata Consult, München (o.J.)
19. Reissner, S.C.: Learning by story-telling? J. Adult Contin. Educ. **10**(2), 99–113 (2004)

The Role of Peer Review in Supporting the Sustainability of Technology-Enhanced Learning Environments

Pantelis M. Papadopoulos[✉] and Antonio Cerone

International Institute for Software Technology, United Nations University,
Macau SAR, People's Republic of China
pmpapad@iist.unu.edu, ceroneantonio@gmail.com

Abstract. We present a series of three studies on the peer review method. We argue that the implementation of such a method in a technology-enhanced learning environment can enhance the learning experience for the students, and consequently affect the sustainability of the learning environment itself. In the context of the paper, sustainability is viewed through a pedagogy lens, describing the property of a learning environment to maintain an active group of students. Finally, we present how different aspects of the peer review process can affect a learning activity.

Keywords: Sustainability · Technology-enhanced learning environments · Peer review · Scripted collaboration

1 Introduction

We present a series of three studies on the peer review method, suggesting that when this kind of instructional intervention is embedded in the design of a technology-enhanced learning environment (TELE) it can enhance the learning experience for the user and, in that way, also affect positively the sustainability of the TELE.

The term sustainability has grown to include different meanings in different contexts and it can suggest various concepts, such as, for example, financial, technical, or institutional sustainability. In the context of this paper, we refer to the longevity of an e-learning environment and the sustainability of the learning process that the environment can support. Even with institutional support and financial viability, a learning environment can fail, if it does not capture the interest of the students. Low engagement can be the result of different factors. While some of these factors may refer to the individual (e.g., low intrinsic motives), others may refer to the characteristics of the learning activity (e.g., scaffolding provided). We maintain that the peer review process can address at least some of the factors related to the activity.

In general terms, a peer review method refers to settings where students (or group of students) review each other's previous work, in order to provide comments and suggestions for improvement. One can find a huge volume of studies focusing on different characteristics of the method. Acknowledged benefits of peer review are, among others, that (a) it can support the collaboration between students (b) structure

A. Cerone et al. (Eds.): SEFM 2012 Satellite Events, LNCS 7991, pp. 89–103, 2014.
DOI: 10.1007/978-3-642-54338-8_7, © Springer-Verlag Berlin Heidelberg 2014

their interaction, and (c) provide an additional channel for feedback (the other being that of the instructor).

In the following, we present the theoretical background of the paper, present a series of three of our studies on the peer review method, provide analysis for the relation between peer review and sustainability, and finally offer conclusive remarks.

2   Theoretical Background

2.1   Sustainability in Educational Technology

Sustainability has become a very broad and ambiguous term, used by researchers of different domains and backgrounds. As Middleton [1] reports, in the educational context the term appears to have oscillated through at least four competing meanings internationally over the last 40 years. The four meanings can be characterized as (a) sustainability as environmental education [2] (b) as sustainable development education [2] (c) as sustainable growth education [3], and (d) as encompassing the concept of social, economic and environmental sustainability [4, 5]. According to Wals and van der Leij [6], determining the meaning of sustainability is a process involving 'all kinds of stakeholders in many contexts'. Most, if not all, calls for proposals in the domain of educational technology explicitly mention the need for sustainability after the completion of the project (e.g., European Commission: FP7 CfP). More specifically, the need for organizational, financial, and institutional sustainability is needed for a proposal to get funded.

Narrowing down the meaning of sustainability, we approach the term from a pedagogical point of view, focusing on the life expectancy of technology-enhanced learning environments (TELEs). The main idea behind our way of thinking is that a learning environment can be sustainable only when there is an active group of students willing to use it. As we have already mentioned, students' motivation for engagement can be affected by many unpredictable factors. So, what is needed is a pedagogical approach that will enhance the learning experience. Our suggestion is that the peer review method can effectively play this role.

2.2   The Peer Review Process in e-Learning

Peer review is a widely used instructional method, focusing both on helping students elaborate on domain-specific knowledge, and also on supporting the development of their methodological review skills. Typically, peer review is a teacher-led activity, where the instructor assigns to each student (or group of students) the review of a piece of work (a written or verbal deliverable produced by another peer/group), according to specific quality criteria. The review then becomes available to the student authors and is used as a means for reflection and revision of the deliverable. However, many variances of this form have emerged over the years. We can identify four major phases in a peer review process: (a) producing initial work (b) assigning reviewers (c) review submission, and (d) revision. The method has been used extensively in various fields [7–9], having a long history in writing instruction and relevant courses at the college level [10–12].

Researchers stress the fact that peer review offers to students the chance of developing a range of skills important in the development of language and writing ability, such as meaningful interaction with peers, a greater exposure to ideas, and new perspectives on the writing process [13–15]. Also, certain researchers emphasize that by implementing peer review students get feedback of greater quantity than a busy teacher could reasonably provide [16, 17]. This gives valuable feedback and the opportunity for development of critical reviewing skills. Others report benefits such as students' improved self-evaluation skills [18] and improved students' attitudes and self-efficacy [19]. However, Turner and Pérez-Quiñones [9] emphasize: "While we have identified a number of potential benefits from reviewing, we have not shown that it is better than or as good as what we currently do. We require some sort of baseline to compare our efforts to. We need a control group in our experiments in order to judge effectiveness." (p. 44).

Based on the above, this paper suggests that the peer review method can also support the creation of sustainable communities of practice in e-learning, and through that the sustainability of the technology-enhanced learning environments used by the communities. In the following, we present three studies on the peer review method. Each study focuses on a different set of research questions, trying to shed light on various aspects of the method.

3 First Study: Peer Review and Script Coercion

The First Study focused on the impact the degree of script coercion can have on the learning outcomes of peer review in a setting of scripted collaboration. A more detailed presentation of the First Study can be found at [20].

3.1 Distance Between External and Internal Collaboration Scripts

"External" CSCL scripts (conceptualized and imposed by teacher or educational designer) need to be adapted to the procedural knowledge and competencies (or "internal" scripts) of learners [21, 22]. Beyond internal and external scripts that represent idealized trajectories of interactions, the observable interactions or "actual" scripts are typically combinations of the various internal and external scripts distributed in small groups of learners [23]. Besides the fact that many internal scripts are typically interacting in any given CSCL scenario, also fine-grained and high-structured external scripts leave some room for students' interpretation of an activity. This script-interpretation and appropriation process depends to a large extent on the degrees of freedom or coercion the script imposes on students and it leads to a difference between the ideal external script from a teacher's or educational designer's perspective and the actual activity as realized by the students. However, this distance should not be interpreted necessarily as instructor's design flaw but as a characteristic inherent in the teaching/learning process (see [24]). The distance "is not a dysfunction of the learner rather than intrinsic to the notion of task and human activity" ([24], p. 36). Likewise, it can be considered an inherent characteristic of external scripts to be interpreted and hence, distance between external and actually emerging script does not indicate a failure of the treatment.

Although educational designers need to design for this distance between external and actual script, there are indications that this distance can be detrimental to learning. In [25], students in a scripted collaboration condition worked in dyads and were guided to (a) read the learning material and answer open-ended questions individually (b) review their partners' answers on the same questions and identify differences and similarities with their own, and (c) discuss their reviews and try to formulate and submit a common final answer to the scenario questions. Students actually followed various paths for realizing the prescribed activity with different degrees of peer interaction. There were four patterns identified: (a) following the ideal external script (b) moderate peer interaction (c) weak peer interaction and (d) no peer interaction. Each of the above mentioned interaction patterns exhibited a different degree of distance from the ideal external script of peer interaction intended by the instructor ranging from small sidesteps to script violation. There are several script characteristics that affect this distance [23, 26]. The three most central ones are: (a) intelligibility (b) fitness between internal and external scripts, and (c) degree of coercion.

In this First Study, we focused on the role of script coercion as a factor affecting the distance between ideal and actual scripts in a CSCL environment, thus becoming a moderator variable between ideal script and learning impact. We hypothesize that increasing script coercion by requiring that learners clearly articulate their mental representations of the subject matter (instead of suggesting this as an option and allowing students to decide whether they implement it or not) should have beneficial impact on learning. In the context of the First Study, we applied this method in a technology-supported peer review scripted task analyzing the collaboration patterns and the group and individual learning outcomes of two student cohorts. Students in the treatment group were coerced to submit their reviews in written form, otherwise they would not be allowed by the system to proceed. By contrast, students in control group were free to choose whether they would submit written reviews or not.

3.2   Method and Results of the First Study

The study involved two groups of juniors majoring in Informatics: 20 students (5 male dyads and 5 female dyads) worked in the Low Coercion (LC) condition, while 22 students (6 male dyads and 5 female dyads) worked in the High Coercion (HC) condition. We used a pre-test post-test experimental research design to compare the performance of the two groups. Students proceeded through the study in five distinct phases: Pre-test, Individual Study, Collaboration, Post-test, and Interview. In the study, we used a technology-enhanced learning environment, designed and developed for our research purposes. The environment was generic and able to support learning in different domains. In the First Study, the domain of instruction was Software Project Management and students had to study different cases of past projects and suggest solutions to realistic open-ended scenarios. The same environment and the same format of cases and scenarios were used actually in all the studies we are presenting here, although system functionality was modified to accommodate the research needs of each study.

In the Pre-test phase, students completed the prior domain knowledge instrument. During the Individual Study phase, all students worked online in the environment (from wherever and whenever they wanted) and answered the questions of 3 scenarios. They were allowed one week to submit their answers. Study conditions were common for all. Next, in the Collaboration phase that also lasted one week, the students worked in dyads. At first, they had to conduct peer review and then discuss, reach a consensus, and provide a common final answer for each scenario. The outline of the collaboration script and the reviewing instructions (microscript) were the same for the two groups, with the only difference being the degree of coercion of the script. Finally, the students took a written post-test in class and shortly after that, we interviewed students from each group to record their opinions and comments on the activity.

Table 1 presents students' scores in the pre-test and post-test instruments. T-test results showed that the groups were comparable regarding students' prior knowledge ($p > 0.05$). ANCOVA results showed a significant difference between groups in the post-test ($p < 0.05$).

We analyzed students' collaboration patterns based, in turn, on: (a) their statements during the interviews (b) the comparison of individual and collaborative answers, and (c) the system log files. Eventually, in the Low Coercion group only 2 dyads demonstrated the "ideal" collaboration pattern, 5 dyads resembled the "moderate" collaboration pattern, and 3 dyads fell into the "weak" collaboration pattern. On the contrary, the patterns identified in the High Coercion group draw a better picture of the actual collaboration, with 5 dyads demonstrating the "ideal" pattern, and 6 dyads the "moderate" one. None of the dyads resembled the "no interaction" pattern.

Our analysis showed that students working in the High Coercion condition applied better collaboration patterns and outperformed students in the Low Coercion condition in acquiring domain conceptual knowledge. Since both groups had the same learning material and the same set of instructions and guidelines, it is clear that these differences occurred because of the imposed requirement for written reviews in the HC group. Submission of reviews in the system was optional for students in the LC group. Although, they were free to use the provided review form, 9 of the 10 dyads chose not to submit their comments in the system. This decision altered significantly the learning setting for the LC students. Of course, LC students stated that they also performed a review process, but they preferred to submit their review comments directly to their peers. Typically, this submission was also in writing, as the majority

Table 1. Students' performance in the First Study.

(Scale:1-10)	High Coercion			Low Coercion		
	M	SD	n	M	SD	n
Pre-test	2.24	(0.71)	22	2.13	(0.59)	20
Post-test	7.42	(1.30)	22	6.36	(0.83)	20

of the dyads used online chat for communication. However, the LC students' contributions were made in a rather reactive mode (that is, in a conversational mode, reacting to their peer's input), lacking structure and, possibly, depth. Through a peer review process, an individual can get multiple perspectives of the domain. As reviewers, students can get new insights by studying others' answers, while as authors they get to know how others view their work. A well-structured, eloquent, and thought-of review, submitted as a separate deliverable that can be accessed multiple times can be more useful for both the author and the reviewer. On the other hand, having the review comments scattered in the online chat log can be counter-productive.

Written reviews can further support collaboration. First, written reviews can inform a student for the peer's opinions and understanding. This way, both students enter the discussion, knowing each other's position. Second, by making their opinions explicit, it is easy for students to identify different views and disagreements. In this case, a written review can trigger the dialogue between peers. Both these points came up in the interviews we held with the HC students, suggesting that the benefits of the written reviews were actually acknowledged.

4 Second Study: The Free-Selection Protocol

This study analyzed the efficiency of an alternative to the commonly used "assigned-pair" peer review protocol, in which students typically work together in instructor-defined dyads, reviewing each other's work. The free-selection protocol allows students to freely browse and select for themselves peer work for review. More on the specifics and the implementation of the free-selection protocol can be found in [27].

4.1 Direct and Indirect Feedback from Peers

While there are studies that assign multiple reviewers to a single peer (e.g., [28, 29]), in the context of our study we used the term "assigned-pair" to refer to a more common research design where students in a dyad are assigned exclusively to each other. In any way, the benefit of the assigned-pair method is that the overhead for the instructor can be well contained and the activity is straightforward for the students. This design, of course, is not without drawbacks. Pairing students means that the author will have just one chance to get valuable comments and suggestions for improvement. On the other hand, the benefit for the reviewer may also be limited. Working in pairs gives the chance to students to improve what they have already wrote, either by getting some useful comments or adopting good ideas from the answers they review. However, when working in a dyad, there is one more point of view provided (the author's). Based on the above, direct feedback is the review comments an author receives from a reviewer, while an indirect feedback is the viewpoint a reviewer gets to see, while reading author's submission.

Our focus was to (a) enhance the learning benefits of peer review for the students, without increasing the minimum amount of work that they had to do, and (b) keep instructor's overhead low. There is already indication in the literature that the "randomly assigned pair" protocol, implemented typically by the instructors, might not be the optimal selection regarding student learning. For example, it is suggested that matching author-reviewer student pairs (depending on student author and reviewer ability) can lead to improved learning outcomes [30]. However, "matching student pairs" results also in additional instructors' workload, since it is necessary for the teacher to somehow model students' author-reviewer ability and apply an optimization algorithm for student matching. Such overhead would make the matching protocol hardly an appealing technique to employ, unless supported by appropriate technology tool. Additionally, the method requires a level of stability in the dyads formation throughout the activity, while a bad pairing may have negative results.

Towards this direction, we decided to investigate the efficiency of a "free-selection protocol", where there are no dyads and students are free to browse all peer work and select what to review. A review can be helpful or not, since it may or may not include good suggestions for improvement. On the other hand, when the students are exposed through reading to many different opinions, they tend to compare and search for the dominant opinion or for the one that fits theirs better. In other words, we believe that students working in a free-selection setting would benefit from the process, even without a policy that ascertains that each answer gets at least one review.

4.2   Method and Results of the Second Study

The study employed two groups of sophomore students majoring in Informatics and Telecommunications Engineering in a 5-year program. We randomly assigned students into two reviewing conditions: 20 students (12 males and 8 females) in the Assigned-Pair (AP) condition, and 17 students (9 males and 8 females) in the Free-Selection (FS) condition. We, once again, used a pre-test post-test experimental research design to compare the performance of the two groups. Students proceeded through the study in five distinct phases: Pre-test, Study, Review & Revise, Post-test, and Interview. The same TELE was used, as in the First Study, modified, of course, to support the new study conditions, while the domain of study was Network Planning and Design.

In the Pre-test phase, we recorded students' prior knowledge on the domain with a test in class. During the Study phase, all students had one week to login into the environment and access the learning material. The idea was, as before to have the students study the available resources and produce their initial deliverables that would later go through the reviewing phase. Up until this point, the conditions were the same for all students. Next, in the Review & Revise phase the students had to review, in a double-blinded process, the answers their peers gave to 3 scenarios in the previous phase. Furthermore, the students were able, in case they wanted to, to revise their own answers according to the comments received from their peers. The Review & Revise phase also lasted one week. More specifically, we allowed a 4-day period for all the reviews, while the parallel revision of the previous answers lasted an additional 3-day period. Students in the AP conditions had access to only their partners' answers, so they could only read and review answers from only one student. On the contrary, all the answers were freely accessible in the FS group and students could read and review as many as they wanted (the bare minimum was one answer per scenario). Finally, after the Review & Revise phase, the students took a written post-test in class and shortly after that, we interviewed the students from each group to record their approaches and comments on the activity.

Table 2 presents students' scores in the pre-test and post-test instruments. The two groups were comparable in the pre-test metric, according to t-test results. On the other hand, ANCOVA results showed that there was a significant difference between groups in the post-test ($p < 0.05$).

Deeper analysis on the review quality also showed that students in the free-selection condition provided more useful comments. Usage data analysis showed that FS students read in average more than 8 answers out of the total 16 (M = 8.25, SD = 2.98) per scenario. Furthermore, FS students reviewed in average almost 2 answers (M = 1.90, SD = 0.92), and of course they received the same number of reviews. We were expecting to have several answers without reviews by the end of the 4-day period of the Review & Revise phase. However, this happened only twice and we asked two students with good review records (number of answer read and submitted reviews above average) to provide the missing reviews.

Another interesting finding was the way students selected the answers to review. According to their statements in the interviews, there were two main trends. Some students selected what they considered good answers, so that they can say positive things about their peers. On the contrary, other students focused on weak answers (again, according to their opinion), so that they could provide some useful review comments. We also asked FS students who submitted more than one review per scenario to explain their motives for such a strategy, especially since they were not awarded extra credit. First, some students said that writing down reviews and explaining their opinions to others was a good exercise to clarify their own understandings. Second, students also mentioned that after reading several answers, and since the answers were relatively short, it was easy for them to spend a little time submitting more reviews. In that way, they thought that they would increase the possibility of everyone receiving at least one review.

Overall the Second Study provided field research evidence that the students who followed the free selection protocol have significant benefits (compared to students who follow the typical "assigned pair" protocol) regarding domain learning and review ability. Students also report encouraging perspectives on their engagement in the activity, such as that writing multiple reviews helped them "clear their own understanding" and "feel members of a community".

Table 2. Students' performance in the Second Study.

(Scale:1-10)	Assigned-pair			Free-selection		
	M	SD	n	M	SD	n
Pre-test	2.69	(1.07)	20	2.59	(0.83)	17
Post-test	7.71	(0.95)	20	8.43	(0.81)	17

5   Third Study: What If There Is Only Indirect Feedback?

Following the findings of the Second Study, we decided to analyze deeper the potential of the free-selection protocol, focusing on settings where there is no direct feedback to the students. In other words, the policy of freely choosing what to read and review makes it possible to have students that submitted answers, but received no comments. In the Second Study, the spread of the reviews was so high that only 2 students did not receive reviews. We addressed that by assigning selected reviewers to these students. However, this does not fully answer the research question regarding the impact of direct and indirect feedback in the free-selection protocol. In the following, we present the background and the ongoing result analysis of the recently conducted Third Study.

5.1   Direct and Indirect Feedback from Peers

At first sight, a certain limitation of the free-selection protocol for peer review settings, as it was implemented in the Second Study, is the need for a strategy that ascertains that each submission will be reviewed. Since the protocol, as we suggest it, is focused more on the students' ability to act freely and much less on guaranteeing review comments for all, one could argue that this could cause serious implementation issues, especially when the reviews distribution is skewed. Our belief, while suggesting the free-selection protocol, was that the benefits provided by an indirect feedback (reading others' submissions and getting multiple viewpoints) could render the absence of direct feedback (review comments from peers) non-significant for the learning outcome.

There are already results in the literature that corroborate the findings of the Second Study. For example, Cho and Schuun [31] reported beneficial learning outcomes when students get multiple reviews (as opposed to getting a single review). Additionally, several studies agree that students that act as "givers" (that is when they provide reviews) demonstrate better learning outcomes than students acting as "receivers" (getting peer feedback) [15, 32, 33]. Furthermore, the students' positive approach to the free-selection method (studying more than asked and submitting more reviews than the lower limit) is also in line with other studies reporting tendency of students to contribute more when not restricted by the assignment protocol [15].

In the free-selection method, as implemented in the Second Study, students assumed both roles of "givers" and "receiver" (reviewers and authors, respectively). This makes our method easier to implement, since there is no need for two different groups. The motive behind the Third Study was to explore the effectiveness of the same method, for students that act only as "givers". For this, we amended the existing method adding a self-review process for all students that do not receive feedback from their peers. So, in the Third Study we tested our initial belief regarding the effectiveness of the free-selection protocol, comparing two groups of students: a group where students act only as "givers" and a control group where students assume both roles.

5.2   Method and Results of the Third Study

The Third Study was conducted a year after the Second one, on the exact same context, meaning the students' year of study, knowledge domain, and material. The study employed 38 sophomore students majoring in Informatics and Telecommunication Engineering. In order to compare the impact of not receiving a review, we needed similar populations of students in the two conditions (review/no review). To do so, we randomly selected 15 students. These students participated as anybody else in the activity, but their answers did not appear to others and thus they did not received reviews. This means that all 38 students submitted reviews, but the answers of only 23 students were available for read and review. We informed students beforehand of this random selection, although we did not divulge the identities of the selected ones. Five students whose answers appeared to others, but did not receive reviews to all their answers were also added to the initial 15. The students that did not receive reviews had to conduct a self-review process, following instructions on analyzing their answers. Eventually, 20 students worked in the Self-Review (SR) group, and 18 students in the Peer-Review (PR) group.

The activity followed the same phase sequence as before (Pre-Test, Study, Review & Revise, Post-Test, Interview). During the first week, students had to study individually in the learning environment and provide answers to open-ended questions regarding 3 realistic scenarios. During the second week, all students followed the free-selection review protocol, freely reviewing at least one answer per scenario. At the end, students in the PR group revised their initial answers based on the comments they received, while students in the SR group based their revisions only on what they read in others' answers and in the self-review form.

One difference between the two studies on the free-selection protocol was the number of available answers to review for each student. In the Second Study, a student had access to all the answers in the group (i.e., 16 peer answers). The log files showed the students read on average half of them. Considering this, we decided to contain the number of answers available to students. Our belief was that a large number of answers could overwhelm the students and affect the selection process, meaning that since it would be difficult for them to get a good idea of what has been said, selecting which answers to review would be done randomly. At the end, out of the total 23 answers, only a random set of 9 answers were available for read and review to each student. Each answer appeared the same number of times and students still had a sense of freely selecting what to read and review.

Table 3 presents students' scores in the pre-test and post-test instruments. T-test and ANCOVA results showed that the two groups were comparable both in the pre-test and the post-test ($p > 0.05$).

Table 3. Students' performance in the Third Study.

(Scale:1-10)	Self review			Peer review		
	M	SD	n	M	SD	n
Pre-test	2.20	(1.09)	20	2.04	(1.06)	18
Post-test	8.19	(1.37)	20	8.13	(1.40)	18

Analysis of the review quality showed that there was no difference between the two groups, but this was already expected, since the review process was identical for all students. Usage data analysis showed that students read almost all the available answers ($M = 8.12$, $SD = 1.45$) and reviewed on average almost 2 answers ($M = 1.74$, $SD = 0.58$). Since all students acted as reviewers, but only 18 of them received reviews, each student in the PR group received on average more than 3 reviews ($M = 3.42$, $SD = 0.75$).

In analyzing the criteria the students used to select which answers to review, the same two trends of the Second Study appeared. Students select answers that are, according to them, correct and adequately supported by argument or incorrect and needing improvement. In the first case the students can praise their peers' effort, and in the second they can provide more useful suggestions in their reviews. Regarding the reasons behind students' attitudes to provide more submissions than asked, student, once more, said that since the task of writing a review was not difficult, they felt that by submitting more reviews they could help others improve their answers. Additionally, they could get benefits for themselves, since the process of explicitly writing down their own opinions helped them understand even better the problem area.

The findings of the Third Study enhanced the value of the free-selection method, as they suggest that this kind of peer review approach can be useful for the students even in a group with low activity and participation. A learner can join at any time, read the material and answer questions. Even in the case where a student does not get comments from peers, the previously submitted answers can provide a valuable feedback.

Finally, it needs to be clear that although our results suggest that the kind of indirect feedback described above can fill the void of personalized comments from peers, the role of an actual collaborator can add even more value. The settings we tested address the specifics of a review process with only one cycle of author-reviewer interaction. Other researchers could use the phase of review submission as a first of many steps towards a dialogue between peers. In these cases, the channel of communication opens up and students are able to discuss in more meaningful ways how to improve their answers. So, in the end, the value of active collaborators cannot be substituted. However, in the absence of them, the indirect feedback that the free-selection protocol supports can be an efficient alternative.

6 Implications for Sustainability

Researchers have repeatedly emphasized that collaborating students may fail to engage in productive learning interactions when left without support and scaffolding (e.g., [25, 34, 35]). This was also evident in the Low Coercion group of the First Study, where students demonstrated suboptimal collaboration patterns. The peer review process can be an effective tool for structuring the interaction between students. However, the researcher needs to strike a balance between the degree of coercion and the freedom of activities allowed to the students. When used right, the degree of coercion can result to deeper engagement and, consequently, to better learning outcomes.

When using a TELE, students' engagement can also affect the sustainability of the learning environment itself. Indifferent students are more likely to abandon the learning activity, thus dropping the usefulness, effectiveness, and efficiency metrics of the system. On the contrary, a vibrant community of active learning can be the drive behind the sustainability of a TELE.

As showed in the last two studies, the degree of students' engagement and involvement can further be enhanced in a peer review setting. We tested two variations of the free-selection protocol and the result analysis showed that in both cases students surpassed the lower limit of workload, choosing to study and review more answers than was mandatory. We believe that the main reason for the positive attitudes recorded is the element of freedom in the protocol. Students take ownership of their learning and they are truly free to apply self-organization. Even if students decide to apply a low effort strategy and study the bare minimum (randomly select one answer to read and review), they will just shift to the assigned-pair condition.

Another strength of the free-selection protocol in supporting the sustainability of a TELE is the nurturing of a community culture. Students explicitly said during the interviews that one of the reasons for their additional effort in the activity was the feeling that they were part of a larger group. This attitude is quintessential in building a learning community and it is important that was observed in several students in both studies. Additionally, the existence of both direct and indirect feedback for the students provides a constant way of support, thus increasing the possibility of students keep using the system.

Finally, when discussing the sustainability of an e-learning system, we should not forget the role of the instructor that has to design and conduct the learning activity. Increased overhead for the instructor could lead to the abandonment of the method or even of the TELE that supports it. The assigned-pair method is straightforward and simple for both the students and the instructors. On the other hand, special attention was given in the design of the free-selection protocol so that the instructor's overhead will remain contained. Actually, since there is no review assignment phase, instructor's role is just to observe students' activity.

A clear benefit of the peer review method would also be to have students willing to keep participating as members of the learning community that was built during the activity, even after their initial involvement is completed. This was for example the case of the OpenSE project [36]. Students participating in the activity had to play different roles (tester, developer, requirements engineer) in real FLOSS project teams. After the semester-long activity, many students continued their involvement in their projects, while others returned to the learning environment of OpenSE to play the roles of mentors and advisors to new students. Although the studies presented here lasted only two weeks each, we believe that there are properties in the peer review process that could support the development of this kind of attitude to the students. The voluntarily increased engagement observed, is already a step towards this direction.

7   Conclusions

This paper presents the case of how pedagogical method of peer reviewing can support (a) deeper engagement (b) structured peer interaction, and (c) efficient collaboration patterns. These can enhance the impact of a learning experience by making the students more active and creating a community culture among them. Focusing on the sustainability of technology-enhanced learning environments from a pedagogical point of view, we suggest that the formation of an active, collaborating group of students can affect the life cycle of system and is essential for its longevity. In these terms, the peer review can be seen as a well-tested pedagogical method that can play a role in the sustainability of e-learning.

Acknowledgments. This work has been partly funded by UNU-IIST and Macao Science and Technology Development Fund, File No. 019/2011/A1, in the context of the PPAeL project.

References

1. Middleton, H.: Problem-solving in technology education as an approach to education for sustainable development. Int. J. Technol. Des. Educ. **19**, 187–197 (2009)
2. Ryan, E.D.: Bucking the system: teacher education for sustainability in the Asia-Pacific region. Unpublished MEE (Hons.) Dissertation. Griffith University, Brisbane (2000)
3. Fien, J.: Education for the Australian Environment. BASSP/Curriculum Development Centre, Canberra (1988)
4. Collins, C.: The problem of cross-purposes—the challenge of our generation. In: Anderson, J. (ed.) Education for a Sustainable Society. Proceedings of the 31st National Conference of the Australian College of Education (ACE). ACE, Canberra (1992)
5. Pavlova, M.: Sustainable development: is it a priority for French students? In: Middleton, H.E., Pavlova, M., Roebuck, R. (eds.) Learning for Innovation in Technology Education. Proceedings of the 3rd Biennial Technology Education Research Conference, vol. 3, pp. 36–45. Centre for Learning Research, Griffith University, Surfers Paradise (2004)
6. Wals, A.E.J., van der Leij, T.: Introduction. In: Wals, A.E.J. (ed.) Social Learning Towards a Sustainable World, Principle, Perspectives and Praxis, pp. 17–32. Wageningen Academic Publishers, Wageningen (2008)
7. Turner, S., Pérez-Quiñones, M.A.: Exploring Peer Review in the Computer Science Classroom, Computing Research Repository. http://arxiv.org/ftp/arxiv/papers/0907/0907.3456.pdf (2009). Accessed 30 November 2009
8. Liou, H.C., Peng, Z.Y.: Training effects on computer-mediated peer review. System **37**, 514–525 (2009)
9. Goldin, I.M., Ashley, K.D.: Peering inside peer review with Bayesian models. In: Biswas, G., Bull, S., Kay, J., Mitrovic, A. (eds.) AIED 2011. LNCS(LNAI), vol. 6738, pp. 90–97. Springer, Heidelberg (2011)
10. DiPardo, A., Freedman, S.W.: Peer response groups in the writing classroom: theoretic foundations and new directions. Rev. Educ. Res. **58**, 119–149 (1988)
11. Haswell, R.H.: NCTE/CCCC's recent war on scholarship. Written Commun. **22**, 198–223 (2005)

12. Cho, K., MacArthur, C.: Student revision with peer and expert reviewing. Learn. Instr. **20**, 328–338 (2010)
13. Hansen, J., Liu, J.: Guiding principles for effective peer response. ELT J. **59**, 31–38 (2005)
14. Mangelsdorf, K.: Peer reviews in the ESL composition classroom: what do the students think? ELT J. **46**, 274–284 (1992)
15. Lundstrom, K., Baker, W.: To give is better than to receive: the benefits of peer review to the reviewer's own writing. J. Second Lang. Writ. **18**, 30–43 (2009)
16. Wolfe, W.J.: Online student peer reviews. In: Proceedings of the 5th Conference on Information Technology Education, pp. 33–37. ACM Press, New York (2004)
17. Silva, E., Moriera, D.: WebCoM: a tool to use peer review to improve student interaction. J. Edu. Resour. Comput. **3**(1), 1–14 (2003)
18. Davies, R., Berrow, T.: An evaluation of the use of computer peer review for developing higher-level skills. Comput. Educ. **30**(1/2), 111–115 (1998)
19. Anewalt, K.: Using peer review as a vehicle for communication skill development and active learning. J. Comput. Small Coll. **21**(2), 148–155 (2005)
20. Papadopoulos, P.M., Demetriadis, S.N.: The impact of script coercion in computer-supported collaboration: a case study on learning benefits when technology makes learners' thinking processes explicit. In: 12th IEEE International Conference on Advanced Learning Technologies – ICALT 2012, Rome, Italy, 4–6 July (2012) (in press)
21. Kollar, I., Fischer, F., Slotta, J.D.: Internal and external scripts in computer-supported collaborative inquiry learning. Learn. Instr. **17**(6), 708–721 (2007). doi:10.1016/j.learninstruc.2007.09.021
22. Fischer, F., Kollar, I., Stegmann, K., Wecker, C.: Toward a script theory of guidance in computer-supported collaborative learning. Educ. Psychol. **48**, 56–66 (2013)
23. Dillenbourg, P. (ed.): Framework for Integrated Learning. Deliverable D23-05-01-F of Kaleidoscope Network of Excellence. http://hal.archives-ouvertes.fr/docs/00/19/01/07/PDF/Dillenbourg-Kaleidoscope-2004.pdf (2004). Accessed 11 September 2008
24. Tchounikine, P.: Computer Science and Educational Software Design – A Resource for Multidisciplinary Work in Technology Enhanced Learning. Springer, Berlin (2011)
25. Papadopoulos, P.M., Demetriadis, S.N., Stamelos, I.G.: Analyzing the role of students' self-organization in scripted collaboration: a case study. In: Proceedings of the 8th International Conference on Computer Supported Collaborative Learning – CSCL 2009, Rhodes, Greece, pp. 487–496. http://portal.acm.org/citation.cfm?id=1600124 (2009)
26. Kollar, I., Fischer, F., Hesse, F.W.: Collaboration scripts - a conceptual analysis. Educ. Psychol. Rev. **18**(2), 159–185 (2006)
27. Papadopoulos, P.M., Lagkas, T.D., Demetriadis, S.N.: How to improve the peer review method: free-selection vs assigned-pair protocol evaluated in a computer networking course. Comput. Educ. **59**, 182–195 (2012). doi:10.1016/j.compedu.2012.01.005
28. Tseng, S., Tsai, C.-C.: On-line peer assessment and the role of peer feedback: a study of high school computer course. Comput. Educ. **49**, 1161–1174 (2007)
29. Tsai, C.-C., Liang, J.-C.: The development of science activities via on-line peer assessment: the role of scientific epistemological views. Instr. Sci. **37**, 293–310 (2009)
30. Crespo, R.M., Pardo, A., Kloos, C.D.: An adaptive strategy for peer review. Paper presented at ASEE/IEEE Frontiers in Education Conference, Savannah, GA (2004)
31. Cho, K., Schunn, C.D.: Scaffolded writing and rewriting in the discipline: a web-based reciprocal peer review system. Comput. Educ. **48**(3), 409–426 (2007)
32. Li, L., Liu, X., Steckelberg, A.L.: Assessor or assessee: how student learning improves by giving and receiving peer feedback. Br. J. Educ. Technol. **41**(3), 525–536 (2010)

33. Reily, K., Finnerty, P.L., Terveen, L.: Two peers are better than one: aggregating peer reviews for computing assignments is surprisingly accurate. In: Proceedings of GROUP'09, Sanibel Island, Florida, USA, 10–13 May 2009

34. Dillenbourg, P.: Overscripting CSCL: the risks of blending collaborative learning with instructional design. In: Kirschner, P.A. (ed.) Three Worlds of CSCL. Can we support CSCL?, pp. 61–91 (2002)

35. Barron, B.: When smart groups fail. J. Learn. Sci. **12**(3), 307–359 (2003)

36. Papadopoulos, P.M., Stamelos, I.G., Meiszner, A.: Students' perspectives on learning software engineering with open source projects: lessons learnt after three years of program operation. In: 4th International Conference on Computer Supported Education – CSEDU 2012, Porto, Portugal, pp. 313–322 (2012)

Creative Classrooms: A Systemic Approach for Mainstreaming ICT-Enabled Innovation for Learning in Europe

Stefania Bocconi, Panagiotis Kampylis[✉], and Yves Punie

European Commission, DG JRC, Institute for Prospective Technological
Studies (IPTS), Seville, Spain
{stefania.bocconi,panagiotis.kampylis,yves.punie}@ec.europa.eu

Abstract. 'Creative Classrooms' (CCR) are conceptualized as innovative learning environments that fully embed the potential of ICT to innovate learning and teaching practices in formal, non-formal and informal settings. The proposed multi-dimensional concept for CCR consists of eight encompassing and interconnected key dimensions. In order to support experimentation and implementation of these key dimensions of CCR, a set of 28 reference parameters ('building blocks') is proposed. The aim is twofold: (i) to unravel the most innovative elements of the multi-dimensional CCR concept and (ii) to depict the systemic approach needed for the sustainable implementation and progressive mainstreaming of Creative Classrooms across Europe. Last but not least, two cases of ICT-enabled innovation for learning are presented showing how CCR building blocks are combined and implemented in real-life settings configuring profoundly diverse types of CCR.

Keywords: Creative classrooms · ICT-enabled innovation for learning · Innovative pedagogies · Systemic change

1 Introduction

The Europe 2020 strategy acknowledges that a fundamental transformation of Education and Training (E&T) is needed to address new skills and competences required if Europe is to remain competitive, overcome the current economic crisis and grasp new opportunities. Innovating in education and training is a key priority in several flagship initiatives of the Europe 2020 strategy, in particular the Agenda for New Skills and Jobs, Youth on the Move, and Digital Agenda. This priority is directly linked to the Europe 2020 educational headline targets regarding early school leaving and tertiary attainment levels.

Educational stakeholders recognize the contribution of ICT to realizing these targets, and more broadly, the role of ICT as a key enabler of innovation and creativity in E&T and for learning at large. In all European countries, national policies for ICT

The views expressed in this article are purely those of the authors and they should not be regarded as the official position of the European Commission.

A. Cerone et al. (Eds.): SEFM 2012 Satellite Events, LNCS 7991, pp. 104–120, 2014.
DOI: 10.1007/978-3-642-54338-8_8, © European Union 2014

in education exist and many activities are undertaken to promote the use of ICT in education and training in Europe [e.g. 1]. It is however also highlighted that, while the infrastructure to promote ICT use for learning is largely available, including a sound research base to guide the process, the full potential of ICT is not being grasped in formal education settings. The vast majority of schools in Europe are not reaping the benefits of new technologies as an enabler to modernize learning and teaching practices [2–4]. Only few innovative projects manage to reach beyond the early adopter stage and become full embedded in educational practice.

In order to move ICT-enabled innovation in E&T to scale, at system level, a holistic approach to contextualized processes is needed, which identifies key dimensions of innovative learning environments that fully embed the potential of ICT (hereafter referred to as 'Creative Classrooms' or CCR) and which gives reasons of the complexity and shifting priorities of implementing sustainable systemic change in education [5–8].

To this end, an overarching conceptualization of 'Creative Classrooms'[1] (CCR) is proposed here, as well as a set of reference parameters that exemplify the enablers of CCR. This conceptualization and the reference parameters are intended to provide the key components of ICT-enabled innovative learning environments, considering the vast diversity of educational contexts across Europe. They also provide a means to develop a sustainable and systemic approach to innovation in formal education.

The present work is part of a larger project on "Up-scaling Creative Classrooms in Europe" (SCALE CCR) recently launched by IPTS[2] on behalf of the Directorate General Education and Culture (DG EAC). The project aims to further define the concept of CCR and to provide a better understanding of ICT-enabled innovation in Education and Training (E&T), as well as in adult education, that can be brought to scale. A set of policy recommendations for mainstreaming of ICT-enabled innovation for learning through the up-scaling of CCR in Europe will also be developed.

In the following sections, the term ICT-enabled innovation for learning is further defined and the key components of CCR are presented. Examples of existing large-scale initiatives implementing ICT-enabled systemic innovation as reflected in the proposed CCR conceptualization are also discussed[3].

---

[1] CCR concept originates from European Commission – DG EAC policies with the aim to support the mainstreaming of ICT-enabled innovation for learning. Currently, an EU funding call is open for policy experimentations on the implementation of innovative learning environments using ICT (http://eacea.ec.europa.eu/llp/funding/2012/call_et_2012_en.php).

[2] The Institute for Prospective Technological Studies (IPTS) is one of the seven scientific institutes of the European Commission's Joint Research Centre (JRC). IPTS consists of five research units, one of which is the Information Society Unit.

[3] The cases presented in this paper have been developed since the time of writing (September 2012). New publications with updated information are made available at http://is.jrc.ec.europa.eu/pages/EAP/SCALECCR.html

2 ICT-Enabled Innovation for Learning at System Level

Nowadays, ICT play an increasingly central role in learners' lives and have the potential to enable changes in formal education settings in order to effectively meet the needs of 21st century [e.g. 9]. Innovative forms of pedagogical practice with ICT encourage learner-centred approaches and group work, as well as promote inquiry-based learning, learning-by-doing, problem solving and creativity [10, 11]. Existing (e.g. mobiles, wikis, 3D virtual worlds) and emerging technologies (e.g. gesture-based, augmented reality, immersive worlds) increasingly empower teachers to create pedagogically effective learning activities [12, 13] that support experimental learning, promoting and improving motivation and learner engagement [14–16].

Attention is thus focused on a new culture of learning afforded by technologies [17], where learners are at the centre of the learning process, participating in ways that were not possible before; where flexibility, personalization and different learning styles are combined; and where learning is authentic, motivational and conceived as a social process [15, 18], enabling peer-to-peer informal interactions that lead them to learn from each other. Interaction with ICT provides learners and teachers with novel ways of dealing with a task, such as enabling to inquire and to gather data in the field, thus changing the nature of the activity itself and fostering creative thinking and meaning-making [19, 20].

In this perspective, the term "ICT-enabled innovation for learning" refers to the profoundly new ways of using and creating information and knowledge made possible by the use of ICT (*as opposed to* using ICT for sustaining or replicating traditional educational practices). It deals with formal, non-formal and informal learning, covering traditional education settings (schools and higher education) and adult education. Last, but not least, this ICT potential for innovation must be realized and accompanied by the necessary pedagogical and institutional change [21]. Hence, the paradigm underpinning ICT-enabled innovation for learning should entail a holistic transformational shift towards connecting learning organizations and processes, being learner's motivation, mindset and competencies crucial aspects [22], such as connecting the realities of learners' lives and their experience of school.

It is claimed here that, for a pedagogical innovation to endure and thrive, this has to be accompanied by changes in values, practices, and infrastructure at the institutional level and beyond, bringing about transformative changes at macro- and micro system level. These principles are reflected in the proposed conceptualization of 'Creative Classrooms', which depicts the systemic approach to sustainable implementation and progressive up-scaling of ICT-enabled innovation for learning. It also conceives innovative pedagogies at the core of CCR innovative, open learning environments.

2.1 Innovative Pedagogical Practices

As documented in the literature [e.g. 9, 23–25] and existing cases from real life educational settings [26–29] technology is just the means towards pedagogical change, driven by participatory practices and approaches that support *innovative teaching* and *creative learning*.

Innovative teaching is any kind of teaching which addresses creativity and applies it to methods and contents. It includes both the processes of *teaching for creativity* and *teaching creatively* [19, 30]: the former refers to any teaching that tries to develop learners' own creative thinking and performance, whereas the latter refers to the implementation of innovative teaching practices to make learning more interesting and effective.

Creative learning refers to the possibility for learners to develop their thinking skills and learn in a new, creative way [23, 31]. As Ferrari et al. [19] highlight, in the educational context, creativity can even be conceptualized as a transversal and cross-curricular skill which everyone can develop. In this perspective, educational actors have the power to unlock (but also inhibit) the creative and innovative potential of the young. However, they require substantial support, especially in terms of training, revision of curricula and assessment, and institutional change.

Craft [32] put forward the suggestion that, to foster creativity in all aspects of life, adequate educational provisions should be developed around key 'Four Ps' principles: plurality, playfulness, possibilities and participation. Interestingly, Teresa Amabile places intrinsic motivation [33] at the core of her componential theory of creativity. She proposes that internal (intrinsic) motivation is beneficial to creativity, over external (or extrinsic) motivation which is detrimental [33, p. 15]. Thus, it appears that because of enjoyment and motivation by their own interests in the task, learners' creativity motivation increases and leads to heightened concentration on the task, which maintains their creative attitudes and behaviours rather than relying upon habitual responses [33, 34].

Therefore, both innovative teaching and creative learning presuppose an active role for the learner and new roles for the teacher who acts mainly as mentor, orchestrator, and facilitator of the learning process. As argued by Loveless [35], creative learning activities need meaningful contexts and ICT can offer tools for creating such contexts. These tools can represent information in a variety of modes that enable learners to make changes, try out ideas and approaches to problem solving. Both learners and teachers need the opportunity to engage, play and become familiar with the distinctive contributions that ICT can make to their creative practices, which other media and tools do not offer. Attention and efforts should thus focus on fostering teachers' preparation for a pedagogy for creativity [36]. Ensuring the necessary accessibility and flexibility can be a challenge for both teachers and schools due to current models of resources, timetables, curriculum, and assessment requirements, which can inhibit learners' engagement with creative processes and lead to a super-ficial or fragmented focus on products [35].

Innovativeness of different pedagogical practices only emerges when teachers use ICT in their efforts to organize newer and improved forms of open-ended, collabo-rative, and extended learning activities, rather than simply to enhance traditional pedagogies, such as expository lessons and task-based learning [21, 27]. Such inno-vative practices require a huge investment of individual and collective effort by all the involved practitioners, as well as adequate support and recognition (e.g. teachers' professional development in the pedagogical use of ICT, changing assessment strat-egies and curricula) at system level [2, 37]. Human factors (vision and expertise) as well as learning materials and infrastructures are decisive success factors concerning the pedagogical use of ICT and, as such, needs to be effectively addressed by policy makers and educational authorities [10].

Innovative pedagogies, as discussed here, thus lie at the core of the multi-dimensional concept of CCR that is presented in the following sections.

3   A Multi-dimensional Conceptualization of Creative Classrooms

'Creative Classrooms' are conceptualized here as innovative learning environments that fully embed the potential of ICT to innovate and modernize learning and teaching practices.

Though the terms 'creativity' and 'innovation' are often used interchangeably [38], here innovation is conceived of as a two-component process, encompassing both the development of creative ideas and the intentional introduction and application of selected creative ideas into teaching and learning practices [31, 39]. Hence, the term 'creative' refers here to the innovation of learning and teaching practices through technologies (collaboration, personalization, active learning, entrepreneurship, etc.). Likewise, the term 'classrooms' is used in its widest sense to include all types of learning environments, formal, non-formal and informal. The focus is not on future scenarios but on what is possible in today's practices, taking advantage of existing technologies.

Creative Classrooms thus can be seen as complex "eco-systems" [27, 28] that evolve over the time, mainly depending on the context and the culture to which they pertain. The proposed *multi-dimensional concept* for CCR puts emphasis on the holistic and systemic nature of these environments, their intended learning outcomes, and their pedagogical, technological, and organizational characteristics that favour innovation.

It consists of *eight* encompassing and interconnected key dimensions (Fig. 1), which capture the essential nature of these learning ecosystems. These are: *Content and Curricula, Assessment, Learning Practices, Teaching Practices, Organization, Leadership and Values, Connectedness,* and *Infrastructure.*

These proposed dimensions (and the related set of reference parameters cf. Sect. 4) build on previous IPTS studies [3, 11, 23, 31] and other relevant works on creative learning and innovative pedagogies using ICT [2, 8, 14, 25]. Furthermore, consultations with educational policymakers, stakeholders and practitioners (e.g. DG EAC Thematic Working Group on ICT in Education consisting of representative of Member States Ministries of Education, eTwinning teachers) contributed to the further development and validation of the CCR concept.

Overall, in CCR open education principles [40] are fully implemented in practice, at all system levels. *Curriculum and content* are open, providing learners with concrete opportunities for developing 21st century skills, such as problem-solving, inquiry, collaboration, and communication. *Learning* is flexible and engaging, meeting students' individual needs and expectations. *Leadership* is open and participatory, supporting teachers/educators' innovative practices. (e-)*Assessment* paradigm

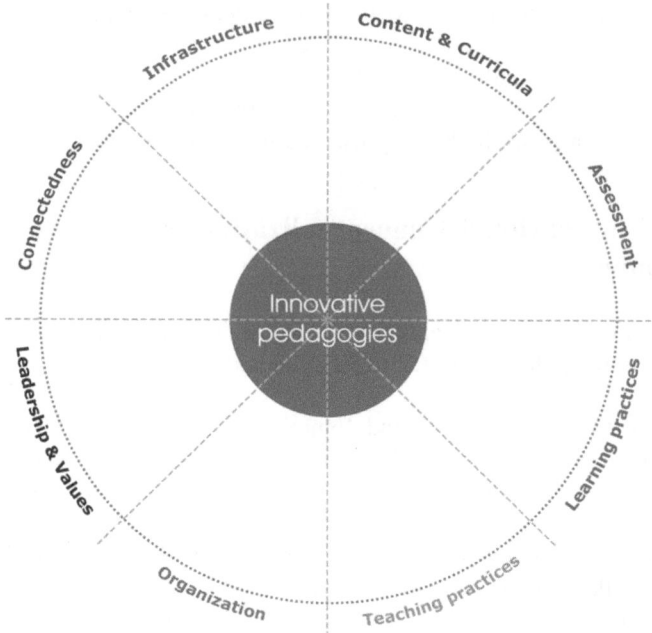

Fig. 1. Key dimensions of Creative Classrooms

now reflects the core competences needed for life in the 21st century. Detailed characteristic of each CCR dimension are described in Bocconi et al. [41] and briefly outlined below:

- *Content and curricula:* The term *Curricula* is conceptualized here as learning objectives and framework for developing activities and the term *Contents* as resources for innovative teaching and creative learning. Content and curricula within the CCR context should be subjects to regular updates, in which education stakeholders and practitioners take an active role, drawing on results from recent evidence-based research [e.g. 10, 24, 27, 42–44].
- *Assessment*: this dimension focuses on the conceptual shift from traditional assessment of knowledge acquisition to innovative ICT-enabled assessment approaches that better capture 21st century skills [45]. In CCR, eAssessment strategies should transcend the testing paradigm and develop integrated, authentic and holistic assessment formats by designing assessment tasks that replicate real life contexts, and are solved by using common ICT tools, such as the Internet and multimedia resources [46, 47]. Moreover, recognition and validation of non-formal and informal learning experience also becomes an essential component of the CCR assessment process [48–50].
- *Learning practices:* this dimension centres on the experience of learning and how learners engaged with it [2, 32]. Personalization, collaboration and informal ways of learning are at the core of creative learning practices [3, 49]. In CCR, learners not only have to take responsibility for their own learning progress, but also have to

support each other in jointly creating the learning content and context. CCR should support more engaging and playful approaches to learning and should foster students' self-directed lifelong-learning abilities [50] and transversal soft-skills.

- *Teaching practices:* In CCR, teachers effectively play new roles as mentors, orchestrators, and facilitators of learning and act as role-models of creativity and innovation [24]. Therefore, the skill sets of professional teachers should shift from subject knowledge towards expertise in pedagogy [51] in order to effectively foster creative learning and innovation attitudes in learners. Besides innovative pedagogies, CCR teachers should also implement creative classroom management strategies and make innovative use of ICT for creative learning [23].

- *Organization:* this dimension captures the organizational practices in CCR - at macro, meso and micro levels, implying a progressive breadth and depth of action to meet local circumstances and needs [52]. At all levels, CCR should adopt a holistic approach to innovation for learning, where all the elements of a learning organization are brought into the picture and considered 'vital' [6, 27]. Continuous monitoring mechanisms should be in place to evaluate progress and effectively refocus organizational practices in order to raise the levels of eMaturity in learning organizations [53, 54].

- *Leadership and Values:* CCR should operate within a context of educational structures and values that strongly influence learning objectives and pedagogies, promote equity and guarantee access to quality education for all [52, 55]. In CCR, school leadership should play a crucial role in orchestrating innovations by initiating and monitoring changes, providing required resources and infrastructure, challenging misconceptions about ICT-enabled innovations for learning by supporting staff professional development and taking advantage of creative partnerships.

- *Connectedness:* This dimension focuses on the social and emotional factors that profoundly affect the relations among members within a learning institution and that have a significant impact on their level of engagement and motivation [2, 27, 56]. CCR should allow new possibilities for students to connect with multiple actors (e.g. peers, parents, external experts and practitioners), opening up alternative channels for gaining knowledge and broadening their horizons, embracing diversity thus anchoring their learning experiences in a rich world of diverse cultures, traditions, languages and opinions.

- *Infrastructure:* CCR need a dynamic ICT infrastructure of adequate performance and reach that can facilitate, communicate and disseminate innovative teaching and creative learning. Effective support structures are also needed to implement smoothly all the necessary technologies. In CCR, ICT infrastructure should also be used to extend the boundaries of the learning space across time (access to resources 24/7). In order to facilitate and inspire innovative teaching and creative learning the physical learning space should be also be (re)arranged, taking advantage of colours, lights, sounds [57].

Innovation goes hand in hand with all these eight dimensions, which are equally necessary and vital within CCR. It is naïve to assume that addressing only one isolated dimension makes innovation happen; evidences from research [2, 15, 25, 27, 54] clearly show that a significant number of these key dimensions -if not all- needs to be tackle based on the common efforts of a critical mass of actors [e.g. 6, 26].

Therefore, CCR innovative learning environments need to be inspired and supported by innovative policies ensuring the progressive implementation at system level of all CCR encompassing elements [41].

4 Fundamental 'Building Blocks' for Creative Classrooms

In order to further clarify and exemplify key enablers of 'Creative Classrooms', a set of reference parameters ('building blocks') complements the proposed CCR conceptualization. The aim is twofold: (i) to unravel the most innovative elements of the multi-dimensional CCR concept and (ii) to depict the systemic approach needed for the sustainable implementation and progressive up-scaling of Creative Classrooms across Europe.

The current set (see Table 1) is composed of 28 reference parameters//building blocks derived from literature in the field [e.g. 3, 23, 32] and existing cases of ICT-enabled innovation for learning [e.g. 27]. The proposed reference parameters thus intend to capture significant changes in *what* we learn, *how* we learn, *where* we learn and *when* we learn in order to achieve educational transformation for a digital world [3].

Table 1 provides an overview of the CCR reference parameters, including the title and a brief description [detailed in 41]. Interrelations of building blocks with the eight key dimensions of the CCR concept are represented by the grey circles in the table background line up under the related dimension (columns). The two different-size circles (large and small) identify main and ancillary interrelations.

As constituents of the "CCR ecosystems", the reference parameters are dynamic by nature, flexible and evolve over time. In other words, these parameters constitute an encompassing list of fundamental building blocks of the CCR: their multiple possible combinations allow configuring a wide variety of Creative Classrooms according to given needs and contexts. Some of them are already well-established in real life practice, whereas others are more at the forefront.

As a strong interrelation exists among the eight key dimensions of the CCR concept (described in Sect. 3), the same applies to the building blocks that are also complementary and cross different CCR key dimensions.

The ultimate scope is to provide educational policy makers, stakeholders and practitioners with an encompassing perspective of ICT-enabled innovation for learning, including key elements that need to be addressed in order to take more strategic decisions within the context of Education & Training in Europe.

A preliminary application of the proposed CCR building blocks has been carried out, and discussed in the next sections, in order to show how the CCR building blocks are combined and implemented in two ongoing cases of ICT-enabled innovation for learning in Europe.

4.1   Example 1 - eTwinning

eTwinning (www.etwinning.net) is the European Commission funded teachers networking platform involving more than 170,000 teachers in 33 European countries. It is recognized by practitioners and stakeholders as a successful ICT-enabled innovation that contributes to the modernization of education in EU [58–60].

Table 1. Overview of the CCR reference parameters

	Content & Curricula	Assessment	Learning Practices	Teaching Practices	Organization	Leadership & Values	Connectedness	Infrastructure
1. Fostering emotional intelligence	Promoting a variety of activities to help learners recognize and manage emotions and form positive relationships. ICT enable the delivery of multimedia learning materials, awareness and control of self, along with empathy for others.							
2. Fostering multiple modes of thinking	Encouraging learners to develop their talents and creative potential in all possible areas (notion of *polymathy*). ICT applications offer unprecedented opportunities for exploratory learning and creative expression.							
3. Building on individual strengths and preferences	Building on learners' strengths, potential and preferences as motivation to learn. ICT offer learners new ways of expressing their interests and preferences.							
4. Fostering soft skills	Designing activities that address transversal soft skills (e.g. problem-solving, collaboration, cultural awareness) and hard, subject-specific skills. ICT provide ways of fostering transversal soft skills in authentic contexts.							
5. Facilitating (social) entrepreneurship	Offering opportunities to implement real-life projects (e.g. innovative products, services for the school community), risk taking, entrepreneurship, and innovation. ICT offer means for both real and/or virtual entrepreneurship							
6. Applying in practice social inclusion and equity	Providing all learners (gifted students, migrants, drop-outs, etc.) with equal opportunities and appropriate means for quality learning. An ICT-based approach offers tailored learning opportunities (and contents).							
7. Recognising non-formal and informal learning	Recognition of non-formal and informal learning as the basis for real-life, context-based, and learner-centred activities for creating innovative solutions to local needs. ICT facilitates ubiquitous learning through open educational resources where and when needed.							
8. Monitoring quality	Developing a clear framework for quality, transparent to all members of the school community, enhancing quality with all its implications for teaching, learning and assessment. ICT offers variety of tools to support incremental approaches to quality.							
9. Innovating timetables	Setting flexible timetables that provide teachers and learners with more opportunities to engage in creative learning in CCR. ICT facilitate time management and offer the possibility of just-in-time learning.							
10. Levelling-up and functioning ICT infrastructure	Providing learners and staff with access to multimedia-rich contents and online services (such as broadband networks, cloud computing, web applications) for innovative teaching and creative learning.							
11. Innovating and renovating services	Making use of ICT infrastructure to modernize existing services and/or offer totally new services both for formal and informal learning. ICT offer powerful tools for updating existing services (e.g. the school library could offer e-books and audio books).							
12. Rearranging physical space	Re-designing physical spaces using colours, lights, sounds, materials, to provide a flexible and stimulating environment, accessible to all learners. ICT tools (e.g. video projectors, tablets) provide new means for easily adaptable physical spaces.							
13. Learning across disciplines /subjects	Using a variety of materials to foster "horizontal connectedness" across knowledge areas and enabling learners to utilize multiple perspectives. ICT offer cost-effective ways to retrieve information from contexts and to create multimodal contents.							
14. Learning-by-exploring	Enabling learners to explore complex concepts and manipulate ideas to make connections about seemingly unrelated concepts. ICT offer new tools for exploratory learning such as online access to remote laboratories.							
15. Learning-by-creating	Engaging learners in producing their own contents in order to nurture their creative imagination, innovation attitude and authentic learning. ICT offer the means for (re)creating, and sharing learner-generated content such as blogs, wikis, and videos.							

Table 1. (Continued)

	Content & Curricula	Assessment	Learning Practices	Teaching Practices	Organization	Leadership & Values	Connectedness	Infrastructure
16. Learning-by-playing	Embedding extensively playfulness (both physical and mental) to fully engage students in the learning process. ICT offer opportunities for playful learning through a great variety of digital games and simulation.							
17. Addressing multiple intelligences and learning styles	Giving value and providing means (i.e. plurality of tasks, educational contents, etc.) to address multiple learning styles and (Gardner's) intelligences to help learners reaching their personal learning objectives. ICT provide the means to support it.							
18. Empowering self-regulated learning	Helping learners to take control of their learning process, promoting self-directed learning skills and supporting reflection and meta-cognition. ICT provide encouraging and engaging environments that foster self-directed skills for life long learning.							
19. Personalised learning	Adapting sensitively curricula and methods to respond to individual learners' needs to foster their intrinsic motivation and allow for self-expression. ICT increases opportunities for personalized learning, both in formal and informal settings.							
20. Meaningful activities	Carrying out activities in an authentic context, encouraging learners to apply their prior knowledge, inquiry and independent thinking. ICT can be used to engage learners in meaningful, authentic learning (e.g. virtual tours in museums, geo-tagging etc.).							
21. Facilitating peer-to-peer collaboration	Fostering learners' ability to think both independently and with others, considering a plurality of points of view that helps creative thinking. ICT provide means for online synchronous and/or asynchronous peer collaborations across networks.							
22. Using/re-using & mixing open educational resources (OER)	Making consistent use/reuse of existing OER to broaden and update the curriculum and achieve the desired/expected learning outcomes. ICT increase the sharing/reuse/adapt of OER, promoting social mechanisms (e.g. recommending, ratings).							
23. Engaging assessment formats	Incorporating creative tasks to engage and motivate learners while assessing complex skills (e.g. collaboration, problem solving) developed inside and outside school. ICT allow to record /retrieve individual learning progress (e.g. e-portfolios).							
24. Embedding formative assessment	Embedding methods and tools to provide a record of learners' thinking and reasoning, assessing competences rather than factual knowledge. Open ICT tools (e.g. web2.0) foster peer2peer assessment and provide meaningful data to teachers.							
25. Learning events	Participating actively and systematically organising learning events (f2f, online and blended) at community level. ICT have the potential to deliver (massive) open educational courses worldwide and offer innovative ways for online lifelong learning.							
26. Engaging through social networks	Using social networks to increase interaction opportunities within the school community, opening up and modernising internal processes. Social computing (blogs, Twitter, LinkedIn, etc.) supports collaboration across borders & cultures.							
27. Implementing innovation management	Implementing a systemic approach to learning, creating a school culture that favours sustainable innovation and makes effective use of human resources. ICT tools help learning organisations become more dynamic, flexible and open.							
28. Networking with real-word context and actors	Interacting effectively and cooperating with a plurality of actors (e.g. industries, museums), on a regular basis to support and foster learners' motivation. ICT offer cost-effective ways for online networking and interaction across time and space.							

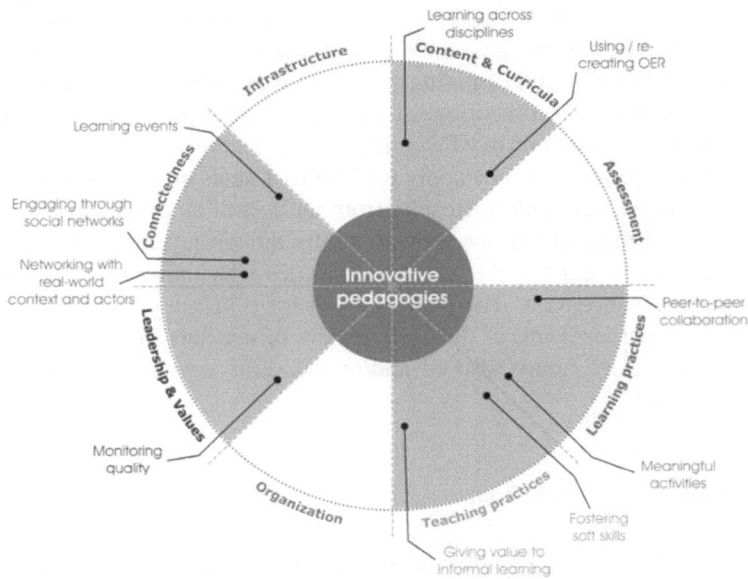

Fig. 2. CCR key dimensions and building blocks covered by eTwinning

Fig. 2 shows which CCR key dimensions and building blocks are mainly covered by eTwinning in its current phase of implementation. By *engaging* teachers *through social networks* mechanisms, eTwinning offers online services that support and foster teachers *peer-to-peer collaboration, networking with real-world context and actors* (e.g. experts, community members), exchanging ideas and practices. It also provides opportunities for teachers to teaming up in groups and training together through both online and face-to-face *learning events* and workshops. Moreover, eTwinning impacts the teaching/learning practices through *meaningful activities* that foster transversal *soft skills* such as problem solving, collaboration and intercultural awareness. The eTwinning projects are mainly *cross disciplinary* and make use and/or *re-use* of *open educational resources* such as lesson plans and worksheets.

Finally, eTwinning projects are based on online and offline work that occurs not only in schools, but also out of them (*informal learning*), in teachers' free time [58].

Data collected from an online survey involving about 100 eTwinning teachers from around Europe shows that, by providing them with concrete opportunities to extend the discussion around ICT-enabled innovation for learning and to share pedagogical know-how, eTwinning helps to accelerate educational change, feeding back into teachers' local communities [59]. However, a wider take-up of eTwinning is needed if it is to have an impact at a systemic/organizational level.[4] For instance,

---

[4] To this end, European Commission has proposed expanding eTwinning as part of the new "Erasmus for all: the EU Programme for Education, Training, Youth and Sport" from 2014-2020 and adopting a more systemic/institutional approach (http://ec.europa.eu/education/erasmus-for-all/doc/legal_en.pdf).

individual teachers currently register in eTwinning and run cross-border projects without the involvement of the wider school community. Thus, the diffusion of innovative characteristics of eTwinning is limited to a small percentage of European education stakeholders and practitioners. Moreover, although at some extent assessment activities are carried out in eTwinning (e.g. at national level, National Support Services assess projects when they apply for Quality Labels or for national/EU prizes), this dimension is not yet exploit. Results from an overall analysis carried out by the eTwinning Central Support Service show that [60], though several positive underlying framework conditions exist, only in some countries eTwinning is acknowledged in terms of career advancement. There is the need for a broader recognition, either at national or cross-border level, of the involvement of teachers in eTwinning projects, as well as of the extra hours worked and/or the skills developed, both inside and outside school [48].

4.2   Example 2 – Vittra Schools

Vittra (http://vittra.se/english/VittraEnglish.aspx) is a private organization that runs a number of Independent State-Funded Schools (ISFS) in Sweden since 1993 [61]. Vittra ISFS follow an innovative educational model based on individual action plans and extensive use of ICT that aim to address the EU's eight key competences [62].

As shown in Fig. 3, Vittra schools adopt innovative practices that cover 6 out of 8 CCR key dimensions and 17 out of 28 building blocks. The majority of building blocks are related to teaching and learning practices: Vittra schools facilitate active and engaging ways of learning such as *learning by exploring*, *learning by creating*,

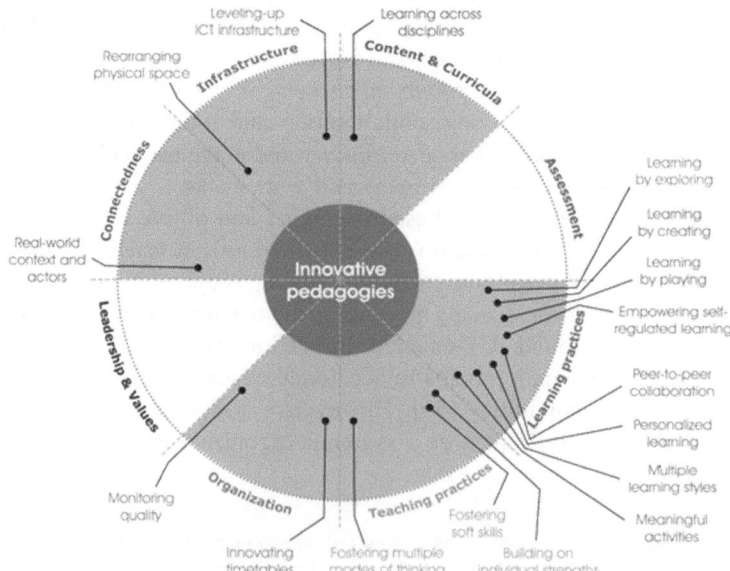

Fig. 3. CCR key dimensions and building blocks covered by Vittra Schools

and *learning by playing*. Moreover, Vittra *innovative timetables* and inspiring and colourful learning spaces (*rearranging physical space*) allow the *self-regulated learning, peer-to-peer collaboration* and *personalized learning* through playful and *meaningful* and *cross-disciplinary activities*.

The Vittra 1-to-1 computer policy and the appropriate *ICT infrastructure* allow the development of students' *soft skills*, such as problem solving and communication with *real-world context and actors*, and the fostering of *multiple modes of thinking* through multimodal teaching and learning materials. Moreover, Vittra students develop effective bilingualism in English and Swedish in order to be equipped for study and work in a multicultural environment and become more self-aware about their strengths and potential through the Individual Development Plans that constantly document and evaluate their development and achievement (*building on individual strengths* and *monitoring quality*).

Thus, according to a preliminary analysis, Vittra schools adopt a wide-ranging innovative model that impacts not only teaching and learning practices, but also content and curricula, connectedness, organization and infrastructure. Following the CCR multidimensional concept, a future take-up should focus on the shift from traditional assessment paradigms to innovative ICT-enabled assessment approaches that better capture 21st century skills and on leadership models that promote equity and guarantee access to quality education for all.

5 Conclusive Thoughts and Future Work

The proposed multi-dimensional concept of CCR and the 28 reference parameters/building blocks were derived from literature in the field, existing cases of ICT-enabled innovation for learning and consultation with education policy makers, stakeholders and practitioners. The aim is to capture the significant changes in *what* we learn, *how* we learn, *where* we learn and *when* we learn in order to achieve a sustainable and systemic change of Education and Training in Europe and effectively meet the needs of 21st century learners. To this end, emphasis is placed on innovative pedagogies that lie at the core of CCR innovative, open learning environments.

Our ongoing research includes the in-depth analysis of a number of existing cases of significant scale and/or impact at system level (such as eTwinning and Vittra), detailing enablers and bottlenecks for further mainstreaming ICT-enabled innovation for learning in Europe. Through this in-depth analysis and through the ongoing wide-ranging consultation process with key stakeholders, policy makers and practitioners in the field of Education and Training (E&T) in Europe, the CCR multi-dimensional concept and reference parameters/building blocks are going to be further developed and validated.

Last but not least, the ongoing research aims also to objectify the desk research findings and draw concrete recommendations for the further development and mainstreaming of CCR in Education and Training in Europe. It demonstrates that a comprehensive and holistic approach is needed that goes beyond isolated and ad-hoc type of policy interventions.

References

1. Eurydice: Key Data on Learning and Innovation through ICT at School in Europe 2011. Education, Audiovisual and Culture Executive Agency (2011)
2. OECD/CERI: Inspired by Technology, Driven by Pedagogy: A Systemic Approach to Technology-Based School Innovations, Educational Research and Innovation. OECD Publishing. doi: 10.1787/9789264094437-en (2010)
3. Redecker, C., Leis, M., Leendertse, M., Punie, Y., Gijsbers, G., Kirschner, P., Stoyanov, S., Hoogveld, B.: The Future of Learning: Preparing for Change. European Commission - Joint Research Center - Institute for Prospective Technological Studies. EUR 24960 EN (2011)
4. European Commission: Learning, Innovation and ICT. Lessons learned by the ICT cluster Education & Training 2010 (2010)
5. Fullan, M.: Whole system reform for innovative teaching and learning. In: Microsoft - ITL Research (ed.) Innovative Teaching and Learning Research: 2011 Findings and Implications, pp. 30–39. Microsoft - Partners in Learning (2011)
6. Levin, B.: How to Change 5000 Schools: A Practical and Positive Approach for Leading Change at Every Level. Harvard Education Press, Cambridge (2008)
7. Coburn, C.E.: Rethinking scale: moving beyond numbers to deep and lasting change. Educ. Res. **32**, 3–12 (2003)
8. Shapiro, H., Haahr, J.H., Bayer, I., Boekholt, P.: Background Paper on Innovation and Education. Danish Technological Institute and Technopolis for the European Commission, DG Education & Culture in the context of a planned Green Paper on innovation (2007)
9. Ferrari, A., Cachia, R., Punie, Y.: Innovation and Creativity in Education and Training in the EU Member States: Fostering Creative Learning and Supporting Innovative Teaching - Literature review on Innovation and Creativity in E&T in the EU Member States (ICEAC). Office for Official Publications of the European Communities (2009)
10. Law, N., Pelgrum, W.J., Plomp, T. (eds.): Pedagogy and ICT use in Schools Around the World. Findings from the IEA SITES 2006 study. Comparative Education Research Centre. The University of Hong Kong, Hong Kong (2008)
11. Redecker, C., Ala-Mutka, K., Bacigalupo, M., Ferrari, A., Punie, Y.: Learning 2.0: The Impact of Web 2.0 Innovations on Education and Training in Europe. Final Report. European Commission - Joint Research Center - Institute for Prospective Technological Studies (2009)
12. Bottino, R.M.: The evolution of ICT-based learning environments: which perspectives for the school of the future? Br. J. Edu. Technol. **35**, 553–567 (2004)
13. Conole, G.: Learning design - making practice explicit. In: ConnectEd 2010: 2nd International conference on Design Education, 28 June - 1 July 2010, Sydney, Australia. http://www.slideshare.net/grainne/conole-connected-final (2010)
14. Johnson, L., Smith, R., Willis, H., Levine, A., Haywood, K.: The 2011 Horizon report. The New Media Consortium, Austin (2011)
15. Punie, Y., Cabrera, M., Bogdanowicz, M., Zinnbauer, D., Navajas, E.: The future of ICT and learning in the knowledge society. Report on a Joint DG JRC-DG EAC Workshop held in Seville, 20-21 October 2005, EUR 22218EN. Technical Report, European Commission - Joint Research Centre - Institute for Prospective Technological Studies (2006)
16. OECD/CERI: The Nature of Learning: Using Research to Inspire Practice. OECD Publishing. DOI:10.1787/9789264086487-en (2010)
17. Thomas, D., Brown, J.S.: A New Culture of Learning: Cultivating the Imagination for a World of Constant Change. CreateSpace, Lexington (2011)

18. Bocconi, S., Trentin, G. (eds.): Wikis Supporting Formal and Informal Learning. Nova Science, New York (2012)
19. Ferrari, A., Cachia, R., Punie, Y.: Innovation and Creativity in Education and Training in the EU Member States: Fostering Creative Learning and Supporting Innovative Teaching. Literature review on Innovation and Creativity in E&T in the EU Member States (ICEAC). JRC-IPTS (2009)
20. Loveless, A.: Creative learning and new technology? a provocation paper. In: Sefton-Green, J. (ed.) Creative Learning, pp. 61–72. Creative Partnerships, London (2008)
21. Kampylis, P., Bocconi, S., Punie, Y.: Towards a mapping framework of ICT-enabled innovation for learning. European Commission, - Joint Research Center - Institute for Prospective Technological Studies, Seville. EUR25445 EN. http://ipts.jrc.ec.europa.eu/publications/pub.cfm?id=5159 (2012)
22. European Commission: Proposal for a Council Recommendation on the validation of non-formal and informal learning. COM(2012) 485 final. http://ec.europa.eu/education/lifelong-learning-policy/doc/informal/proposal2012_en.pdf (2012)
23. Cachia, R., Ferrari, A., Ala-Mutka, K., Punie, Y.: Creative learning and innovative teaching: Final Report on the Study on Creativity and Innovation in Education in EU Member States. European Commission - Joint Research Center - Institute for Prospective Technological Studies. EUR 24675 EN (2010)
24. Kampylis, P.: Fostering creative thinking: the role of primary teachers (Jyväskylä Studies in Computing No. 115, S. Puuronen, Ed.). University of Jyväskylä. Available at http://urn.fi/URN:ISBN:978-951-39-3940-3, Jyväskylä, Finland (2010)
25. Microsoft: Innovative Teaching and Learning research: 2011 Findings and Implications. ITL research and Microsoft (2011)
26. Fullan, M.: All Systems Go: The Change Imperative for Whole System Reform. Corwin, Thousand Oaks (2010)
27. Law, N., Yuen, A., Fox, R.: Educational Innovations Beyond Technology - Nurturing Leadership and Establishing Learning Organizations. Springer, New York (2011)
28. Luckin, R.: The learner centric ecology of resources: a framework for using technology to scaffold learning. Comput. Educ. 50(2), 449–462 (2008)
29. Leadbeater, C.: Innovation in Education - Lessons From Pioneers Around the World. Bloomsbury Qatar Foundation Publishing, Doha (2012)
30. Jeffrey, B., Craft, A.: Teaching creatively and teaching for creativity: distinctions and relationships. Educ. Stud. 30, 77–87 (2004)
31. Ferrari, A., Cachia, R., Punie, Y.: ICT as a driver for creative learning and innovative teaching. In: Villalba, E. (ed.) Measure Creativity: Proceedings for the conference, Can creativity be measured? Brussels, 28–29 May 2009, 345–368. Publications Office of the European Union, Luxembourg (2009)
32. Craft, A.: Creativity and Education Futures: Learning in a Digital Age. Stoke-on-Trent, Trentham, (2011)
33. Amabile, M.T.: The Social Psychology of Creativity. Springer, New York, ISBN 0-381-90830-1 (1983)
34. Csikszentmihalyi, M.: Creativity: Flow and the Psychology of Discovery and Invention, 1st edn. Harper Collins, New York (1996)
35. Loveless, A.: Creativity, Technology and Learning – A Review of Recent Literature. Futurelab, Ciena (2007)
36. Loveless, A.: Didactic analysis as a creative process: pedagogy for creativity with digital tools. In: Hudson, B., Meyer, M.A. (eds.) Beyond Fragmentation: Didactics, Learning and Teaching in Europe, pp. 239-251. Barbara Budrich Publishers, Leverkusen (2011)

37. Ottestad, G.: Innovative pedagogical practice with ICT in three Nordic countries – differences and similarities. JCAL-J. Comput. Assist. Learn. **26**, 478–491 (2010)
38. Kahl, C.H., Fonseca, L.H.D., Witte, E.H.: Revisiting creativity research: an investigation of contemporary approaches. Creativity Res. J. **21**, 1–5 (2009)
39. West, M.A.: Sparkling fountains or stagnant ponds: an integrative model of creativity and innovation implementation in work groups. Appl. Psychol.: Int. Rev. **51**, 355–424 (2002)
40. Iiyoshi, T., Kumar, M.S.V.: Opening Up Education: The Collective Advancement of Education Through Open Technology, Open Content, and Open Knowledge. MIT Press, Cambridge (2008)
41. Bocconi, S., Kampylis, P., Punie, Y.: Innovating Learning: Key Elements for Developing Creative Classrooms in Europe. European Commission - Joint Research Centre - Institute for Prospective Technological Studies, Seville. EUR 25446 EN. ISBN 978-92-79-25744-5. http://ipts.jrc.ec.europa.eu/publications/pub.cfm?id=5181 (2012)
42. Hattie, J.: Visible Learning for Teachers: Maximizing Impact on Learning. Routledge, London (2012)
43. OECD: Innovating to Learn, Learning to Innovate. OECD Publishing. DOI: 10.1787/9789264047983-en (2008)
44. Vosniadou, S.: The cognitive-situative divide and the problem of conceptual change. Educ. Psychol. **42**, 55–66 (2007)
45. Griffin, P., McGaw, B., Care, E. (eds.): Assessment and Teaching of 21st Century Skills. Springer, New York (2012)
46. Villalba, E.: On Creativity - Towards an Understanding of Creativity and its Measurements. EUR 23561 EN. Office for Official Publications of the European Communities, Luxembourg (2008)
47. Redecker, C., Punie, Y., Ferrari, A.: eAssessment for 21st Century Learning and Skills. Paper accepted for publication at ECTEL 2012 (2012)
48. Werquin, P.: Recognising Non-Formal and Informal Learning. Outcomes, Policies and Practices. OECD Publishing, Paris. DOI : 10.1787/9789264063853-en (2010)
49. Ott, M., Pozzi, F.: Getting Ready for the "School of the Future": Key Questions and Tentative Answers. In: Lytras, M.D., De Pablos, P.O., Avison, D., Sipior, J., Jin, Q., Leal, W., Uden, L., Thomas, M., Cervai, S., Horner, D. (eds.) Technology Enhanced Learning. Quality of Teaching and Educational Reform, vol. 73, pp. 495–502. Springer, Heidelberg (2010)
50. Zimmerman, B.J., Schunk, D.H. (eds.): Handbook of Self-Regulation of Learning and Performance. Routledge, New York (2011)
51. Hannon, V.: Only connect!: A new paradigm for learning innovation in the 21st century. Occasional Paper No. 112,. Centre for Strategic Education (2009)
52. OECD: Equity and Quality in Education: Supporting Disadvantaged Students and Schools. OECD Publishing, Paris. DOI: 10.1787/9789264130852-en (2012)
53. Durando, M., Blamire, R., Balanskat, A., Joyce, A.: E-mature Schools in Europe. Insight - Knowledge Building and Exchange on ict Policy and Practice. European Schoolnet, Brussels (2007)
54. Vanderlinde, R., Braak, J.v.: The e-capacity of primary schools: development of a conceptual model and scale construction from a school improvement perspective. Comput. Educ. **55**, 541–553 (2010)
55. Alexander, R.: Education for All, the Quality Imperative and the Problem of Pedagogy. University of London, Institute of Education (IOE) (2008)
56. ACOT2: Apple Classrooms of Tomorrow-Today: Learning in the 21st Century. http://images.apple.com/education/docs/Apple-ACOT2Whitepaper.pdf. (2008)

57. Burke, C.: Inspiring spaces: creating creative classrooms. Curriculum Briefing **5**, 35–39 (2007)
58. Cachia, R., Bacigalupo, M.: Teacher Collaboration Networks in 2025 - What is the role of teacher networks for professional development in Europe? Notes from the Workshops held on the 6th and 7th June 2011 at the Institute for Prospective Technological Studies of the European Commission Joint Research Centre. European Commission - Joint Research Center -Institute for Prospective Technological Studies, EUR 25025 EN (2011)
59. Kampylis, P., Bocconi, S., Punie, Y.: Fostering innovative pedagogical practices through online networks: the case of eTwinning. In: Proceedings of the SQM / INSPIRE 2012 Conference, Tampere, Finland, 21–23 August, 2012. School of Information Sciences of the University of Tampere and the British Computer Society, Tampere (2012, in press)
60. Crawley, C., Gilleran, A., Scimeca, S. (eds): Teachers' professional development. An overview of current practice. Central Support Service for eTwinning (CSS), European Schoolnet. http://desktop.etwinning.net/library/desktop/resources/5/55/955/43955/etwinning_report_teachers_professional_development_en.pdf (2010)
61. Meyland-Smith, D., Evans, N.: A guide to school choice reforms. Policy Exchange. http://www.policyexchange.org.uk/images/publications/a%20guide%20to%20school%20choice%20reforms%20-%20mar%2009.pdf (2009)
62. European Commission: Key Competences for Lifelong Learning - European Reference framework. Office for Official Publications of the European Communities, Luxembourg (2007)

FLOSS in Technology-Enhanced Learning

Sara Fernandes[1,2(✉)], Antonio Cerone[1(✉)], Luís Soares Barbosa[2(✉)],
and Pantelis M. Papadopoulos[1]

[1] United Nations University – International Institute for Software Technology,
Macao SAR, China
{sara.fernandes,pmpapad}@iist.unu.edu,
ceroneantonio@gmail.com
[2] HASLab/INESC TEC, University of Minho, Braga, Portugal
lsb@di.uminho.pt

Abstract. This paper presents a comparative analysis of Free/Libre Open Source Software (FLOSS) Learning Management System (LMS). Following a selection process we analyze the functionalities and characteristics of 8 tools commonly used in formal and informal education. More specifically we focus on the availability of different tools concerning communication and assistance, such as, forum, email, calendar, portfolios, etc. Our analysis showed that despite their similarities, the appropriateness of different FLOSS LMSs can be greatly affected by the specific needs of students, instructors and institutions.

Keywords: FLOSS · Learning management system · e-Learning

1 Introduction

Adopting online education can be regarded as a natural transition for the 21st century institutions. It is perceived as an innovation that has considerable potential for enhancing teaching and learning, promoting lifelong learning and reaching out to non-traditional learners [1].

With the current international crisis, cuts in funding for education have a very high adverse impact [2]. The need to reduce costs, maintaining educational quality, gathered with the fact that institutions rely on the Internet to perform many of their activities, makes it necessary to introduce new approaches into education that will enable governments to continue promoting high-level education. Free/Libre Open Source Software (FLOSS) [32] is regarded as the solution that emerges from these needs.

FLOSS is a result of a development process that respects freedom and takes place within a community of practice. It allows institutions to be more independent from the pricing and licensing policies of software companies, and empowers users with independency to run, copy, distribute, study, change, and improve it according to their needs.

Hence, institutions' need to reduce costs, provide students access to new ways of learning, and follow up with the advance in technology, suggest that applying the FLOSS paradigm to education may be an advantage to explore. Not only the FLOSS paradigm can be modeled according to the needs of specific Higher Education

A. Cerone et al. (Eds.): SEFM 2012 Satellite Events, LNCS 7991, pp. 121–132, 2014.
DOI: 10.1007/978-3-642-54338-8_9, © Springer-Verlag Berlin Heidelberg 2014

Institutions (HEIs), but also adapted to other educational contexts such as informal learning and long life learning.

The research addressed by this paper is how to assess LMS projects based on experiences of their use in higher education. Addressing such a problem, we analyze a set of FLOSS LMS and their social and economic impact. The main contribution of the paper is to provide an assessment framework for analyzing LMS and some assessment results that can assist teachers and HEI decision makers in the selection of the suitable LMS.

The rest of the paper is structured as follows. Section 2 presents the background of our study, Sect. 3 the proposed methodology. Results and their analysis are detailed in Sect. 4. Finally, Sect. 5 concludes and lists some topics for future work.

2 Background

The use of Information and Communications Technology (ICT) in educational contexts often requires the use of terminology whose meaning may depend on the context in which they are used. The following definitions are adopted in this paper.

- Learning management systems (LMS) are software systems designed to support student learning. They contain a number of presentation, assessment, communication, and management tools. Examples include Moodle, Sakai and OpenSE.
- e-Learning is the use of Information and Communication Technologies (ICT) to assists the teaching/learning process [3].
- Technology-Enhanced Learning (TEL) is any online facility or system that directly supports learning and teaching. This may include a formal virtual learning environment (VLE), an institutional intranet with learning and teaching components, a system that has been developed in house, or a particular suite of specific individual tools [4].
- Technology Enhanced Learning Environment (TELE) is a learning environment that uses technology to enhance and enrich the learning process [5].
- Computer-supported collaborative learning (CSCL) is a pedagogical approach where learning takes place via social interaction using a computer or through Internet. This kind of learning is characterized by sharing and construction of knowledge among participants, using technology as their primary mean of communication or as a common resource [28].
- Instructional Methods [6] are methods used in teaching which include:

  - Explaining, by oral explanations on the subject to be learned;
  - Demonstrating [29], through examples or experiments;
  - Collaborating, allowing students to actively participate in the learning process by talking with each other and listening to others points of view;
  - Learning by Teaching, by making students to assume the role of teacher and teach their peers.

Technological tools in education have a considerable impact and can be regarded as facilitators during the teaching and learning process [30]. They promote collaboration between students as well as collaboration between students and teachers. In Educational Studies this is designated as collaborative learning [31].

e-Learning 2.0 led to the concept of social learning. Social learning refers to the perspective that states that people learn within a social context and it is facilitated by concepts such as modeling and observational learning [26]. From an e-Learning 2.0 point of view, conventional e-Learning systems were based on instructional packets, which were delivered to students using assignments. A teacher was up to the task to evaluate these assignments [7]. Therefore, e-Learning 2.0 lead to the concept of *social learning* through the use of social software tools such as blogs, wikis, forums, and chats, promoting learning at a wider scale than individuals or learning groups, up to a societal scale, through social interaction between peers [8].

FLOSS is software that is both Free and Open, and is liberally licensed to grant users the right to use, copy, study, change, and improve its design through the availability of its source code. This approach has gained both momentum and acceptance. As the potential benefits increased, the recognition by individuals and corporations also increased [9].

Depending on the level of political correctness and the intention of the author, the terms Free Software (FS), Open Source Software (OSS), Free and Open Source Software (FOSS) or Free/Libre Open Source Software (FLOSS) are more or less, used interchangeably in the literature. As Richard Stallman puts it, "Open Source is a development methodology, free software is a social movement" [10].

We will use the acronym FLOSS throughout this paper.

As far as development is concerned, FLOSS is developed inside communities in the precise sense of "collectives of individuals that cohere around a shared spirit" [11]. Most of the existing open source software is developed in such communities. Its code is typically created as a collaborative effort in which programmers improve code, test, document, discuss and share changes.

Although FLOSS products are perceived as being of high quality [12], they present pros and cons. On one hand, FLOSS products are popular, because they are free of costs, developed by volunteers with different backgrounds that bring positive contributions to the project, and, hopefully, are always updated and with constantly new features. On the other hand, because of the different backgrounds, the releases of new features can be delayed; volunteers can stop their contribution, killing, in this way, the project [13].

3   Method

3.1   Pre-selection

We have initially searched for educational projects in the SourceForge [14] repository. Then, we have refined our selection by searching for the keywords Learning Management System (LMS). The initial list had over 30 LMS projects and we narrowed it down to 11 by selecting only those open source Learning Management System projects that have downloads on a weekly basis. We argue that the number of downloads per week is a parameter that should be considered as a mere indicator of the LMS acceptability. Moreover, we understand this as an indicator of the number of users that are aware of the considered LMS.

After the pre-selection of the LMSs, we gathered more information using UrlSpy [15], a database containing information on hundreds of thousands of websites.

As shown in Table 1, for each project we considered the following data:

- World Wide Rank, i.e. the position of the website in the world wide rank of most visited website;
- Total No of Years, i.e. the number of years the tool as been available;
- External Links, means the number of websites that refer the project website;
- Number of Pages visited by users within the tool website.
- Estimated Daily Users, i.e. the estimated number of users of the website tool;
- Downloads per week from SourceForge,

From the selected LMSs, Moodle is number one in the World Wide Rank, with 37300 External Links. The number of External Links can be regarded as a measure to analyze the impact of the project worldwide. It is interesting to notice that almost all LMSs have been available for more than 10 years. The most recent ones are Dokeos and Open Elms. Since data from e-Learning Applications Suite, Docebo reborn and Brilhaspati were not available, we decided to narrow the sample to the 8 LMSs: Moodle, ILIAS, Claroline, Open Elms, ATutor, Dokeos, EClass.Net and Sakai.

By narrowing the sample we consider a relationship between the data presented in Table 1 and the social impact of these projects. For example, the Estimated Daily Users is considerably higher for Moodle. Data in Table 1 prove the popularity of Moodle. However, drilling down in the analysis, it is clear that Dokeos, with 7 years

Table 1. FLOSS LMS projects data using SourceForge and UrlSpy.

LMS	World wide rank	Total no of years	External links	Number of pages	Estimated daily users	Downloads per week from SourceForge
Moodle	5717	<11	37300	28650	71370	16796
Dokeos	68947	7	3221	3345	6388	53
Claroline	110 846	<10	2829	821	4165	597
ATutor	154563	>11	2426	345	2948	224
Sakai	206 726	>11	2127	1386	2551	3
ILIAS	292 306	<11	813	356	1240	428
Open Elms	989 640	4	92	35	398	104
EClass.Net	14 019 198	<9	36	6	16	25
e-Learning applications suite	n/a	>5	n/a	n/a	n/a	17
Docebo reborn	n/a	<1	n/a	n/a	n/a	28
Brilhaspati	n/a	>7	n/a	n/a	n/a	19

of existence, is gaining popularity very fast, considering that the closest player, Claroline, has been available for almost 10 years.

Next, the selected LMSs are briefly described.

Moodle – is an LMS for producing Internet-based course websites. It has been designed to support modern pedagogies based on social constructionist theory, and includes activity modules such as forums, resources, journals, quizzes and others. Also, Moodle allows developers to extend it by creating plug-ins for new functionalities. Moodle is written in PHP [16].

ILIAS – is an LMS based on the concepts of Personal Desktop and repository. While the Repository contains all content, such as courses and other material structured in categories, the Personal Desktop is an individual workspace for each learner, author, tutor and administrator. A Personal Desktop contains the selected items from the Repository as well as certain tools like mail, tag-in, calendar and also a portfolio and personal blogs. ILIAS is written in PHP [17].

Claroline – specific for educational purposes, this system is based on some specific principles of Moodle. It supports SCORM content as well as a built-in wiki and other online content tools. It is developed on PHP/MySQL and allows teachers or educational institutions to create and administer courses through the Web. It provides group management, forums, document repositories and calendar [20].

Open Elms – although an LMS for training and business it is, in fact, known as the first open source Learning Management System aimed at business. It is also known because of its 3D virtual room [19]. Open Elms is written in ASP and Java.

ATutor – is a platform to develop and deliver online courses. It is possible to install it within minutes and supports easy distribution of web-based instructional content for online courses. It is written in PHP [18].

Dokeos – is an e-Learning and course management web application, translated into 34 languages and used by multinational companies, government agencies and universities. It is written in PHP, using MySQL as database backend [21].

EClass.Net – is a platform for users to build a set of easy to use, cross-platform software tools for developing e-books and learning modules. It is written in Python. [22].

Sakai – is a free educational software platform and is used for teaching, research and collaboration. Sakai is written in Java [23].

3.2   Assessment Criteria

To assess the 8 pre-selected LMS tools we propose an assessment framework, as the one depicted in Fig. 1.

The main concepts of our framework are: Selected Tools (as explained in Sect. 2), Functionality Criteria, and Impact Criteria.

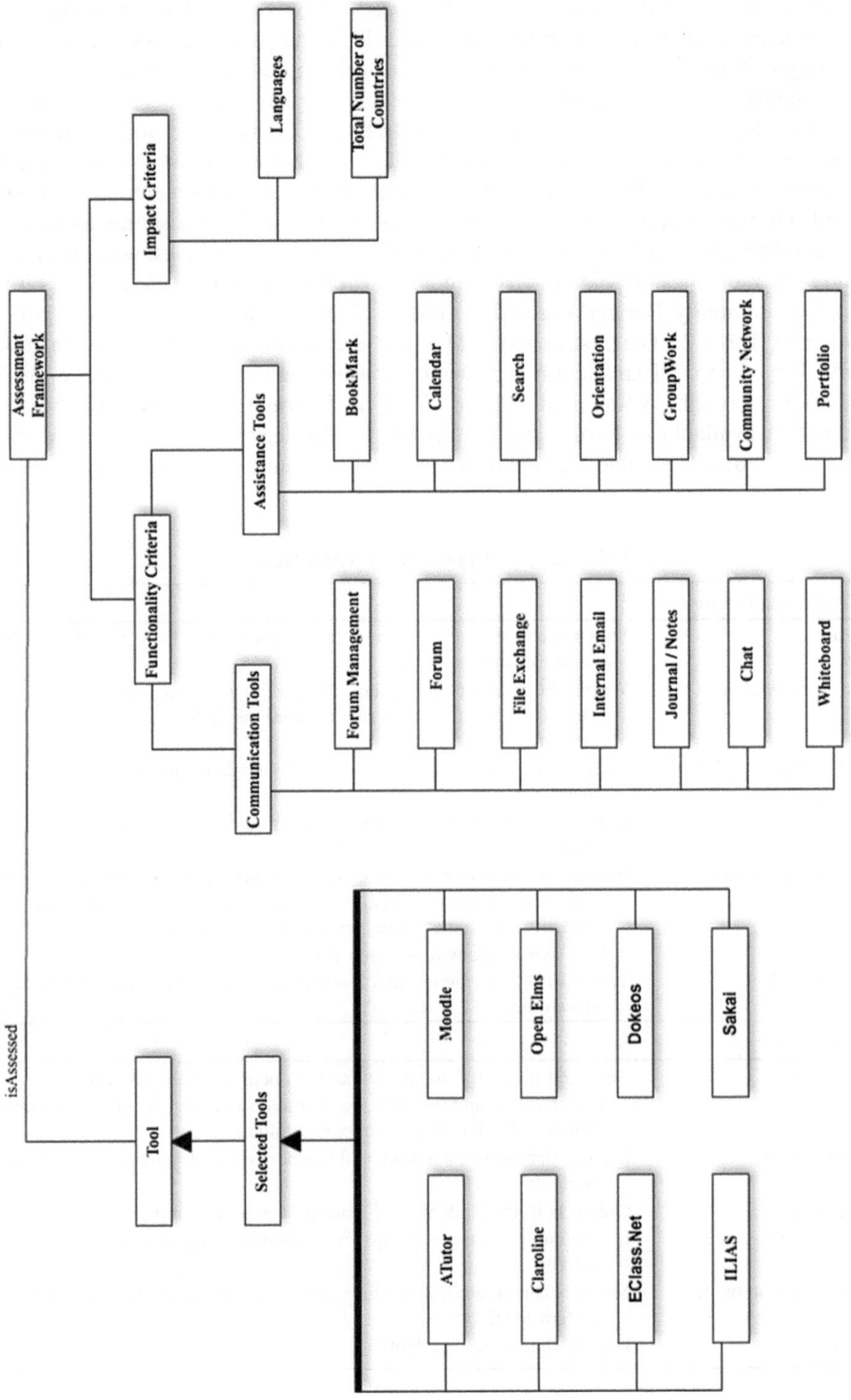

Fig. 1. Assessment framework.

Functionality Criteria correspond to features of the software. They are categorized in two main areas [24]: communication tools [27] and assistance tools [25]. Functionality Criteria allow to determine if Instructional Methods used in formal education are available or not in e-Learning tools. In Sect. 2, we have introduced the following Instructional Methods: Explaining, Demonstrating, Collaborating and Learning by Teaching [6]. Within the communication tools, tools that help users to communicate, we considered the following requisites: Forum, Forum Management, File transfer, Email, Online journals/Notes, Chat and Whiteboard. For the Assistance tools, tools that assist teachers and students during the performance of their tasks, we consider the following requisites: Bookmarks, Calendar, Search of content, Orientation, Group Work, Community Networking and Portfolios. The description of each category is shown in Table 2. The Instructional Methods are available in the communication tools. For example, Explanation and Demonstration methods are available in almost all LMSs through Whiteboard, Group Work and Orientation. The Collaborative Method is available in Forum and Group Work. The learning by teaching method, where the students assume the role of teacher, can be found on Community Network.

Table 2. Description of the LMS features.

Communication tools	
Forum	Students can submit posts in a discussion forum. They can also enable and/or disable posts
Forum management	Within the forum management, teachers or instructors can create discussion forums, moderate discussions and access to statistical information
File exchange	Files can be uploaded and download by students and teachers or instructors
Email	Teachers or Instructors can email an entire class by using a single email alias
Online journal/notes	Enables students to make notes in a personal or private journal. Students can share personal journal entries with their instructor or other students but cannot share private journal entries
Chat	Allows synchronous messaging discussion groups
Whiteboard	Tool used by instructors and learners in synchronous modes (virtual classroom)
Assistance tools	
Bookmarks	Accessed through a menu, bookmarks help organize contents
Calendar	Allows students and teachers (or instructors) to create events in the online course calendar. It also supports announcements
Content search	Feature that allows students and teachers (or instructors) to search for contents
Orientation	Online help for students and teachers (or instructors)
Group work	It is possible to create groups for discussions, assignments, or any other activity
Community network	Students can create online clubs, interest groups, and study groups at the system level
Portfolios	Feature that allows students to collect their work

Hence, the large range of available Instructional Methods make all considered LMSs effective tools to support both formal and informal education.

With respect to Impact Criteria, we determined the impact of each project by analyzing data presented in Table 1, as well as the Number of Languages in which they are available, and the Total Number of Countries in which they are established. We consider Impact Criteria as the most relevant for the analysis of the concept of e-Learning 2.0 and the concept of *social learning* since, with these parameters, we can determine the range of a certain tool.

4   Results and Analysis

Functionality Criteria cover two main areas: (a) Communication Tools, and (b) Assistance Tools. We analyze the existence or absence of Instructional Methods.

For the Impact Criteria analysis, a broader analysis aims at presenting the impact of each LMS tool. Hence, we conclude our analysis by presenting recommendations for the choice and usage of LMS according to social and economic viewpoints.

As shown in Table 3, with the exception of Open Elms and EClass.Net, the tools fulfill all requisites for communication tools introduced in Sect. 3.2. EClass.Net does not provide clear information about the communication tools since the LMS from the project has been discontinued and is now an application to create e-books. Note that only some of the Instructional Methods are available in the communication tools. For example, Explanation and Demonstration methods are available in almost all LMSs through Whiteboard, and the Collaborative Method is available in Forum.

As shown in Table 4, Explaining and Demonstrating are available in almost all LMSs through Group Work and Orientation, which allows oral explanations and examples. The collaborative method is present, for example, in Group Work. Finally, the learning by teaching method, where the students assume the role of teacher, can be found on Community Network. Hence, the large range of available Instructional Methods make all considered LMSs effective tools to support both formal and informal education.

Table 3. LMS tools analysis according to the communication tools.

Features	Communication tools							
	Moodle	ILIAS	Claroline	Open Elms	ATutor	Dokeos	EClass.Net	Sakai
Forum	X	X	X	n/a	X	X	n/a	X
Forum management	X	X	X	n/a	X	X	n/a	X
File transfer	X	X	X	X	X	X	n/a	X
Online journals/ notes	X	X	X	X	X	X	n/a	X
Share online journal	X	X	X	X	X	X	n/a	X
Chat	X	X	X	X	X	X	n/a	X
Whiteboard	X	X	X	n/a	X	X	n/a	X

Table 4. LMS tools analysis according to the assistance tools.

Features	Assistance tools							
	Moodle	ILIAS	Claroline	Open Elms	ATutor	Dokeos	EClass.Net	Sakai
Bookmarks	n/a	X	X	X	X	X	X	X
Calendar	X	X	X	X	X	X	n/a	X
Search for content	X	X	X	X	X	X	n/a	X
Orientation	X	X	n/a	X	X	n/a	n/a	X
Group work	X	X	X	X	X	X	n/a	X
Community network	X	X	n/a	X	X	X	n/a	X
Portfolios	n/a	n/a	n/a	X	X	X	n/a	X

Table 5. Impact criteria data.

Features	Impact criteria							
	Moodle	ILIAS	Claroline	Open Elms	ATutor	Dokeos	EClass.Net	Sakai
Languages	78	26	35	1	20	20	n/a	12
Number of countries	216	53	71	156	58	60	n/a	17

For analyzing the Impact criteria data was extracted from each LMS website and UrlSpy.

Table 5 shows, for each LMS, the number of languages in which it has been translated and the number of countries in which it is used. Moodle is in the first position with respect to both these parameters. Therefore, data presented in Tables 1 and 5, show that Moodle is the LMS with higher impact, and, thence, the number one open source LMS. However, this does not mean that others LMSs should not be taken into consideration.

Working with Table 1, we start grouping tools according to the proximity on the Work Wide Rank, the number of External Links and the number of Estimated Daily Users. Then we compared Dokeos with Claroline, ATutor with Sakai, and ILIAS with Open Elms.

Dokeos vs Claroline – These two platforms have the same communication tools, but Claroline lacks some of the features in assistance tools (Orientation, Community Network and Portfolios). Although Claroline is available in 35 languages (20 for Dokeos), and is used in 71 countries (Dokeos is used in 60), Dokeos is better classified in the World Wide Rank (Table 1). According to the number of External Links, Dokeos has more external references to its homepage than Claroline, although it is more recent.

ATutor vs Sakai – These two platforms have been available for over 11 years and have the same functionality features. From Table 5 we can observe that ATutor is available in more languages and present in more countries. Also, based on Table 1 we can observe that ATutor is better classified in the World Wide Rank than Sakai. The number of External Links is very similar for these two platforms, having ATutor just a slight advantage. The number of Estimated Daily Users is also very similar.

ILIAS vs Open Elms – Although Open Elms is available in more countries than ILIAS, it is only available in English language. This makes this tool less interesting than ILIAS. Open Elms is in the 989640th position on the World Wide Rank. Being ILIAS on the 206726th position means that ILIAS is better positioned than Open Elms. Moreover, the difference between the number of External Links is considerable for these two platforms. ILIAS has 813 external Links compared to only 92 for Open Elms, as a clear indicator of the impact of these platforms.

Although these LMSs are free and open source, this does not mean absence of any sort of exploration cost. In particular, the support service of ATutor and Open Elms is not free of charge Hence, the tools we suggest are: Moodle, Dokeos, Claroline, Sakai and ILIAS. The decision on which tool to choose relies on requirements such as: if a Portfolio is needed, then Moodle, ILIAS and Claroline are not suitable options. If Orientation is required, then Claroline and Dokeos are not an option. If, for example, Bookmarks are required, Moodle is not an option. By analyzing Tables 3 and 4, we observe that Sakai is a more complete tool, and therefore easier to adopt than Moodle, even if the latter is available in several languages.

It is interesting to analyze that according to the size of the institution and the number of students, some platforms become more suitable than others. For example, as far as the Calendar is concerned, it is an effective way to announce new events and schedule activities within the courses. The Calendar not only allows students to keep track of all activities of the course, but also promotes awareness of new activities. With an increase of activities, announcements and documents the search for data may be difficult. The Content search allows a faster way to track it.

Portfolios are an effective way to gather information about students work. However, they may not be relevant for an institution with thousands of students' to keep all students' records. When it comes to smaller institutions, the Portfolio can actually be a good feature since it can give the teacher more information on the tasks each student performs. Among all relevant features, Community Networks can be regarded as a supporting tool for collaborative learning. In a Community Network, students can create online clubs, groups of interest and study groups. This feature along with, for example, Group Work, is very relevant when it comes to the social learning. It allows a peer-to-peer learning, were all students gather with the same purpose and the same interest.

5   Conclusion and Future Work

In this paper, we present an explorative data analysis of several FLOSS LMSs, in order to define some guidelines to help educational institutions to make a choice between them. We showed that different LMSs address different needs. We analyzed each tools independently, and in comparison with others. The analysis was performed using two sets of Criteria: Functionality and Impact. For the Functionality Criteria, we were able to determine the features available in each tool, assessing, in this sense, their relative characteristics. For the Impact Criteria, we analyzed different and relevant statistics of each tool, showing the relevance and importance of the LMS. We started the analysis with the World Wide Rank, to obtain an overall view of the importance of the tool. Then, we analyzed the number of External Links, meaning how many websites refer to each tool. We also analyzed the number of countries and the number of languages in which each tool is available. Also, and due to our interest on the FLOSS paradigm, we examined whether the tools are free of costs. We were able to determine that, although some tools are free of costs and developed under the FLOSS paradigm, their support is not free.

For future work, we intend to pursue the analysis of the 8 selected tools. In particular, a usability study from both the teachers' and students' perspective seems most relevant now. We also intend to conduct further analysis from an educational point of view concerning the support of instructional methods, such as individual and collaborative learning using survey techniques.

Acknowledgments. This work has been supported by Macao Science and Technology Development Fund, File No. 019/2011/A1, in the context of the PPAeL project, as well as by ERDF - European Regional Development Fund through the COMPETE Programme (operational programme for competitiveness) and by Portuguese National Funds through the FCT (Portuguese Foundation for Science and Technology) within project FCOMP-01-0124-FEDER-007254.

References

1. Virkus, S.: (2004) Review of: Online education and learning management systems: global e-learning in a Scandinavian perspective. Oslo: NKI Gorlaget, 2003. Information Research, 9(2), review no. R126. http://informationr.net/ir/reviews/revs126.html
2. de Koning, M.: Survey: The Global Economic Crisis and its Impact on Education. EUNEC SEMINAR Education and Training in Period of Economic crisis (2010)
3. HEFCE. http://www.hefce.ac.uk
4. Hewitt, R., Walker, R.: Technology enhanced learning (TEL) survey 2010. In: UCISA User Support Conference 2010, 20–22 July 2010. St Anne's College, Oxford (2010)
5. Hinton, H.S., Gonzalez, R., Tedder, L.L., Karandikar, S., Behl, H., Smith, P.C., Wilbanks, J., Humphrey, J., Gordon, M., Lightner, M.: A technology-enhanced learning environment for a graduate/undergraduate course on optical fiber communications. In: Proceedings of the 30th Annual Frontiers in Education - Volume 01 (FIE '00), vol. 1, pp. F1E/1–F1E/6. IEEE Computer Society, Washington, DC (2000)
6. Wikipedia.   http://en.wikipedia.org/wiki/Teaching_method#Methods_of_instruction. Accessed 17 June 2012
7. Brown, J.S., Adler, R.P.: Minds on fire: open education, the long tail, and learning 2.0. Educause Rev. Mag. **43**(1), 16–32 (2008)
8. Reed, M.S., Evely, A.C., Cundill, G., Fazey, I., Glass, J., Laing, A., Newig, J., Parrish, B., Prell, C., Raymond, C., Stringer, L.C.: What is social learning? Ecol. Soc. **15**(4), r1 (2010)
9. Wikipedia. http://en.wikipedia.org/wiki/Free/Libre_Open_Source_Software. Accessed 7 June 2012
10. GNU. http://www.gnu.org/philosophy/free-software-for-freedom.html. Accessed 7 June 2012

11. Hollenbeck, C.R., Peters, C., Zinkhan, G.M.: Gift giving: a community paradigm. Psychol. Mark. **23**(7), 573–595 (2006)
12. Michlmayr, M.: Quality improvement in volunteer free software projects: exploring the impact of release management. In: Proceedings of the First International Conference on Open Source Systems, pp. 309–310 (2005)
13. Ghosh, R.: Understanding free software developers: findings from the FLOSS study. In: Feller, J., Fitzgerald, B., Hissam, S.A., Lakhani, K.R. (eds.) Perspectives on Free and Open Source Software, pp. 23–46. MIT Press, Cambridge (2008)
14. Source Forge. http://sourceforge.net/
15. URLSpy. http://urlspy.co.uk. Accessed 12 June 2012
16. Moodle. http://moodle.org/. Accessed 9 June 2012
17. ILIAS. http://www.ilias.de/. Accessed 9 June 2012
18. ATutor. http://atutor.ca/. Accessed 9 June 2012
19. Open Elms. http://www.openelms.org. Accessed 9 June 2012
20. Claroline. http://www.claroline.net. Accessed 9 June 2012
21. Dokeos. http://www.dokeos.com. Accessed 11 June 2012
22. E.Class. http://www.eclass.net/. Accessed 11 June 2012
23. Sakai Project. http://www.sakaiproject.org. Accessed 11 June 2012
24. Konstantinidis, A., Papadopoulos, P.M., Tsiatsos, T., Demetriadis, S.: Selecting and evaluating a learning management system: a Moodle evaluation based on instructors and students. Int. J. Distance Educ. Technol. (IJDET) **9**(3), 13–30 (2011). doi:10.4018/jdet. 2011070102
25. EduTools Course Management System Comparisons. http://www.edutools.info. Accessed 9 June 2012
26. Ormrod, J.E.: Human Learning, 3rd edn. Prentice-Hall, Upper Saddle River (1999)
27. Blurton, C.: New directions of ICT-use in education. http://www.unesco.org/education/educprog/lwf/dl/edict.pdf. Accessed 7 August 2012
28. Stahl, G., Koschmann, T., Suthers, D.: Computer-Supported Collaborative Learning: An Historical Perspective. Cambridge University Press, Cambridge (2006)
29. McKee, E., Williamson, V.M., Ruebush, L.E.: Effects of demonstration laboratory on student learning. J. Sci. Educ. Technol. **16**(5), 395–400 (2007)
30. Alejandro, L., Liliana, M.: The impact of technological tools in the teaching and learning of integral calculus (2010)
31. Sing, C.C., Lim, W.-Y., So, H.-J., Mun, C.H.: Advancing Collaborative Learning with ICT: Conception, Cases and Design. Ministry of Education, Singapore (2011)
32. European Commission: Free/Libre and open source software: survey and study. http://flossproject.org/. Accessed August 2012

A Preliminary Analysis of Learning Awareness in FLOSS Projects

Sara Fernandes[1,2(✉)], Antonio Cerone[1(✉)],
and Luís Soares Barbosa[2(✉)]

[1] United Nations University – International Institute for Software Technology,
Macao SAR, People's Republic of China
Sara.fernandes@iist.unu.edu, ceroneantonio@gmail.com
[2] HASLab /INESC TEC, University of Minho, Braga, Portugal
Lsb@di.uminho.pt

Abstract. It can be argued that participating in free/libre open source software
(FLOSS) projects can have a positive effect in the contributor's learning process. The need to interact with other contributors, to read other people's code,
write documentation, or use different tools, can motivate and implicitly foster
learning. In order to validate this statement we design an appropriate questionnaire asking FLOSS contributors about their experience in FLOSS projects.
In this paper, we illustrate how this questionnaire was designed and what we
expect to learn from the answers. We conclude the paper with a preview of the
results from three cases studies.

Keywords: FLOSS participants · FLOSS community · Communities of
practice · Learning awareness

1 Introduction

FLOSS communities consist of heterogeneous groups of independent volunteers, who
interact even if driven by different motivations [1]. FLOSS provides an example of
peer-production, which is driven by collaborative, social modes of interaction and
knowledge exchange [2].

The above characteristics raise interesting questions related to education, in particular concerning the analysis of how contributors collaborate and learn [3]. These
questions have the goal to analyze if FLOSS contributors recognize a learning environment in their FLOSS community, and if activities performed in a FLOSS community enable knowledge sharing and collaboration between contributors. In fact,
FLOSS communities collaborate in a wide range of activities, which are by no means
restricted to software development. Such activities include exchange of information,
reciprocal support and technical assistance, planning, code review, testing, and use
and sometime even development of several kinds of tools. It is therefore important to
understand how people learn and produce knowledge, and how communities collaborate and work to solve problems while performing these activities.

FLOSS can be regarded as an instantiation of the Common-based Peer Production
(CBPP) model. CBPP [8] refers to the collaborative efforts based on sharing
information and outcomes of a large number of people working incrementally on a

A. Cerone et al. (Eds.): SEFM 2012 Satellite Events, LNCS 7991, pp. 133–139, 2014.
DOI: 10.1007/978-3-642-54338-8_10, © Springer-Verlag Berlin Heidelberg 2014

problem [2]. Yochai Benkler, who first introduced the CBPP model, considered FLOSS "as an emerging third model of production which maximizes human creativity". Dillon identifies four key characteristics of CBPP that underlie the FLOSS approach to software production [3]:

- **Motivation** where individuals are not driven by money to work on a project;
- **Chunking** where many individuals work incrementally and asynchronously on a problem;
- **Multi-disciplinary** where peer-production projects include a large number of contributors, complementing expertise and solving problems;
- **Integration of** successful peer production products.

Hence, FLOSS can be considered as the prime example of CBPP [9]. CBPP is a new model of economic production based on a theory that, in addition to market, signals or managerial commands, individuals can organize their productive behavior based collective action. The latter occurs when a large numbers of people work independently on a single project "following a diverse cluster of motivation drives and social signals" often without traditional hierarchical organization or financial compensation [6]. More specifically, CBPP has been defined as any coordinated mainly "internet-based efforts whereby volunteers contribute project components, and there exists some process to combine them to produce a unified intellectual work" [7].

This paper presents three case studies that enable to show the positive impact on contributor's learning by being a member of a FLOSS community.

The FLOSS community itself provides a valuable, though partisan, source of information. This paper focuses on the FLOSS community and its contributors. As a way to analyze whether FLOSS has a positive effect on contributors' learning we decided to run an online questionnaire that allows us to address this issue in a simplified manner (although the results in this case depend on contributors' answers and their reliability).

The rest of the paper is structured as follows. In Sect. 2, we present the motivations and scope of the questionnaire. In Sect. 3, we present some results from the questionnaire. Finally, in Sect. 4 we present our Conclusions and Future Work.

2 Approach

Participation in FLOSS projects can have a positive effect in contributor's learning process. Our main goal with this questionnaire is to understand how contributors learn and whether they recognize the learning process they experience. Hence, in order to analyze if contributors are compelled to learn, we designed a questionnaire that addresses our questions concerning contributors' ability to interact with other contributors, contributors' documentation of their own achievements or doubts, contributors' level of commitment in the FLOSS project, and, ultimately, contributors' awareness of learning mechanisms within their contribution to the project.

We divided the questionnaire into three sets of questions.

The first set of questions is titled "*About you as a FLOSS contributor*" and concerns personal information. Contributors are not only requested to present themselves, through name, academic background, etc., but also to describe a list of FLOSS projects to which they have contributed. Examples of questions are: *"Name"*, *"Country"*, *"Education level"*, and *"List all FLOSS projects that you were involved in"*. Out of this first set of questions we expect to characterize types of contributors in terms of their background and level of involvement in FLOSS projects.

The second set of questions is titled *"Your involvement as a FLOSS contributor"* and is related to a specific project chosen by the contributor. Here the contributor describes the project and its community, and presents his current role in the project. There are also questions about how the interaction between community members works. For instance, how it is organized (is there a hierarchy of some kind?) or how contributors deal with internal problems (if problematic members are ignored, invited to leave, or managed in any other way). The questions that address these issues are, for example, "Project Name", "Project community name", "How many members does the community have", "How long did you first start as a member of this community / project?" "How often do you communicate with other group members?" "What is the structure of the project community?" With this set of questions, we aim to analyze the characteristics of the project and its community. Moreover we aim to study the subject's engagement in the community. These issues are addressed by questions such as *"What is the project name?"* *"What is the name of the community?"* and *"How many members does the community have?"* Also, the subject personal experience within the community is addressed by questions such as *"How do you relate with other contributors within the community?"* or *"What sort of relationship do you have with other community members?"*

The third set of questions is titled *"FLOSS communities as possible learning contexts"*. It is related to FLOSS communities as a possible learning context, as well as an educational tool. In this set we address questions such as: "Did the fact of being in a FLOSS community provide any relevant learning opportunity for you?" "What did you learn while engaged in a FLOSS project and its community?" or "Did your involvement as a contributor to this project changed the way you assess your own formal education?". With these questions we expect FLOSS contributors to assess their own experience as learners. We also intend them to provide us with feedback concerning the learning effect within the community and while working for the project.

3   Partial Results - Case Studies

We tested the questionnaire on a limited number of subjects. The questionnaire was sent to approximate 15 subjects. We consider here three of these subjects and present them as case studies.

Case 1 - The subject is a male who is currently a Ph.Dstudent. He has been contributing to several FLOSS projects, including Perl, Parrot and Debian.

In the second set of questions he selected the Parrot project. Parrot is a register-based process virtual machine designed to run dynamic languages. The project started in 2006 and the community is called Parrot users. It has more than 10 active members.

The subject became a member of this community as a tester. Currently he is a developer. The means this community uses to communicate include wikis, forums and chats. Moreover, the community has vis-à-vis meetings.

For this subject, a FLOSS project and its community can be regarded as a learning environment, where he is able to develop skills as a tester, programmer, code reviewer and/or analyst. He is aware of the fact that his background highly contributes to his success within the FLOSS project. He also reported in the questionnaire that FLOSS project communities have a relevant role in his learning experience. For him the community has "a lot of knowledge that can be externalized and shared". He also states that the involvement in a FLOSS project can be regarded as a possible alternative and/or complement to formal education. Alternative to formal education because the contributor have the opportunity to work with some programming language, applications and technology, and can get support in his FLOSS community for this learning process. Complement to formal education because it can be regarded as a practical assessment of the learning process. The feedback presented by the subject is positive and, for him, a FLOSS project can have a positive effect in contributor's learning process.

Case 2 - The subject is a male who currently works as a software developer. He contributed to several FLOSS projects, such as, gwibber, bigodejs, plone and django. He holds a degree in Mathematics and Computer Sciences.

In the second set of questions he selected the Plone project. Plone is a Web CMS based on the Zope application server. This project was created in 2001 and there are currently more than 10 active members in the Plone community. The subject became a member of this community as an observer, driven by the novelty of the challenge. Currently he is a developer. The community uses mailing lists as the main communication means.

For this subject, a FLOSS community provides a relevant learning opportunity. He recognizes that he improved skills such as testing, programming and performing code analysis while contributing to the community. He also perceives his interactions with the community as good way to share knowledge. He recognizes that his involvement in FLOSS projects not only changed the way he thinks about software engineering education, but also, has enabled him to understand how FLOSS communities work and develop software. Moreover, the subject changed the way he assesses his own formal education.

Despite all personal changes, he does not regard his involvement in FLOSS project as an alternative to formal education but as a complement that provides him with an environment in which usability and collaboration skills can be improved. The feedback presented by the subject is, in general, positive and, for the subject, a FLOSS project can have a positive effect in contributor's learning process if it is combined with formal education.

Case 3 - The subject is a male who holds a PhD in computer sciences. He is currently a NLP researcher. He worked for several FLOSS projects, such as, Perl Dancer, Perl Lingua:: Jspell, Perl Lingua:: NATools and Perl Lingua::FreeLing3.

In the second set of questions he selected the Perl Dancer project. Perl Dancer is a web framework based on Sinatra. This project community is called Perl Community.

Although this project exists since 2008 it has currently less then 5 active members. The subject became a member of this community as an observer, driven by the topic. Currently he is a developer and considers producing documentation as a very important activity. The communication means this community uses include chats, mailing lists and wikis. The community members physically meet once a year and have regular online meetings.

The subject recognizes that being part of a FLOSS community provided him with an important learning opportunity as a tester, programmer, code reviewer and analyst. He shares his knowledge of programming and writing documentation with the community members through wikis, mailing lists and chat.

The subject does not feel that the Perl Dancer project contributed to change the way he assesses formal education; universities should teach how to think independently of the used technology. However, he also believes that FLOSS communities can be regarded as educational communities, since they provide a platform where to learn technology and social skills. In his opinion a FLOSS project cannot be considered as an alternative to formal education but represents a complement to it in the sense that it contributes to improve collaboration and technological skills.

The feedback presented by the subject is positive. For the subject, a FLOSS project can have a positive effect to the contributor's learning process while representing complement to a formal education.

We can observe that in all three case studies the subject (1) sees his participation in the FLOSS project as a learning experience; (2) started participation in the community either as tester or observer rather than directly as developer; (3) is currently able to perform a much larger variety of tasks than before: testing, programming, code review, code analysis or writing documentation. These observations suggest that individuals' participation in a FLOSS community evolves through time. The initial stage of such evolution is characterized by activities that aim to observe community processes rather than producing code. Therefore, the evolution toward the more mature stage of contribution that the three subjects describe through their answers in the questionnaire can be seen as a learning process.

Another interesting observation is that subject in case 3, who belongs to the smallest community, perceives that the quality of the product developed in his project is just average. Subjects in cases 1 and 2, who belong to communities with more than 10 members, perceive instead that the quality of the products developed in their projects is good. This seems to confirm what Raymond wrote in the essay The Bazaar and the Cathedral: "given enough eyeballs, all bugs are shallow" [4].

4   Conclusion and Future Work

The goal the questionnaire considered in this paper is to understand whether and to which extent participation in FLOSS projects may effectively contribute to the individual's learning process.

Although the questionnaire is still in testing phase, we can observe that in the three cases presented in this paper subjects express consensus on the fact that FLOSS communities provide experiences that can be regarded as a complement to formal education. Furthermore, in their answers, all three subjects express the belief that participation in FLOSS projects fosters the development of competence in important areas, such as usability, that are seldom addressed by formal education.

The three case studies present participation in a FLOSS community as a good way to share knowledge and develop skills. All three feel that knowledge sharing occurs naturally and easily within FLOSS communities. We conjecture that this happens because contributors' freedom in joining projects, which is usually driven by strong intrinsic and extrinsic motivations.

Since the questionnaire is still in testing phase, our statements rely on weak results and need further validation. Therefore, as part of our future work, we intend to improve the questionnaire and apply it to a significant sample of FLOSS contributors. Also, we intent to distinguish between formal, informal, and non-formal aspects of learning, as in recent approaches to life-long learning contexts. Moreover, since this is an online questionnaire, answers may not be entirely reliable. Hence, we intend to select some subjects and run personal interviews.

This work has been supported by Macao Science and Technology Development Fund, File No. 019/2011/A1, in the context of the PPAeL project, as well as by ERDF - European Regional Development Fund through the COMPETE Programme (operational programme for competitiveness) and by Portuguese National Funds through the FCT (Portuguese Foundation for Science and Technology) within project FCOMP-01-0124-FEDER-007254.

Acknowledgments. This work has been supported by Macao Science and Technology Development Fund, File No. 019/2011/A1, in the context of the PPAeL project, as well as by ERDF - European Regional Development Fund through the COMPETE Programme (operational programme for competitiveness) and by Portuguese National Funds through the FCT (Portuguese Foundation for Science and Technology) within project FCOMP-01-0124-FEDER-007254.

References

1. Kumar, R.: Research Methodology-A Step-by-Step Guide for Beginners, 2nd edn. Pearson Education, Singapore (2005)
2. Benkler, Y.: The Wealth of Networks: How Social Production Transforms Markets and Freedom. Conn: Yale University Press, New Haven (2006)
3. Cerone, A., Sowe, S.K.: Using free/libre open source software projects as learning tools. In: OpenCert 2010. vol. 33 of ECEASST (2010)
4. Dillon, T.: The potential of open source approaches for education. http://archive.futurelab.org.uk/resources/publications-reports-articles/opening-education-reports/Opening-Education-Report200 (2006). Accessed May 2012
5. Raymond, E.S.: The Cathedral and The Bazaar, 1st edn. Tim O'Reilly (Ed.). O'Reilly and Associates, Inc., Sebastopol (1999)
6. Krowne, A.: The FUD-based encyclopedia: dismantling fear, uncertainty, and doubt, aimed at Wikipedia and other free knowledge resources. Free Software Magazine, N. 2. (2005)
7. Benkler, Y.: Common Wisdom: Peer Production of Educational Materials. COSL Press, Logan (2005)

8. Krowne, A.: The FUD based encyclopedia: dismantling the fear, uncertainty and doubt aimed at Wikipedia and other free knowledge sources. Free Software Magazine (2005)
9. Magrassi, P.: Free and open-source software is not an emerging property but rather the result of studied design. In: Proceedings of the 7th International Conference on Intellectual Capital, Knowledge Management and Organisational Learning, ICICKM10. Hong Kong Polytechnic, Hong Kong (2010)

Concept and Experiences on Using a Wiki-Based System for Software-Related Seminar Papers

Dominik Franke$^{(\boxtimes)}$ and Stefan Kowalewski

RWTH Aachen University, 52074 Aachen, Germany
{franke,kowalewski}@embedded.rwth-aachen.de
http://embedded.rwth-aachen.de

Abstract. Wikis and tools like Apache Subversion are wide-spread and used in various application areas. This paper presents a concept based on DokuWiki and Apache Subversion (SVN) to create and manage software-related seminar papers. While DokuWiki presents the content of the seminar paper, SVN manages referenced source code from the DokuWiki pages. The paper presents also experiences on applying this concept to a student seminar. It concludes the advantages and drawbacks of this concept in practice, based on student and advisor evaluations. The outcome is a well-working combination of Wiki and SVN, which in advance requires agreements on some usage-guidelines.

1 Introduction

In the following a *seminar* refers to a course with 5-20 students, where at the beginning each student participant gets a particular topic to work out. Then the students have to write a paper-like elaboration on the topic and present the content of the elaboration in a presentation at the end of the semester to all other participants and the advisors. Traditionally seminar papers are written on printed paper. Regular references are attached in a reference list and Internet sources often given as footnotes. Small parts of the source code are printed in an appropriate formating style and static images are added to increase comprehensibility and perfect the reader's impressions.

In one of the seminars at our chair we combined some tools to give students a different experience and possibilities on seminar papers. As a central element for their seminar paper we used a Wiki, a website which allows users to add and modify its content using a Wiki-specific syntax [1]. The seminar students were able to create their own Wiki page for their seminar topic, add Wiki-internal as well as external HTTP links, attach various files (e.g. audio and video material), embed images in their text and create subpages. The images could be static, dynamic (e.g. including an animation) and even interactive. Since the seminar had a practical orientation, we also provided the students an Apache Subversion (SVN) repository [2], where they could commit their source code and keep track of previous source code versions. Additionally we used a SVN-plug-in for the Wiki, to connect the SVN to the Wiki. The students were able to reference and

A. Cerone et al. (Eds.): SEFM 2012 Satellite Events, LNCS 7991, pp. 140–146, 2014.
DOI: 10.1007/978-3-642-54338-8_11, © Springer-Verlag Berlin Heidelberg 2014

embed source code files of a specific version into their seminar paper. The reader was able to browse through the linked source code and if desired, he could see other parts of the source code (e.g. super or associated classes) by browsing the SVN repository, too.

This paper presents our concept and experiences on using this Wiki-based system for education in a student seminar. We present the benefits which result from using recent technologies, but also some drawbacks in contrast to traditional printed paper methods.

The paper is structured as follows. Section 2 gives an overview of the setup we used and gives background information to all used technologies. Our experiences on applying this concept to a computer science seminar and the evaluation of the students and advisors are given in Sect. 3. Section 4 concludes this work.

2   Concept

In this section we present our conceptual setup and also make it concrete introducing the tools we used. Since there are various Wikis with different functionalities available, for reasons of comprehensibility and due to page limitations we do not keep it abstract - i.e. talking about Wikis in general - but make it concrete by naming immediately the used tools.

The conceptual setup is presented in Fig. 1. The central element of the concept is the Wiki. For our seminar we chose *DokuWiki* [3], since we already had good experiences with it at our chair. But other Wikis might work as well and often provide other functionality and a different Wiki-specific syntax for creating Wiki pages. The Wiki-requirements for our setup were:

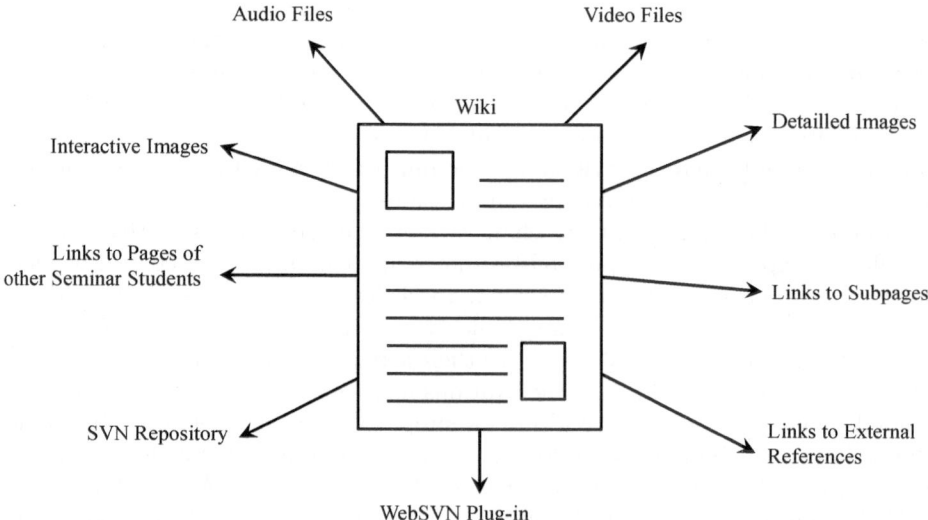

Fig. 1. Conceptual setup including concrete tools

- Easy to learn and use
- Graphical user interface for managing files and internal links
- Rights management for pages and trees of subpages
- Possibility to link to SVN
- Embed code from SVN in a Wiki page

DokuWiki is one of the Wikis which fulfills these requirements. Using DokuWiki the students were able to upload and link audio- and video-files by the click of a button. The files were then accessible to the reader by clicking on the corresponding inline-link. Images uploaded by the students could be enlarged by clicking on them. Students used this possibility to present larger images, e.g. system architectures, in a small preview and after a click a detailed enlarged view. Additionally they were also able to design interactive images, which were then linked in the DokuWiki. For instance, by moving the mouse pointer over a pie chart, the corresponding parts enlarged and displayed additional information. The students were free to use the technique they wanted, e.g. drawing gif-, svg- or interactive diagrams with Google Chart Tools[1]. The seminar, which we used the Wiki-solution in, was about testing mobile devices. As with many other seminars, some students present related work of other students. With this Wiki-solution the students have been able to set links to pages and chapters of other students. The reader then could follow the link to get more information on a specific topic, written by a different student. To structure the work, the students introduced links to subpages, which handled either a chapter of their work, a certain tool or topic. So each paper in this Wiki was structured like a tree with links between the different pages. External sources and references have been placed in the text and in the reference list as external links. These external links would lead the reader to either a project page of an interesting tool, recent press releases about the smartphone market or abstracts of referenced papers.

To handle source code and version control it, we used a SVN repository. Each user got a folder in this repository, where only he had write-permissions. Until this point the SVN and DokuWiki are separate components, both on the same server[2]. To connect the SVN and DokuWiki we used the WebSVN[3] plug-in for DokuWiki. This plug-in allows to set links in DokuWiki directly to source code files of a specific revision. By clicking on such a link the reader sees the source file in an integrated WebSVN view. Additionally the students had the possibility to embed source code files into their DokuWiki pages. In this case the reader did not had to follow a link, but he could inspect a source code file within an integrated source code view embedded in the DokuWiki page.

There are various tools available to manage user rights of an SVN repository. However, we did not find one integrated solution which handles user rights of the DokuWiki and SVN together. But this is not a big issue, so we managed the rights of the SVN repository and DokuWiki separately and synchronized them manually. A clear and strict rights management is important for seminar papers,

---

[1] See https://developers.google.com/chart.

[2] We used a virtual server running Ubuntu 10.04 32-bit version.

[3] See http://websvn.tigris.org.

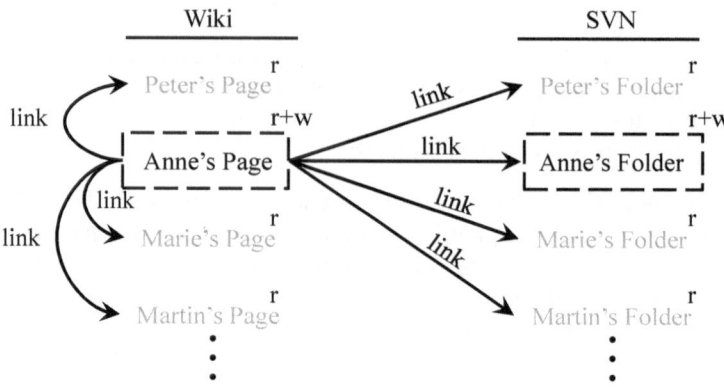

Fig. 2. Wiki and SVN rights management from *Anne's* point of view

which have to be marked afterwards. It was important for us that students could not edit and delete source code and DokuWiki pages of other students. But they should be able to view the source code and DokuWiki pages of the other students, e.g. to check for related work and learn from the way the other participants design their pages.

This requirements lead to the rights management presented in Fig. 2. Each student has the same access rights. Figure 2 highlights the access rights of the student *Anne*. Each student has read- and write-access to his main DokuWiki page, all subpages and to his SVN-folder. Additionally he can link and embed source code from his SVN-folder. But each student can also read and link the content of SVN-folders and DokuWiki pages of other students. But the SVN- and DokuWiki-content of other students cannot be edited or deleted, just read. This rights management gives each student the freedom to browse transparently through the content of the other seminar participants, but prevents the modification of their material.

3 Evaluation

This evaluation is based on interviews and reports of the student participants of the seminar, as well as the advisors' experience while working with the presented solution. The particular course we are referring to, took place at our University RWTH Aachen, in Germany. The students were mostly working on their seminar topics at home. Meetings were held whenever students required some feedback or had some questions. Additionally there was one meeting at the beginning of the seminar, where the topics have been given to the students, and one large meeting at the end of the seminar, where the students presented their work to each other and the advisor. Seven students participated in the seminar and were assigned to one advisor. Five of them were Master- and two Bachelor-students. Where appropriate, as a comparison we use the traditional printed paper seminar solution, where each student has to submit a certain number of printed pages to be reviewed. We structure the evaluation by first naming the experienced advantages and then the disadvantages of the concept.

3.1 Advantages

There are various advantages for the students. One clear advantage is that students learn from each other by simply browsing through the pages of other students. This leads to a reduced load on the seminar advisor, since he is not confronted few times with the same question. Another advantage is that students learn new tools (e.g. SVN and DokuWiki) by using them for writing a seminar. All of our computer science students felt comfortable with this learning process, although some of them never used a Wiki before. Due to its good usability, a great community and numerous available plug-ins, DokuWiki seems to be a good choice. Tools as Wiki and SVN are usually not taught in courses, but very wide-spread and thus our students were happy to learn them by the way in a seminar. By having the possibility to link to related work of other students, the amount of redundancy in multiple seminar papers about related topics is reduced. This also reduces for the advisor the amount of similar text to check. And the students learn by reading the related work of other students. By not having to submit a printed and static paper version, the students have more possibilities to individually style and decorate their papers. Animations, interactive and detailed images, videos and audio files at the right positions in a seminar paper, often make a paper more interesting, readable and comprehensible than a static printed version. Additionally printing of a wrong version is omitted, since a Wiki usually shows the most recent version of a document. Few students have also made use of the possibility to reset a DokuWiki page to a previous version, which can be done in DokuWiki with few clicks.

One advantage for the advisor of a seminar course is that he always has access to the most recent version of the seminar paper. He does not require the student to send him the latest paper, but he simply can access it through DokuWiki. This also helps to solve issues quickly. Since the advisor has the role of a super-user in the DokuWiki, he can e.g. solve technical or syntactical issues with DokuWiki by accessing the corresponding page from his workspace. Another advantage for advisors is the available of timestamps and document versions for both, the SVN and DokuWiki pages. If the students have a deadline to submit a version with specific requirements (e.g. camera ready version until 12 a.m.), the advisor has two possibilities: Either he can check when the last version has been submitted, and if it was after 12 a.m. he can reset the DokuWiki pages of the student to the last version before 12 a.m.. Or he removes the write-access rights from all seminar participants immediately after 12 a.m.. The same can be done with the SVN-material. For revising the DokuWiki seminar papers, advisors can use various markup tools and e.g. mark text passages or add notes. The student can see the notes immediately and react correspondingly.

3.2   Disadvantages

During our seminar course the advisors as well as students also experienced some disadvantages of this system. One clear disadvantage for the students became clear when the advisor did not regularly check the different DokuWiki pages. At some point a student started to use a wrong reference style. Other students, who didn't know how to reference, checked his page and copied his style, trusting it was the right one. After a while a whole part of the course had adapted the wrong style, until the advisor noticed. So checks by the advisor are necessary and the students should be made aware of such frequent problems at the beginning of the seminar. Another question that the seminar participants raised was how to measure the amount of the written text and images. Since it is not a static document with a certain length, the advisors cannot restrict it to 12 pages. One solution is to simply count the words in the DokuWiki pages of each student and to define a range in which the number words must be within. Another solution is to print the DokuWiki pages as a pdf-Document with well defined rules, as size of text, if images are included, if linked and embedded source code is included or not. These rules have to be clearly defined at the beginning of the seminar.

One disadvantage experienced as advisors is the separate rights management between DokuWiki and SVN. For instance, if a user wants to access a DokuWiki page where source code from the SVN is embedded, the user has to authenticate twice: Once for DokuWiki and once for SVN. Since this is a technical issue, we are sure that there is a solution for it, but it is not integrated in the presented tools. Another disadvantage is that printing of DokuWiki pages with images and embedded source code is not easy. We did not find any integrated tool or solution for this. For instance, printing a DokuWiki page with embedded source code leads to printer-adjusted formatting - which is different from the web browser formatting - and only the visible part of the embedded source code view is printed, not the code which requires to scroll in the embedded code view. We also did not find any solution for this issue. A third disadvantage for advisors might result in various reference styles, if the advisor does not give clear instructions, how to reference in a DokuWiki document. At the beginning of the seminar the advisor should make clear how books, proceedings, Internet links etc. have to be referenced. But after a corresponding introduction into consistent referencing in DokuWiki, this should not be an issue. Additionally the advisor can create a DokuWiki page, which is readable by all seminar participants and explains the way of referencing with corresponding DokuWiki-code examples.

4   Conclusion

Well-established tools like Wikis and SVN can be used in teaching for seminar papers. They present a refreshing and interactive alternative to printed paper seminar papers but also raise some issues. Using a Wiki in combination with SVN for seminar papers requires a good preparation of the tools, a well-defined rights management and guidelines for the seminar participants, e.g. how to reference and what the maximum size of this digital seminar paper is. However, for advisors, seminar participants and each interested reader, it is a different experience of reading such an interactive paper instead of a printed static version. It is not just reading from top to bottom, but following different links, interacting with images, listening to sounds and reading references, all by one click. The seminar paper gets more dynamic and vital. For us it was an interesting experience, which requires some preparation and planning, but quickly leads to acceptance and interests on the students side. We are in the process of optimizing this concept and planning to reuse it in various future seminars.

Acknowledgments. This work was supported by the UMIC Research Centre, RWTH Aachen University, Germany.

References

1. Leuf, B., Cunningham, W.: The Wiki Way: Quick Collaboration on the Web. Addison-Wesley Professional, Indianapolis (2001)
2. Pilato, C.M., Collins-Sussman, B.: Version Control with Subversion. O'Reilly Media, Sebastopol (2008)
3. Victorino, T.J.: DokuWiki. Log Press, Saarbrücken (2012)

MoKMaSD 2012 —
1st International Symposium on Modelling and Knowledge Management for Sustainable Development

Modelling and Knowledge Management for Sustainable Development

Antonio Cerone[1] and Alexeis Garcia-Perez[2]($\boxtimes$)

[1] UNU-IIST — International Institute for Software Technology,
United Nations University, Macau SAR, China
ceroneantonio@gmail.com
[2] Faculty of Engineering and Computing, Coventry University, Coventry, UK
ab1258@coventry.ac.uk

Abstract. This paper introduces the motivation and aim of the *1st International Symposium on Modelling and Knowledge Management for Sustainable Development (MoKMaSD 2012)*, inspired by the POST-2015 UN Development Agenda. Then the keynote paper and the four contributed papers presented at the Symposium are summarised and related to the POST-2015 UN Development Agenda.

1 Introduction

The 2012 Report to the UN Secretary-General "Realizing the Future We Want for All" by the UN System Task Team on the POST-2015 UN Development Agenda [6] identifies and elaborates the four core dimensions "where progress will be needed in coming years and decades in order to build a rights-based, equitable, secure and sustainable world for all people":

1. *inclusive social development*;
2. *environmental sustainability*;
3. *inclusive economic development*;
4. *peace and security*.

Inclusive social development aims to ensure people's rights to health and education through preventive, curative and promotional health services, intervention on the environment to provide sanitation and hygienic standards as well as training, childhood education and lifelong learning. Prevention and long-term planning require the ability to manage and integrate rapidly changing information about both natural environment and social development, and create computational models to simulate the implementation of preventive measures, human intervention on the environment and government policies.

The core dimension of *environmental sustainability* is essential in achieving success in inclusive social development. Humans live in a global environment and their survival depends on the sustainability of such global environment, which includes land, water, natural resources, biomass and climate. Damage

A. Cerone et al. (Eds.): SEFM 2012 Satellite Events, LNCS 7991, pp. 149–153, 2014.
DOI: 10.1007/978-3-642-54338-8_12, © Springer-Verlag Berlin Heidelberg 2014

to any component of the global environment affects all other components and, as a consequence, threatens the integrity of the global environment. Therefore "immediate priorities in preserving environmental sustainability include ensuring a stable climate, stopping ocean acidification, preventing land degradation and unsustainable water use, sustainably managing natural resources and protecting the natural resources base, including biodiversity." Furthermore "ecosystem-based approaches to adaptation can provide a win-win opportunity for reducing vulnerabilities, as part of national adaptation strategies" [6].

"Sustainable development involves stable, equitable and inclusive economic growth, based on sustainable patterns of production and consumption." Any modelling approach and policy analysis has to aim to *inclusive economic development*, through sustainable development and better governance, and align "the imperatives of macroeconomic stability and financial sustainability with broader structural development policies enabling adequate generation of productive employment and decent work, reduction of poverty and inequalities, low-carbon as well as resource-and waste-efficient economic growth, and welfare protection" [6].

Better governance also means compliance with and adaptability to international laws and principles of inclusion and participation as prerequisites to maintain *peace and security*.

The *1st International Symposium on Modelling and Knowledge Management for Sustainable Development (MoKMaSD 2012)* was inspired by the POST-2015 UN Development Agenda and originated as a development of the special track on "Modelling for Sustainable Development" of the 9th International Conference on Software Engineering and Formal Methods, held on 14–18 November 2011, in Montevideo, Uruguay. The aim of the Symposium, held on 2 October 2012 in Thessaloniki, Greece, was to bring together practitioners and researchers from academia, industry, government and non-government organisations to present research results and exchange experience, ideas, and solutions for modelling and analysing complex systems and using knowledge management strategies, technology and systems in various domain areas, including economy, governance, health, biology, ecology, climate and poverty reduction, that address problems of sustainable development.

The keynote paper and the four contributed papers presented at *MoKMaSD 2012* show how to use modelling techniques (Sect. 2) or knowledge management frameworks (Sect. 3) to address the core dimensions of the POST-2015 UN Development Agenda.

2 Modelling for Sustainable Development

The formalisation of process calculi in both constructive and classical logics, as carried out in recent years, may be combined with other techniques such as concurrency and individual-based modelling, to develop knowledge representation schemes which could help overcome some of the challenges of current knowledge management systems. In their keynote paper, Kahramanoğullar, Lynch and Priami [5] present an integrated approach to ecosystem modeling from an algorithmic systems biology point of view. They use a modelling interface, called LIME, to provide models written in a narrative style, which are then automatically translated into stochastic programming languages.

Individual-based modelling can be used to model and understand how biological or social systems are organised and governed, but they can also help study individual aspects of population dynamics and their interaction with the surrounding environment, including human beings and their interventions and policy enforcement. Barbuti, Cerone, Maggiolo-Schettini, Milazzo and Setiawan [1] present a new formalism, Grid Systems, aimed at modelling population dynamics, which uses rewrite rules to integrate capabilities of membrane computing, spatiality dynamics and stochasticity. Such integrated approach supports the inclusion in the ecosystem model of aspects of the interaction between the population under analysis (here a mosquito population, vector of fatal diseases) and the human population. This makes the approach suitable not only for analysis of population dynamics but also for epidemiological simulation.

The two works above provide modelling frameworks that address the core dimension of *inclusive social development*. System dynamics is an interdisciplinary method to enhance learning about dynamic complexity and sources of policy resistance in complex systems. Because system dynamics draws on cognitive and social psychology, organisation theory, economics and other social sciences, studying system dynamics may help the Knowledge Management community understand and influence change in organisations. In this sense, the use of system dynamics yields models that aim to address *environmental sustainability*. Bernardo and D'Alessandro [2] analyse various policies that may promote the transition to sustainability, with a particular focus on the energy sector, and present a dynamic simulation model where three strategies for sustainability are identified (eduction in GHG emissions, improvements in energy efficiency and the development of the renewable energy sector) and the dynamics they may produce in the economy is evaluated.

3   Knowledge Management for Sustainable Development

Knowledge management includes important dynamic aspects, such as knowledge transfer and adaptivity, which requires a synergistic approach that incorporates modelling.

Bolisani, et al. [3] consider knowledge transfer between distant organizations and explore recent literature with the purpose to highlight relevant formal approaches that can help model and analyse the processes of inter-organisational knowledge transfer for sustainable development. In this context, modelling and simulation may help investigate

- the effectiveness of knowledge transfer mechanisms that can be adopted in the light of potentially conflicting stakeholders goals;
- how beneficial protective mechanisms may be for economic development;

- the role of co-operation where companies with complementary competencies can fruitfully share and integrate their knowledge, and can benefit of mutual learning.

This analysis represents a first step towards a synergistic approach to modelling and knowledge management. In addition, it addresses the first three core dimension of the POST-2015 UN Development Agenda described in Sect. 1.

Adapting to and complying with frequently changing legislation quickly against low costs is an important pre-requisite to guarantee *peace and security* in governance. Moreover, this requires organizations to adapt their business processes automatically. Gong and Janssen [4] use semantic representation of legal knowledge and present a modelling framework that enables the automatic creation of business process by invoking Semantic Web Services (SWS).

4   Conclusion

The works presented at the *1st International Symposium on Modelling and Knowledge Management for Sustainable Development* show that development of synergistic approaches to modelling and knowledge management can be very effective in supporting Sustainable Development.

However, there are other important aspects of Development, both in science and society, that go beyond Sustainability and generally benefit of such synergistic approaches. In biology and medicine, large amounts of data are analysed, often using data mining techniques, to extract pattern and organise and manage knowledge to be then used, for instance, as a basis for the selection of optimal genetic engineering techniques and drug dosages. At the same time, but in separate studies, modelling techniques are used for similar purposes. Analogously, behaviour and interaction within societies are investigated through sentiment analysis to extract moods, learning attitudes as well as various indicators of social processes such as collaboration, while in alternative studies evolution and adaptation within societies are investigated through modelling and simulation. Therefore, in the future, we would like to enlarge the scope of the MoKMaSD symposia towards such more general directions.

References

1. Barbuti, R., Cerone, A., Maggiolo-Schettini, A., Milazzo, P., Setiawan, S.: Modelling population dynamics using Grid Systems. In: Cerone, A., et al. (eds.) SEFM 2012 Satellite Events, LNCS, vol. 7991, pp. 172–189. Springer, Heidelberg (2012)
2. Bernardo, G., D'Alessandro, S.: Transition to sustainability: Italian scenarios towards a low-carbon economy. In: Cerone, A., et al. (eds.) SEFM 2012 Satellite Evens, LNCS, vol. 7991, pp. 190–197. Springer, Heidelberg (2014)
3. Bolisani, E., Scramoncin, F., Shaikh, S.A.: Models of knowledge transfer for sustainable development. In: Cerone, A., et al. (eds.) SEFM 2012 Satellite Events, LNCS, vol. 7991, pp. 198–203. Springer, Heidelberg (2014)

4. Gong, Y., Janssen, M.: A framework for translating legal knowledge into administrative processes: dynamic adaption of business processes. In: Cerone, A., et al. (eds.) SEFM 2012 Satellite Events, LNCS, vol. 7991, pp. 204–211. Springer, Heidelberg (2014)
5. Kahramanoğulları, O., Lynch, J.F., Priami, C.: Algorithmic systems ecology: experiments on multiple interaction types and patches. In: Cerone, A., et al. (eds.) SEFM 2012 Satellite Events. LNCS, vol. 7991, pp. 154–171. Springer, Heidelberg (2014)
6. UN System Task Team on the POST-2015 UN Development Agenda. Realizing the future we want for all - report to the secretary-general. Technical report. United Nations, New York, June 2012

Algorithmic Systems Ecology: Experiments on Multiple Interaction Types and Patches

Ozan Kahramanoğulları[1](✉), James F. Lynch[2], and Corrado Priami[1,3]

[1] The Microsoft Research – University of Trento Centre for Computational and
Systems Biology, Trento, Italy
`ozan@cosbi.eu`
[2] Department of Computer Science, Clarkson University, Potsdam, NY, USA
[3] Department of Mathematics, University of Trento, Trento, Italy

Abstract. Dynamic behavior in ecosystems can emerge as a result of multiple interactions of different types as well as movements of the ecosystem species between different patches. The extinction behaviors in ecosystem models, which can result from the small species numbers, bring stochasticity to the foreground as they are often not observable in deterministic representations. To this end, we demonstrate an integrated approach to ecosystem modeling from an algorithmic systems biology point of view. We use a modeling interface, called LIME, which allows us to give biologically intuitive models of a plant-pollinator system's descriptions with varying interaction types and patches. Our models, written in a narrative style, are automatically translated into stochastic programming languages. The discrete stochastic nature of the models brings about the possibility to analyze the models with respect to their simulations as well as various graph representations. Our analysis provides an assessment of the functional dynamics of ecosystems with respect to the influence of various interaction patterns and patch links.

Keywords: Ecosystem modeling · Plant-pollinator networks · Multiple interactions · Stochasticity

1 Introduction

Systems biology is established as a methodology that assists investigations for obtaining knowledge on dynamics and functioning of biological systems at various levels. Recent developments in computational methods now offer new avenues of investigation that provide contributions to long standing discussions also in ecology. Individual based models (IBMs) [3,9,10] have been instrumental in addressing different issues on ecosystems such as the relationship between patterns and processes [23]. Similar considerations that are centered around complex adaptive systems view of ecosystems have also been proven useful in addressing dynamical properties of ecosystems [19].

Until relatively recently, ecosystem modeling has been dominated by continuous deterministic representations that provide estimations of populations'

A. Cerone et al. (Eds.): SEFM 2012 Satellite Events, LNCS 7991, pp. 154–171, 2014.
DOI: 10.1007/978-3-642-54338-8_13, © Springer-Verlag Berlin Heidelberg 2014

dynamics with respect to the species interactions. However, the greater availability of powerful computers made a departure from more traditional considerations feasible with the availability of new capabilities.

A point of interest in IBMs is on capturing certain sources of noise, which can be important in small populations [24]. This is because the same amount of living biomass can have a noisy behavior if it corresponds to an individual of an ecosystem rather than millions of individuals of the same system, for example, as in the relationship between whales and planktons. Stochasticity, which is exploited in some IBMs, is an instrumental feature for studying the inherent noise in ecosystems, both at individual level and at the population level. In contrast to deterministic population-level models, stochastic models make it possible to simulate actual extinction events. In this respect, generalistic discussions of ecosystem models are limited in both handling the noisy behavior of small populations and modeling extinction. However, the extinction of rare species is at the frontier of applied ecological research and conservation biology.

Another challenge that is confronting ecosystem models is the representation of different types of concurrent interspecific interactions [21]. In ecology literature the focus is on single interaction types, with an emphasis on food webs, and an increasing focus on plant-pollinator networks in isolation. However, in ecosystems, different kinds of interactions always happen in parallel. The capability to model them simultaneously is important for a better understanding of ecosystems.

In this paper, we present an algorithmic systems biology approach [26] for compositional stochastic modeling of ecosystems with different kinds of interactions between species and movement of species between patches, that is, spatial regions [14]. For our ecosystem models, we use the CoSBiLab LIME (Language Interface for Modeling Ecology) [14], which is designed for modeling ecosystems with multiple interaction types and patches. The LIME language allows the user to give a biologically intuitive model description in a narrative style. This makes it possible to specify in the same model multiple parallel ecological interactions.

The LIME language is designed to perform static analysis on the model structures prior to the translation of the model description into a program suitable for stochastic dynamical simulation. These features make it possible to design, simulate and analyze ecosystem models with varying patterns of interactions and structures without dealing with the technicalities of specialized programming languages. In LIME, composability of the used language constructs play a key role in expressing the different kinds of interactions in a unified manner in a single model [15].

Besides mathematical approaches based on continuous differential equations, and experimental approaches of biology, which are however difficult in ecology, our algorithmic systems biology approach provides a discretized point of view of the models. This in return makes it easier to adapt computational analysis techniques for querying to the models and simulations with them. As an illustrative example for this, we discuss how an approach for discrete stochastic flux analysis can be used to obtain various graph representations of the models that display the resource flows in the modeled systems, and the causal reading of these flows.

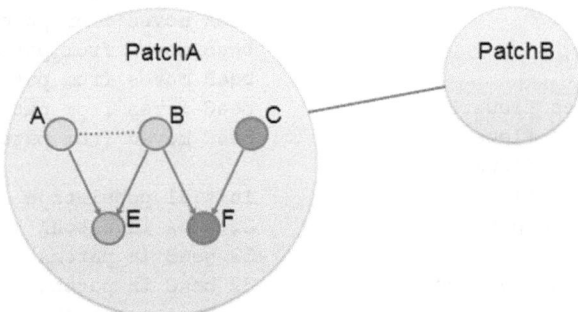

Fig. 1. The graphical representation of a pollinator network on two patches, given with the LIME model in Fig. 2. The species A and B are pollinators for the plant E, whereas B and C are pollinators for the plant F. There is direct competition between the species A and B. The pollinator species can move between the two patches A and B.

As an example case study of an ecosytem with multiplicity of ecological interactions acting in parallel, we present models of a plant-pollinator system with varying interaction patterns and patch structures. Because ecological systems and processes are inherently variable, composability of the LIME language and the constructs of the underlying framework help to manage the emerging complexity. This way, we discuss and illustrate how these features can be used for the construction of complicated ecosystem models together with their simulation and analysis while keeping track of stochasticity and quantifying its consequences.

2   Algorithmic Modeling with LIME

We use a programming language that is based on process algebras. Process algebras are formal languages, which were originally introduced as a means to study the properties of complex reactive systems by providing rigorous discrete syntactic representations of these systems. In process algebra, concurrency, that is, the view of systems in which interacting computational processes are executing in parallel, is a central aspect. Stochastic extensions of these languages are now broadly used tools for describing the dynamics of biological systems [27], as they faithfully capture mass action kinetics with a continuous time Markov chain semantics. While continuous and discrete representations approximate each other, discrete representations are more realistic for the case of biological systems, because populations are described by discrete variables and both continuous and discrete representations are continuous in time. Moreover, discrete representations provide the expressive power to model otherwise challenging structures [2,17].

The algebraic operators and the language constructs of the specialized stochastic process algebra languages allow them to capture the structural and functional aspects of the systems that they model. The biological system models written in these languages vary within a spectrum that spans from molecular

```
duration time 1.0                    beeA moves from patchB to patchA
                                     beeB moves from patchA to patchB
interactions                         beeB moves from patchB to patchA
beeA pollinates flowerE              beeC moves from patchA to patchB
beeB pollinates flowerE              beeC moves from patchB to patchA
beeB pollinates flowerF
beeC pollinates flowerF              initial population
beeA and beeB compete                32 beeA in patchA
                                     32 beeB in patchA
birth and death dynamics             32 beeC in patchA
beeA dies                            32 beeA in patchB
beeB dies                            32 beeB in patchB
beeC dies                            32 beeC in patchB
flowerE dies
flowerF dies                         1000 flowerE in patchA
                                     1000 flowerF in patchA
patch dynamics                       1000 flowerE in patchB
beeA moves from patchA to patchB     1000 flowerF in patchB
```

Fig. 2. LIME description of the model depicted in Fig. 1. The rates values are not specified, they are thus set to the default value 1.0 for this case.

biology to ecology with respect to their levels of abstraction. However, the mathematical syntax of these languages makes them difficult to make modifications on the models. When the modifications on the models involve functional phenomena such as patterns of interactions, for example, as in ecosystem models, the syntax of these languages becomes even more challenging. This creates obstacles for these languages to be used effectively in experiments that involve variations of the same model. As a result of this, specialized high level languages that provide user friendly interfaces to these languages are developed and used for modeling biological systems at these different levels of biological systems for expressing various phenomena [11, 13, 14].

We describe our model in the language of LIME (Language Interface for Modeling Ecology) [14, 15]. After performing static analysis on the model structure, the LIME translation software tool translates the model description into the stochastic process algebra languages BlenX [6] and SPiM for simulation. In Appendix A, we give a short introduction to BlenX. For an indepth exposure to BlenX we refer to [5, 6], and for SPiM to [1, 13, 17, 22]. A graphical representation of a model is depicted in Fig. 1, and its complete LIME description is given in Fig. 2. There, the rates are not specified, they are thus set to the default value of 1.0 for this case.

A LIME input file can consist of five parts that describe different aspects of the model. Some of these parts are optional, therefore they can be excluded in models. However, the model in Fig. 2 includes all these parts. The first part,

```
duration time 1                          birth and death dynamics
interactions                                beeA dies with rate 2.4
  beeA pollinates flowerE with rates        beeB dies with rate 2.0
    0.00294651236 and 0.00240000000         beeC dies with rate 2.4
  beeB pollinates flowerE with rates        flowerE dies with rate 0.7
    0.0146105379 and 0.00191794978          flowerF dies with rate 0.7
  beeB pollinates flowerF with rates
    0.0163731225 and 0.0000820502154     initial population
  beeC pollinates flowerF with rates        32 beeA   32 beeB 32 beeC
    0.00301982726 and 0.00240000000         1000 flowerE 1000 flowerF
```

Fig. 3. A model obtained from the one depicted in Fig. 1, however on a single patch, without competition interactions, and with explicit rate values.

initiated with the keyword `duration`, is a single statement on the simulation duration. In this model, the simulations are specified to run until time point 1.0.

The second part, initiated with the keyword `interactions`, consists of the sentences that describe the interactions of the individuals of the modeled ecosystem. Each sentence describes an interaction in the ecosystem together with the ecological patch where it happens and its rate. The interactions can be of four different kinds: *predator-prey*, *plant-pollinator*, *direct competition*, and *facilitation*. The model in Fig. 2 contains only plant-pollinator and direct competition interactions. There are three pollinator species, that is, `beeA`, `beeB`, `beeC`, and two flower species `flowerE` and `flowerF`. The species `beeA` is a pollinator for the `flowerE`, and `beeC` is a pollinator for the `flowerE`, whereas `beeB` is a pollinator for both `flowerE` and `flowerF`. `beeA` and `beeB` have a direct competition interaction between each other.

The optional third part of the input file, initiated with the keywords `birth and death dynamics`, collects the information on the birth and death rates of the species. Each sentence in this part describes the birth rate or the death rate of a species in each habitat patch. Without habitat patch specification, a rate is distributed and applies to all patches: this way, general rates can be defined. In the model in Fig. 2, death rates for all the species `beeA`, `beeB`, `beeC`, `flowerE` and `flowerF` are defined as the default rate value 1.0.

The optional fourth part of the input file, initiated with the keywords `patch dynamics`, contains the information on the rates of the movements between patches of the ecosystem: each sentence here describes the migration rate between two particular patches of a given species. In the model in Fig. 2, the bee species can move between connected patches as depicted in Fig. 1. `patchA` and `patchB` are connected such that `beeA`, `beeB` and `beeC` can move between them.

The fifth part, initiated with the keywords `initial population`, provides the information on the initial population sizes at the beginning of a simulation. In the model in Fig. 2, there are 1000 flowers and 32 bees of each species in each patch at the initial state.

LIME translation algorithm maps the sentences of the model into program code that implements the corresponding reactions. For example, each sentence of the form

Pollinator pollinates Plant with rates rate1 and rate2

is mapped to two reactions

$$\text{Pollinator} + \text{Plant} \rightarrow_{rate1} \text{Pollinator} + \text{Plant} + \text{Plant}$$
$$\text{Pollinator} + \text{Plant} \rightarrow_{rate2} \text{Pollinator} + \text{Pollinator} + \text{Plant} + \text{Plant}.$$

Each sentence of the form

SpeciesA and SpeciesB compete with rate rate1

is mapped to a reaction

$$\text{SpeciesA} + \text{SpeciesB} \rightarrow_{rate1} \cdot$$

In the model, when movement of species between spatial regions, given with patches, are defined or interactions are defined specific to certain patches, the LIME translation algorithm distributes these patches to the reactions with respect to the model.

Due to these features, LIME models can be written, extended and modified with a great ease with almost no prior knowledge of this language. As we illustrate below, this capability makes it very easy to experiment with variations of models.

3   In Silico Experiments

As a first step for an analysis of the model, we work with a single-patch model, given in Fig. 3, as in PatchA of the model depicted in Fig. 1, however we exclude the direct competition between beeA and beeB. That is, there are only plant-pollinator interactions, where beeA is a pollinator for flowerE, beeC is a pollinator for flowerF, and beeB is a pollinator for both flowerE and flowerF.

We instantiate the rates of the model such that the simulations display a close to stable behavior. For this, we obtain the rates by fitting the ODE representation of the model to steady state, where the death rates and initial quantities are fixed as in Fig. 3. For the fitting, we used the least-squares method provided by the PET tool [28]. We assume that the time unit of the simulations is one year. This provides realistic death rates for the bee populations in accordance with their average lifespans within a season, and allows us to observe the population behavior in response to interactions within that season. With stochastic simulations, we obtain a close to stable level for the time interval from 0 to 1, however as the simulation continues, the levels of the species depart from the steady state values due to the fluctuations in the system. These simulations result either in an exponential growth of the numbers of some or all of the species or in extinctions, depending on the initial bias given by the fluctuations.

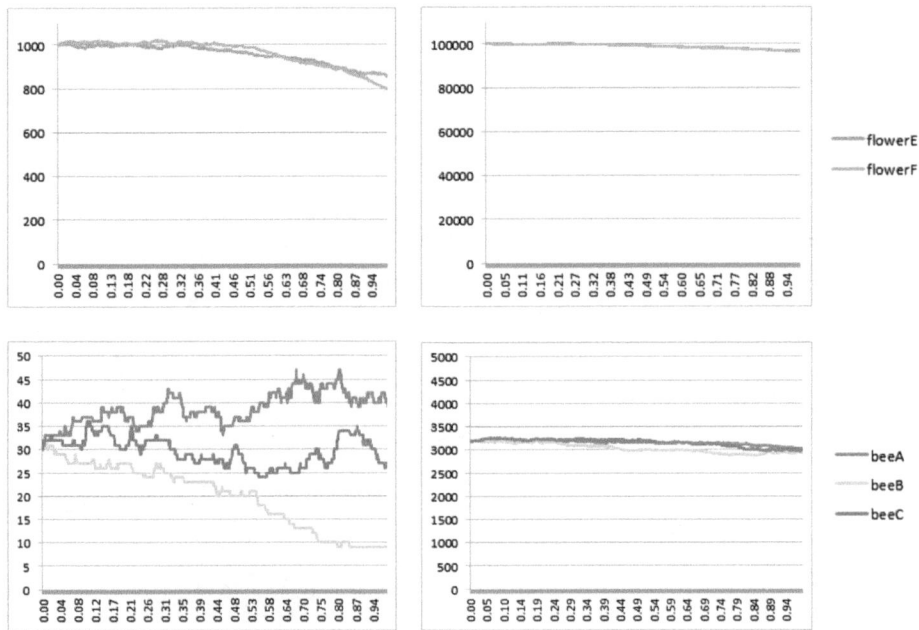

Fig. 4. The plots on the left are from a simulation with the model in Fig. 3. The plots on the right are from a simulation with a version of the model, which is scaled by 100. The upper plots display the behavior of the flower species, whereas the lower plots display the behavior of the bee species.

As we scale the model by multiplying the initial numbers by a scaling factor, we observe extended stability with respect to simulation time as depicted in Fig. 4, however with an increased tendency towards extinctions as the simulation continues. This contrasts with the exponential increases often observed with lower species numbers in the non-scaled model. Because our focus of interest is the behavior within a season, the model does not factor for the seasonal changes between two years. The model thus gives an estimate of the tendencies within one time unit after the start of the simulation that are delivered by the interaction patterns and also patch structures as we analyze below.

In order to analyze the effect of direct competition to the system behavior, we introduce a direct competition interaction between the species beeA and beeB by adding the following sentence to the interactions of the model: "beeA and beeB compete with rate 0.1". The direct competition interactions can be seen as a mechanism that stresses beeA and beeB concomitantly when they are present at the same patch. With the introduction of this interaction, as depicted in Fig. 5, we observe that in the simulations the numbers of the species beeA and beeB reduce until at least one of them goes extinct. As a result of this the numbers of the species flowerE and flowerF reduce as their pollination by beeA and beeB becomes hampered. When we increase the rate of the direct competition inter-

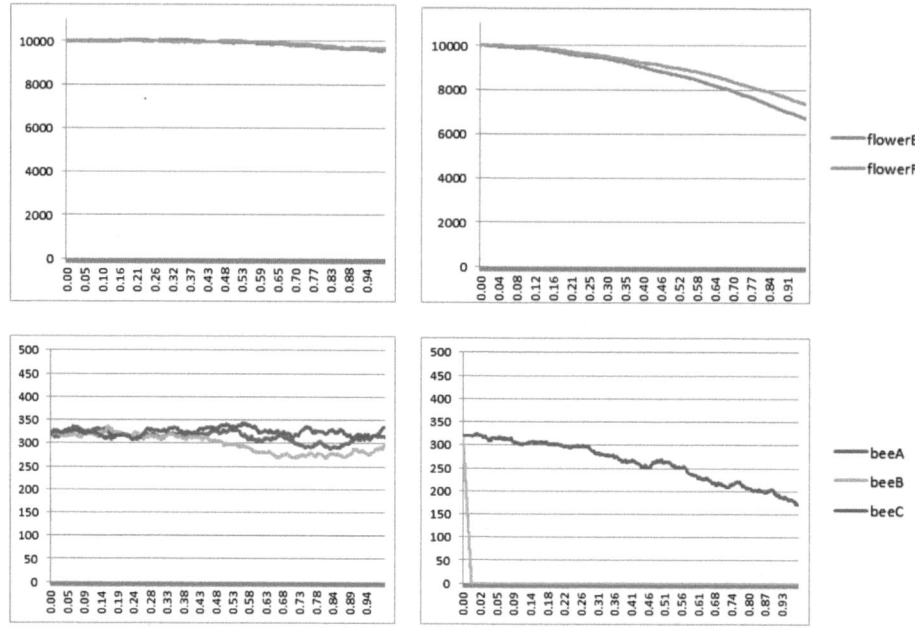

Fig. 5. The plots on the left are from a simulation with the model in Fig. 3. The plots on the right are from a simulation with a model that extends the model in Fig. 3 with competition between **beeA** and **beeB**. The upper plots display the behavior of the flower species, whereas the lower plots display the behavior of the bee species. The simulations are with the versions of the models, which are scaled by 10.

action from 0.1 up to ten orders of magnitude, we observe that this increases the extinction of the competing species within the considered time interval, however it does not accelerate the extinction drastically in comparison to original rate. Decreasing the competition rate more than two orders of magnitude brings the behavior of the system close to the levels that are observed without competition.

In order to observe the effect of the availability of patches, between which the bee species can move, we extend the model to two patches. The simulations with the different versions of this model are depicted in Fig. 6. In the first version of this extension, we consider a model without competition. This model is obtained by extending the model in Fig. 3 with the sentences in Fig. 7. The simulation plot, depicted on the left-hand-side of Fig. 6, is with this model. As a second step for a consideration of patch dynamics, we extend this model with direct competition. The plot on the right-hand-side of Fig. 6 is with the model, which extends patch dynamics with direct competition between **beeA** and **beeB** as above. Both models behave similar to their single patch versions as can be seen by comparing these plots with those in Fig. 5. However, for the case of the model without competition, the movement between patches provides a minor stabilizing effect to the pollination in comparison to the single patch version.

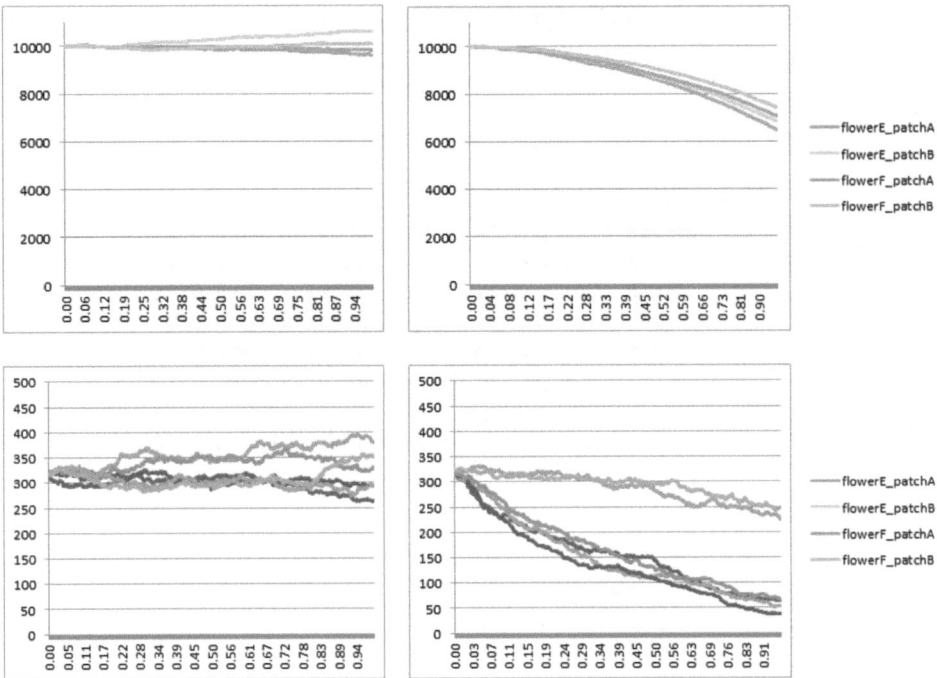

Fig. 6. Simulation plots with the model that extends the model in Fig. 3 to two patches, named A and B. The plots on the left are without competition, whereas the ones on the right include the competition between beeA and beeB. The upper plots display the behavior of the flower species and the lower plots display the bee species. The simulations are with the versions of the models, which are scaled by 10.

In order to model the different conditions on different patches, we restrict the competition between beeA and beeB to patch A. We then performed experiments, where we restricted the movement of species. These variations of the model are as follows: (1) only beeA and beeB can move between patch A and patch B, and beeC is stationary on both patches; (2) only beeA moves between patch A and patch B; (3) only beeB moves between patch A and patch B. Example simulation plots with these variations of the models are depicted in Fig. 8, where the plot on the left is for the case where all the bee species can move between two patches, whereas the plot on the right is for the case where only beeA and beeB can move between patches.

In all these variations of the model, the restriction of competition to a single patch provides a safe environment for the pollination in the patch without competition, which is patch B. Apart from this, the two models with the simulations in Fig. 8, have similar behaviors since the movement of beeC between two patches does not strongly hamper the competition between beeA and beeB, however their movement has a minor influence that reduces the effect of the competition.The cases where either only beeA or only beeB can move between two patches display similar behaviors to the simulation depicted on the left-hand-side of Fig. 8.

```
patch dynamics
    beeA moves from patchA to patchB with rate 0.1
    beeA moves from patchB to patchA with rate 0.1
    beeB moves from patchA to patchB with rate 0.1
    beeB moves from patchB to patchA with rate 0.1
    beeC moves from patchA to patchB with rate 0.1
    beeC moves from patchB to patchA with rate 0.1
```

Fig. 7. The sentences that extend the model in Fig. 3 with patch dynamics

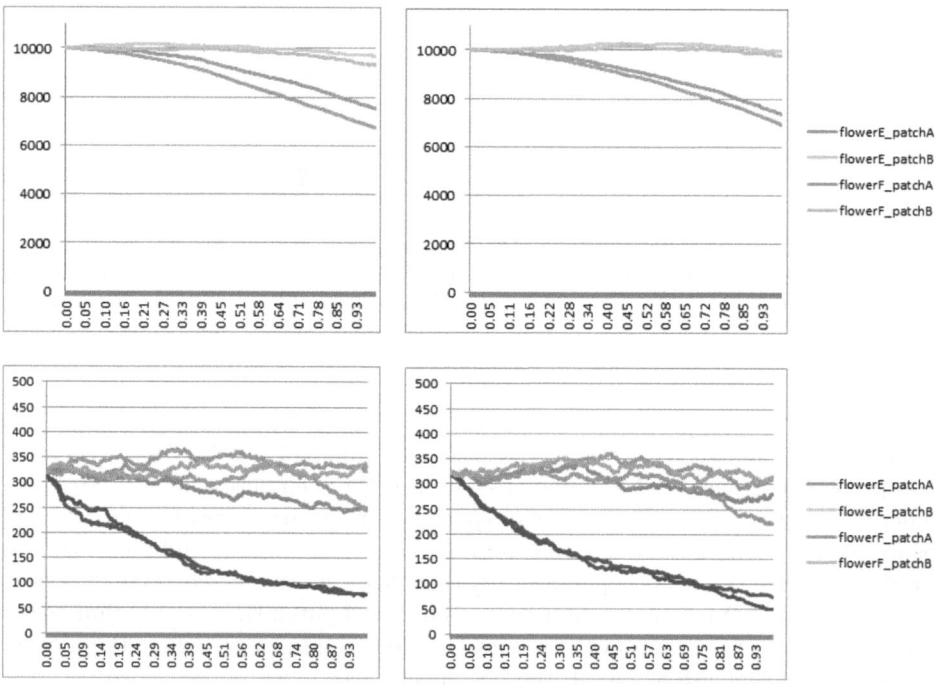

Fig. 8. Simulation plots with the model that extends the model in Fig. 3 to two patches, named A and B. In these models, there is competition between beeA and beeB, however only in patch A. The simulation plots on the left are with a model where all the bee species can move between both patches, whereas the plots on the right are with a model where the movement between patches is restricted to only beeA and beeB, and beeC are stationary on both patches. The upper plots display the behavior of the flower species, whereas the lower plots display the behavior of the bee species. The simulations are with the versions of the models which are scaled by 10.

$$1 : \texttt{beeA+} \rightarrow \qquad\qquad\qquad\qquad\qquad\qquad\qquad\qquad \times\, 70$$

```
 1 : beeA+ →                                                    × 70
 2 : beeA + flowerE → beeA + beeA + flowerE + flowerE          × 71
 3 : beeA + flowerE → beeA + flowerE + flowerE                 × 72
 4 : beeB →                                                    × 58
 5 : beeB + flowerE → beeB + beeB + flowerE + flowerE          × 42
 6 : beeB + flowerE → beeB + flowerE + flowerE                 × 333
 7 : beeB + flowerF → beeB + flowerF + flowerF                 × 389
 8 : beeC →                                                    × 67
 9 : beeC + flowerF → beeC + beeC + flowerF + flowerF          × 49
10 : beeC + flowerF → beeC + flowerF + flowerF                 × 57
11 : flowerE →                                                 × 669
12 : flowerF →                                                 × 642
```

Fig. 9. The reactions that occur during a simulation and their numbers of occurrences.

4   Flux Analysis

The reactions that are given by a LIME model are interpreted by the stochastic simulation algorithm as a continuous time Markov chain (CTMC). A simulation with a model can thus be seen as reduction of this complex structure, that is, the model, into a simpler structure, that is, the simulation trajectory, which is a path in the CTMC. However, during this process, some of the information on the simulation can be lost. In particular, the causality between the reactions with respect to the flow of resources during simulation remains hidden in the total order of the reaction instances of the simulation trajectory, which is emphasized by the unique time stamps of these reaction instances.

In [16], Kahramanoğulları and Lynch have introduced a method for flux analysis on stochastic simulations with reaction networks, where flux is the flow of resources between reactions of the network. The approach of [16] is based on inspecting the reaction instances from the point of view of their dependencies on one another during simulation, and relaxing their total order into a partial order structure. The method then uses this partial order as a representation of causal dependencies in the simulation, and processes it further to observe the flux in the network with respect to the flow of the resources from a reaction to another in arbitrary time intervals. The notion of flux obtained this way does not only approximate the notion of flux given by continuous deterministic representations, but also reveals other information that are not given by differential equation analysis.

We perform flux analysis for the simulation time interval from 0 to 1. Figure 9 gives a list of the reactions together with their ids and their number of occurrences during a simulation. The flux graphs of this simulation within the considered time interval are depicted in Figs. 10, 11, 12.

Figure 10 shows how resources present at the beginning of the simulation are distributed to the reactions of the network. Here, 0 denotes the initial state, and the directed edges of the graph display how resources at the initial state are

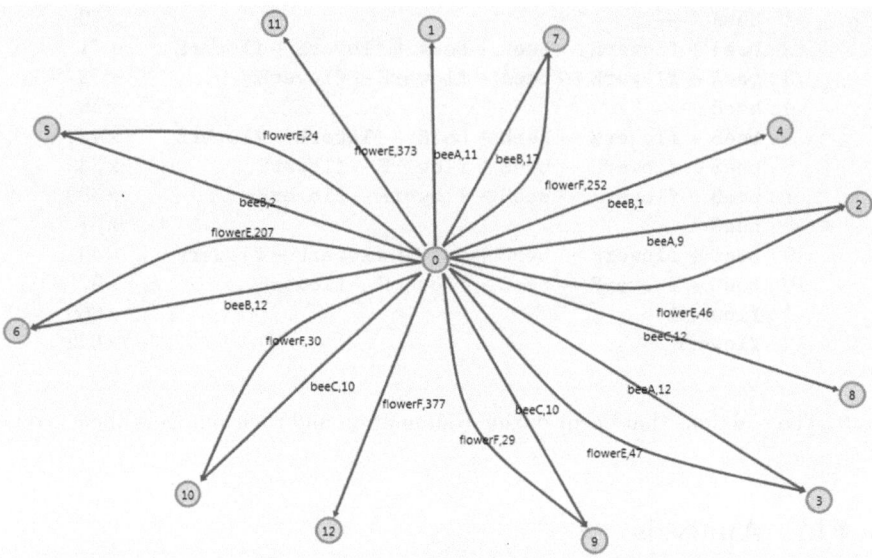

Fig. 10. Flux analysis graph for the simulation time interval from 0 to 1, indicating the quantity of the resources distributed from the initial state to the reactions of the network. Here, 0 denotes the initial state, and Fig. 9 gives a list of the reactions together with their ids.

consumed by the reactions listed in Fig. 9. As shown by this graph, 11 of beeA, 1 of beeB, 12 of beeC, 373 of flowerE and 377 of flowerF die without participating in any pollination interaction. An implication of this observation is that substantial fractions of the beeA and beeC populations die without participating in any pollination interaction, which removes one third of these species. However, almost all of the beeB participate in the reactions. A possible interpretation of these facts is that beeB is the most important bee species for maintaining the system. In order to check this hypothesis, we modified the pollination rates of beeA, beeB, and beeC in three different versions of the model. The simulations showed that lowering the rates of beeA and beeC by a third of the original rates does not affect the stability as much as doing the same to beeB as this causes a rapid decline in the levels of all the species. This observation agrees with the evidence provided by the flux analysis indicating that beeB plays a more important role in maintaining the system.

Figure 11 shows for different species the resources flowing from other reactions to death reactions. We observe that 59 of beeA participate in a pollination before they die, however 38 of these pollination interactions result in a reproduction of beeA. Similarly, 55 of beeC participate in a pollination before they die, and 40 of these pollination interactions result in a reproduction of beeC. On the other hand, while 57 of beeB participate in a pollination before they die, only 40 of these pollination interactions result in a reproduction of beeC. From these observations, it follows that although comparable numbers of beeA, beeB and

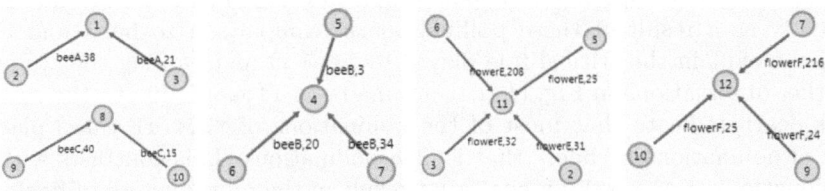

Fig. 11. Flux analysis graphs for the simulation time interval from 0 to 1, indicating the quantity of species flowing from other reactions of the network, excluding the initial state, to those for the death of the species. These are, respectively, for `beeA`, `beeC`, `beeB`, `flowerE` and `flowerF`. Figure 9 gives a list of the reactions and their ids.

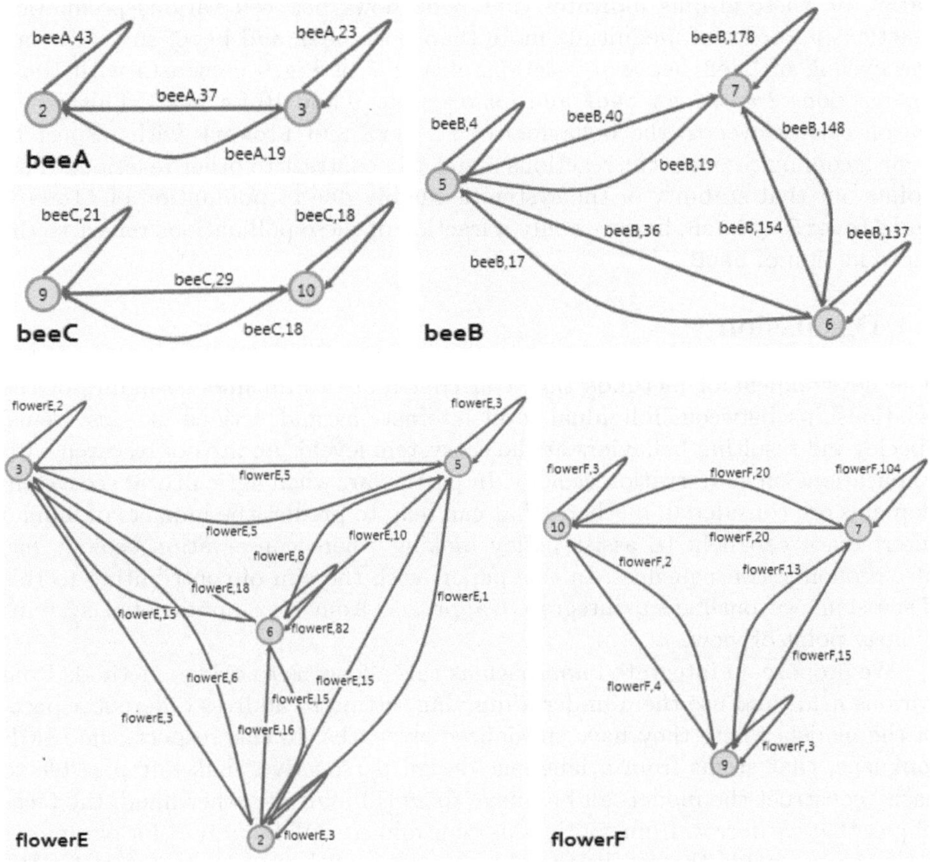

Fig. 12. Flux analysis graphs of different species for the simulation time interval from 0 to 1. The graphs indicate the quantity of species flowing between the pollination reactions of the network. These exclude the initial state and the reactions for the death of the species. Figure 9 gives a list of the reactions and their ids.

beeC die after participating in a pollination interaction, beeB reproduces less frequently as a result of these pollinations in comparison to beeA and beeC, which can explain the critical role played by beeB in maintaining the system.

Other observations in Fig. 11 that are made on flowerE due to the reaction for its death indicate that most of the pollinations of flowerE takes place as result of pollinations by beeB, that is, 208 pollinations. This contrasts with the 25 pollinations of flowerE by beeB that result in the reproduction of beeB, and the other 63 pollinations by beeA. Similarly, for the case of flowerF, 216 of the death reactions occur after having participated in a pollination by beeB, which does not result in a pollination. This contrasts with the total of 49 reactions that occur after a pollination by beeC.

Figure 12 shows for different species the resources flowing between the reactions of the network that model the pollination of the flower species. An observation on these graphs indicates that beeB flows between various pollination reactions an order of magnitude more than both beeA and beeC. In particular, the cycling of beeB between reactions 6 and 7 of Fig. 9 contrasts with those for reactions 2 and 3 for beeA and for reactions 9 and 10 for beeC. This observation carries over to the behaviors of flowerE and flowerF with respect to their incoming resources at reactions 6 and 7 in contrast to other reactions. This points out that stability of the system is mainly due to pollination of flowerE and flowerF by beeB, however only a fraction of these pollinations reflect to the reproduction of beeB.

5   Discussion

The development of methods that can contribute to an understanding of the relationships between individual level interactions and actions of ecosystems' species and resulting behaviors at the ecosystem level is an area of research with implications on conservation ecology. In particular, when agricultural ecosystem domains are considered, methods that can help to predict the impacts of human interference can help to assist policy making where conservation ecology has also economic consequences. In this paper, with the aim of contributing to this discussion, we outline an integrated approach from a computational systems biology point of view.

We propose an integrated approach as this allows us to bridge methods from various fields and use them under a unifying setting to address different aspects of the models where they have specialized strengths. In this respect, the LIME language, that stems from a language-design perspective, makes it possible to easily construct the models and manage them [14]. On the other hand, the techniques that we borrow from continuous deterministic ODE analysis for parameter estimation provide the means to calibrate our model in order to factor for the context, that is not included in the model structure, of the modeled ecosystem [28]. Our flux analysis brings together ideas from concurrency theory that allows us to exploit the discrete structures of the stochastic simulations to analyze them as graphs that explain the flow of species. This is done by treating the species as resources that flow between ecosystem events [12, 16].

Besides the other methods, which are standard in systems biology, our stochastic flux analysis is prone to potential uses in ecology. With respect to the case analysis of the present paper, an example is the identification of the species that are critical to the robustness of the system. As our flux analysis showed, beeB, which pollinated both flower species, is more important in this regard than the other two species, which each pollinated only one species. This agrees with the observations of [20] stating that removal of generalist pollinators had the greatest effect on plant survival. Another potential application is on the movement of individuals between patches, which can be important to ecosystems [18]. Stochastic flux analysis can help to determine which movements have major consequences for the populations, as this makes it possible to monitor the movements at arbitrary time intervals as in our case study.

In the present paper, we have illustrated our approach on an hypothetical ecosystem model. Future work includes applying the methods here to study actual plant-pollinator systems by relying on field data, and also including other kinds of interactions between ecosystem species. In this respect questions of interest include the conditions that lead to stability or extinction, and identification of the keystone species. In our case study, also in order to factor for the non-modeled ecosystem context, we used a parameter estimation method in order to determine the rates of interactions. An alternative or complementary approach can be based on exploiting field data to assist the estimation of these rates. However, typically field data shows the rates at which the various pollinator species visit the plant species [7]. This poses other questions, as the available data does not reflect the quantitative effect of the visitations on their reproductive rates. Directions of future investigation include an investigation on stochastic simulations to be used to infer the reproductive rates from the field data.

Appendix A

BlenX shares features with the process algebra languages stochastic pi-calculus [25] and Beta-binders [4], it thus keeps a strong focus on the interactions of entities. Stochasticity is given by a continuous time Markov chain semantics, and it is realized by an efficient implementation of the Gillespie algorithm [8]. BlenX is a part of the software platform *COSBILAB*.

In BlenX, each individual of the modeled system is described as an abstract entity called *box*. Each box can interact with others via its connectivity interfaces called *binders*, and the result of the interactions and also other autonomous actions are determined by the user defined internal program of the box, which employs the stochastic semantics. As an example, consider the two boxes in Fig. 13, where each box has only one binder that is identified by its name, e.g., binder x and its type, e.g., X.

The internal program of a box describes the effect of the interactions and the autonomous actions that the box can undertake. Every time when such an action takes place with respect to the underlying stochastic semantics, the effect of the action is reflected to the interfaces, and this way the new state of the box is computed. This is performed by the simulation engine by picking an action of the model with respect to the Gillespie algorithm by taking the rates of the available actions of all the boxes at that state. This results in a model behavior in the form of a sequence of model actions that can be read as a time series of the model individuals, i.e., boxes.

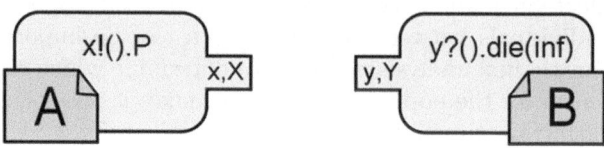

Fig. 13. Two BlenX boxes representing two interacting species A and B.

A BlenX model is written as two separate files, where the first file is the description of all the boxes of the model and their binders. The second file of the model contains a list of pairs of binder types together with their binding, unbinding, and interaction rates, which can all be 0. With respect to the compatibilities given by this list, binders can bind or unbind with binders of other boxes, or interact to exchange information communications with other boxes. As an example for this, consider the model given in Fig. 13, where the expression $(X, Y, 0, 0, 1)$ indicates that the binders with types X and Y can interact with a rate 1. The third and forth parameters of this expression state the binding and unbinding rates are 0.

The interaction of a predator A and its prey B can be described in a BlenX model with the boxes depicted in Fig. 13. The interaction rate, specified in the BlenX code, determines the rate of the predation being modeled. The internal program, which can be `nil`, describes this interaction and its consequences in terms of the *actions* the box can undertake. The `nil` action does nothing. Other stochastic *actions* that a BlenX box can perform are summarized as follows: a box can

(i.) communicate with another box (or with itself) by performing an input action, e.g., `x?(message)` that is complementary to the output action, e.g., `x!(message)`, of the other box, or vice versa, and this way send or receive a message;

(ii.) perform a stochastic `delay` action;

(iii.) change (`ch`) the type of one of its interfaces;

(iv.) eliminate itself by performing a `die` action;

(v.) `expose` a new binder;

(vi.) `hide` one of its binders;

(vii.) `unhide` a binder which is hidden.

In addition to these actions, there are also other programming constructs available such as if-then statements and state-checks. For example, let us consider the box A in Fig. 13. We can define the program P such that it changes the type X to Z if this box is bound to another species via its interface x:

$$\text{if } (x, X) \text{ and } (x, \text{bound}) \text{ then } ch(x, Z) \text{ endif}$$

As BlenX is a process algebra based language, internal programs can be written as compositions of actions by using algebraic composition operators in order to define increasingly complex behaviors. We can sequentially compose actions by using the prefix-operator, written as an infix dot. For example, ch(x,Z).hide(x).nil denotes a program that first performs change action and then hides the changed binder. Programs can be composed in parallel. Parallel composition (denoted by the infix operator |, for instance P|Q) allows the description of programs, which may run independently in parallel and also synchronize on *complementary actions* (i.e., *input* and *output* over the same channel). Programs can also be composed by *stochastic choice*, denoted with the summation operator "+". The sum of processes P and Q, P + Q behaves either as P or as Q, determined by their stochastic rates, and selection of one discards the other forever.

References

1. Cardelli, L., Caron, E., Gardner, P., Kahramanoğulları, O., Phillips, A.: A process model of Rho GTP-binding proteins. Theoret. Comput. Sci. **410**(33–34), 3166–3185 (2009)
2. Cardelli, L., Zavattaro, G.: Turing universality of the biochemical ground form. Math. Struct. Comput. Sci. **20**(1), 45–73 (2010)
3. DeAngelis, D.L., Gross, L.J.: Individual-based Models and Approaches in Ecology. Chapman and Hall, New York (1992)
4. Degano, P., Prandi, D., Priami, C., Quaglia, P.: Beta binders for biological quantitative experiments. ENTCS **164**(3), 101–117 (2005)
5. Dematté, L., Larcher, R., Palmisano, A., Priami, C., Romanel, A.: Programming biology in BlenX. Syst. Biol. Signal. Netw. **1**, 777–821 (2010)
6. Dematté, L., Priami, C., Romanel, A.: The BlenX language: a tutorial. In: Bernardo, M., Degano, P., Zavattaro, G. (eds.) SFM 2008. LNCS, vol. 5016, pp. 313–365. Springer, Heidelberg (2008)
7. Forup, M.L., Henson, K.S.E., Craze, P.G., Memmott, J.: The restoration of ecological interactions: plant-pollinator networks on ancient and restored heathlands. J. Appl. Ecol. **45**, 742–752 (2008)
8. Gillespie, D.T.: Exact stochastic simulation of coupled chemical reactions. J. Phys. Chem. **81**, 2340–2361 (1977)
9. Grimm, V.: Ten years of individual-based modelling in ecology: what have we learned and what could we learn in the future? Ecol. Model. **115**, 129–148 (1999)
10. Grimm, V., Berger, U., Bastiansen, F., Eliassen, S., Ginot, V., Giske, J., Goss-Custard, J., Grand, T., Heinz, S.K., Huse, G., Huth, A., Jepsen, J.U., Jørgensen, C., Mooij, W.M., Müller, B., Peer, G., Piou, C., Railsback, S.F., Robbins, A.M., Robbins, M.M., Rossmanith, E., Rüger, N., Strand, E., Souissim, S., Stillman, R.A., Vabø, R., Visser, U., DeAngelis, D.L.: A standard protocol for describing individual-based and agent-based models. Ecol. Model. **198**(1–2), 115–126 (2006)

11. Guerriero, M.L., Dudka, A., Underhill-Day, N., Heath, J.K., Priami, C.: Narrative-based computational modelling of the gp130/jak/stat signalling pathway. BMC Syst. Biol. **3**(1), 40 (2009)
12. Kahramanoğulları, O.: Flux analysis in process models via causality. In: Proceedings of the 3rd Workshop from Biology to Concurrency and Back, vol. 19, pp. 20–39. EPTCS (2010)
13. Kahramanoğulları, O., Cardelli, L.: An intuitive modelling interface for systems biology. Int. J. Softw. Inform. (2011) (in press)
14. Kahramanoğulları, O., Lynch, J., Jordán, F.: CoSBiLab LIME: a language interface for stochastic dynamical modelling in ecology. Environ. Model Softw. **26**(5), 685–687 (2011)
15. Kahramanoğulları, O., Jordán, F., Priami, C.: Composability: perspectives in ecological modeling. In: Horimoto, K., Nakatsui, M., Popov, N. (eds.) ANB 2010. LNCS, vol. 6479, pp. 136–148. Springer, Heidelberg (2012)
16. Kahramanoğulları, O., Lynch, J.: Stochastic flux analysis of chemical reaction networks. BMC Syst. Biol **7**(133) (2013)
17. Kahramanoğulları, O., Phillips, A., Vaggi, F.: Process modeling and rendering of biochemical structures: actin. In: Biomechanics of cells and tissues: experiments, models and simulations. Lecture Notes in Computational Vision and Biomechanics. vol. 9, Springer (2013)
18. Knight, T.M., McCoy, M.W., Chase, J.M., McCoy, K.A., Holt, R.D.: Trophic cascades across ecosystems. Nature **437**, 880–883 (2005)
19. Levin, S.A.: Ecosystems and the biosphere as complex adaptive systems. Ecosystems **1**(5), 431–436 (1998)
20. Memmott, J., Waser, N.M., Price, M.V.: Tolerance of pollination networks to species extinctions. Proc. R. Soc. Lond., Ser. B, Biol. Sci. **271**, 2605–2611 (2004)
21. Olff, H., Alonso, D., Berg, M.P., Eriksson, B.K., Loreau, M., Piersma, T., Rooney, N.: Parallel ecological networks in ecosystems. Philos. Trans. R. Soc. B **364**(1524), 1755–1779 (2009)
22. Phillips, A., Cardelli, L.: Efficient, correct simulation of biological processes in the stochastic pi-calculus. In: Calder, M., Gilmore, S. (eds.) CMSB 2007. LNCS(LNBI), vol. 4695, pp. 184–199. Springer, Heidelberg (2007)
23. Pimm, S.L.: The Balance of Nature?. The University of Chicago Press, Ecological Issues in the Conservation of Species and Communities (1991)
24. Powell, C.R., Boland, R.P.: The effects of stochastic population dynamics on food web structure. J. Theor. Biol. **257**(1), 170–180 (2009)
25. Priami, C.: Stochastic π-calculus. Comput. J. **38**(6), 578–589 (1995)
26. Priami, C.: Algorithmic systems biology. Commun. ACM **52**(5), 80–89 (2009)
27. Regev, A., Shapiro, E.: Cellular abstractions: cells as computation. Nature **419**, 343 (2002)
28. Shaffer, C.A., Zwolak, J.W., Randhawa, R., Tyson, J.J.: Modeling molecular regulatory networks with jigcell and pet. Methods Mol. Biol. **500**, 1–31 (2009)

Modelling Population Dynamics Using Grid Systems

Roberto Barbuti[1]([✉]), Antonio Cerone[2]([✉]), Andrea Maggiolo-Schettini[1]([✉]),
Paolo Milazzo[1]([✉]), and Suryana Setiawan[1,2]([✉])

[1] Dipartimento di Informatica, Università di Pisa, Pisa, Italy
{barbuti,maggiolo,milazzo,setiawan}@di.unipi.it
[2] UNU-IIST — International Institute for Software Technology,
United Nations University, Macau SAR, China
ceroneantonio@gmail.com, setiawan@iist.unu.edu

Abstract. A new formalism, *Grid Systems*, aimed at modelling population dynamics is presented. The formalism is inspired by concepts of Membrane Computing (P Systems) and spatiality dynamics of Cellular Automata. The semantics of Grid Systems describes how stochasticity is exploited for reaction duration as well as reaction selection. Grid Systems perform reactions in maximally parallel manner, imitating natural processes. Environmental events that change population behaviour can be defined in Grid Systems as rewrite rules.

A population model of a species of mosquitoes, *Aedes albopictus*, is presented. The model considers three types of external events: temperature change, rainfall, and desiccation. The events change the behaviour of the species directly or indirectly. Each individual in the population can move around in the ecosystem. The simulation of the model was performed by using a semantics based tool.

1 Introduction

An important component of Sustainable Development, sometimes called Ecologically Sustainable Development, is the use of strategies and measures to prevent environmental degradation [1]. A critical aspect of the use of preventive strategies and measures is the evaluation of their effectiveness as well as their global long-term impact on the ecosystem. In this respect, ecological modelling may represent an important tool to compare the effect of alternative prevention measures before they are implemented in the actual ecosystem.

Ecological modelling requires analytical tools able to deal with the representation of complex real world parameters. Among them we can cite parameters depending on environment characteristics (light, humidity, presence or absence of water, ...) and parameters depending on periodic or non-periodic events (temperature, level of water bodies,...). Thus, formalisms designed for ecological computational modelling should provide mechanisms for representing the influence of these parameters on the model outcome. Recently, some new formalisms were introduced [2,20,26,33]. Many of them were inspired by biological phenomena

A. Cerone et al. (Eds.): SEFM 2012 Satellite Events, LNCS 7991, pp. 172–189, 2014.
DOI: 10.1007/978-3-642-54338-8_14, © Springer-Verlag Berlin Heidelberg 2014

such as cells structure [31] and DNA chains [3]. Some were intended as new computing paradigms and others were defined to provide biologists with a modelling framework for analysing phenomena. For instance, stochastic P Systems [10] and BlenX [12,21], a modelling language inspired by π-calculus, along with its interface language LIME, have been used to model population dynamics. However, none of these works takes spatiality into account. In fact, most of the formalisms designed for describing biological systems were tailored for specific applications, thus lacking features for representing all the parameters that are crucial for modelling ecological systems.

In this paper we present a new formalism, *Grid Systems*, inspired by concepts of Membrane Computing (P Systems) [28,31]. A Grid System consists of an envelop compartment (the outer membrane) containing a grid of adjacent inner compartments (inner membranes). Each inner membrane is characterized by its position in the grid, and, as in P Systems, owns its rules and objects. Rules are applied with maximal parallelism and can be promoted or inhibited by objects in the system. The outer membrane has rules too, which represent events common to the entire Grid System. Differently from standard P Systems, the application of Grid System rules has a duration, which can be different for each rule.

Grid Systems can easily model the heterogeneity of environments. Each membrane in the grid may represent a distinct part of the environment with specific parameters and behavioural rules. Rules can move objects across membranes, thus describing the migration of resources or individuals. To illustrate these features, we use Grid Systems to model the ecology of the Asian tiger mosquito (*Aedes albopictus*). Spatiality aspect, such as the movement of individual mosquitos are described as movement among grid's cells.

The paper is organized as follows. Section 2 formally introduces Grid Systems and discusses some features such as stochasticity and spatiality. Section 3 shows how to use Grid Systems for illustrative model of mosquito. Finally, Sect. 4 reports the results of stochastic simulations performed using our model.

2   The Grid Systems

Several existing formalisms for modelling concurrent as well as biological systems embody the concepts of spatiality and stochasticity [4,9,18,20,22,23,25,30–34].

P Systems (Membrane Computing) are appropriate for ecological modelling for their ability in describing dynamics at object level as reactions: each reaction performs its action according to the principle of maximal parallelism [31]. Formal semantics of P Systems have been defined in [5–7]. Pardini extended P Systems with spatiality [28], but the introduced concept deals with objects position, which cannot easily represent environment heterogeneity. Cellular Automata have the ability of describing systems in which the dynamics can vary spatially according to local/neighbouring situations [2,27,35]. Grid Systems combine features of P-systems and Cellular Automata in order to model ecological systems. The independence of events occurring at the same time is modelled by maximal parallelism, while different zones of the environment are modelled by adjacent membranes, like cells in a Cellular Automaton. A variant of Gillespie's Stochastic Simulation Algorithm [15,16] is used to model stochasticity.

2.1 Syntax

Definition 1. *A Grid System* $G(N, M, \Sigma, R, A, C^{(0)})$ *is defined as follows:*

- *G is the grid name;*
- *N and M are two integers indicating that G has $N \times M$ cells, also called local membranes;*
- *Σ is the alphabet of object types;*
- *R is a set of transition rules;*
- *A is the set of associations of the rules with the membranes, i.e.*

$$A = \{(\rho, \gamma) \mid \rho \in R, \ \gamma \in \{G_{i,j} | 0 \leq i < N, \ 0 \leq j < M\} \cup \{G_E\}\};$$

   where
       - *$G_{i,j}$, with $0 \leq i < N$ and $0 \leq j < M$, denotes the cell in position (i, j);*
       - *G_E is the global membrane surrounding the cells;*
- *$C^{(0)}$ is the initial configuration of the grid.*

A graphical representation of a Grid System is illustrated in Fig. 1. The global membrane describes the environment and is represented by a dashed square. Local membranes are represented by a grid of squares. The two associations $(r_k, G_{3,1})$ and $(r_k, G_{2,3})$ in Fig. 1 indicate that r_k is applicable in local membranes $G_{3,1}$ and $G_{2,3}$.

A transition rule, or a rule for short, defines how a reaction can be performed in its associated membrane. Therefore a reaction is an instance of a rule.

Definition 2. *A transition rule* $\rho : \alpha \xrightarrow{c,\pi} \beta \ [\psi \mid \chi]$ *is defined as follows:*

- *ρ is the unique identifier of the rule;*
- *α is a non-empty multiset of reactants;*
- *β is a multiset of products;*
- *ψ is a multiset of promoters;*
- *χ is a multiset of inhibitors;*
- *$c \in \mathbb{R}^+$ is the rate with which the rule may be applied to perform a reaction.*
- *$\pi \in \{M, D\}$, with M indicating that the elapsed time of the rule is an exponential random variable with parameter c, and D indicating that the elapsed time of the rule is exactly $1/c$.*

Reactants must be in the membrane with which the rule is associated, promoters and inhibitors may be in any membrane, and products can be sent into any membrane. Note that the positions of promoters, inhibitors and products can be either absolute or relative to the current membrane.

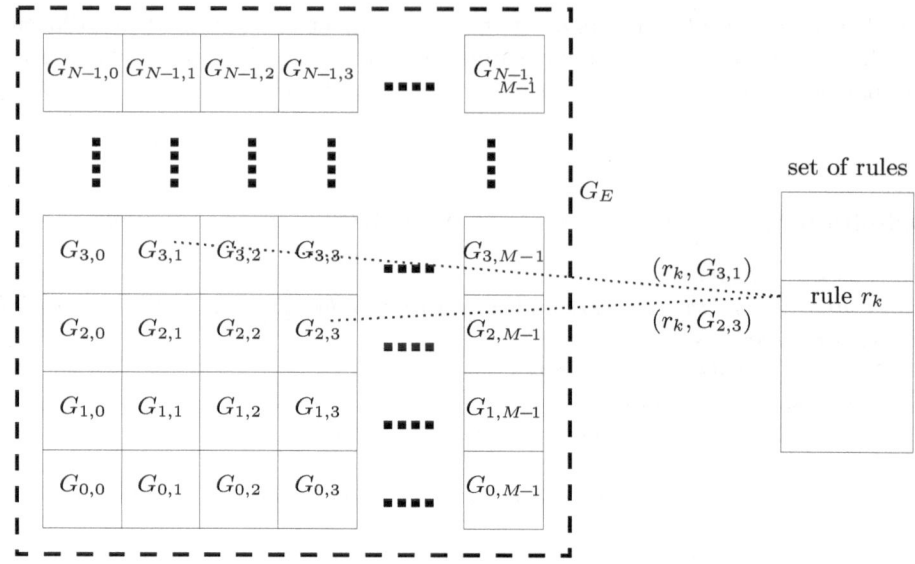

Fig. 1. Grid of membranes and association of rules with membranes

In the rest of the paper we will be using the following notations:

- $[m]_{G_A}$ refers to a membrane $m \in \{G_{i,j} | 0 \le i < N, 0 \le j < M\} \cup \{G_E\}$ of Grid System G_A;
- $[m]$ can be used instead of $[m]_{G_A}$ when the name of the Grid System is obvious from the context;
- $\alpha(r)$ is the multiset of reactants required by rule r;
- $\beta(r)$ is the multiset of products given by rule r;
- $\psi(r)$ is the multiset of promoters required by rule r;
- $\chi(r)$ is the multiset of inhibitors of rule r;
- $Assoc(r)$ is the set of membranes that are associated with reaction r;
- $Assoc([m])$ is the set of rules that are associated with membrane $[m]$.

The multiset of n instances of object a in membrane $G_{i,j}$ is denoted by $a_{i,j}^n$. An alternative notation for $a_{i,j}^n$ is $(a, n, G_{i,j})$. Analogously n instances of object a in membrane $[m]_{G_A}$, or $[m]$ for short, is denoted by $(a, n, [m]_{G_A})$, or by $(a, n, [m])$ for short. Finally, for a promoter, inhibitor or product a of a rule, $a_{\langle \pm v, \pm h \rangle}$ denotes that a is in $G_{i \pm v, j \pm h}$, being $G_{i,j}$ the cell in which the rule is applied; thus a can be seen as short form for $a_{\langle +0, +0 \rangle}$.

2.2   Semantics

The evolution over time of a Grid System starts from an initial configuration $C^{(0)}$ to be defined by the modeller. The system evolves passing through a trajectory of configurations $C^{(0)}, C^{(t_1)}, C^{(t_2)}, ...$, where, $0 \le t_1 \le t_2....$ An evolution step at time t_k consists in a maximally parallel application of rules to available objects in all membranes of the system. In order to apply a rule, reactants have to be present among available objects. Application of rules with maximal parallelism means that several rules can be applied (also more than once) to different objects in the same evolution step until no further rule is applicable. Because rules have a duration, reactants of the applied rules become committed objects of the configuration, and they remain committed until the completion of the rules. For each applied rule a termination time is computed and a new entry in the list of ongoing reactions $\Omega^{(t_k)}$ is created.

Once all applied rules of the current evolution step have been handled, the set of rules to be completed first, $\{(r_i, t, [m_i])$ such that t is minimal in $\Omega^{(t_k)}\}$, is extracted from $\Omega^{(t_k)}$. Rules in this set are the next ongoing reaction to be completed in membrane $[m]$, and t is the time of the next evolution step, namely $t_{k+1} = t$. Completion of reactions consists in the removal of its reactants from the committed objects and in the addition of the products to the available objects. Note that if there exist in $\Omega^{(t_k)}$ several ongoing reactions associated with the same time t all of these will be extracted and handled. Subsequently, the procedure is repeated to perform the next evolution step.

Definition 3. *A Configuration $C^{(t)}$ is a pair*

$$(\{C^{(t)}_{[m]}| \ m \in \{G_{i,j}|0 \le i < N, 0 \le j < M\} \cup \{G_E\}\}, \Omega^{(t)})$$

where

- *$C^{(t)}_{[m]}$ is the multiset over objects that exist inside membrane $[m]$ at time t;*
- *$\Omega^{(t)} = \{(r_k, t_k, [m_k])|k = 1, ..., n$ and $t \le t_1 \le ... \le t_n\}$ is the set of ongoing reactions where each $(r_k, t_k, [m_k])$, $k = 1, ..., n$, denotes ongoing reactions that instantiate rule r_k in membrane $[m_k]$ and will terminate at time t_k.*

Moreover,

- *$Committed^{(t)}_{[m]}$ denotes objects of $C^{(t)}_{[m]}$ that are committed to any of the $(r_k, t_k, [m_k]) \in \Omega^{(t)}$ such that $m = m_k$;*
- *$Avail^{(t)}_{[m]} = C^{(t)}_{[m]} \setminus Committed^{(t)}_{[m]}$.*

Given a transition rule r and a membrane $[m]$ of a configuration $C^{(t)}$, let $applicable(r, [m])$ be a predicate that holds if and only if r is applicable in membrane $[m]$. Formally:

$$applicable(r, [m]) = \alpha(r) \subseteq Avail^{(t)}_{[m]}$$
$$\wedge \ \forall(a, n, [p]) \in \psi(r).a^n \subseteq (Avail^{(t)}_{[p]} \cup Committed^{(t)}_{[p]})$$
$$\wedge \ \forall(a, n, [q]) \in \chi(r).a^n \not\subseteq (Avail^{(t)}_{[q]} \cup Committed^{(t)}_{[q]})$$

Note that both available and committed objects can provide promoters and inhibitors.

2.2.1   Evolution Algorithm

The evolution of a Grid System starts from a given initial configuration $C^{(0)}$ in which $\Omega^{(0)}$ is assumed to be an empty list.

Given a configuration $C^{(t_k)}$ at time t_k, the evolution step giving $C^{(t_{k+1})}$ as result is obtained by performing the following steps (where $+$ and $-$ denote multiset union and subtraction, respectively):

– Step-1: For each membrane $[m]$, compute a maximal multiset $Cand([m])$ of candidate reactions (transition rule instances) over $Assoc([m])$. Each reaction in $Cand([m])$ must be an instance of an applicable rule, namely $Cand([m]) \subseteq \{r \mid applicable(r, [m])\}$. Maximality is defined as follows: let $\alpha(Cand[m]) = \bigcup_{r \in Cand([m])} \alpha(r)$, it must hold:

$$\forall r \in Assoc([m]).$$
$$\left(applicable(r, [m]) \implies \alpha(r) \not\subseteq (Avail_{[m]} - \alpha(Cand([m])))\right)$$

Namely, it must be impossible to apply any rule to the objects to which no candidate reaction is applied.

– Step-2: For each membrane $[m]$, perform each reaction $r \in Cand([m])$ by changing the states of its reactants from available to committed. Compute the duration of the reaction $elapsed(r)$ as will be described later in Subsect. 2.2.2. Insert into $\Omega^{(t_k)}$ the new tuple $(r, term(r), [m])$, where $term(r) = t_k + elapsed(r)$. Formally, for each $r \in Cand([m])$ perform the following assignments:

$$Avail_{[m]} := Avail_{[m]} - \alpha(r)$$
$$Committed_{[m]} := Committed_{[m]} + \alpha(r)$$
$$term(r) := t_k + elapsed(r)$$
$$\Omega^{(t_k)} := \text{insert } (r, term(r), [m]) \text{ into } \Omega^{(t_k)}$$

– Step-3: Compute the multiset $First(\Omega^{(t_k)})$ of earliest reactions to terminate in $\Omega^{(t_k)}$. This set is formally defined as follows:

$$First(\Omega^{(t_k)}) = \{(r_i, t, [m_i]) \mid (r_i, t, [m_i]) \in \Omega^{(t_k)} \text{ and}$$
$$\forall(r', t', [m']) \in \Omega^{(t_k)}.t \leq t'\}$$

– Step-4: For each reaction $(r_i, t, [m_i]) \in First(\Omega^{(t_k)})$, remove its reactants from the committed objects, add its products to the available objects (by taking into account the target membrane of each product) and remove the corresponding entry from $\Omega^{(t_k)}$. Formally, for each $(r_i, t, [m_i]) \in First(\Omega^{(t_k)})$ perform the following assignments, where $[m]$ is the membrane associated with r:

$$Committed_{[m]} := Committed_{[m]} - \alpha(r)$$
$$\forall(a, n, [p]) \in \beta(r).Avail_{[p]} := Avail_{[p]} + a^n$$
$$\Omega^{(t_k)} := \text{remove } (r, t, [m]) \text{ from } \Omega^{(t_k)}$$

– Step-5: Let t_{k+1} be the termination time t associated with reactions in $First(\Omega^{(t_k)})$ in Step-3. The configuration obtained after the assignments in the previous steps has to be considered as configuration $C^{t_{k+1}}$ to be used in the next evolution step.

If $\Omega^{(t_{k+1})}$ is empty and for each membrane $[m]$ no rule is applicable in $C^{(t_{k+1})}$ (namely $\forall[m].Cand[m] = \emptyset$) then the evolution terminates with $C^{t_{k+1}}$ as final configuration.

We remark that in Step-2 and in Step-4 of the algorithm the state of a reactant is changed from being available to being committed then to being removed. During its committed state, a reactant cannot be involved in other reactions as a reactant, but it can still affect any reaction as promoter or inhibitor.

2.2.2 Stochasticity and Reaction Duration

The Grid Systems enable stochasticity in two aspects: resolving non-deterministic choices and computing reaction elapsed times.

Nondeterministic choices may arise when some possible reactions from different rules are conflicting/competing to consume the same available objects as their reactants. In this case, reaction propensities are computed as in Gillespie's Stochastic Simulation Algorithm (SSA) as follows: for each reaction r, assume $a_r(t) = h_r(t)c_r$, where, c_r is the rate of the rule r and $h_r(t)$ is the number of different combination of reactants that can be taken from available objects at the time t. The reactions to be applied are then randomly chosen with a probability proportional to their propensities.

When a reaction r is selected to be included in $Cand([m])$, its duration $elapsed(r)$ has to be computed in Step-2 of the algorithm. The way in which $elapsed(r)$ is computed depends on the parameter π of the transition rule:

– For fixed elapsed time ('D' in the rule notation), $elapsed(r) = 1/c$, where c is the rule's rate.
– For exponentially distributed time ('M' in the rule notation), $elapsed(r)$ is an exponential random number with rate c.

This exponential random number can be generated be using the inverse method, i.e., $elapsed(r) = -1/c \log(X)$, where X is a uniform random number from the interval $[0, 1)$.

2.2.3 Discrete Time Approximation

In a Grid System consisting mostly of rules with exponentially distributed duration there is a very small probability of having more than one reaction in $First(\Omega^{(t_k)})$. Stochasticity will cause reactions to terminate at different times, and consequently at each evolution step a single terminating reaction is handled.

In this situation the Evolution Algorithm of Grid Systems from the efficiency viewpoint behaves similarly to Gillespie's SSA (in which one reaction per step is handled). Several approximated variants of Gillespie's SSA have been proposed to improve performances [14,17,24,29]. However, such approximations are not applicable to Grid Systems because of the differences in rule selection of the latter due to maximal parallelism.

For the sake of improving simulation performances we consider a simple approximation approach for Grid Systems that consists in discretizing the simulation time. In particular, we assume time to consist of a sequence of time intervals of a fixed duration. All reactions terminating in the same time interval are then considered as terminating at the same time. This causes a simulation error proportional to the duration of the time interval.

Given an interval length δ_t, the discrete time approximation can be included in the Evolution Algorithm by replacing the definition of $First(\Omega^{(t_k)})$ in Step-3 with the following new definition:

$$First(\Omega^{(t_k)}) = \{(r,t,[m]) \mid (r,t,[m]) \in \Omega^{(t_k)} \text{ and}$$
$$\forall(r',t',[m']) \in \Omega^{(t_k)}.(t \leq t' \text{ or } SameTime(t,t'))\}$$

where $SameTime(t,t')$ is $true$ when $\exists k \in I^+$, such that $k\delta_t \leq t, t' < (k+1)\delta_t$.

Moreover, the assignment to $\Omega^{(t_k)}$ in Step-4 of the evolution algorithm has to be modified as follows:

$$\Omega^{(t_k)} := \text{remove } (r,t',[m]) \text{ from } \Omega^{(t_k)} \text{ s.t. } SameTime(t,t') = true.$$

The interval length should be defined as a trade off between simulation performance and its precision.

2.3 Additional Notation

To ease the writing of the model by using the formalism of Grid Systems some additional notation is introduced:

Region. A group of local membranes may be identified as a region, and rules can be associated to regions. Therefore, for region R, membrane $[m]$ and rule r:
if $[m] \in R$, and $r \in Assoc(R)$, then $r \in Assoc([m])$.

Constant. A constant is an identifier that can be associated with a value (either number or string). Constants provide values to variables used within rule templates.

Rule Template. Rules with similar structures may be identified as a single template containing one or more template variables $\langle X \rangle$, each representing a finite set of values. Rules can be obtained by instantiating each $\langle X \rangle$ in the body of the template with one of its possible values.

3 Modelling: *Aedes albopictus*

3.1 Population Behaviour

Species may be potential vectors for diseases or they may be considered as endangered. Both situations are likely to have a negative impact on the ecosystem to which these species belong. It is therefore important to develop strategies to control disease vectors and preserve endangered species. Modelling population dynamics provides a way to test and compare alternative strategies and support the process of defining and implementing policies in population control and reintroduction biology.

Models of population dynamics range from differential equation to general stochastic models [11]. Recently, Bearded Vulture population was modelled using P Systems [10] where a probability measure was attached to each rule in a Markov Chain model. *Aedes albopictus* population was modelled using Stochastic CLS [8].

Some species might be endemic in one wide area due to specific local conditions that affect population behaviour spatially. Spatiality based on Cellular Automata was used for computing population coverage on a specific area [27].

Aedes albopictus, also known as Asian tiger mosquito, is a mosquito species that originated from Asia [13,19]. This species is an important subject of study since it is well-known as vector of some deadly pathogens, such as the West Nile virus, Yellow fever virus, St. Louis encephalitis, Dengue fever and Chikungunya fever. *Aedes albopictus* life-cycle has 4 phases: egg, larval, pupa, and adult [19].

Our model consists of a simple mosquito life cycle: an egg becomes an immature (first larva, then pupa), which becomes an adult. The ecosystem affects the population in terms of volume of water containers and temperature. Temperature affects the population behaviour directly by changing reaction rates. Higher temperatures will increase the rates of the transition in the life cycle. Temperature affects the population indirectly by changing desiccation rate of water in the containers. Temperature in the environment may increase or decrease through temperature change events. Water volume in the environment may increase or decrease through rainfall events.

3.2 Formal Model

We consider a 5×5 *grid* to model the space where the mosquito population lives. However, the actual movement area is 3×3. Additional rows (top and bottom) and columns (leftmost and rightmost) are set for isolating the movement area. Access to these additional cells is denied to mosquito by an initial state in which such cells contain inhibitor Z. We assume that only the central cell contains water, although we do not model how the water is distributed within the cell (e.g. uniformly or in separate containers).

We use *object E* to represents eggs, I to represent immatures and A to represent adults. The environment state is defined by the temperature level and the quantity of water. Temperature is represented by the number of objects T located in the global membrane and the quantity of water is represented by the number of objects W located in central cell $G_{2,2}$.

Environmental state may change depending on events that are either continuously triggered by the environmental state itself or are scheduled to occur at specific times. For instance, desiccation is a continuous event triggered by temperature and quantity of water while rainfall and temperature change are scheduled events. Objects $Rain100$ and $Rain200$ represent light rain and heavy rain, respectively; their affect the environment by increasing the quantity of water (number of objects W). Objects $TempUp1$ and $TempUp2$ represent increases of temperature of two different scales. Objects $TempDwn1$ and $TempDwn2$ represent decreases of temperature of two different scales. They modify the number of objects T.

We consider the following *regions*.

- $MovingSpace = \{G_{1,1}, G_{1,2}, G_{1,3}, G_{2,1}, G_{2,2}, G_{2,3}, G_{3,1}, G_{3,]}, G_{3,3}\}$ consists of all cells that adult mosquitoes may access.
- $WaterContainer = \{G_{2,2}\}$ is the central cell.
- $Boundary = \{G_{0,0}, G_{0,1}, G_{0,2}, G_{0,3}, G_{0,4}, G_{1,0}, G_{1,4}, G_{2,0}, G_{2,4}, G_{3,0}, G_{3,4}, G_{4,0}, G_{4,1}, G_{4,2}, G_{4,3}, G_{4,4}\}$ consists of the boundary cells, inaccessible to mosquitoes.

In Sects. 3.2.1 and 3.2.2 we define the rules that model the dynamics of our ecosystems. Such rules are written using templates. Table 1 shows the constants that instantiate the variables used in templates.

Table 1. Constants that instantiate the variables used in templates

$\langle L \rangle$	1	2	3	4
$Prom\langle L \rangle$	λ	T_E	T_E^3	T_E^5
$Inh\langle L \rangle$	T_E	T_E^3	T_E^5	λ
$Hatchrate\langle L \rangle$	0.3	0.4	0.45	0.5
$Failrate\langle L \rangle$	0.3	0.4	0.45	0.5
$Metarate\langle L \rangle$	0.1	0.2	0.5	1.0
$Deathimrate\langle L \rangle$	0.2	0.25	0.3	0.35
$Deathadrate\langle L \rangle$	0.4	0.45	0.5	0.55
$Ovirate\langle L \rangle$	0.1	0.2	0.33	0.5
$Desicrate\langle L \rangle$	0.75	1.0	1.5	2.5

3.2.1 Population Dynamics

In this section we introduce the rule templates that define the dynamics of *Aedes albopictus* population. Dependence of rates on temperature is expressed by combining instantiations of variables $Prom\langle L \rangle$ (promoters) and $Inh\langle L \rangle$ (inhibitors), which define ranges of temperature, and instantiations of variable for rates, as shown in Table 1.

Hatched eggs become immature mosquitoes. Reaction rate depend on temperature. Egg hatching is modelled by the following rule template.

$$\forall \langle L \rangle \in \{1, 2, 3, 4\}. \; Hatch\langle L \rangle : E \xrightarrow{\;hatchrate\langle L \rangle, M\;} I \; [\, Prom\langle L \rangle | Inh\langle L \rangle \,]$$

if $Hatch\langle L \rangle \in Assoc(WaterContainer)$.

If we consider the following instantiations of the above template for $L = 1, 2$, according to the constants in Table 1,

$$Hatch1 : E \xrightarrow{0.3,M} I \quad [\lambda | T_E] \quad and \quad Hatch2 : E \xrightarrow{0.4,M} I \quad [T_E | T_E^3]$$

we can observe that a temperature up to T_E corresponds to rate 0.3 for rule $Hatch1$ and a higher temperature, over T_E and below T_E^3, corresponds to higher rate 0.4 for rule $Hatch2$.

Eggs failing to hatch are modelled by the following rule template, whose death rate depends on temperature.

$$\forall \langle L \rangle \in \{1, 2, 3, 4\}.\ Fail\langle L \rangle : \quad E \xrightarrow{failrate\langle L \rangle, M} \lambda \quad [Prom\langle L \rangle | Inh\langle L \rangle]$$

if $Fail\langle L \rangle \in Assoc(WaterContainer)$.

When water level is extremely low (below a minimum threshold) eggs may die due to dehydration. Moreover, when water level is extremely high (above or equal a maximum threshold) eggs may be flooded away.

$$DryE : \quad E \xrightarrow{8.000,M} \lambda \quad [\lambda | W^{500}]$$
$$FloodE : E \xrightarrow{8.000,M} \lambda \quad [W^{1500} | \lambda]$$

if $DryE, FloodE \in Assoc(WaterContainer)$.

In this rule template the maximum threshold W^{500} for dehydration is modelled as an inhibitor and the minimum threshold W^{1500} for flooding is modelled as a promoter. Here rates are much higher than 0.5 and dominate the effect of $Hatch\langle L \rangle$ and $Fail\langle L \rangle$ rules above.

Immature mosquitoes may become adult with a rate that depends on temperature.

$$\forall \langle L \rangle \in \{1, 2, 3, 4\}.\ Meta\langle L \rangle : \quad I \xrightarrow{metarate\langle L \rangle 0, M} A \quad [Prom\langle L \rangle | Inh\langle L \rangle]$$

if $Meta\langle L \rangle \in Assoc(WaterContainer)$.

Immature mosquito failing to become an adult are modelled by the following rule template, whose rate depends on temperature.

$$\forall \langle L \rangle \in \{1, 2, 3, 4\}.\ DeathI\langle L \rangle : \quad I \xrightarrow{deathimrate\langle L \rangle, M} \lambda \quad [Prom\langle L \rangle | Inh\langle L \rangle]$$

if $DeathI\langle L \rangle \in Assoc(WaterContainer)$.

Moreover, immature mosquitoes may be either flooded away or dehydrated by extreme water conditions.

$$DryI : \quad I \xrightarrow{8.000,M} \lambda \quad [\lambda | W^{500}]$$
$$FloodI : I \xrightarrow{8.000,M} \lambda \quad [W^{1500} | \lambda]$$

if $DryI, FloodI \in Assoc(WaterContainer)$.

Mosquitoes may either move from one cell to one of its four adjacent cells or remain in the initial cell. Boundary cells cannot be entered.

$$Move1 : A \xrightarrow{0.500, M} A_{\langle -1, +0 \rangle} \quad [\lambda | Z_{\langle -1, +0 \rangle}]$$

$$Move2 : A \xrightarrow{0.500, M} A_{\langle +0, -1 \rangle} \quad [\lambda | Z_{\langle +0, -1 \rangle}]$$

$$Move3 : A \xrightarrow{0.500, M} A_{\langle +0, +1 \rangle} \quad [\lambda | Z_{\langle +0, +1 \rangle}]$$

$$Move4 : A \xrightarrow{0.500, M} A_{\langle +1, +0 \rangle} \quad [\lambda | Z_{\langle +1, +0 \rangle}]$$

$$Move5 : A \xrightarrow{0.500, M} A$$

if $Move1, Move2, Move3, Move4, Move5 \in Assoc(MovingSpace)$.

For example, $Move1$ models the movement of object A to the cell immediately to the left of the cell where the rule is applied (from $A = A_{\langle +0, +0 \rangle}$ to $A_{\langle -1, +0 \rangle}$), provided that the arrival cell does not contain inhibitor Z ($Z_{\langle -1, +0 \rangle}$).

Adults may lay eggs only in the cell containing water. We assume that every individual lays exactly 20 eggs.

$$\forall \langle L \rangle \in \{1, 2, 3, 4\}. \quad Ovi\langle L \rangle : \quad A \xrightarrow{ovirate\langle L \rangle, M} A \, E^{20} \quad [W \, Prom\langle L \rangle \mid Inh\langle L \rangle]$$

if $Ovi\langle L \rangle \in Assoc(WaterContainer)$.

Adult death rate depends on temperature.

$$\forall \langle L \rangle \in \{1, 2, 3, 4\}. \quad DeathA\langle L \rangle : \quad A \xrightarrow{deathadrate\langle L \rangle, M} \lambda \, [Prom\langle L \rangle | Inh\langle L \rangle]$$

if $DeathA\langle L \rangle \in Assoc(MovingSpace)$.

3.2.2 Environment Dynamics

Desiccation is a continuously occurring event that decreases the volume of water according to a desiccation factor. Such factor depends on temperature. We assume that a desiccation event decreases the quantity of water by 4 %. This is modelled in the following rule template by removing one object W out of 25.

$$\forall \langle L \rangle \in \{1, 2, 3, 4\}. \quad Desic\langle L \rangle : W^{25} \xrightarrow{desicrate\langle L \rangle, M} W^{24} \, [Prom\langle L \rangle | Inh\langle L \rangle]$$

if $Desic\langle L \rangle \in Assoc(WaterContainer)$.

Scheduled events, such as rainfalls and temperature changes, are defined by rules that consume dummy object that are in the initial environmental state and produce rain or temperature change objects. In this way, if the rule deterministically spends time t to consume the dummy object, then the rain or temperature change object is produced exactly at the scheduled time t. Once the dummy object is produced, the rule that has produced it is disabled forever. For example, a high increase of temperature ($TempUp2$) at time $\langle S \rangle$ is modelled by the following rule template

$$\forall \langle S \rangle \in \mathbb{N}. \quad SchedTempUp2\langle S \rangle : TempUp2At\langle S \rangle \xrightarrow{1/\langle S \rangle, D} TempUp2$$

if $SchedTempUp2\langle S \rangle \in Assoc(G_E)$.

Exactly one dummy object $TempUp2At\langle S\rangle$ in the initial state enables rule $SchedTempUp2\langle S\rangle$ just once at time $\langle S\rangle$, thus producing temperature increase object $TempUp2$ at time $\langle S\rangle$.

For simplicity we assume that each rainfall lasts 1/5 of a day (4.8 h) and that water flows away without being collected in all cells apart from central cell $G_{2,2}$.

$$\forall\langle V\rangle \in \{100, 200\}.SchedRain\langle V\rangle : Rain\langle V\rangle \xrightarrow{5,D} W_{2,2}^{\langle V\rangle}$$

if $SchedRain\langle S\rangle \in Assoc(G_E)$.

The number of objects T represents four temperature thresholds as shown by the values for promoter and inhibitor variables in Table 1. We model two possible decrement or increment of temperature using the following rule templates

$$\forall\langle C\rangle \in \{1,2\}.\ SchedTempDwn\langle C\rangle : TempDwn\langle C\rangle\ T^{\langle C\rangle} \xrightarrow{10,D} \lambda$$
$$SchedTempUp\langle C\rangle :\ \ TempUp\langle C\rangle \xrightarrow{\ 10,D\ } T^{\langle C\rangle}$$

if $SchedTempDwn\langle C\rangle, SchedTempUp\langle C\rangle \in Assoc(G_E)$.

4   Model Simulation

A running prototype for simulating the model was developed using Java. The input is a system model defined using Grid Systems; the output is the population size. Values are tabulated in text format, which can then be fed to a data visualiser or a charting tool, such as MS Excel for previewing or TikZ for embedding it inside a LaTeX document (as we did in this paper).

4.1   Results

Data in Figs. 2, 3, 4 were produced by a simulation with initial objects: 2000 eggs, 1000 immatures and 400 adults.

The simulation run for 190 time units (i.e. 190 days) using data for temperature and rainfalls collected in the period May–November 2009 in the province of Massa-Carrara (Tuscany, Italy). By running the simulation several times (using the same initial objects), it was observed that shapes of output curves presents only small differences. Differences become smaller for larger numbers of initial objects (e.g., 4000 eggs, 2000 immatures and 800 adults) and bigger for smaller numbers of initial objects (e.g., 50 eggs, 30 immatures and 20 adults).

Figure 5 shows the plot of sampling data collected during May–November 2009 in the province of Massa-Carrara using 11 CO_2 mosquito traps.

Spatiality representation can be appreciated by considering the number of adults in each cell. Since the spatial model is very simple this number tends to be stable over time, i.e. forming a bell shape distribution, unless extreme conditions of the environment occur. In our model the water level directly affects the number of eggs and immatures, and consequently, after some delay, the number of adults.

The simulation was performed using a PC (Pentium D 3 GHz, 1 GB RAM, Windows XP SP3), for about 32 s. By doubling each time the initial population the simulation takes respectively 47, 70, 100, 155 s.

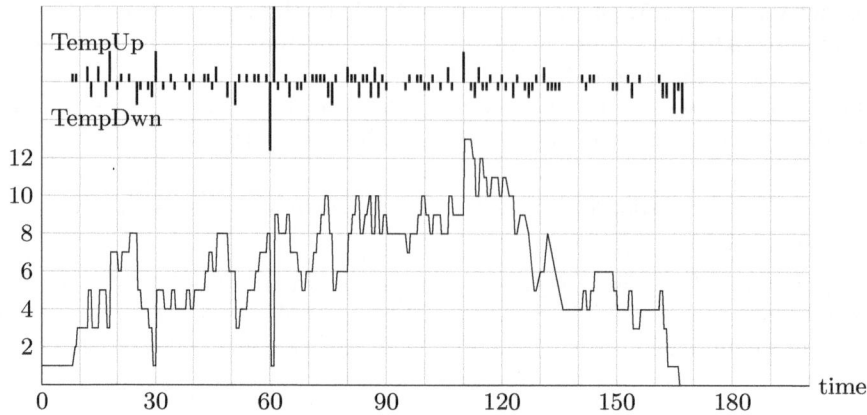

Fig. 2. Temperature level fluctuation

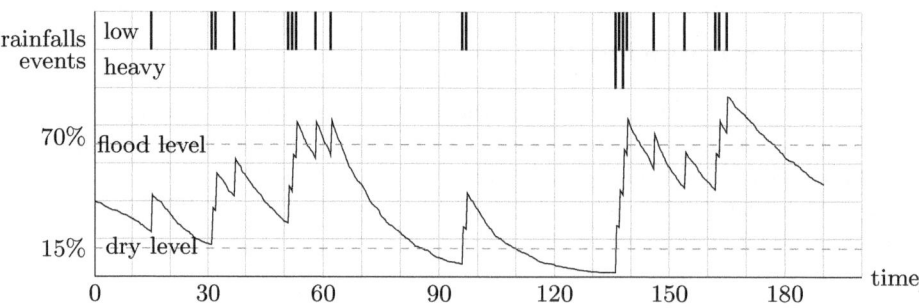

Fig. 3. Water level fluctuation due to desiccation and rainfalls

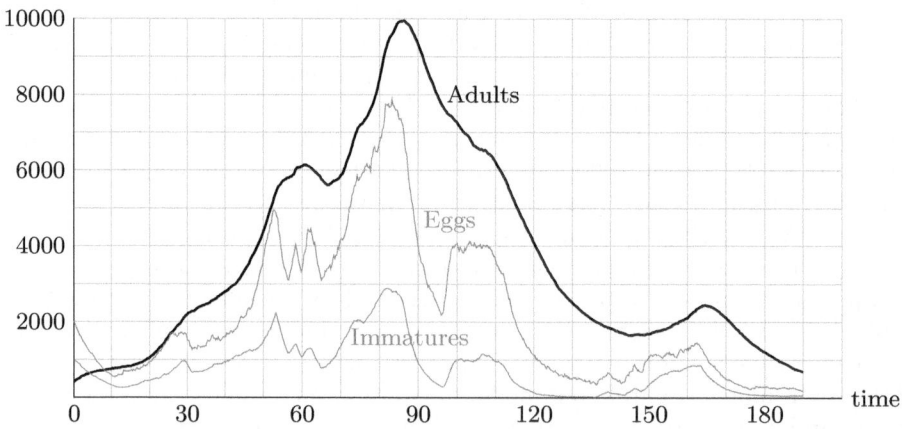

Fig. 4. Population growth: adult mosquitos, immature mosquitos (Pupae/Larvae) and their eggs

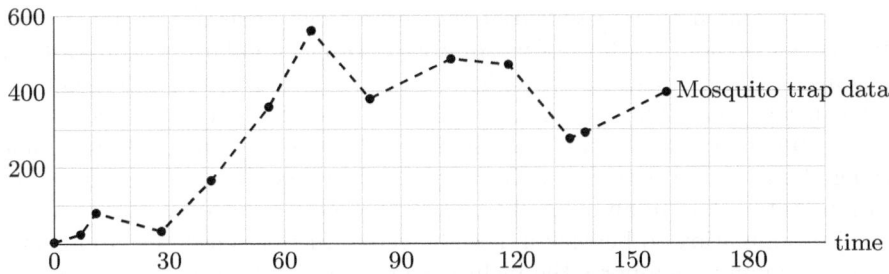

Fig. 5. Plot of CO_2 trap data: number of adults

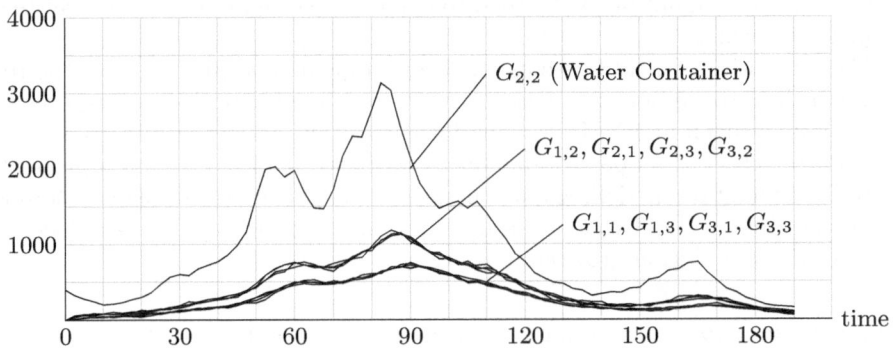

Fig. 6. Spatial distribution of adult mosquitoes over time

5 Conclusion and Future Work

Grid Systems, a new formalism for modelling population dynamics, has been presented. It supports modelling of spatiality in terms of cells in a grid. Objects may move between cells. Spatiality dynamics is obtained through transition rules. Location or time may change the applicability of rules. Grid Systems consider two aspects of stochasticity: choice and duration of rules. The enabling of rules depends on the presence/absence of promoters/inhibitors.

We have illustrated the use of Grid Systems by modelling the dynamics of an *Aedes albopictus* population. Although our model of biological aspects of the mosquito population is simpler than the model developed by Basuki *et al.* [8], the use of spatiality address a wider range of practical applications.

In our simple case study spatiality is used to model an isolated area (e.g., an island), which mosquitoes cannot enter or exit. This spatiality aspect is modelled by using *boundary cells*, which do not contain mosquitoes but, instead, contain inhibitors that prevent rules from moving mosquitoes into them. A more sophisticated use of promoters and inhibitors could support the modelling of occasional or regular flows of individuals between specific areas. For example, mosquitoes may occasionally move beyond their flight range carried inside vehicles; however, when there is a considerable traffic of vehicles between two specific areas (e.g., daily traffic between residential and commercial areas or through a bridge between two islands) the flow of mosquitoes becomes regular and facilitates the spreading of diseases associated with the vector. More generally, human movement can also contribute to the spreading of diseases carried by mosquitoes, even in absence of movement of mosquitoes beyond their flying range. Blood sucking of an infected human coming from an area where the disease is endemic by a mosquito living in an area where the disease is absent may cause the local mosquito population to become a disease vector. In this sense, our approach to spatiality dynamics supports the inclusion in the ecosystem model of aspects of the interaction between mosquito population and human population. This makes our approach suitable not only for analysis of population dynamics but also for epidemiological simulation. We intend to explore this capability of Grid Systems in our future work.

The semantics of Grid Systems has been implemented into a prototype tool written in Java to support simulation. The current version of the tool requires the model to be written in a XML tagging format to take advantages of using Javax XML Parser classes. As part of our future work we plan to develop a graphical interface to facilitate modelling and simulation control as well as display modules to provide direct visualisation through spatial animation and to produce the charts of the population growths.

Acknowledgments. This work has been supported partly by UNU-IIST and partly by Macao Science and Technology Development Fund, File No. 07/2009/A3, in the context of the EAE project. Suryana Setiawan is supported by a PhD scholarship under I-MHERE Project of the Faculty of Computer Science, University of Indonesia (IBRD Loan No. 4789-IND & IDA Credit No. 4077-IND, Ministry of Education and Culture, Republic of Indonesia).

References

1. Rio Declaration on Environment and Development. United Nations Conference on Environment and Development (UNCED), Rio de Janeiro, Brazil (1992)
2. Adamatzky, A.: Identification of Cellular Automata. Taylor and Francis, London (1994)
3. Barbuti, R., Caravagna, G., Maggiolo-Schettini, A., Milazzo, P., Pardini, G.: The calculus of looping sequences. In: Bernardo, M., Degano, P., Zavattaro, G. (eds.) SFM 2008. LNCS, vol. 5016, pp. 387–423. Springer, Heidelberg (2008)
4. Barbuti, R., Maggiolo-Schettini, A., Milazzo, P., Pardini, G., Rama, A.: A process calculus for molecular interaction maps. In: Membrane Computing and Biologically Inspired Process Calculi (MeCBIC), pp. 35–49 (2009)
5. Barbuti, R., Maggiolo-Schettini, A., Milazzo, P., Tini, S.: Compositional semantics and behavioral equivalences for p systems. Theor. Comput. Sci. **395**(1), 77–100 (2008)
6. Barbuti, R., Maggiolo-Schettini, A., Milazzo, P., Tini, S.: A p systems flat form preserving step-by-step behaviour. Fundam. Inform. **87**(1), 1–34 (2008)
7. Barbuti, R., Maggiolo-Schettini, A., Milazzo, P., Tini, S.: An overview on operational semantics in membrane computing. Int. J. Found. Comput. Sci. **22**(1), 119–131 (2011)

8. Basuki, T.A., Cerone, A., Barbuti, R., Maggiolo-Schettini, A., Milazzo, P.: Modelling the dynamics of an aedes albopictus population. In: Proceedings of Application of Membrane Computing, Concurrency and Agent-based Modelling in Population Biology (2010)

9. Cardelli, L., Gardner, P.: Processes in space. In: Ferreira, F., Löwe, B., Mayordomo, E. (eds.) CiE 2010. LNCS, vol. 6158, pp. 78–87. Springer, Heidelberg (2010)

10. Cardona, M., Colomer, M.A., Perez-Jimenez, M.J., Sanuy, D., Margalida, A.: A P system modeling an ecosystem related to the bearded vulture. In: Proceedings of Sixth Brainstowming Week on Membrane Computing, pp. 52–66 (2008)

11. Chaloupka, M.: Stochastic simulation modelling of southern great barrier reef green turtle population dynamics. Ecol. Model. **148**, 79–109 (2001)

12. Dematté, L., Priami, C., Romanel, A.: The BlenX language: a tutorial. In: Bernardo, M., Degano, P., Zavattaro, G. (eds.) SFM 2008. LNCS, vol. 5016, pp. 313–365. Springer, Heidelberg (2008)

13. Focks, D.A., Daniels, E., Haile, D.G., Keesling, J.E.: A simulation model of the epidemiology of urban dengue fever: literature analysis, model development, preliminary validation, and samples of simulation results. Am. J. Trop. Med. Hyg. **53**, 489–506 (1995)

14. Gibson, M.A., Bruck, J.: Efficient exact stochastic simulation of chemical systems with many species and many channels. J. Phys. Chem. **104**, 1876–1889 (2000)

15. Gillespie, D.T.: A general method for numerically simulating the stochastic time evolution of coupled chemical reactions. J. Comput. Phys. **22**, 403–434 (1976)

16. Gillespie, D.T.: Exact stochastic simulation of coupled chemical reactions. J. Phys. Chem. **81**, 2340–2361 (1977)

17. Gillespie, D.T.: Approximate accelerated stochastic simulation of chemically reacting systems. J. Chem. Phys. **115**, 1716–1733 (2001)

18. Goss, P.J., Peccoud, J.: Quantitative modeling of stochastic system in molecular biology by using Petri Nets. J. Bioinform. Comput. Biol. **95**, 6750–6755 (1990)

19. Hawley, W.A.: The biology of aedes albopictus. J. Am. Mosq. Control Assoc. **4**, 1–39 (1988)

20. John, M., Ewald, R., Uhrmacher, A.M.: A spatial extension to the π-calculus. Electron. Notes Theoret. Comput. Sci. **194**, 133–148 (2009)

21. Kahramanoğullari, O., Jordan, F., Lynch, J.: CoSBiLab LIME: a language interface for stochastic dynamical modelling in ecology. Environ. Model Softw. **26**, 685–687 (2011)

22. Kohn, K.W., Aladjem, M.I., Weinstein, J.N., Pommier, Y.: Molecule interaction maps of bioregularity networks: a general rubric for systems biology. Mol. Biol. Cell **17**, 1–13 (2005)

23. Lanotte, R., Tini, S.: Probabilistic bisimulation as a congruence. ACM Trans. Comput. Log. **10**(2), 1 (2009)

24. Li, H., Petzold, L.: Logarithmic Direct Method for Discrete Stochastics Simulation of Chemically Reacting Systems. Technical report, University of California Santa Barbara (2006)

25. Milazzo, P.: Qualitative and quantitative formal modeling of biological systems. Ph.D. thesis, Università di Pisa (2007)

26. Milner, R.: Communication and mobile systems: the π-calculus. In: Proceeding of the Pacific Symposium on Biocomputing, pp. 459–470 (2001)

27. Moreno, D.H.R., Federico, P., Canziani, G.A.: Population dynamics models base on cellular automata that includes habitat quality indices defined through remote sensing. In: ISRSE RM (2001)

28. Pardini, G.: Formal modelling and simulation of biological systems with spatiality. Ph.D. thesis, Università di Pisa (2011)
29. Pineda-Krch, M.: Gillespie SSA: implementing the stochastic simulation algorithm in R. J. Stat. Softw. **25**, 1–18 (2008)
30. Priami, C., Regev, A., Silverman, W., Shapiro, E.Y.: Application of a stochastic name-passing calculus to representation and simulation a molecular processes. Inf. Process. Lett. **80**, 25–31 (2001)
31. Păun, G.: Computing with membranes. J. Comput. Syst. Sci. **61**, 108–143 (2000)
32. Păun, G.: Twenty six research topics about spiking neural P systems. In: Proceeding of Sixth Brainstowming Week on Membrane Computing (2008)
33. Regev, A., Silverman, W., Shapiro, E.Y.: Representation and simulation of biochemical processes using the π-calculus process algebra. In: Proceeding of the Pacific Symposium on Biocomputing, pp. 459–470 (2001)
34. Tini, S.: Non-expansive epsilon-bisimulations for probabilistic processes. Theor. Comput. Sci. **411**(22–24), 2202–2222 (2010)
35. Wolfram, S.: A New Kind of Science. Wolfram Media, Champaign (2002)

Transition to Sustainability: Italian Scenarios Towards a Low-Carbon Economy

Giovanni Bernardo and Simone D'Alessandro(✉)

Dipartimento di Scienze Economiche, Università degli Studi di Pisa,
Via Cosimo Ridolfi 10, 56124 Pisa, Italy
g.bernardo@ec.unipi.it, s.dale@ec.unipi.it

Abstract. This paper analyzes different policies that may promote the transition to sustainability, with a particular focus on the energy sector. We present a dynamic simulation model where three different strategies for sustainability are identified: reduction in GHG emissions, improvements in energy efficiency and the development of the renewable energy sector. Our aim is to evaluate the dynamics that those strategies may produce in the economy, looking at different performance indicators: rate of growth, unemployment, fiscal position, GHG emission, and transition to renewable energy sources.

Keywords: Energy transition · System dynamics · Scenario analysis

1 Introduction

After twenty years since the 1992 "United Nation Conference for the Environment and Development" in Rio de Janeiro, the awareness on climate change and mass poverty is widespread and debated. However, the results in terms of emissions reduction and eradication of poverty are unsatisfactory. There was no radical political change able to invert the unsustainable trend followed by our societies. Beyond the lack of audacity of public authorities, there is a strong need for analytical tools that address, in an integrated way, the dynamics that policy changes can trigger at a macroeconomic level.

A wide range of models take into account issues such as energy transition, pollution and environmental limits, but only a few integrate the economic and the environmental spheres by considering the influence of energy policies. Several approaches are used to investigate the issue of energy transition, e.g. assessment management, agent based model, DSGE, econometrics and system dynamics. The latter seems a suitable tool to study complex systems, since it is characterized by flexibility and a simple recognition of feedback mechanisms. Moreover, the multidisciplinary nature of the possible applications allows for the integration of socio-economic and natural systems. Furthermore, scenario analysis gives the opportunity to deal with the uncertainty that characterizes societal behavior, availability of fossil energy source and climate change.

A. Cerone et al. (Eds.): SEFM 2012 Satellite Events, LNCS 7991, pp. 190–197, 2014.
DOI: 10.1007/978-3-642-54338-8_15, © Springer-Verlag Berlin Heidelberg 2014

In this approach, a first class of models focuses on the issue of peak oil and energy transition without analyzing the economic sphere [1–3]. A second group of contributions focuses on the economic and technological aspects but do not take into account the limits of fossil energy supply [4–6]. A third class of models investigates, in an integrated approach, energy, economy, and the environmental system. A well-known model is *World 3*, the dynamic simulation model used in the "Limits to Growth" [7]. That model was further improved thought the *World3/91* model used in "Beyond the Limits" [8] and the *World3/2000* model distributed by the *Institute for Policy and Social Science Research*. Recently, Millennium Institute's "Threshold 21" model was applied to energy policies in U.S. and North America [9,10]. Those contributions investigate the interdependence between the economic, social, and environmental spheres focusing on the role of energy policies in each one. Furthermore, Victor and Rosenbluth [11] and Victor [12] investigate how no- and low-growth scenarios for Canada can affect macroeconomic and environmental variables such as income, poverty, unemployment, government expenditure, and greenhouse gas emissions.

Following this stream of literature, the focus of this paper is to evaluate different policies that may promote the transition to sustainability, with a particular focus on energy sector. Indeed, people's well-being and economic stability are dependent on safe and sustainable energy availability. Our aim is to analyze the dynamics that those strategies may produce in the economy, looking at different performance indicators: rate of growth, unemployment, fiscal position, GHG emission, and transition to renewable energy sources.

Sustainability is a complex concept. In our framework we aim to take into account this complexity in three stages. First, we build a macroeconomic model where disequilibrium between aggregate demand and supply is possible since aggregate demand has autonomous components. Adjustments in consumption and investment shape the demand for production factors, in particular labour. This model allows us to analyze the dynamics of GDP, unemployment and public and private debt, when different policies are implemented.

Secondly, we integrate the core of the model, with an analysis of the energy sector. While this sector is often underestimated in economic analysis, some recent publications of European Commission recognize as a priority goal for Europe, the development of an efficient energy system. We investigate three different strategies: abatement in GHG emissions, investment in energy efficiency and the development of renewable energy sources (see, for instance, [13]). Those strategies can be seen as complementary in the transition to sustainability. Indeed, they aim both, to control climate change and to reduce the dependency of the economy from fossil energy sources. However, given budget constraints, there is a quite strong competition among those strategies. Scenario analysis is a powerful tool to evaluate the dynamics generated by alternative policies which tend to favor one of those strategies. Furthermore, an increase in public expenditure in the energy sector (e.g. through monetary incentives) may reduce the availability of resources for improvements in other performance indicators such as unemployment, inequality and poverty. The model allows for the investigation of this kind of trade-offs.[1]

Finally, while the model can be easily adapted to different countries, we apply it to Italy, making calibration and robustness analysis of the crucial parameters.

Preliminary results show that *business as usual* scenario is not able to attain European Commission prescriptions on renewable energy sources and emissions standard [14]. Moreover, limits on the exploitation of fossil resources generate irreversibility thresholds which may induce the collapse of the whole economy (see, for instance, [15]). Policies must take into account those thresholds and induce a significant increase in the investment in the renewable energy sector. However those investments are costly, and may reduce the rate of growth and increase unemployment at least in the short run.

At this stage of the analysis, we get that the three strategies have different outcomes. Abatements in GHG emissions and increases in energy efficiency are effective in the short run, while the development of renewable energy sector has higher effects in the long run.

The paper is organized as follow. Section 2 presents the essential theoretical structure of the model. Section 3 discusses the main results of the dynamic simulation model through scenario analysis. Section 4 concludes.

2   The Model

Production takes place according to the following technology

$$Y_t = \min\left\{A_t L_t^\alpha K_t^{1-\alpha}, \epsilon_t E_t\right\}, \tag{1}$$

where the subscript t indicates the time, Y is the GDP, L is the employment, K is the available capital, A captures the productivity of production factors, $\alpha \in (0,1)$ is a technological parameter. Furthermore, production needs energy: E is the flow of energy, ϵ measures energy efficiency.

In every period, capital accumulates according to

$$K_{t+1} = (1 - \delta^k)K_t + I_t^k, \tag{2}$$

where $\delta^k > 0$ is the depreciation of capital per unit of time, and I_t^k is the level of investment in the capital sector.

We consider two composite energy sources, fossil fuels and renewable energy, and we use the standard, although strong, assumption that the two types of energy are perfect substitutes

$$E_t = Q_t + H_t, \tag{3}$$

where Q and H are the services of fossil fuel extraction and renewable energy resource harnessing respectively.

---

[1] At this stage, the analysis of inequality and poverty is not included in the simulation model.

The harnessing of renewable energy sources depends on "renewable energy source capacity" (henceforth RESC) and is indicated as R. For simplicity, we assume that renewable energy flow is produced through a linear technology which employes R_t and labour L_t^R,

$$H_t = h \min\{R_t, L_t^R\}. \tag{4}$$

In the model we assume that only fossil energy flows (Q_t) produce GHG emissions (P_t). Thus

$$P_t = \phi_t Q_t, \tag{5}$$

where ϕ_t indicates the technology available in period t.

We explore through a simulation model which size of investments in RESC (I_t^R), in energy efficiency (I_t^ϵ) and in the abatement of greenhouse gas emissions (I_t^ϕ) are necessary for moving Italian economy to a low-carbon economy in 2050.[2]

As we pointed out in the previous section, we allows for disequilibrium between aggregate demand and GDP. In particular, aggregate demand is given by

$$D_t = C_t + I_t^K + I_t^R + I_t^\epsilon + I_t^\phi + G_t + B_t, \tag{6}$$

where B_t is given by exports minus imports in period t, G_t is the public expenditure, C_t is the level of consumption. In the simulation we make a detailed specifications of the autonomous component of those variables. Given a certain cost of fossil energy $c(Q)$, at any period differences between net income $(Y - c(Q))$ and aggregate demand (D_t) generates a change in the stock of inventories. Those variations induce firms to adjust the demand of labour and the size of investment. We describe this process in the following section.

3   Dynamic Simulation and Scenario Analysis

Two main feedback loops drive the model outcomes. The first feedback is an engine of economic growth. If aggregate demand is higher than aggregate supply, then the stock of inventories decreases. Thus suppliers tend to increase the demand for production factors. Labour and investment increase inducing a further increase in the aggregate supply, if energy is available. Since some components of aggregate demand, such as consumption and investment, are positively related to production, demand increases. This process without continuous shocks or public intervention tends to converge in the long run (see Fig. 1).

The second feedback takes into account government expenditure and public incentive to the development of RESC. We assume that as long as unemployment increases, government expenditure has to increase to subsidize new unemployed and their families. Thus under budget constraint, government may renounce to stimulate energy transition. However, a positive feedback may emerge (see Fig. 2). An increase in the incentive for investment in RESC has two positive

---

[2] In this short paper we have no space for explicitly analyzing our analytical assumption about the impact of the investment on the three variables R, ϵ and ϕ.

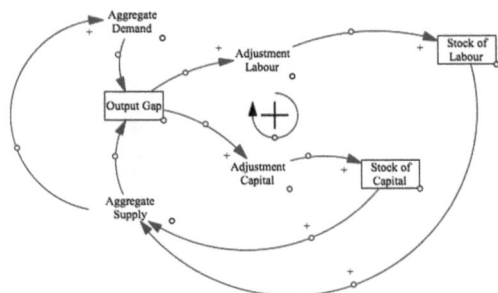

Fig. 1. Positive feedback through output gap.

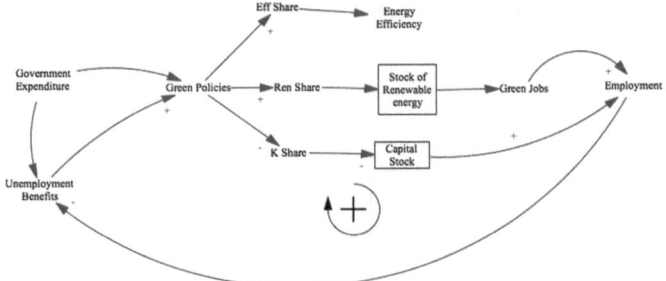

Fig. 2. Positive feedback through an increase in the incentive for renewable energy source.

effects on employment: (i) it directly promotes green jobs, (ii) it diverts part of the investment in capital to investment in RESC, reducing the accumulation of capital. Such change may induce firms to substitute labour for capital. Those two effects tend to increase the level of employment, thus government may further provide incentives for RESC without compromising its fiscal position.

At this stage of the project we are still working on the robustness analysis and in the choice of parameters through Italian statistics (from the ISTAT website). Hence, scenarios results are a qualitative analysis of the size of the investments in energy efficiency, in RESC and in physical necessary to follow the roadmap prescriptions for a low-carbon economy in 2050 rather than a quantitative answer to this problem. The Italian National agency for new technologies, Energy and sustainable economic development (ENEA) presents the possible evolution of National energy system in a time horizon of 30 years following three scenarios (see Fig. 3). The first one, Reference Scenario, adopts the set of policies at the end of 2009 and describes the evolution of the system following the actual trend. The second one, Current Policies Scenario, describes the effect of new actual policies. The third one, the Roadmap Scenario, evaluates the additional investment needed to reduce green house gas emissions following the prescriptions of the Impact Assessment for 2050 of [14].

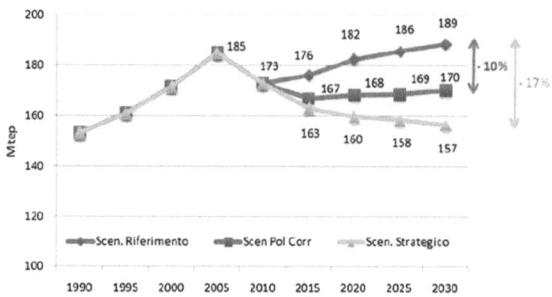

Fig. 3. Source [13]. Primary energy demand 1990–2030. Reference Scenario (blue); Current Policies Scenario (red); Strategic Scenario (green).

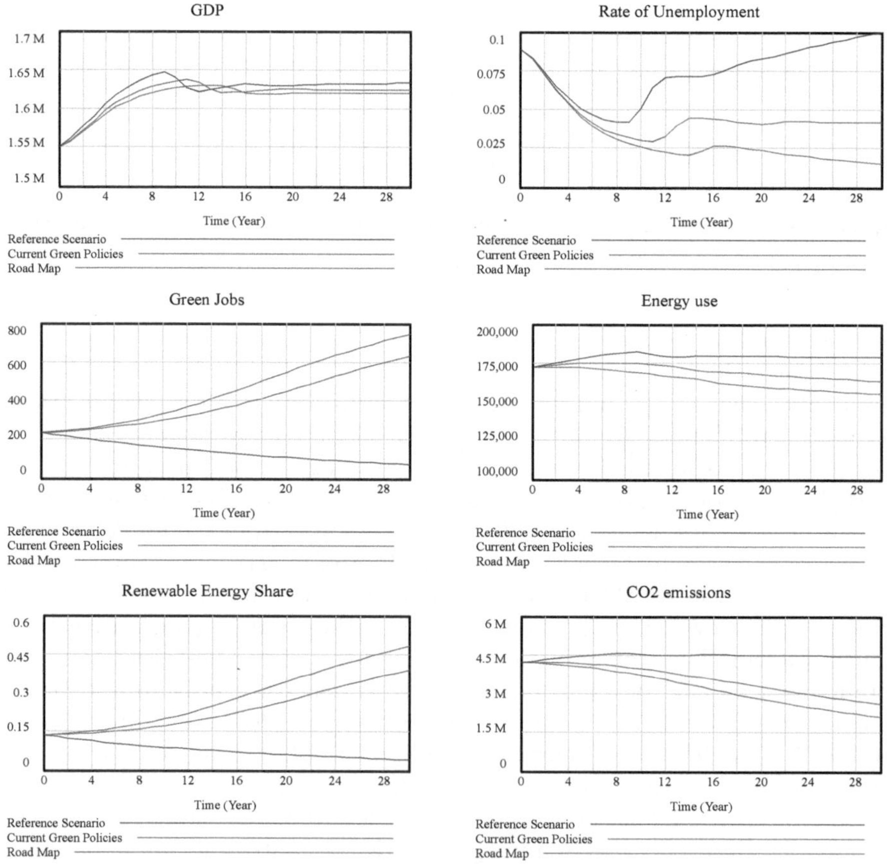

GDP

Reference Scenario
Current Green Policies
Road Map

Rate of Unemployment

Reference Scenario
Current Green Policies
Road Map

Green Jobs

Reference Scenario
Current Green Policies
Road Map

Energy use

Reference Scenario
Current Green Policies
Road Map

Renewable Energy Share

Reference Scenario
Current Green Policies
Road Map

CO2 emissions

Reference Scenario
Current Green Policies
Road Map

Fig. 4. Scenario analysis.

In our model those scenarios can be replicated by choosing a certain level of investment in the three areas stressed above. Figure 4 presents the results in terms of GDP, unemployment, green jobs, energy use, renewable energy share and CO_2 emissions. In order to following the roadmap scenario, investment in RESC must significantly increase in the percentage of total investment. In order to get such a result government has to divert public resources to support the profitability of investment in RESC.

4   Concluding Remarks

Preliminary results shows that *business as usual* scenario is not able to attain European Union prescriptions on renewable energy sources and emissions standard neither through the implementation of current policies. Investment in renewable energy source capacity (RESC) has to increase significantly in order to approach the roadmap for moving to a low-carbon economy in 2050. We obtained that investments in energy efficiency and greenhouse gas emission abatements are more effective in the short run, while the development of a large renewable energy sector is more effective in the long run by reducing the dependence on foreign sources of energy. This result raises several questions which we are aiming to deal with in the development of this research.

References

1. Nail, R., Budzik, P.: Fossil1: a policy analysis model of the U.S. energy transition. In: WSC 1976 Proceedings of the 76 Bicentennial Conference on Winter Simulation, pp. 145–152 (1976)
2. ASPO: Aspo newsletter no 95. Technical report, http://www.aspo-ireland.org (2008)
3. Bentley, R.: Global oil & gas depletion: an overview. Energy Policy **30**, 189–205 (2002)
4. Sterman, J.: A dynamic, disequilibrium model of energy-economy interactions. Int. J. Energy Syst. **2**, 159–163 (1982)
5. EIA: International energy outlook 2007, energy information administration. Technical report, US Department of Energy (2007)
6. IPCC: Ipcc special report on emissions scenarios. Technical report (2001)
7. Meadows, D., Meadows, D., Randers, J.: The Limits to Growth. Universe Books, New York (1972)
8. Meadows, D., Meadows, D., Randers, J.: Beyond the Limits: Global Collapse or a Sustainable Future. Earthscan, London (1991)
9. Bassi, A.: Modeling US Energy Policy with Threshold 21. VDM, Saarbrcken (2008)
10. Bassi, A., Powers, R., Schoenberg, W.: An integrated approach to energy prospects for North America and the rest of the world. Energy Econ. **32**, 30–42 (2010)
11. Victor, P., Rosenbluth, G.: Managing without growth. Ecol. Econ. **61**, 492–504 (2007)
12. Victor, P.: Managing Without Growth: Slower by Design, not Disaster. Edward Elgar, Cheltenham (2008)

13. ENEA: Rapporto energia ambiente. Technical report, National agency for new technologies, Energy and sustainable economic development (2012)
14. European Commission: A roadmap for moving to a competitive low carbon economy in 2050. Technical report, SEC 288 (2011)
15. D'Alessandro, S., Luzzati, T., Morroni, M.: Energy transition towards economic and environmental sustainability: feasible paths and policy implications. J. Clean. Prod. **18**, 291–298 (2010)

Models of Knowledge Transfer
for Sustainable Development

Ettore Bolisani[1]([✉]), Francesca Scramoncin[1], and Siraj Ahmed Shaikh[2]

[1] Department of Management and Engineering, Faculty of Engineering,
University of Padua, Padova, Italy
ettore.bolisani@unipd.it, jjceska@libero.it
[2] Digital Security and Forensics (SaFe) Research Group, Department of Computing,
Faculty of Engineering and Computing, Coventry University, Coventry, UK
s.shaikh@coventry.ac.uk

Abstract. Sustainable development requires that distant organisations connect to one another and exchange knowledge. Online social networks have the potential to support these processes. It is however important to understand and model the processes of knowledge transfer that can effectively occur on the Internet. This paper explores recent literature with the purpose to highlight relevant formal approaches that can help to model and analyse the processes of inter-organisational knowledge transfer for sustainable development.

1 Introduction

Sustainable development requires that distant organisations, specialising in complementary areas, connect to one another. Knowledge transfer mechanisms can, in principle, help sustainable development [15]. In addition, online social networks, by design, have the potential to be adopted by the developing parts of the world given the accessibility through the mobile platform.

It is therefore important to understand and model the processes of knowledge transfer that can occur on the Internet [16]. This paper explores recent literature with the purpose to highlight relevant notions and formal models that can help to understand and analyse the processes of inter-organisational knowledge transfer for sustainable development. The purpose is to underline some basic points that can be helpful for supporting business management and policy making for favouring sustainable development. Particularly attention is paid to aspects of (a) social networking, (b) knowledge flows, and (c) knowledge protection and disclosure, as relevant to our position.

2 Social Networking

Modern communication has been transformed by the advent of the Internet. The extent of this transformation allows for truly global and open innovation to be a reality. The Internet has allow for media of all types (including video, audio and text) to be

A. Cerone et al. (Eds.): SEFM 2012 Satellite Events, LNCS 7991, pp. 198–203, 2014.
DOI: 10.1007/978-3-642-54338-8_16, © Springer-Verlag Berlin Heidelberg 2014

- globally accessible, communicated and created anywhere in the world,
- exchanged in higher volume, allowing high-scale storage and transfer,
- communicated at higher speeds, providing very fast speeds links to all kinds of devices,
- open for interaction and integration, to allow for various kinds of devices to share the same platform ranging from PCs to tablets to phone and other consumer devices,
- collaborative, allowing multi-user environments through chat and voice communication tools, and
- pervasive, such that this media is present anywhere and everywhere thanks to mobility and the concept of Internet of Things (IoT) that brings on all kind of unconventional devices connected to the Internet.

One of the notable trends over the last decade has been the emergence of Web 2.0. Ian Davis [7] describes the notion as such

> "Web 2.0 is an attitude not a technology. It's about enabling and encouraging participation through open applications and services. By open I mean technically open with appropriate APIs but also, more importantly, socially open, with rights granted to use the content in new and exciting contexts."

Undoubtedly, Web 2.0 helps to readjust the focus of the Internet from *information* to *people*, who are the producers and consumers of information, and more importantly, have the ability to innovate. This is achieved by

- the growth of Web authoring styles that enables people to collectively create and maintain shared content,
- people's personal data moving online from their computers to the services and cloud, and
- a growing trend of linking styles that provides for online connections between people (and not just between web pages and documents).

Online social networks, such as Facebook and Twitter, are successful manifestations of Web 2.0. Such networks provide for a great opportunity for developing and emerging countries to participate in the global process of knowledge transfer and innovation. This appears particularly promising as the Internet becomes reachable over mobile platforms, which have achieved remarkable penetration in some of the developing regions of the world. Mobile data traffic is expected to grow to 10.8 exabytes per month by 2016, an 18-fold increase over 2011 [6], and estimates suggest that by 2015, mobile access will become more widely available than electricity in the regions of Middle East, Sub-Saharan Africa, and South- and Southeast Asia [6].

Social network theory provides an insight into how communities emerge. The principle of *triadic closure* suggests that if two people in a social network have a friend in common, then there is an increased likelihood that they will become friends themselves at some point in the future [10]. This principle is illustrated

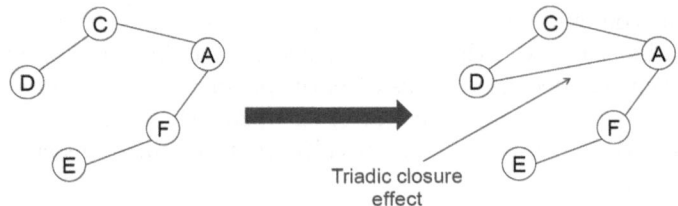

Fig. 1. The principle of triadic closure in social network theory

in the simple diagram in Fig. 1, where the theory suggests that A and D have an *opportunity* to form a link due to a common link with C and a basis for *trusting each other* due to this common link, along with C also having an *incentive* to bring A and D closer.

This provides an insight into how communities with similar interests emerge and become a critical mass to sustain knowledge and promote cross-beneficial innovation [9]. Such communities have the potential to connect people into far reaching places of the globe, as per the *small world* phenomenon [10] that suggests that any two nodes in a social network are separated by no more than a few degrees of separation.

3   Knowledge Transfer and Its Relevance for Economic Development

To connect into social networks by means of new Web 2.0 applications is important for local economies, provided that the relevant interacting players are willing to share their knowledge. The possibility for companies to get access to the results of knowledge production performed by others, and especially by "big" labs and high tech companies [1,4,8,11] is a fundamental ingredient of economic development. The purpose of this section is to highlight formal models that can help to understand knowledge transfer mechanisms and their economic implications.

A first important issue is that organisations can engage in different kinds of interactions involving knowledge flows [2,3]. In a strict sense, knowledge transfer can be seen as the situation where a subject possesses a piece of knowledge and gives it to another subject (a payback is not explicitly considered here). An important aspect of knowledge transfer is that this process is really effective under specific conditions: the receiver has to assimilate the piece of knowledge, which implies an active process of learning. While knowledge transfer is generally a bilateral model, knowledge sharing is, instead, a situation where a piece of knowledge is shared between two or more subjects: the assumption is that all the subjects share not only the knowledge but also the appropriate mechanisms to understand and use it. Also, all the parties can act as sources and receivers. Knowledge exchange is a mechanism where a source gives a piece of knowledge to a receiver, provided that the latter pays it back. This situation is particularly significant in economic terms, because it implies the existence of a "market" for knowledge. The last case is that of knowledge transaction, that is different from knowledge exchange because, in this case, the payment is represented by another piece of knowledge that flows back: in other words, the source is willing to give a piece of knowledge to a receiver provided that the latter teaches something useful to the former.

This formal distinction is useful for the topic treated in this paper, because it helps to underline some basic questions that need resolving. For example: how do interacting organisations communicate knowledge effectively? When can this be useful for economic development? How do companies in developed countries can pass useful knowledge on to developing countries? What infrastructures and mechanisms are more appropriate for this? For example a case of knowledge transfer is that of a research institution that publishes the results of some scientific activity: in this case, the transfer is really effective only when the receiver (for instance, a company in a developing country) is able to assimilate that knowledge content properly. This means that simply diffusing technical or business information can be not enough, unless the receiver is properly trained to assimilate that content. An example of knowledge exchange is, instead, that of a company selling a patent to another company: in this case, it is the financial capability that allows the second company to really gain the economic benefits of the technical/scientific invention. Again, this raises special questions: can companies in a developing country have the financial resources to buy knowledge from abroad? What policies can help this process? Another emerging approach used to formally analyse the effectiveness of knowledge flows is that of agent-based simulation. For example, Strohmaier *et al.* [14] use an agent-based simulation model to investigate the effectiveness of knowledge transfer mechanisms that can be adopted in the light of potentially conflicting stakeholders goals. As a matter of fact, while research on the effectiveness of knowledge transfer is often based on empirical observations (i.e. case-studies or surveys), the authors claim that a knowledge-based simulation can help to explore the conditions under which a particular mechanism of knowledge transfer can be effective.

A second issue that is relevant to our analysis is that of the strategies of knowledge protection/disclosure. This is clearly associated to the issue of knowledge flows. Knowledge protection is generally intended as a way to protect the capability of a company to produce or commercialise innovations: by protecting knowledge, a company avoids that precious knowledge is unintentionally transferred to others for free. It is clearly not possible to protect all the knowledge that a company produces [13], but there are popular mechanisms like patents, confidentiality agreements, secrecy, etc. that are often used by innovative companies, sometimes very effectively. Patents are the norm in some industries, for instance Pharmaceutics or Biotechnologies, and it is often matter of debate if this protection mechanism is fair (think, for instance, to the case of orphan diseases) or beneficial to economic development.

Conversely, the recent literature highlights that there are situations in which a strategy of knowledge disclosure can be beneficial not only to the potential receiver but also to the source: in the open innovation model [5] it is assumed that the complexity and high risks of innovative activities call for an open co-operation where companies with complementary competencies can fruitfully share and integrate their knowledge, and can benefit of mutual learning.

Given the critical question about whether protection or disclosure is more beneficial, several studies have attempted to formally model the mechanisms of knowledge protection or disclosure and their potential effect on knowledge transfer efficiency. A common formal approach is that of game theory, which is used to investigate the situation of equilibrium between protecting and disclosing knowledge in terms of the relative distributions of advantages and disadvantages. An example of study is that by Ponce [12], who analyses a case of two companies, one of which can imitate the innovation discovered by the other, and explores different combinations of protection/disclosure. From this study, it may be concluded that, without proper incentives, the inventor may be not willing to accept a transfer of knowledge towards others. This highlights the importance of policies to support transfer of knowledge.

4   Conclusion

In this position paper, we argue that a reflection on the mechanisms that can allow effective knowledge transfer can be useful to understand how innovations can be effectively flow from sources (i.e. developed countries) and receivers (namely, developing countries), and how this can help to identify proper management strategies and public policies. Assuming that this process of innovation transfer is essential for a sustainable and balanced development, it is therefore important to analyse the conditions that can make it successful. Today, IT applications (and, especially, Web 2.0 social networking applications) are of great help for connecting companies and organisations across time and space. However, simply "connecting companies" is not the solution. The use of IT systems can be more or less effective depending on the networking structures within companies and the kind of knowledge flows that occur. Modelling how knowledge can effectively flow from a source to a receiver, and understanding what effects a policy of innovation protection or disclosure can have, are absolutely necessary to implement appropriate supporting policies that can help a balanced economic development. The examples of formal modelling approaches presented here are an essential starting point.

References

1. Ballantyne, P.: Accessing, sharing and communicating agricultural information for development: emerging trends and issues. Inf. Dev. **25**(4), 260–271 (2009)
2. Bolisani, E.: Capitalising knowledge exchanges: an interpretative model. In: 11th European Conference on Knowledge Management (ECKM), September 2010
3. Boyd, J., Ragsdell, G., Oppenheim, C.: Knowledge transfer mechanisms: a case study from manufacturing. In: 8th European Conference on Knowledge Management (ECKM), September 2007

4. Chan, L., Costa, S.: Participation in the global knowledge commons: challenges and opportunities for research dissemination in developing countries. New Library World **106**(3/4), 141–163 (2005)
5. Chesbrough, H.: Open Innovation: The New Imperative for Creating and Profiting from Technology. Harvard Business School Press, Boston (2003)
6. Cisco. Cisco visual networking index: global mobile data traffic forecast update, 2011–2016. Technical report, Cisco (2012)
7. Davis, I.: Internet Alchemy: Talis, Web 2.0 and All That. http://blog.iandavis.com/2005/07/04/talis-web-2-0-and-all-that/
8. Garcia-Penalvo, F.J., De Figuerola, C.G., Jose Merlo, A.: Open knowledge: challenges and facts. Online Inf. Rev. **34**(4), 520–539 (2010)
9. Guest, R.: Borderless Economics: Chinese Sea Turtles, Indian Fridges and the New Fruits of Global Capitalism. Palgrave Macmillan, New York (2011)
10. Kleinberg, J., Easley, D.: Networks, Crowds, and Markets: Reasoning About a Highly Connected World. Cambridge University Press, Cambridge (2010)
11. Maskus, K.E., Reichman, J.H.: The globalization of private knowledge goods and the privatization of global public goods. J. Int. Econ. Law **7**, 279–320 (2009)
12. Ponce, C.J.: Knowledge disclosure as intellectual property rights protection. J. Econ. Behav. Organ. **80**(3), 418–434 (2011)
13. Stiglitz, J.: Public policy for a knowledge economy. Technical report, OECD Report (2007)
14. Strohmaier, M., Yu, E., Horkoff, J., Aranda, J., Easterbrook, S.: Analyzing knowledge transfer effectiveness-an agent-oriented modeling approach. In: Proceedings of the 40th Annual Hawaii International Conference on System Sciences, HICSS '07, p. 188b. IEEE Computer Society, Washington, DC (2007)
15. Tong, J., Shaikh, S.A.: ICT driven knowledge management in developing countries: a case study in a Chinese organisation. In: Pont, A., Pujolle, G., Raghavan, S.V. (eds.) WCITD 2010. IFIP AICT, vol. 327, pp. 60–71. Springer, Heidelberg (2010)
16. Tong, J., Shaikh, S.A., James, A.E.: A formal approach to analysing knowledge transfer processes in developing countries. In: Barthe, G., Pardo, A., Schneider, G. (eds.) SEFM 2011. LNCS, vol. 7041, pp. 486–501. Springer, Heidelberg (2011)

A Framework for Translating Legal Knowledge into Administrative Processes: Dynamic Adaption of Business Processes

Yiwei Gong[✉] and Marijn Janssen

Faculty of Technology, Policy and Management, Delft University of Technology,
Jaffalaan 5 2628 BX Delft, The Netherlands
{Y.Gong,M.F.W.H.A.Janssen}@tudelft.nl

Abstract. Adapting to and complying with frequently changing legislation quickly against low costs requires organizations to adapt their business processes automatically. Semantic representation of legal knowledge is a prerequisite for the automatic creation of business processes. Business Rules (BR) can be used to capture legal knowledge and business processes can be created by selecting, composing and invoking Semantic Web Services (SWS). In this paper, a modeling framework is presented that enables the automatic creation of business process by invoking SWSs. Process creation is conducted by BRs derived from legislation. The framework addresses the modeling of legal knowledge representation and service descriptions that are required for creating operational processes at runtime. The framework is briefly illustrated by a legislation implementation case study which shows how compliance between business processes and legislation is ensured.

Keywords: Business process management · Business rule · Semantic Web Service · Legal knowledge representation · Administrative organization

1 Introduction

Legislation is formulated as law, regulations or guidelines that need to be implemented by administrative organizations. Legislation typically changes frequently and these changes need to be adopted by administrative organizations. This often demands changes in business processes supported by software applications. As such there is a need for business process management (BPM) systems that are able to adapt to these changes against low costs and within a short time frame. This is complicated as multiple sources of legislation often need to be included and processes might vary based on specific circumstances.

Building and maintaining long-living processes for delivering services that can easily adopt to changes is a challenge [1]. In the effort of achieving higher process flexibility, Semantic Web Service and Business Rule technologies can be used. Business rules can be used to capture legal knowledge and business processes can be created by selecting services and composing them in a sequence.

A. Cerone et al. (Eds.): SEFM 2012 Satellite Events, LNCS 7991, pp. 204–211, 2014.
DOI: 10.1007/978-3-642-54338-8_17, © Springer-Verlag Berlin Heidelberg 2014

Semantic Web Services (SWSs) are an emerging approach for designing an architecture that would provide flexible integration and adaptability to changes in the processes [2]. The advantage of using SWSs is that semantically described services (which are human and computer readable) can be composed into complex processes corresponding to the needs of a service request. By using their semantic descriptions, services can be automatically selected based on their functionality, input set, output set and composed into a process (see for example [3]).

A *Business Rule* (BR) is a directive intended to influence or guide business process behavior [4]. Although there is no unified classification of rules, BRs can be generally categorized into declarative rules which define the goal of an operation, and operative rules which describe how an operation should be done [5]. The forms or formats of business rules are various depending on the technologies in use.

There has been much work in which BRs are used to create business processes. For example, BRs can be used to determine how a Web service composition should be structured and scheduled [6], or realize dynamic service composition [7]. Yet business processes in administrative organizations have to comply with legislation, which is hardly given attention in research. Current approaches in a governmental context largely focus on operational processes or knowledge representation of laws without considering its possible use in the creation of business processes [1]. There is limited research into how business rules can be used by administrative organizations to describe their legal knowledge and to use them to create business processes.

Administrative organizations take legislation as input, interpret it and implement it in their operational processes. Translating legislation into BRs is done by deriving the rules from multiple sources rather than just from legislation. According to Goedertier and Vantienen [8], other sources include the business strategy, internal directives, procedures, information prerequisites: the information required to start an activity, and technical and common-sense constraints.

In this paper, we propose a framework which is able to derive business processes from legal knowledge described by BRs. Our framework integrates SWS and BR technology to create administrative processes automatically. Both Web services and BRs are used to execute processes. BRs that are derived from legislation and those derived from other sources are clearly separated to allow the traceability between legislation and BRs. During process execution, Web services are invoked according to their semantic description and related BRs. A domain ontology that provides unified vocabulary and taxonomy is used to provide interoperability between SWSs and BRs. This framework is not an all-in-one solution or type of technology, instead, a reference framework is developed which allows various technologies to fulfill their roles at different levels.

2   Challenges in Implementing Legislations

When adapting to changes in legislation the first step is to let legal experts analyze the text of legislation and interpret them with necessary extra information. Then IT personnel build BRs models according to their interpretation using certain knowledge representation techniques (e.g. semantic network [9]). Finally, these BRs are deployed into a BR engine and tested. At runtime, the engine is used in business processes for making decisions. Although this process looks easy, it is complicated as there are often multiple sources of legislation which might not be consistent and have different demands. Our framework is aimed at managing BRs at all levels to maintain the consistency and separate legislation-derived and non-legislation-derived BRs. Such a framework should provide a clear implementation of legislation which allows an easy maintenance of legal compliance of the business processes.

3   A Framework for Automatic Creation of Processes

BRs can be derived from different sources and can be represented in different forms. The essence of BRs is that they determine the behavior of processes. The core concept in BRs is the *"separation of concerns"* [10]. Current BR approaches allow the separation of *"knowledge"* (the business logic used by a decision making task) and *"process"* (the sequence of all tasks). The consideration of this separation is that in many knowledge-intensive organizations, large sets of rules are involved. Rules may change frequently and should be separated from the applications which execute them. In a service-oriented system, the "separation of concerns" can be further explained as the separation of not just process flow and knowledge but also of *"resource"* [11]. The notion of resource can be considered as an component of a software application that needs to be used or addressed [12]. In a service-oriented system, services can be invoked from anywhere and managed independently. This allows the encapsulating of all forms of resources (provided by either humans or computers) into Web Services, uses Semantic Web technology to describe them and compose them into a process by a BPM engine.

BRs that have different sources can also be clearly separated by locating them into different services to ensure a high level of reuse. Taylor and Raden [13] used the term *"decision service"* to describe a self-contained callable component with a view of all conditions and actions that need to be considered in making an operational business decision. To execute decision services supportive services are needed which can include infrastructural services like identification, information retrieval, storing etc.

An overview of the framework is given in Fig. 1. In our framework, there are three knowledge repositories: domain ontology, SWS description and BR models. A *domain ontology* has been indicated as necessary for interoperability. A domain ontology refers to the knowledge elements that comprise the conceptualization of the domain where the architecture is going to be applied [14]. A domain ontology shared by all the components enables communication and avoids conflicts and mismatching of concepts. It provides vocabulary and taxonomy (or concept hierarchy) to facilitate communication between BR models and SWS descriptions. The vocabulary provided by the domain ontology can be and should be used by the description of BRs and SWSs.

SWS descriptions semantically describe Web services. Dietze et al. [15] claimed that "a SWS description is formally represented within a particular ontology that complies with a certain SWS reference model such as OWL-S or WSMO" (p. 248).

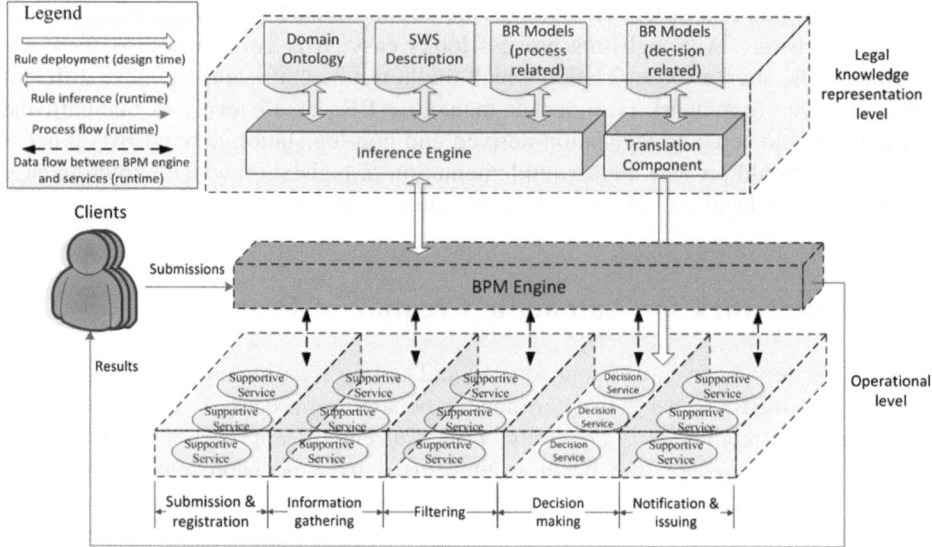

Fig. 1. A framework for automatic creation of administrative processes

Such a description is suitable for both service supply and request. All relevant aspects of a Web service should be described including the distinguishing of a decision service or a supportive service. The use of SWS description separates the management of resources.

BR models are the semantic presentation of BRs. In our framework we focus on two kinds of BRs. The first one is operational rules which are used in the decision making and which are involved in the execution of decision services. The other one is declarative rules which describe the process logic, e.g. what decision service should be select for a certain type of clients. Both these two kinds of BRs are derived from legislation and should maintain traceability and compliance with the legislation. Distinguishing decision and process related BRs enables the separation of process flows and knowledge.

For the BRs that are encapsulated in Web services, a translation component is useful for the construction of the Web services by, e.g. generating codes to assist their development.

The above mentioned knowledge entities should be presented in proper formats that allow an inference engine to perform reasoning operations on them. The inference engine uses the knowledge presented with semantic technologies and BRs to generate service invocation prescription that can be executed by the BPM engine. In our framework we use a common process pattern in this domain [16] to form operational processes. By making use of this pattern, the goal of each task in the process is clear for the BPM engine. The creation of a certain process is done by selecting proper decision or supportive services for each task and composing them, in this way creating a process. The selection of supportive services is based on their semantic descriptions, whereas the selection of decision services is controlled by process related BRs. During the creation of processes, the inference engine works out the service selection and create a temporary invocation prescription for each task. Given the prescription, the BPM engine is able to invoke proper services in each task. The process creation is dynamic as it does not require a fully pre-defined process model. Instead, the process is created and executed step after step. Adaption in legal knowledge representation will be automatically reflected in the creation of operational processes.

4   Illustration

We use an implementation of the Highly Skilled Migrant (HSM) policy in the Netherlands to illustrate how the framework creates operational processes. According to the HSM legislation for 2012, non-EU foreigners are granted resident permits if they have an annual income no less than €37575 (applicant younger than 30) or €51239 (from the age of 30). But for persons who graduated in the Netherlands and who graduate from top foreign universities with master or PhD degree (under Highly Educated Migrant Schema[1]), the annual income requirement is €26931. To implement this legislation using the proposed framework, we performed the following steps: (1) building a domain ontology, (2) defining business services, (3) defining business rules and (4) testing process creation.

In our approach, the first step is to define a domain ontology to provide consistent understanding of concepts. In Fig. 2 most concepts used in service description and business rules are involved and connected. For space reason, we could not include every detail and its intention is only to demonstrate the structure of a domain ontology. For the business processes in a typical case handling system, the domain ontology contains the identification of different clients under the *Person* class. Similar to the Object-Oriented programming, its subclasses inherit all its properties. We also defined an Action concept, and its several subclasses with different semantic meanings.

To create processes for serving different types of clients, the immigrant office can create three decision services: one for regular HSM applicants (DS01), one for local graduate applicants (DS02), and one for highly educated migrates (DS03). Supportive services that provide income information (SS02) and diploma checking (SS03, 04) are needed to gather information for the related decision service. A supportive service for filtering is also needed for risk control, e.g. blacklist checking (SS05). For all kinds of processes, supportive services for submission intake (SS01) and returning result of decision (SS06) are required. The system then creates operational processes to provide services for applicants according to their situations: being a regular applicant or Dutch graduate or foreign graduate.

Process related BRs describe which decision service should be invoked by the BPM engine to deal the submission that they are processing. As the functions of

---

[1] Policy and criteria of Highly Skilled Migrant and Highly Educate Migrant can be found at www. ind.nl

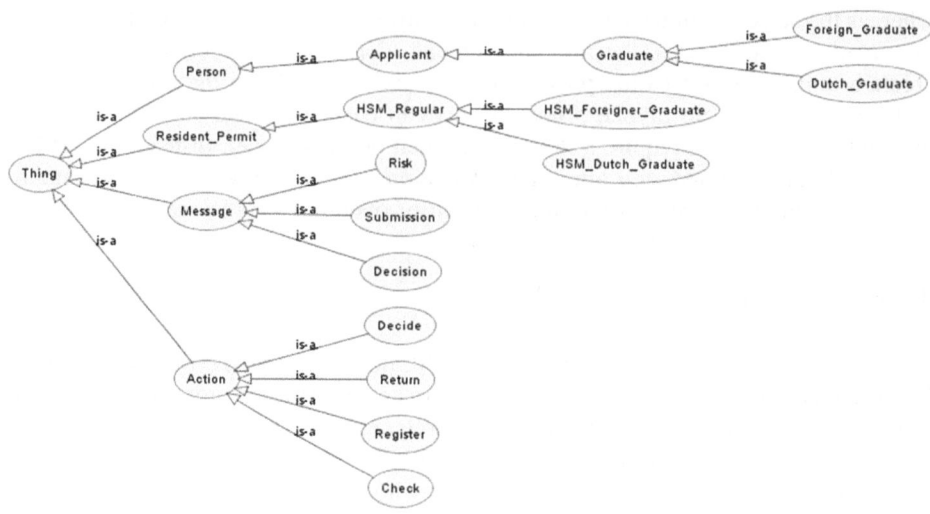

Fig. 2. Illustrative domain ontology (created using Protégé)

decision services have been semantically described, the BRs should indicate which decision service can be used for which kind of immigrant applications. We use the following RIF-core [17] rules for giving an example.

```
Prefix(act <http://example.com/action#>)
Prefix(per <http://example.com/person#>)
Base(<http://example.com/service#>)

Forall ?Applicant(
    act:decide(?Applicant <hsm_Regular>):-
?Applicant#per:applicant
    act:decide (?Applicant <hsm_Dutch_Graduate>):-
?Applicant#per:dutch_graduate
    act:decide (?Applicant <hsm_Foreign_Graduate>) :-
?Applicant#per:foreign_graduate
    )
```

Figure 3 demonstrates the interactions between the BPM engine and the Web services to create dynamically the process for regular HSM applications.

The use of our framework to translate legal knowledge into operational processes makes the processes more adaptive. If the income requirement is changed, the new income requirement can be easily adapted by changing decision related BRs. In case that a new type of applicants is added to the legislation, a new operational process can be created by adding a new decision service containing this logic and reusing the

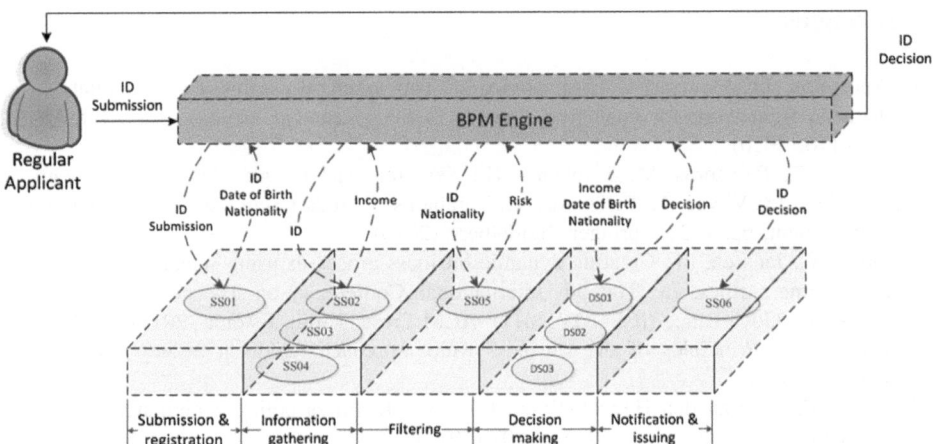

Fig. 3. An example of dynamic creation of the business process for regular HSM applicant

existing supportive services like income and diploma checking services, if they are applicable. Legal compliance can be maintained easily because the decision service only contain BRs derived from legislation and separated from supportive services for information gathering and other activities.

5   Conclusion and Future Research

With the aim of automatic creation of operational processes to satisfy requirements from frequently changed legislation, the proposed framework combines BR and SWS technology. The framework enables a clear integration of BRs between legal knowledge representation and operational levels and allows BRs to conduct the invocation of SWSs to create a business process. Web services are used as the way to manage resources which are invoked to create a process. SWS technology is used to describe decision and supportive services. Processes are created by a BPM engine that takes BRs as an input to invoke Web services making up a business process. When legislation is changed, BR can be easily updated in order to include the new or changed legislation in the process. This should not only allow to quickly adopt new legislation at low cost, but also ensure the compliance of business processes with legislation.

For future research, our framework can be used for a variety of legislation used in different settings and situations. A further research direction is to use the framework for translating strategy into operational processes to investigate its suitability for cross-organizational systems.

Acknowledgement. This work is supported by AGILE project (Advanced Governance of Information services through Legal Engineering, details can be found on the web page http://www.jacquard.nl/?m=426).

References

1. Apostolou, D., Mentzas, G., Stojanovic, L., Thoenssen, B., Lobo, T.P.: A collaborative decision framework for managing changes in e-Government services. Gov. Inf. Q. **28**, 101–116 (2010)
2. Vitvar, T., Peristeras, V., Tarabanis, K.: Semantic technologies for e-Government: an overview. In: Vitvar, T., Peristeras, V., Tarabanis, K. (eds.) Semantic technologies for e-Government, pp. 1–22. Springer, Heidelberg (2010)
3. Gong, Y., Janssen, M.: Creating dynamic business processes using semantic web services and business rules. In: The 5th International Conference on Theory and Practice of Electronic Governance (ICEGOV 2011). ACM Press, Tallin, Estonia (2011)
4. Ross, R.G.: Principles of the Business Rule Approach. Addison-Wesley Professional, Boston (2003)
5. Weigand, H., Van den Heuvel, W.-J., Hiel, M.: Business policy compliance in service-oriented systems. Inf. Syst. **36**, 791–807 (2011)
6. Orriëns, B., Yang, J., Papazoglou, M.P.: A Framework for business rule driven service composition. In: Benatallah, B., Shan, M.-C. (eds.) TES 2003. LNCS, vol. 2819, pp. 14–27. Springer, Heidelberg (2003)
7. Weigand, H., Van den Heuvel, W.-J., Hiel, M.: Rule-based service composition and service-oriented business rule management. Regulations Modelling and Deployment (ReMoD'08). CEUR (2008)
8. Goedertier, S., Vanthienen, J.: Declarative process modeling with business vocabulary and business rules. In: Meersman, R., Tari, Z., Herrero, P. (eds.) OTM 2007 Ws, Part I. LNCS, vol. 4805, pp. 603–612. Springer, Heidelberg (2007)
9. Kordelaar, P., van Teeseling, F., Hoogland, E.: Acquiring and modelling legal knowledge using patterns: an application for the Dutch immigration and naturalisation service. In: Cimiano, P., Pinto, H.S. (eds.) EKAW 2010. LNCS(LNAI), vol. 6317, pp. 341–349. Springer, Heidelberg (2010)
10. Lienhard, H., Künzi, U.-M.: Workflow and business rules: a common approach. In: Fischer, L. (ed.) Workflow Handbook 2005, pp. 129–140. Future Strategies Inc., Lighthouse Point (2005)
11. Gong, Y., Janssen, M.: From policy implementation to business process management: principles for creating flexibility and agility. Gov. Inf. Q. **29**, S61–S71 (2011)
12. Guinard, D., Trifa, V., Wilde, E.: A resource oriented architecture for the Web of Things. Internet of Things (IOT). IEEE (2010)
13. Taylor, J., Raden, N.: Smart (Enough) Systems: How to Deliver Competitive Advantage by Automating Hidden Decisions. Prentice Hall, New York (2007)
14. García-Sánchez, F., Sabucedo, L.Á., Martínez-Béjar, R., Rifón, L.A., Valencia-García, R., Góme, J.M.: Applying intelligent agents and semantic web services in eGovernment environments. Expert Systems **28**, 416–436 (2011)
15. Dietze, S., Benn, N., Domingue, J., Conconi, A., Cattaneo, F.: Two-fold service matchmaking – applying ontology mapping for semantic web service discovery. In: Gómez-Pérez, A., Yu, Y., Ding, Y. (eds.) ASWC 2009. LNCS, vol. 5926, pp. 246–260. Springer, Heidelberg (2009)
16. Bouwman, H., Van Houtum, H., Janssen, M., Versteeg, G.: Business architectures in the public sector: experiences from practice. Commun. Assoc. Inf. Syst. **29**, 411–426 (2011)
17. W3C: RIF Core Dialect (W3C Proposed Recommendation 22 June 2010). World Wide Web Consortium (2010). http://www.w3.org/TR/2010/REC-rif-core-20100622/

OpenCert 2012 —
6th International Workshop
on Foundations and Techniques
for Open Source Software Certification

Model-Based Tool Qualification
The Roadmap of Eclipse Towards Tool Qualification

Oscar Slotosch$^{(\boxtimes)}$

Validas AG, Munich, Germany
slotosch@validas.de

Abstract. In this paper we describe the model-based approach to tool qualification starting from the process model for the determination of the qualification need until the model for test and qualification. The model-based
approach can automate many steps from checking the syntactical requirements
completeness until the determination whether all requirements have been
implemented and successfully tested. Many required documents like the "Tool
Requirements Specification" or "Tool Test Specification" can be generated
from the model. The model-based approach has been shown to fulfill all
requirements from the DO-330 standard which describes tool qualification for
avionic, automotive and other industries. Therefore the Eclipse Foundation has
chosen this standard and proposed a roadmap to provide support for the
development of qualifiable Eclipse-based tools. This paper describes the
model-based approach and the roadmap of Eclipse to support this process.

Keywords: Tool qualification · Model-based · Eclipse · Roadmap · DO-330

1 Introduction

The amount of software in our world increases very fast. The usage of tools in the
development of this software in systems increases also. Therefore the correctness of
the software does not only depend on the development process of the software but also
of the tools used for the development of the software. For example static analyzers can
check the reachability of code or some potential errors in the code that had to be
detected using reviews. Test generation tools can automatically generate tests that
completely cover formalized requirement specifications and simulators allow to verify
software without their surrounding systems. However those tools can introduce or hide
safety relevant errors in the software.

This fact is reflected new standards for the development of safety critical systems
as the ISO 26262 [ISO26262], the DO-178C /DO-330 [DO330] and the IEC 61508
[61508]. These standards require to analyze all tools that are used within the development process of the software. This includes also the integration and verification of
the software. All these standards have a three phase approach for using tools safely:

(1) Classification: the tools are classified into classes that describe the confidence
     (certification credit) they require in the development process of the system.

A. Cerone et al. (Eds.): SEFM 2012 Satellite Events, LNCS 7991, pp. 215–228, 2014.
DOI: 10.1007/978-3-642-54338-8_18, © Springer-Verlag Berlin Heidelberg 2014

The classification is based on the analysis of potential errors in the tool and their detection or prevention probability within the process. Note that the confidence classes for tools differ among the different standards: tool confidence levels in the ISO 26262, tool criteria in the DO-178C and tool classes in the IEC 61508. Tools that do not require confidence since they have either no impact or a high detection probability for all their potential errors in the process can be used without qualification in the analyzed processes.

(2) Qualification: Tools that require confidence in the analyzed processes have to be qualified. Qualification might be restricted to the identified use cases and to show the absence of critical errors. In the ISO 26262 there are many qualification methods suggested (proven in use, process assessment, validation and development according to a safety standard). All qualifications methods require a tracing from the use cases to the known bugs and mitigations. The safety standards are the clearest approach, since they prescribe all actions in detail which does not leave so much room for interpretations and makes the tool qualifications better comparable.

(3) Usage: The tools can be used according to the known or found restrictions in the development process. There should be a documentation that contains the constraints from the process that have been considered in the analysis phase and workarounds for all restrictions found during tool qualification.

The tool qualification (required for certification) has been considered to be difficult since there were many unclear specified steps in the standards that left much space for interpretation and since the amount of requirements that have to be considered manually was very high.

In this paper we present a model-based approach for tool qualification. This has the following advantages:

- Clarity: the model has precisely defined elements and leaves (together with it's documentation) not much space for interpretation,
- Reusability and Transparency: since the model clearly states which requirements and functions have been qualified the qualifications can be easily checked for their reuse in different tool chains,
- Completeness: the model covers all phases in the development process and has been successfully traced against all requirements in the DO-330 standard and
- Automatization: the model can be automated in the following ways:

  - Consistency and completeness checks,
  - Inference of confidence requirements from the process model part,
  - Generation of documents from the model and
  - Integration into development environments.

Therefore the model-based approach can reduce the qualification (and certification) efforts dramatically and reduces tool qualification from a research topic to the essence of correct software development which is well known since many years.

This paper presents the model-based approach that has been proposed for the integration into the Eclipse development environment but can also be used in a stand-alone version for tools implemented using other IDEs or programming languages.

The model-based approach consists of the description and the model for the qualification data. The paper is structured as follows: Sect. 2 describes the purpose and the structure of the DO-330 standard. Section 3 describes the structure of the model and different parts of the model are presented in Sect. 4, while Sect. 5 roughly describes the tool qualification process. Section 6 describes the roadmap to enable Eclipse to support the model-based approach in an optimal way by integrating this model into the meta-model of Eclipse plugins. Section 7 describe the used support tools and Sect. 8 summarizes the approach.

2 DO-330

The DO-330 is called "Software Tool Qualification Considerations". It has been created to factor out the tool qualification topic from the standards DO-178C and DO-278A and it is also applicable to automotive and other applications as well. Since these other applications have different risk classes (for example ASILs in ISO 26262) there is an interface to other standards and processes in the DO-330. It is called the tool qualification level (TQL). There are five different TQLs (TQL-1 to TQL-5) that have different rigorous approaches. TQL-1 is the most rigorous level with the most requirements. The decision which TQL shall be used for which standard to create sufficiently tool confidence depends on the risk class and the determined qualification need. This mapping from tool criteria and risk class has to be defined in every standard. DO-178C and DO-278A contain such mappings (see Fig. 1), the ISO 26262 currently has no such mapping, since it appeared some weeks after the DO-330. A possible mapping for the ISO 26262 from ASILs and the tool confidence levels (TCL) to the DO-330 TQLs would be the only necessary adaptation of the ISO 26262 to use this standard with all it's positive aspects mentioned in the previous section. Such a mapping could be as defined as proposed in Fig. 1.

The structure of the DO-330 is according to the processes that shall be applied to develop and qualify tools. As every safety standard it does not prescribe a concrete process but poses requirements to processes that have to be satisfied. The structure of the DO-330 is depicted in Fig. 2. It contains processes in sections and sub-processes in subsections. The requirements within the DO-330 can be identified quite well using the numbers in it's sections and enumerations.

While the ISO 26262 determines the tool confidence level based on a detailed analysis of use cases, potential errors and applied checks and mitigations the DO-178C and IEC 61508 have a rather fixed classification from the tools into tool criteria

ASIL	TCL 1	TCL 2	TCL 3
D	TQL-5	TQL-2	TQL-1
C	TQL-5	TQL-3	TQL-2
B	TQL-5	TQL-4	TQL-3
A	TQL-5	TQL-5	TQL-4

Table 3: Determination of Tool Qualification Levels for DO-330

Table 12-1 Tool Qualification Level Determination

Software Level	Criteria		
	1	2	3
A	TQL-1	TQL-4	TQL-5
B	TQL-2	TQL-4	TQL-5
C	TQL-3	TQL-5	TQL-5
D	TQL-4	TQL-5	TQL-5

Fig. 1. TQL-Mappings for ISO 26262 (proposed) and DO-178C

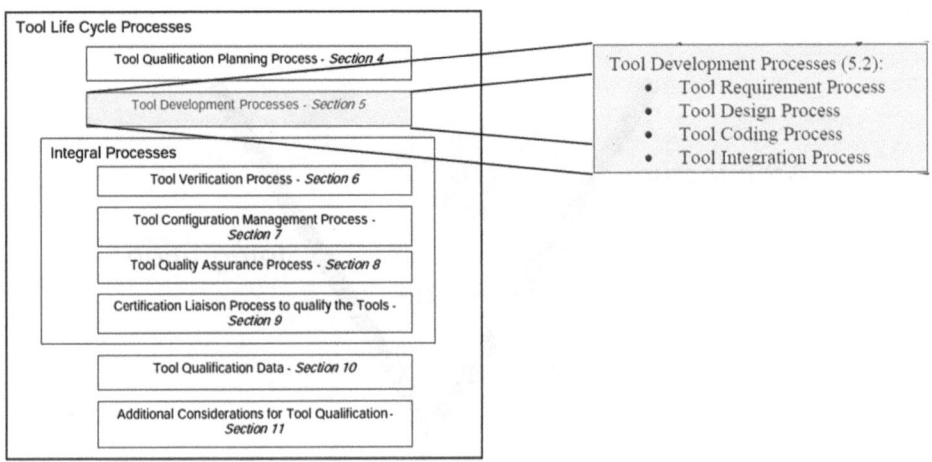

Fig. 2. Structure of DO-330

and tool classes. However the detailed analysis of the ISO can be applied also for the other standards, since it is a typical safety technique. The DO-330 states in FAQ D.3 that the tool criteria classification can be reduced by analyzing all uses cases of the tool and their potential errors. Therefore we integrated this approach into the model and we can reduce the tool criticality with this analysis for example by using redundancy.

3   Model-Based Qualification Approach

Model-based development is increasingly used in more and more processes, for example model-based code generation, model-based testing, model-based risk analyses, model-based design, documentation models, etc. The success of the models is caused by the appropriateness of the models, the automatized model analyses and the outputs of the models.

The Eclipse development tool (and other IDEs) are based on a meta model. It consists of classes, packages, etc. The Eclipse meta model covers also many design aspects using the plugin architecture, their export and import interfaces and contributions of other plugins to tool's functionality. The Eclipse modeling framework allows to generate code from design models. Also the integration process is specified using a meta model. Therefore the current model of Eclipse covers some aspects to satisfy the DO-330 (parts of architecture, design and integration) already. It can be depicted in Fig. 3. Note that the development process does not need to be a strict V, but can be differently organized. This meta models have been proved useful in the development with Eclipse, however they cover only small parts of the DO-330. Therefore we propose to extend the current meta model by new elements to cover also the missing phases of the DO-330.

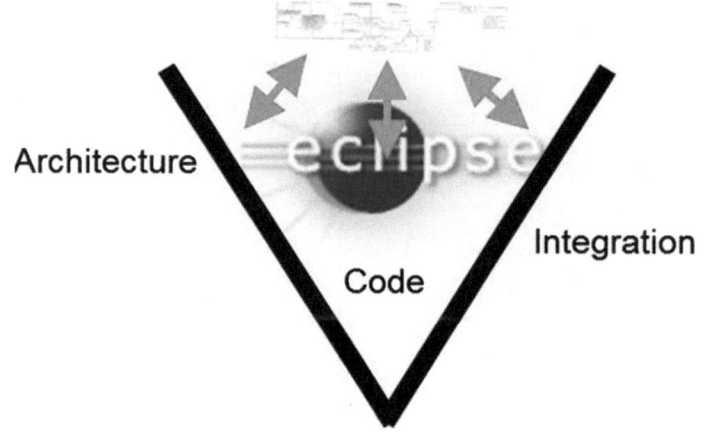

Fig. 3. Meta model and process phases of eclipse

In addition to the extended meta model we also need some instructions how to use the model correctly. These are documented in the following three documents:

- Howto Qualify Eclipse-based Tools [HowTo]: Contains the liaison process between the authority and the developer and some other steps like the application of the qualification kits. Furthermore it contains a complete tracing from all requirements in the DO-330 to the documents describing the model.
- Development Plan for every Qualifiable Eclipse Plugin [TDP]: Describes how to develop the plugins and how to model development artifacts to satisfy the corresponding DO-330 requirements.
- Verification Plan for every Qualifiable Eclipse Plugin [TVP]: Describes the generic verification activities and artifacts.

Note that these generic documents can be applied for every plugin of Eclipse. The plugin specific elements (plugin requirements, plugin design, code, tests,...) are modeled as described in the generic documents. All plugin specific documents (from the tool analysis in the plan of software aspects in certification (PSAC), until the verification reports can be generated from the meta model and the integrated verification tools.

The extended meta model covers the tool operational requirements (use cases), the tool requirements (functions and architecture) and the low-level requirements (code documentation in Eclipse) and the verification and qualification data. Also the other processes are covered from the model (see Sect. 4) (Fig. 4).

4   The Tool Qualification Model

The tool qualification model contains all data that are required for tool qualification. It is modeled with the Eclipse Modeling Framework [EMF] in a class diagram. Every artifact required for qualification is contained as a class in the qualification model. The

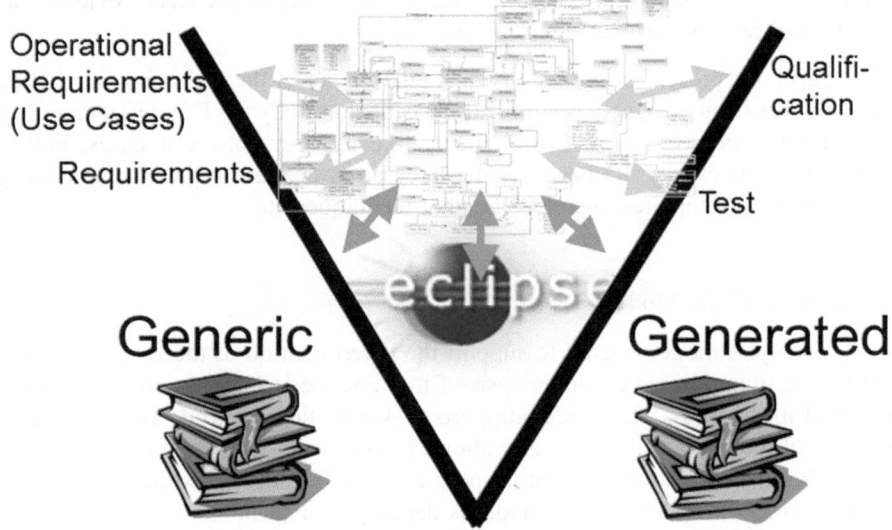

Operational
Requirements
(Use Cases)

Requirements

Qualifi-
cation

Test

Generic

Generated

Fig. 4. Extended meta model, documents and process phases of eclipse

tracing between the artifacts is modeled using associations. This allows a tracing from the process model for the usage of the tools via a stepwise refinement into requirements, code and test cases. Verification data classes for reviews and tests are added to the model and have to be populated from the verification activities. Even if the model is integrated in one big class diagram, it needs to be presented in several parts corresponding to different process areas of the DO-330. Therefore the generic tool development and the verification plans (see Sect. 3) have the following parts that contain the description of details (attributes and relations) of the model:

- Tool Analysis Model: It describes the artifacts and potential errors and error classes for the automated determination of the required tool confidence, see Sect. 4.1,
- Tool Operational Requirements (TORs): It describes the different TORs required from the DO-330 and the assumptions for the user, see Sect. 4.2,
- Tool Requirements (TRs): It describes the different kind of requirements of the tool,
- Tool Design: It contains the elements to describe the architecture of the tool and integrates many design elements of plugins, EMF, xText, packages, ecore diagrams, etc.
- Low Level Requirements (LLRs): It contains the LLRs that are an extension of the Javadoc formatted comments within Eclipse code,
- Implementation: It contains stubs to refer to the existing code in Eclipse like classes, methods etc. The stubs will be replaced with the existing models, once the model has been integrated into Eclipse by QPP (see Sect. 6),
- Quality Assurance: It contains the models of existing problem reports, their severity and the relations to tests and potential errors. This model has to be filled from problem reporting system and

- Test and Verification: They describe the model to represent tests, reviews, their results and relations to the requirements, etc.

In this paper we present only some parts of the model in the following subsections. The model has been designed as simple as possible to satisfy the DO-330 using simple strings for the description of the elements like requirements, test cases, problem reports, etc. This can be the basis for the integration of more sophisticated concepts like requirement templates, test specification techniques etc.

4.1   Tool Analysis Model

The tool analysis model is used to support the determination of the tool qualification level for the plugin based on an analysis of the functions of the plugin their potential errors and mitigations. The model supports a systematic way to derive the potential errors (black-box and white-box) and allows to compute the TQL automatically (see the tool chain analyzer tool for that purpose in [TCA]) as described in the ISO 26262 and allowed in the DO-330. The model is depicted in Fig. 5.

The tool analysis model is depicted using pink color. It is contained in the plugin project model (gray color) in two containers: **Artifacts**: contains all artifacts used by this plugin and **ToolAnalysis** containing the potential errors, their mitigations etc. Both containers are contained in the **Project** model that represents the information of the plugin project required for tool qualification, for example the **TQL** and the maximal risk level (**MaxRiscLevel**). The **TQL** is computed as described in [ISO26262], while the maximal risk level is a uniform interface to the risk levels of the different standards (Risk class in DO, SIL in IEC 61508 and ASIL in ISO 26262) and is used to compute the TQL from the maximal required confidence according to

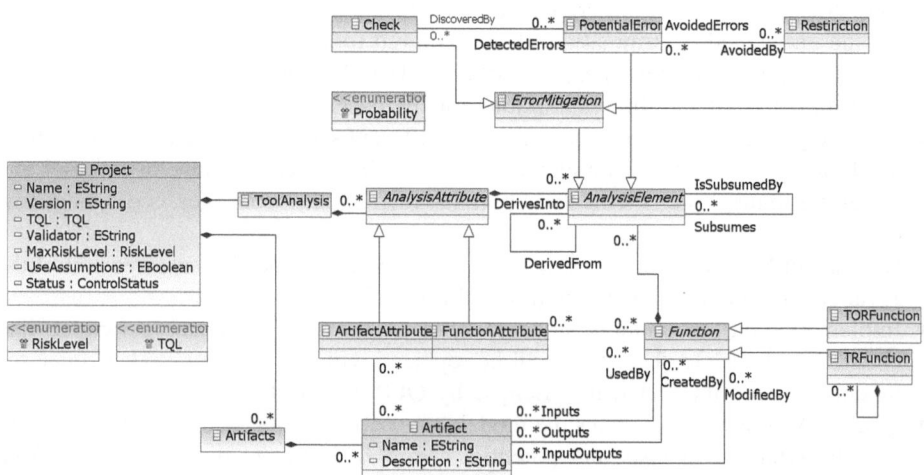

Fig. 5. Tool analysis model

Confidence Need	No Impact	LOW	MEDIUM	HIGH
Risk Level 1	No TQL	TQL 5	TQL 2	TQL 1
Risk Level 2	No TQL	TQL 5	TQL 3	TQL 2
Risk Level 3	No TQL	TQL 5	TQL 4	TQL 3
Risk Level 4	No TQL	TQL 5	TQL 5	TQL 4
No Level	No TQL	No TQL	No TQL	No TQL

Fig. 6. Determination of the TQL

the table in Fig. 6. Note that some standards might have deviations from this table, for example in ISO 26262 a low confidence need (TCL 1) requires no tool qualification.

In contrast to [WPJSZ12] where the functions are guessed manually from an assumed structure or the user manual of the tool, the analysis model in Fig. 5 has a well-defined interface to the functions developed. The used functions in a plugin are modeled as tool operational requirements (*TORFunction*) and refined to tool functions (*TRFunction*) during the requirements engineering. Those two parts are modeled in different colors (blue and green). Both elements have a common analysis interface *Function* that is used to assign the input/output artifacts to the functions and to assign the attributes that characterize the functions (*FunctionAttribute*) to them. Beside the *FunctionAttribute* elements that characterize a function (white box strategy), a function can also be analyzed as black box by just considering it's output *Artifacts*. The *Artifacts* are also characterized by attributes (*ArtifactAttribute*). Both *FunctionAttribute*s and *ArtifactAttribute*s are *AnalysisAttribute*s and contain the following *AnalysisElement*s: *PotentialError*, *Check* and *Restriction*. *AnalysisAttribute*s can be derived from other *AnalysisAttribute*s and can be subsumed to simplify the mitigation. Furthermore assumptions can be used in plugins (*UseAssumption* in *Project*) and the analysis (*Assumption* in *ErrorMitigation*) to model constraints the user of the tool has to respect.

The required confidence of a plugin is determined automatically from the given model as follows: all functions are characterized by function attributes and artifact attributes of their outputs and each analysis attribute has a set of typical errors. Those errors have to be assigned to mitigations that have *Probability* elements to detect or prevent the error if it would occur. The best mitigation for an error determines the probability to mitigate the error, while the worst error mitigation probability determines the confidence need as follows:

- If all errors in a plugin have a **high** mitigation probability the plugin has LOW qualification need /or confidence level,
- If at least one error has a **medium** mitigation probability the plugin has MEDIUM qualification need /or confidence level and
- If at least one error has no or **low** mitigation probability the plugin has HIGH qualification need /or confidence level.

The tool transition criteria (see Sect. 5) ensure that the functions are analyzed systematically within the tool qualification alpha state.

4.2   Tool Operational Requirements

The TORs describe how the tool is operating in it's environment. They can be seen as a description of the use cases of the tool. The provider of a plugin describes the developer use cases (from his point of view), while the user of the tool can use those unchanged or adapt it to his needs. The TORs are the top level requirements. The model of the TORs and some related elements is depicted in Fig. 7. Note that there are further requirements, not depicted in this overview, for example to describe interfaces, the architecture etc.

The TOR model is structured similar to the tool analysis model. All elements are in containers that are contained in the *Project* element that contains the plugins qualification data (grey color). The TORs (blue) consists of an abstract class *Tool-OperationalRequirement*. It has different sub classes for different kinds of requirements required from the DO-330. For example the functional operational requirements (*TORFunction*) are required to be considered in the tool operational requirements definition process (DO-330-5.1) in the consistency verification step (DO-330-5.1.2.b) and shall be contained in the tool qualification plan (DO-330-10.1.2.c). The format requirements (*TORFormat*) are required from the DO-330 in section 10.3.1 where the formats of input and output files in the operational environment shall be contained. The *TORAssumption* class is used to model assumptions to the usage of the tool, for example to avoid some constructs or to perform checks to verify the output of the tools. The assumptions are the interface from the tool to the user of the tool to ensure a save development process. Furthermore there are operational requirements on the context in which the system should run (*TORContext* for example required by DO-330-10.3.1.b) and there are other requirements (*TOROther*) that can be used to model other operational requirements of the tool.

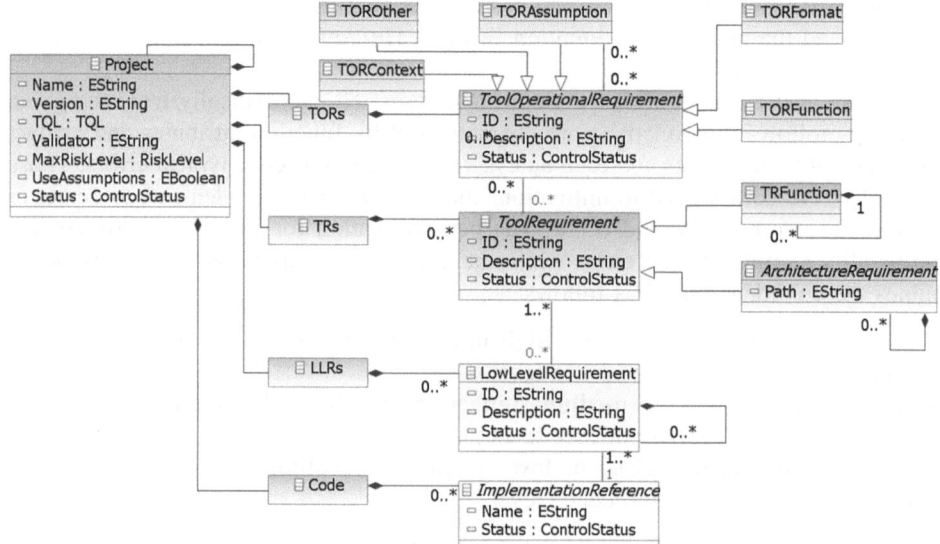

Fig. 7. Tool operational requirements model

All TORs (use cases) have to be mapped to tool requirements (functions) are that implemented in the tool using LLRs (*LowLevelRequirement*) and have references to the code (*ImplementationReference*). The architecture requirements (*Architecture-Requirement*) are modeled as special cases of tool requirements (*ToolRequirement*). These elements are modeled like the TORs. However Fig. 7 shows only the abstract elements to illustrate the structure. More details can be found in the tool development plan.

5 Tool Development and Qualification Process

The tool development process is not restricted except that it is required to use the model to document the development steps. This can be done before, during or after the development of the code, thus supporting also the qualification of existing tools and plugins. However it is recommended to stick to established software-engineering processes.

The qualification process makes use of the tool qualification model. Especially the tool life cycle and the transition criteria can be determined automatically based on the model. The transition criteria define different development stages of the tool/plugin from the qualification point of view. This has the advantage that the well working development processes of the Eclipse community do not need to be changed, but they are enriched by an addition attribute the "qualification stage" that is independent from the other processes. Qualified tools/plugins must have the stage "Qualification Release".

The following qualification stages are defined for each plugin and have a formal definition that is based on the qualification mode:

- **Unqualified Pre-Alpha Release:** The plugin is an undefined, unknown qualification state, for example if the model is missing,
- **Qualification Alpha-Release:** The TORs are defined and TQL is determined for the plugin. It is "analyzed",
- **Qualification Beta-Release:** All requirements (TORs and TRs) are described and have links to LLRs and Code. The plugin is "feature complete",
- **Qualification Release Candidate:** All required verification steps are defined. No open bugs of the category Blocker are available. The plugin is "Verification Defined" and
- **Qualification Release:** Verification has been successfully executed and is documented within the qualification kit. The plugin is "Successfully Verified".

The qualification stages are based on each other, i.e. the qualification beta-release requires the alpha release and additional constraints. If some elements, e.g. requirements are changed this invalidates the verification data that bases on this element such that the qualification stage is reduced.

The transition criteria are defined on the qualification data using their attributes and relations from the qualification model. For example the transition into the alpha release requires (among other similar checks) that the qualification model of the plugin has at least one *TORFunction* element defined in the plugin and that this has a nonempty name and description and the CM status is reviewed. The TORFunction element should have an Artifact element assigned as input or output and at least one potential error. All details of the transition criteria are described in the tool development plan.

The qualification process for a tool is as follows:

(1) Determine the plugins required for the tool,
(2) Classify the plugins, i.e. reach the qualification alpha state in the corresponding qualification models and determine the TQL of the plugins and
(3) Qualify the plugins that require confidence according to the determined TQL.

The assumptions of the required plugins under which the TQL is computed have to be satisfied. If they are not satisfied by construction of the tool they will correspond to assumptions of the tool that have to be satisfied from the user of the tool.

Similar to the development of Eclipse-based tools, where plugins can be integrated and reused the qualification information (classification and qualification kit) can also be reused in several tools. This enables a modular qualification approach and makes the qualification of plugins that are used in many tools to a common interest of all users of those plugins that want to qualify their tools.

6   Roadmap of Eclipse

Since currently Eclipse does not support tool qualification but many tools that require tool qualification base on Eclipse there should be tool qualification support for Eclipse to ease the qualification of those tools. Validas AG has developed a roadmap towards the qualification of Eclipse-based tools within the automotive industrial working group of Eclipse [AutoIWG]. It consists of the following steps:

- Goals Agreement: The goals of the roadmap are to enable the tool qualification of Eclipse-based tools according to the DO-330 which is applicable to all domains. This shall not change the normal process of Eclipse, but gives the possibility to analyze, develop and qualify critical parts of Eclipse-based tools.
- Concept Elaboration: The concept is to use the model-based tool qualification on the level of Eclipse plugins as presented in this paper.
- Concept validation: The concept will be validated in two steps, that both will improve the concept:
  - Demonstrator: A small tool will be developed and qualified according to the concept. We selected the implementation of the transition criteria checker of the DO-330 model as demonstrator application. This will show the feasibility of the concept and provide us with estimations on the required effort,
  - DO-330 Review: The DO-330 review shall review the presented concept and the work products produced during the demonstrator and shall verify if the DO-330 is covered correctly by the concept and the demonstrator,
- Qualifiable Plugin Projects (QPP): This will be a typical Eclipse project that will extend the current plugin mechanism such that it supports the creation of the

qualification model (with the tools mentioned in Sect. 7) during the development and the generation of the plugin specific documents from the model and

- Qualification: Selected plugins of Eclipse will be qualified. For the selection and the qualification there will a business model and an eco system of people ("Validators") that qualify tools and verify the necessary conditions. Note that there are some mechanism of Eclipse that ensure the modularity and the correctness of the approach that are of highest priority to qualify.

Eclipse follows this roadmap towards tool qualification within the work package 5 of the automotive IWG [AutoIWG] for an actual status of the roadmap and some presentations of the topic.

7   Tools

There are many tools that can be used with a model-based tool qualification. The tools may also differ in different IDEs. However it is required to integrate them into the generic development plan such that the plan satisfies the DO-330 requirements. For Eclipse we propose a configuration and description of supporting tools that has been successfully checked to fulfill the DO-330 requirements in the chosen configuration. The proposed tools are: Git, [Gerrit], Bugzilla and [CodeCover].

8   Conclusion

New Standards like the ISO 26262 allow to classify the tools according to the used processes and also the DO-330 states in FAQ D.3 that this is possible. Therefore the presented model-based tool qualification approach seems to be very promising, especially since the integration into Eclipse can reduce the overhead for qualification significantly. Currently the approach is evaluated by developing a Eclipse plugin according to it. Of course further relevant plugins of Eclipse and some Eclipse parts need qualification as well [HowTo] but this work enables the model-based tool qualification and will be the basis for all further qualification activities of Eclipse.

This classification approach has been applied from many users [HRMSP11], [WPJSZ12], but the combination of the classification model with the development model is new and also for the Eclipse tool there is neither a classification, nor a qualification model available.

The effort for development of qualifiable tools can be split into the effort for developing a reliable tool (starting from the requirements until the test that completely cover the code) and the effort for providing the documentation to make it evident to the user of the tool or a certification authority. While the effort for developing a reliable tool is high, the additional effort for documenting this should be quite low. Therefore the development of qualifiable tools should not be much more work than the development of reliable tools. For non-reliable tools the effort for making it reliable is surely higher.

The development of reliable systems is something quite well studied based on the domain specific standards. Speaking in terms of [Rus11], this work is the construction of a specific safety case [BB98], however focused on tools and not on systems such that the safety claim is that the used tools must not corrupt the safety of the developed systems. The development of reliable tools requires many verification steps like reviews and tests that should be performed by trustworthy persons.

For that purpose we propose to create the role "Validator" in the Eclipse community that is a specialization of the "Committer" role for tool validation. The Validators task is to validate that the required verification steps are executed correctly. This can be supported with a public visible profile like the traders in eBay have. The Validators can gain positive ratings if they successfully verify activities. If their verification turns out to be false they will get negative feedback. Being a positive Validator will be even more desirable than being an active committer.

Acknowledgments. We would like to thank the Eclipse Foundation and it's automotive industrial working group for supporting us in the development, especially Mario Driussi. Furthermore we like to thank Stefan Dirix and Natacha Tchebetchou for their contributions to the roadmap and BMW CarIT (Michael Rudorfer und Tilmann Ochs) to support the development of the demonstrator. For review comments we would like Jan Philipps and the unknown reviewers of this paper.

Especially we would like to thank all authors of the DO-330 to provide the first general safety standard for tool qualification that could be adopted for Eclipse so easily.

References

[61508] International Electrotechnical Commission, IEC 61508, Functional safety of electrical/electronic/programmable electronic safety-related systems, 2nd edn, April 2010

[AutoIWG] Automotive Eclipse Automotive Industrial Working Group for tool qualification. http://wiki.eclipse.org/Auto_IWG_WP5

[BB98] Bishop, P., Bloomfield, R.: A methodology for safety case development. In: Safety-Critical Systems Symposium, Birmingham, February 1998. http://www.adelard.com/resources/papers/pdf/sss98web.pdf (1998)

[CodeCover] An open source glass-box testing tool. http://codecover.org/

[DO330] RTCA. DO-330: Software Tool Qualification Considerations, 1st edn, 13 December 2011

[EMF] The Eclipse Modeling Framework. http://www.eclipse.org/modeling/emf/

[Gerrit] Code Review Tool for Git. http://code.google.com/p/gerrit/

[HowTo] Eclipse (Proposal): How-To Qualify Eclipse-Based Tools, Version 1.0, to be published when reviewed

[HRMSP11] Hillebrand, J., Reichenpfader, P., Mandic, I., Siegl, H., Peer, C.: Establishing confidence in the usage of software tools in context of ISO 26262. In: Flammini, F., Bologna, S., Vittorini, V. (eds.) SAFECOMP 2011. LNCS, vol. 6894, pp. 257–269. Springer, Heidelberg (2011)

[ISO26262] International Organization for Standardization. ISO 26262 Road Vehicles – Functional safety–, 1st edn, 15 November 2011

[Rus11] Rushby, J.: New challenges in certification for aircraft software. In: EMSOFT'11, 9–14 October 2011, Taipei (2011)

[TCA] Tool Chain Analyzer Tool. http://www.validas.de/TCA.html

[TDP] Eclipse (Proposal): Tool Development Plan for every Qualifiable Eclipse Plugin, Version 1.0, to be published when reviewed

[TVP] Eclipse (Proposal): Tool Verification Plan for every Qualifiable Eclipse Plugin, Version 1.0, to be published when reviewed

[WPJSZ12] Wildmoser, M., Philipps, J., Jeschull, R., Slotosch, O., Zalman, R.: ISO 26262 - Tool chain analysis reduces tool qualification costs. In: SAFECOMP (2012)

Secure Migration of Legacy Applications to the Web

Zisis Karampaglis[1], Anakreon Mentis[1], Fotios Rafailidis[1]([✉]),
Paschalis Tsolakidis[2], and Apostolos Ampatzoglou[1]

[1] Department of Informatics, Aristotle University of Thessaloniki,
Thessaloniki, Greece
{zkarampa,anakreon,frafaili,apamp}@csd.auth.gr
[2] Chalmers University of Technology, Gothenburg, Sweden
pastso@chalmers.student.se

Abstract. In software engineering, migration of an application is the process of moving the software from one execution platform to another. Nowadays, many desktop applications tend to migrate to the web or to the cloud. Desktop applications are not prepared to face the hostile environment of the web where applications frequently receive harmful data that attempt to exploit program vulnerabilities such as buffer overflows. We propose a migration process for desktop applications with a text-based user interface, which mitigates existing security concerns and enables the software to perform safely in the web without modifying its of the source code. Additionally, we describe an open source tool that facilitates our migration process.

Keywords: Software migration · Web application · User interface · Legacy application

1 Introduction

Migration of a software application is the process of moving it from one execution platform to another that is thought to be a more fitting one for the purpose of its operational use. For example, migration could mean replacing a Windows-based environment with a Linux-based environment or vice versa.

Nowadays, the growing trend for providing Software as a Service (SaaS) and the globalization of modern economy, demand the transfer of many systems to the web or even to the cloud. Such a transfer involves obvious implementation costs and security-related risks as well. Web applications are exposed to a large and distributed user base that, by accident or malice, can provide input that is harmful to the application execution and stored data.

In this paper we propose a migration process for *legacy* applications to the web, that protects the application from harmful user provided input. The proposed process uses an open-source tool developed by the authors for automatically adapting the text-based user interfaces to web-based UI without changing the program code.

A. Cerone et al. (Eds.): SEFM 2012 Satellite Events, LNCS 7991, pp. 229–243, 2014.
DOI: 10.1007/978-3-642-54338-8_19, © Springer-Verlag Berlin Heidelberg 2014

In Sect. 2, we discuss the current state of the art on how to modernize legacy applications and on data sanitization techniques. In Sect. 3, we describe the proposed migration process, along with a qualitative evaluation. Section 4 precuts the developed tool. Section 5 examines threats to validity while Sect. 6 provides conclusions derived from the outlined research and proposes future research and development prospect.

2 Related Work

In this section of the paper we provide background information and related work on the problems addressed in this paper, i.e. modernization of legacy applications and data sanitization. More specifically, in Sect. 2.1 we provide a literature review of studies on processes for migrating legacy applications to more modern environments. In Sect. 2.2, we describe basic concepts of data sanitization and related work on tools that perform these tasks.

2.1 Modernization of Legacy Application

Bringing legacy applications at par to the latest technological standards has been the focus of many research efforts. They propose a wide variety of processes and methods to modernize the software components of the legacy applications as well as the hardware they perform on. Modification of legacy code is an expensive and error-prone task which most research efforts address only partially. A middleware is usually introduced to provide the necessary stepping stone for the migration of the application into a modern execution platform. Software modernization is achieved by enhancing application properties such as availability, usability, security, flexibility, interoperability, expandability and maintainability.

Modern operating systems prevent or limit direct access to system components that raise interoperability issues with some legacy applications. In [19], the authors propose the use of a Virtual Desktop Infrastructure that executes the legacy application in its own OS. In [12], the authors propose the use of a POSIX shell interpreter and an applet to allow the execution of an application from different operating systems. In our approach we achieve migration of desktop applications to the Web by introducing a TUI middleware maintaining platform independency. Similarities with our approach can be found in [13], where the authors describe two problems that legacy applications must surpass to achieve web-integration: platform dependencies and quality requirements that the application should meet. The authors show that both problems are efficiently resolved by a middleware product.

In [10], several case studies of test-driven methods are presented to define the flexibility of a legacy application in terms of security, by determining the degree of coupling between business logic and access control. Highly coupled applications are less flexible and require more modifications in the implementation to enhance security. In [9], the author presents an Interface Adapter Layer to enable communication between a Common Object Request Broker Architecture

(CORBA) platform and a legacy application. With this technique, the legacy application maintains its autonomy, enhances its availability and improves its security. The TUI library in this paper operates as a communication bus between the Web and the legacy application, obtaining the aforementioned benefits.

Approaches to increase flexibility appear in [18] where the authors propose a framework to enable Quality of Service (QoS) based on a network layer mechanism, for legacy applications. The main constraint of introducing such a framework is the inflexibility to modification and recompilation that comes with legacy code. In order to surpass this obstacle the authors use a middleware component that bridges the gap between the application and the network QoS entities. The same applies for the Web implementation of our approach, which needs only the recompilation of the UI Library and not of the legacy code.

An approach to usability comes from [7] where the authors suggest two proof-of-concept techniques to change the user interface of legacy applications into an innovative one. They separated the graphic output subsystem and the user interface from the application and modified them to support modern ways of interaction without changing the core of the application. In this paper the API/TUI is used in the same way to allow interaction from the Web without altering the code of the legacy application.

An upward trend exists that supports the transition of legacy applications towards a Service Oriented Architecture (SOA). Legacy applications are usually transformed into Grid services or services of cloud computing. In [1], the authors propose three approaches to transition legacy applications to Web Services through Service Oriented Architecture (SOA). The reason for this transition is the increased need for new features in organizations legacy IT infrastructure. The three approaches are: a session based approach that changes only the Graphical User Interface (GUI) keeping the code of the legacy application unmodified, a transaction based approach to cover security issues that come with the transition and a data based approach that expose the data of the application to the Web.

In [21] the authors propose a method for migrating legacy applications into Grid Services. The otherwise standalone applications are reused and wrapped into the Grid technology by using the Globus Toolkit. The main benefit of this approach is that multi-user access can be achieved without modifying the code of the application for Internet functionality. Similar to [21], the authors of [6,8,11] present their proposals for migrating legacy code into Grid services without changing the source code of the application. The architecture of such an approach is identical to the architecture of our tool. In [20], the authors provide a solution to migrate a legacy application to the cloud. The Application Migration Solution (AMS) reconstructs the GUI of the application without changing its source code. The solution also supports the compilation of more than one application together, in order to create a more powerful, in terms of features, application.

The authors of [4] use the Ubiquitous Web Application (UWA) framework to reengineer a legacy application into the web. The benefits of their approach are good documentation and high usability/maintainability for the reengineered application as opposed to a production-oriented approach based on studies from past years. An extension of the above work from the same authors is in [5]. They used the Ubiquitous Web Applications Design Framework (UWA) and an extended version with Transaction Design Model (UWAT+). Through this approach they leveraged legacy applications into rich Internet ones and due to the formality of the framework they minimized the time needed for the transition.

Expandability towards modern technologies seems that is not a top priority for legacy applications. The authors of [2] present a solution to the problem of continuous re-engineering for legacy applications. With constant maintenance to keep an application up to date with the latest technological standards, its architectural structure becomes more difficult to expand. To mitigate the problem they suggest the use of ArchJava in order to ensure the integrity of the original architectural structure.

2.2   Data Sanitization

Sanitization takes user input and transforms it in order to eliminate potential threats for the data and operation of the application. Threats exist due to the use of characters known as *metacharacters* that have special meaning, when processed by the various parts of a system. The transformation of user input is applied by removing characters based on two methods. These methods are distinguished by using a white or black list of characters, which contain characters that respectively can or cannot be harmful for the application.

For example, an SQL Injection attack consists of insertion or "injection" of a SQL query via the input data from the client to the application using meta-characters or special characters of SQL, such as ', ', AND, =. An SQL injection attack can read sensitive data, modify data, and execute administration operations. The example from [15] in Listing 19.1 uses a *Prepared Statement.* Consider the string *john* is the value for input parameter *user_name*, which is a valid input. The application will search a user with the *user_name john* and will return all information for this user. On the opposite, if someone passes the string *1 OR 1=1*, this leads to an attack because the query that the program submits to the database contains a tautology in the WHERE clause and gain access to sensitive information regarding database users.

Listing 19.1. Sample code for SQL Injection

```
String firstname = req.getParameter("firstname");
String query = "SELECT * FROM authors
        WHERE firstname = ? ";
PreparedStatement pstmt =
        connection.prepareStatement( query );
pstmt.setString( 1, firstname);
ResultSet results = pstmt.execute( );
```

To prevent an SQL Injection Attack, we apply data sanitization. The quotes ', ' and = are removed from the string and the sanitized string will be *1OR11*, which cannot be a tautology. Several characters can be meta-characters depending on the language of the application. Data sanitization aims to prevent harmful input data to be inserted in an application. In [14] the authors propose a technique of automatic query sanitization to prevent SQL Injection attacks. They use a combination of static analysis and program transformation to automatically instrument web applications with sanitization code.

There are three different ways to apply data sanitization to the user data. The first way is to use tools, which take user data, sanitize them and produce as output the sanitized user data to be sent to the web application. *Urlrewritefilter* is based on a tool that rewrites url using certain filters and sends the modified url to the web application. Another tool for sanitizing html tags, attributes and values is *jsoop*. *Jetscripts* Data Sanitizer and XSS cleaner prevents SQL Injection and XSS attacks by cleaning or sanitizing user-submitted data. This tool is intended for users who write or modify scripts, or want an extra measure of protection against malicious users. It requires some knowledge in php scripting. The sanitizer can work in various modes such as numeric only, alphabetic only, alphanumeric only, alphanumeric with punctuation and email validation mode. Additionally to the above modes common command entities and Javascript specific entities are removed.

The second way is to use libraries that offer functions which sanitize input data. The ESAPI library by OWASP provides libraries for many programming languages such as Java, .net, ASP, PHP, PHP, ColdFusion, Python, JavaScript, Objective-C, Ruby, C, CPP and Perl.

The third way is to use embedded functions in various languages that sanitize input data depending on special characters for each language. At php, function *mysql_real_escape_string()* sanitizes special character of mysql at a string, which is proposed to be sent to the mysql database. Other functions are *filter_input()*, *escapeshellarg()* and *urlencode* for php, etc. Finally, tools that are used to statically analyze the vulnerabilities of code written in C are presented and compared in [3].

Security issues caused by invalid sanitization of user-provided input is the focus of [16]. Cross-site scripting (XSS) exploits is prevented without any modifications to the application implementation.

3   Migration Process

A typical architecture for desktop applications is shown in Fig. 1. The application receives input from the keyboard and renders the output on the user's screen. Both input and output are handled by a TUI library responsible for the translation of user input into a series of events and the application output into user interface elements such as windows, labels and buttons. The application interaction with the user consists of appropriate reactions to the events generated by the TUI library.

On the other hand, in a web–based architecture the user–provided data are encoded as POST or GET variables transferred via the HTTP protocol. An

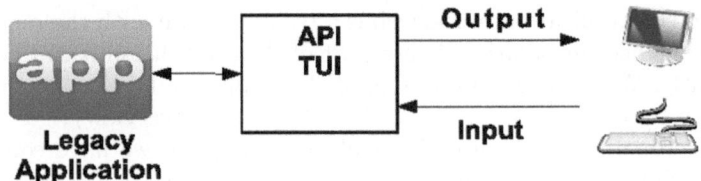

Fig. 1. Legacy application architecture

application residing on the server processes the received user input and responds with an HTML document displayed to the user by a web browser. To compensate for the stateless nature of the HTTP protocol, web applications store information that are required in conversations between the client and the server in cookies or include the values in POST or GET variables in every exchange of data. Clearly, this is in contrast with desktop applications that can preserve state between subsequent user interactions.

Desktop applications operate in a relatively secure environment where the user–provided input can be trusted and is checked only for accidental mistakes. In contrast, malformed user input is often deliberately sent to web applications with the explicit goal to disable it's normal operation or to gain access to sensitive data managed by the considered web application.

The proposed migration process aims at (a) transferring the application to the web without modifying the application code base and (b) secure the application from harmful input received from the web interface.

We propose a two step process to achieve those goals. To fulfill the first goal we replace the TUI library with a modified version that does not receive the user–provided input from the keyboard; instead it uses the information provided by the GET and POST variables. Moreover, the modified TUI library produces an HTML document which, when rendered by the browser, displays the application output and TUI elements that enable further interactions. The second goal is realized by the sanitizer component that blocks malformed input or transforms potentially dangerous input into harmless data. The application architecture produced from the proposed method is shown in Fig. 2.

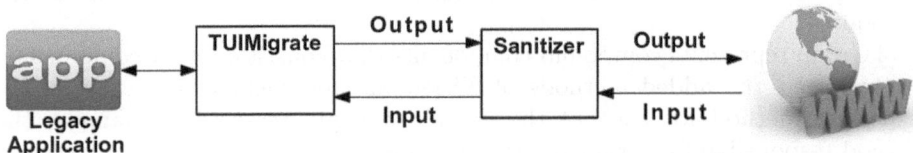

Fig. 2. The architecture of the web–enabled legacy application

The proposed process clearly addresses both migration goals. The modified TUI library retains the same API with the original version. All that is required for enabling the application in the web is a recompilation with the modified TUI library. Also, since the sanitizer is not part of the application it can be modified independently. We could integrate one of the many available open source tools that provide sanitization services (see Sect. 2.2 for an overview).

In order to validate the usefulness of our approach, we have conducted an interview with the project manager of a CRM created in the early 1980s for the DOS operating system. After three years of development, the CRM was migrated to the Windows OS. Currently, they are considering migrating the application to the web which they estimate it will require an additional five year period. The duration of migrating from Windows to the Web is estimated to be as long as the transition from DOS to Windows, because of increased security threats in the execution environment of web applications.

The above case suggests that an automated process for a secure migration of legacy applications to the web would be useful for the software industry.

4   The Modified UI Library

In this section we show in detail the required process for modifying a Text User Interfaces (TUI) library in order to enable applications that use it in the web. The process is applied on an open source TUI named Turbo Vision [17], a framework developed by Borland and later placed in the public domain. It provides a reach user interface with various components such as menus, check boxes, buttons, and many others. Figure 3 shows a Turbo Vision application.

The modified library expects user input not from input devices such as the keyboard or the mouse but from a file or the standard input. Also, the application output is not rendered on the screen. Instead, it is transformed into an XML document which can be rendered to the user's browser with the help of style sheets or some other method able to produce an HTML document. Our library is currently in beta version and is distributed[1] freely under a permissive free software license.

TVision components correspond to C++ classes that form the hierarchy shown in Fig. 4. TView is the base class inherited by all components. We declared additional methods in this class responsible for exporting the component's state into XML and for recovering a previous state from a textual format. When needed, derived classes modify accordingly the implementation of the added methods.

TGroup represents compound components that consist of other components. In this class, the added methods of TView are reimplemented to invoke the respective method for each of the contained components. For example, the method responsible for serializing the component's state into XML invokes the same method of each contained component and returns the merged obtained output.

TVision applications consists of one or more TDialog instances where only one of them is active at any time. Dialogs are modal, the user can interact only

---

[1] http://sourceforge.net/projects/tuimigrate

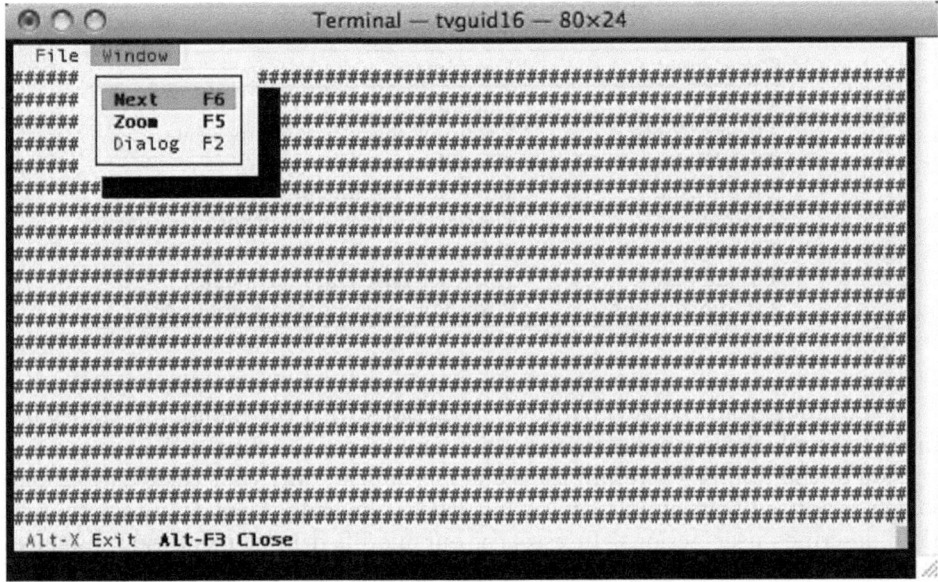

Fig. 3. An example TUI application

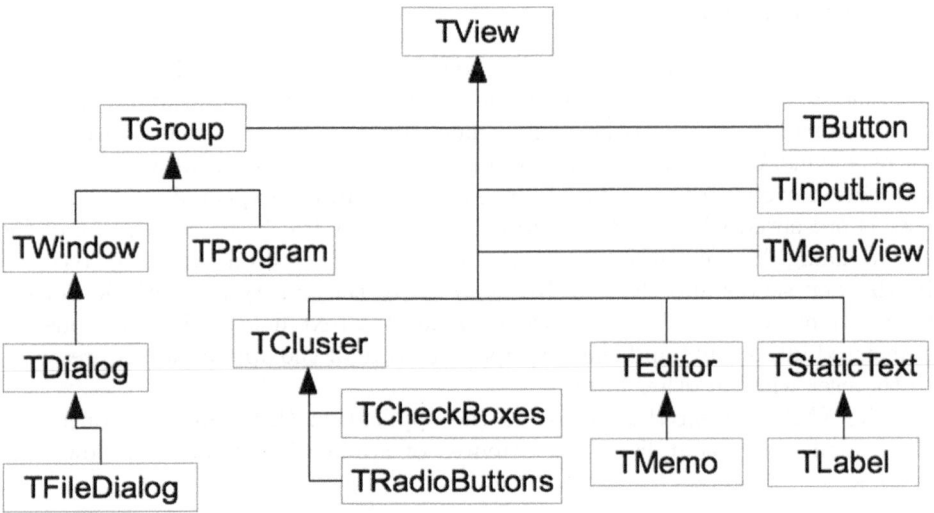

Fig. 4. TVision classes and their hierarchy

with the active dialog and the other dialogs of the application are inaccessible until the active one is closed. TDialog is a container for other components shown in Table 1.

Table 1. Main TVision components

Component	Description
TButton	Buttons
TCheckBoxes	Group of check-box components
TFileDialog	File selector
TInputLine	Input for one line of text
TLabel	Descriptive labels for other components
TMemo	Multi-line text input control
TMenuView	Abstract base class for menus
TRadioButtons	Group of radio button components

User input from the keyboard or interactions with the mouse are translated into events which the application can bind and react accordingly. In our modified version of the library we retain the same mechanism only that the events are no longer produced from input devices but from a specially formatted text content that describes user actions. In essence, our modified implementation emulates the user interactions and as far as the application code is concerned, nothing is changed.

4.1 Input/Output

The library binds a port in order to communicate with the client application (e.g. the sanitizer) and accepts two commands. One command produces an XML description of the currently accessible dialog and the components it contains (e.g. forms, menus, buttons etc.), while the other command asks the library to produce interaction events from a textual representation. In the expected work-flow, the user is presented with an HTML form produced by the XML description of the active dialog, his interactions with the form are reflected on the values received by the web server and the sanitizer submits to the library a description of the user actions (e.g. the button clicked, value of a text field). Those actions are translated into events and the new updated state of the application is presented to the user with an other form.

The XML content that describes the application User Interface consists of three main parts that list the attributes of application menus, windows and dialogs:

Menu. Menus contain menu items as well as nested menus. Menu items can be identified by a name or by an identifier and the schema defines the two respective attributes. Moreover, menu items can be associated with an action performed when the user selects it.

Window. This part describes the windows of the application. Windows have a title and contain other components.

Dialog. The document contains a dialog description only if there is an active dialog and describes all the components contained in the dialog. Since dialogs are modal, the previous two sections of the document are not included in order to prevent the user from accessing menu entries or windows.

All elements (windows, dialogs, menus and components) have the following common attributes: a unique identifier, a type, a content attribute that stores the component's value and a name. In Listing 19.2 we show an excerpt of the XML Schema that defines in detail the structure of the XML document produced by the library.

Listing 19.2. A small part of the output XML schema

```
<xs:element name="dialog">
    <xs:complexType>
        <xs:choice maxOccurs="unbounded">
            <xs:element ref="label"/>
            <xs:element ref="text"/>
            <xs:element ref="button"/>
            <xs:element ref="checkbox"/>
            <xs:element ref="radiobutton"/>
        </xs:choice>
    </xs:complexType>
    <xs:key name="formItemKey">
        <xs:selector xpath="*"/>
        <xs:field xpath="@id"/>
    </xs:key>
    <xs:keyref name="formItemRef" refer="formItemKey">
        <xs:selector xpath="label"/>
        <xs:field xpath="@idref"/>
    </xs:keyref>
</xs:element>
<xs:element name="checkbox">
  <xs:complexType>
    <xs:sequence maxOccurs="unbounded">
      <xs:element name="item">
        <xs:complexType>
          <xs:simpleContent>
            <xs:extension base="xs:string">
              <xs:attribute name="selected"
              type="xs:boolean"/>
              <xs:attribute name="id"
              type="xs:int" use="required"/>
    ....
    </xs:sequence>
    <xs:attribute ref="id" use="required"/>
  </xs:complexType>
</xs:element>
```

User actions are provided in a textual description where each line corresponds to an action. Lines are expected to have one of the forms shown in Table 2.

Table 2. Available instructions for altering the TUI state

Form	Description
name :: value	Assigns a value to the component identified by the given name.
id <: value	Assigns a value to the component identified by the given id.
name :> index	Activates a component with the given index contained in a component identified by the provided name.
id <> index	Has the same effect as the previous command for the container with the provided unique identifier.

Let us examine a user session to demonstrate our approach and see how user interactions are handled by the application with the help of the modified TUI library. At first the user is presented with an HTML form produced by the window shown in Fig. 3 and selects the "Dialog" menu. The form is submitted to the web server and the sanitizer components delivers to the application the following instruction:

```
m202 <: active
```

which selects the application's "Dialog" menu and performs the associated action. The performed action creates a new modal dialog shown in Fig. 5 described in XML in Listing 19.3. After the user modifies the values of the various controls, it submits the form with the "OK" button delivering to the application the following action description:

```
1  Delivery Instructions : : Hurry!
2  Cheeses :> 0
3  8 <> 2
4  6 <: Runny
5  OK : : true
```

In the first line, the library is instructed to set the value of the text component associated with the label named "Delivery Instructions" to "Hurry!". In Listing 19.3, the "idref" attribute of the label shows which component is associated with the label. In the second line, the library finds the check box group component associated with the label "Cheeses" and selects the first check box (index zero). The third line performs the same action but it refers to the check box group by id and selects the third check box. As a result of lines two and three, "Tilset" is the only unselected check box. The fourth instruction sets the value of the component with id 6 to "Runny" effectively selecting the second radio button of the radio group labeled "Consistency". Finally, the last action selects the button labeled "OK" and performs its associated actions.

Listing 19.3. XML produced from TUI of figure 5

```xml
<?xml version="1.0" encoding="UTF-8"?>
<program xmlns:xsi=
        "http://www.w3.org/2001/XMLSchema-instance">
  <dialog>
    <button id="1">Cancel</button>
    <button id="2">OK</button>
    <label id="3" idref="4">Delivery Instructions</label>
    <text id="4"><![CDATA[Phone Mum!]]></text>
    <label id="5" idref="6">Consistency</label>
    <radiobutton id="6">
        <item selected="false" id="0">Solid</item>
        <item selected="false" id="1">Runny</item>
        <item selected="true" id="2">Melted</item>
    </radiobutton>
    <label id="7" idref="8">Cheeses</label>
    <checkbox id="8">
        <item selected="true" id="0">Hvarti</item>
        <item selected="false" id="1">Tilset</item>
        <item selected="false" id="2">Jarlsberg</item>
    </checkbox>
  </dialog>
</program>
```

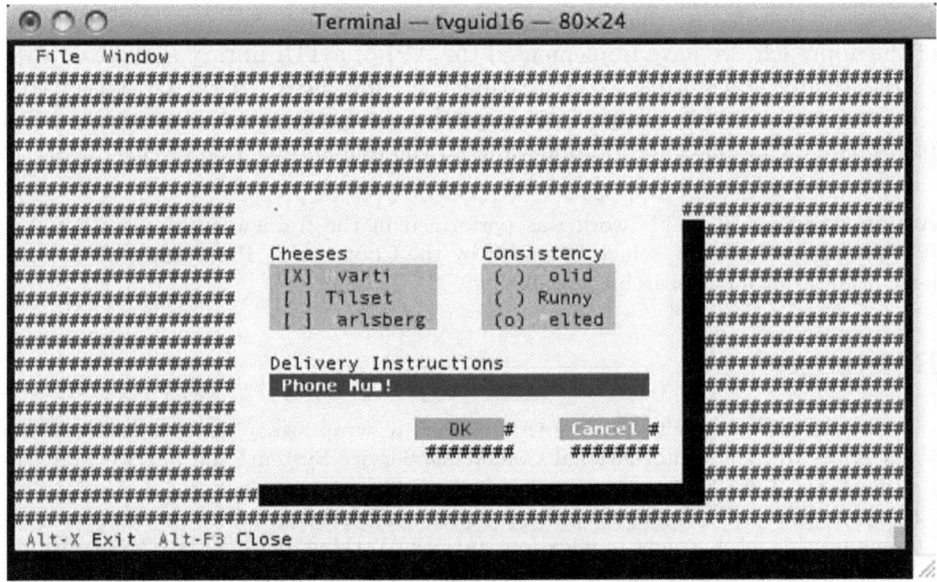

Fig. 5. An example of a modal dialog

5   Future Work

At the current preliminary stage of development, we have provided an alternative implementation of a TUI library API that enables legacy applications to operate in a Web environment. We are currently extending the sanitization component with functionality offered by the OWASP security library which detects and blocks user input that cause SQL injection attacks. When all components of the architecture of the proposed migration approach are completed, we could demonstrate a more detailed example with a web interface and the communication between the interface and the application. Then, we will be able to validate empirically whether TUI application users are equally satisfied by the automatically generated web-based UI. In addition, we will use the Turbo Vision library for more applications and try to apply the above method to other TUI libraries.

6   Conclusions

This work proposes a process for automatically migrating legacy applications to the web. It is a general method in the sense that it places no constraints on the design and implementation of a legacy TUI application. As far as the application is concerned, nothing is changed. It still invokes the same methods provided by the TUI API although the user input is now provided by data sent remotely with HTTP requests and the produced output is now transformed into HTML instead of being displayed on the user's screen. Also, the received data is cleared of special characters that may threaten the integrity of the application data or the security of the application. Common cases of errors such as SQL injection attacks are handled by the data sanitizer. In order to demonstrate the feasibility of the approach, we have implemented the API of a TUI library and a tool that automatically transforms TUIs (textual user interfaces) to HTML based UIs. The proposed process, reduces the migration cost and enables secure access to previously locally executed applications in the demanding web environment.

Acknowledgement. This work was performed in the framework of the TRACER (09SYN-72-942) project, which is funded by the Cooperation Programme of the Hellenic Secretariat for Research & Technology.

References

1. Al Belushi, W., Baghdadi, Y.: An approach to wrap legacy applications into web services. In: 2007 International Conference Service Systems and Service Management, pp. 1–6 (2007)
2. Abi-Antoun, M., Coelho, W.: A case study in incremental architecture-based re-engineering of a legacy application. In: 5th Working IEEE/IFIP Conference on Software Architecture, 2005, WICSA 2005, p.p. 159–168 (2005)

3. Chatzieleftheriou, G., Katsaros, P.: Test driving static analysis tools in search of C code vulnerabilities. In: Proceedings of the 35th IEEE Computer Software and Applications Conference Workshops (COMPSACW), Munich, Germany, pp. 96–103. IEEE Computer Society (2011)

4. Distante, D., Perrone, V., Bochicchio, M.A.: Migrating to the Web legacy application: the Sinfor project. In: Proceedings of the Fourth International Workshop on Web Site Evolution, 2002, pp. 85–88 (2002)

5. Distante, D., Tilley, S., Canfora, G.: Towards a holistic approach to redesigning legacy applications for the Web with UWAT+. In: Proceedings of the 10th European Conference on Software Maintenance and Reengineering, 2006, CSMR 2006, pp. 5–10 (2006)

6. Lu, F., Huang, H., Xu, Z., Yu, H.: A middleware for legacy application wrapper. In: First International Conference on Semantics, Knowledge and Grid, 2005, SKG '05, pp. 47 (2005)

7. Besacier, G., Vernier, F.: Toward user interface virtualization: legacy applications and innovative interaction systems. In: EICS '09: Proceedings of the 1st ACM SIGCHI Symposium on Engineering Interactive Computing Systems, pp. 57–166. New York (2009)

8. Kacsuk, P., Goyeneche, A., Delaitre, T., Kiss, T., Farkas, Z., Boczko, T.: High-level grid application environment to use legacy codes as OGSA grid services. In: GRID '04: Proceedings of the 5th IEEE/ACM International Workshop on Grid Computing, pp. 428–435. Washington (2004)

9. Konstantas, D.: Migration of legacy applications to a CORBA platform: a case study. In: Proceedings of the IFIP/IEEE International Conference on Distributed Platforms: Client/Server and Beyond: DCE, CORBA, ODsanitP and Advanced Distributed Applications, pp. 100–112 (1996)

10. Le Traon, Y., Mouelhi, T., Pretschner, A., Baudry, B.: Test-driven assessment of access control in legacy applications. In: 2008 1st International Conference on Software Testing, Verification, and Validation, pp. 238–247 (2008)

11. Zhu, L., Matsunaga, A., Sanjeepan, V., Lam, H., Fortes, J.A.B.: Application modeling and representation for automatic grid-enabling of legacy applications. In: First International Conference on e-Science and Grid Computing, pp. 8–31 (2005)

12. Marosi, A.C., Balaton, Z., Kacsuk, P.: GenWrapper: a generic wrapper for running legacy applications on desktop grids. In: IEEE International Symposium on Parallel & Distributed Processing, 2009, IPDPS 2009, pp. 1–6 (2009)

13. Mondal, S.A., Gupta, K.D.: Choosing a middleware for web-integration of a legacy application. SIGSOFT Softw. Eng. Notes 25(3), 50–53 (2000). (New York)

14. Mui, R., Frankl, P.: Preventing SQL injection through automatic query sanitization with ASSIST. In: Fourth International Workshop on Testing, Analysis and Verification of Web Software, EPTCS 35, Antwerp, pp. 27–38 (2010)

15. Owasp. https://www.owasp.org/

16. Saxena, P., Molnar, D., Livshits, B.: SCRIPTGARD: automatic context-sensitive sanitization for large-scale legacy web applications. In: CCS '11: Proceedings of the 18th ACM Conference on Computer and Communications Security, pp. 601–614. New York (2011)

17. Sigala Turbo Vision. http://www.sigala.it/sergio/tvision/index.html

18. Tsetsekas, C., Maniatis, S., Venieris, I.S.: Supporting QoS for legacy applications. In: Lorenz, P. (ed.) ICN 2001. LNCS, vol. 2094, pp. 108–116. Springer, Heidelberg (2001)

19. Wong, D.: Kickin' it old school!: dealing with legacy applications. In: SIGUCCS '08: Proceedings of the 36th Annual ACM SIGUCCS Fall Conference: Moving Mountains, Blazing Trails, pp. 55–58. New York (2008)
20. Meng, X., Shi, J., Liu, X., Liu, H., Wang, L.: Legacy application migration to cloud. In: 2011 IEEE International Conference on Cloud Computing (CLOUD), pp. 750–751 (2011)
21. Xiong, Y., Su, D.: Wrapping legacy applications into grid services: a case study of a three services approach. In: Shen, W., Luo, J., Lin, Z., Barthès, J.-P.A., Hao, Q. (eds.) CSCWD. LNCS, vol. 4402, pp. 520–529. Springer, Heidelberg (2007)

A Web Portal for the Certification of Open Source Software

Pedro Martins$^{(\boxtimes)}$, João P. Fernandes, and João Saraiva

HASLab / INESC TEC, Universidade do Minho, Braga, Portugal
{prmartins,jpaulo,jas}@di.uminho.pt

Abstract. This paper presents a web portal for the certification of open source software. The portal aims at helping programmers in the internet age, when there are (too) many open source reusable libraries and tools available. Our portal offers programmers a web-based and easy setting to analyze and certify open source software, which is a crucial step to help programmers choosing among many available alternatives, and to get some guarantees before using one piece of software.

The paper presents our first prototype of such web portal. It also describes in detail a domain specific language that allows programmers to describe with a high degree of abstraction specific open source software certifications. The design and implementation of this language is the core of the web portal.

Keywords: Software analysis · Software certification · Open source software · Programming languages

1 Introduction

The advent of the internet is changing our lives. Not only is it changing the way we live, but also the way we develop our software. In the last century, developing software was mainly performed using programming languages and their libraries, which provided the necessary support to build software applications. Nowadays, the way we develop software is changing: programming languages still offer supporting libraries, but there are many more resources available in the internet. These wide set of resources can be other powerful off-the-shelf reusable libraries and tools, usually available as Open Source Software (OSS).

This fact influences the way we program since developing a particular software tool/library may be, in most cases, a matter of looking for the right (open source) software/libraries solutions already available. Indeed, the internet encourages sharing our software. This new style of developing software, however, needs to handle three important issues:

This work is funded by ERDF - European Regional Development Fund through the COMPETE Programme (operational programme for competitiveness) and by National Funds through the FCT - Fundação para a Ciência e a Tecnologia (Portuguese Foundation for Science and Technology) within project FCOMP-01-0124-FEDER-010049.

A. Cerone et al. (Eds.): SEFM 2012 Satellite Events, LNCS 7991, pp. 244–260, 2014.
DOI: 10.1007/978-3-642-54338-8_20, © Springer-Verlag Berlin Heidelberg 2014

- Firstly, because there is so much OSS available in the internet it is difficult to select the right tool/library. Thus, we need an appropriate framework to support the analysis of the available alternatives.
- Secondly, because we may reuse different software artifacts, developed in different contexts, we need to integrate them into a coherent piece of software.
- Thirdly, because we are reusing OSS, we may need to guarantee that it satisfies certain properties before reusing it. For example, when developing software that handles credit card information we may need the guarantee that a piece of software to be reused conforms to specific security guarantees. On a different context, if we if we are developing software for embedded systems, we may need to guarantee that a reused library implements optimal memory management.

In this paper we present a web portal for the analysis and certification of Open Source Software that aims at improving on these three issues. The portal works as a repository for tools that analyze source code. By the certification of a piece of source code software we understand the process of analyzing the its code while producing an information report about it.

The usage of our portal is heterogeneous in that it supports the analysis of any programming language and distributed in the sense that it makes software analysis available in the web. Also, while already incorporating several pre-defined certifications, the portal makes it very simple for any user to re-arrange these certifications and to develop new ones: we designed and implemented a Domain Specific Language (DSL) that allows portal users to define, in a high level and abstract way, how certifications and software tools that analyze source code can be integrated and combined. This allows the creation of personalized analysis closely tied to the scope and nature of the necessary feedback.

This paper is organized as follows: in Sect. 2 we introduce the web portal together with the software analysis scenarios it supports. In Sect. 3 we introduce the DSL that allows the creation of new analysis suites, together with its underlying working mechanisms. In Sect. 4, we describe the validations that are ensured by the used of our combinators, and in Sect. 5 we introduce implementation and usage issues of the portal. Finally, in Sect. 6 we conclude the paper.

2   An Open Source Software Certification Portal

Software analysis is an interesting topic of research, whose motivations range from the need to maintain software as easily as possible to the removal of its bugs and the improvement of its overall characteristics [1–5]. While tools and techniques for program analysis are very diverse, the fact is that they are often too restrictive to gain wide acceptance. This has two main causes, in that tools are often: (i) designed for a specific programming language; (ii) not flexible enough to be tailored when the particular needs of a user differ from the built-in analysis.

In this section, we introduce the portal that we have constructed to act as a repository for tools that are freely available and to enable the certification of open source software based on such tools. By a Certification we mean the

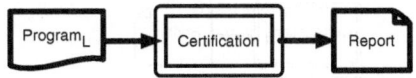

Fig. 1. The flow of information in our portal when analyzing a single source code file.

execution of a software analysis tool that is capable of processing a source code file and of producing an information report about it.

Our portal was constructed to make no distinction with respect to the programming language or scope of the tools it hosts. Also, the tools that are hosted can easily be combined therefore allowing the fast creation of test suites that perfectly match the needs of different programmers. The combination possibilities, that we describe in the remaining of this section, include the possibility of analyzing software components written in multiple programming languages. To enable the definition of certifications and their composition, we have designed a domain specific language, that we describe in the next section.

The portal that is the result of our work can be found at:

http://www.cross.di.uminho.pt/

Analyzing a Single Open Source File. The simplest way to use our portal is to analyze a single source code file. This simple test, that is depicted in Fig. 1, may be useful to identify performance opportunities or to validate security requirements, for example.

In this illustration, a **Certification** is being used on a **Program** written in language L, leading to a **Report** being produced. In the context of our portal, reports are always defined as elements conforming to our **XML Schema** for reports.

We have chosen an XML-based representation since it allows storing information in different formats such as charts and images. Also, **XML Schemas** are widely used, easily understood, and can be translated to different representations. Indeed, we show our reports as **HTML** pages that are produced using **XSLT**.

Our portal is not only suitable for one isolated certification of a program. Indeed, we show next how the same program can have several of its characteristics certified at the same time by a set of certifications, that are combined into a larger certification, while producing a single information report.

Multiple Analysis for a Single Source Code File. Analyzing software usually implies running a number of tests provided by a set of tools which, together, allow us to obtain information about diverse aspects of the software. Our system provides a simple interface to agglomerate and run multiple certifications while creating a single information report, as sketched in Fig. 2. In this particular case, the submitted $Program_L$ is subject to three independent analyses, $Certification_1$, $Certification_2$ and $Certification_3$, but the number of certifications that can be composed is arbitrary.

We observe that a set of reports is aggregated into a single final report. This is a strategy that always needs to be followed in our setting, and that we have

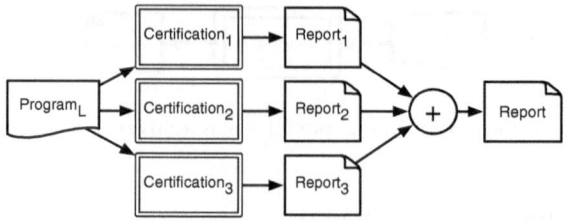

Fig. 2. Multiple analysis for one single source code file.

adopted since analyzing multiple reports individually would become a tedious
and confusing task, for growing numbers of such reports.

The mechanisms presented so far allow a simple analysis of source code single
files. We, however, often want to certify software repositories, i.e., software artifacts that are composed of several pieces, each of which in (at least) one different
file, and possibly expressed in a different programming language. Next, we show
how our web portal allows analyzing a set of source code files of this kind.

Analyzing Multiple Source Files. Our web portal supports the analysis of a set
of different source files, and in Fig. 3 we show an example of this type of analysis
being performed.

In our system, uploading a set of files is achieved through an archiving format,
being it ZIP, Tar or RAR. Our web portal automatically infers information from
the compressed archive, extracts its regular files and parses them.

Again, the results of all certifications need to be aggregated into a single
report file. In this case, the final report groups either the results of applying
the certification individually to each file, or the results provided by certifications
analyzing all the source files of the same type at the same time. The produced
reports will be as big as demanded by the certifications that are executed. While
sometimes their information is going to be too large for manual inspection, the
fact is that having them under XML files allows users to easily automate the
process of analyzing the information reports that are produced. In fact, the last

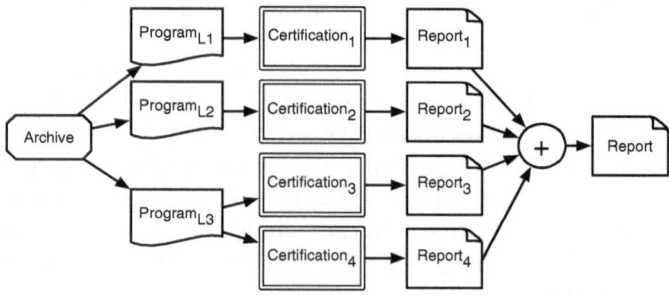

Fig. 3. A testing suite for multiple source files expressed in different languages.

step of analyzing the report might be integrated into the certifications themselves, as we will see next, where we describe how to personalize and customize certifications to the individual needs of each user.

Creating Customized Certifications. So far, we have seen how our web portal provides different types of analyzes for source code. These analyzes are supported by the certifications that we have already integrated in our portal, a subset of which we now present.

Certification	Input	Description
sLOCJavaFiles	-java	Lines of code of a Java file
sLOCCFiles	-c	Lines of code of a C file
sLOCHaskellFiles	-hs	Lines of code of a Haskell file
zips	-zip	CRC32 checksum, size (zipped and unzipped)
fleschKincaid	-txt	The Flesch/Flesch-Kincaid readability test
emptyCellSmell	-xlsx	The empty cell spreadsheet *bad smell* [6,7]

While the certifications that have thus far been built-in the portal already allow for several analysis, the fact is that within the framework described so far, users do not have the possibility of combining the available certifications according to their own particular needs. Furthermore, analyzing software is not usually achievable by a single certification: it often implies using a variety of tools and techniques, whose results, unified, provide the programmer with the necessary feedback.

Ideally, we want to use the results of a certification as input to another, which requires, apart from being able of performing a series of tasks through the use of several tools, aggregating and treating the results obtained. Examining and dealing with the information that is produced is as important as the results themselves. Just as an example, some analyses derive results that are not quantifiable, and no information can be obtained from them. It is their treatment and analysis through comparison that provides good feedback to the user[1].

To solve the limitations described above, we have created a domain specific language that we have integrated in our system. This language allows the customization of each step of the process of analyzing software, which include data extraction, treatment of the results and the analysis itself.

In Fig. 4 we show how to implement a certification, Certification$_1$, that is composed of other simpler certifications.

In our setting, certifications are often composed by smaller units capable of communicating among themselves to achieve a state where the overall mechanics of each unit and the flow of information among them is capable of producing quantifiable results (Certifications). A Component is one of this smaller software units. A Component is therefore a tool, capable of assessing and producing metadata but that is not powerful enough so that a whole analysis, i.e., a Certification,

---

[1] An example of such case are the Halstead Complexity Measures [8].

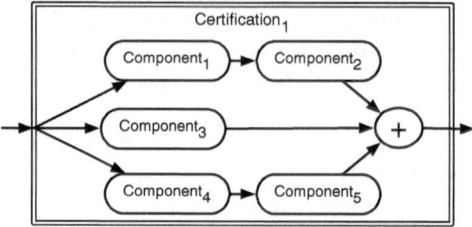

Fig. 4. An example of a certification composed by five components.

is made out of it. Examples of components that we have already integrated in our portal are shown next.

Component	Input	Output	Description
readFile	`-c, -hs, -xml, -java`	`-string`	Reads a file.
text2NLines	`-string`	`-int`	Calculates the number of lines
int2Report	`-int`	`-rep`	Creates a Report from a value
text2NFors	`-string`	`-int`	Calculates the number of 'fors'
text2NIfs	`-string`	`-int`	Calculates the number of 'ifs'
text2Report	`-string`	`-rep`	Creates a Report from text

The concept of a component makes our system more powerful and configurable: not only the programmers and uploaders of tools are able of creating small software units, but also end users have access to a wide number of this specific tools that can easily be configured and adequate to concrete needs.

Using existing components, our DSL provides an environment where the user has the possibility to create customized certifications. Furthermore, the mechanisms inherent to the DSL ensure that such components are isolated for errors and that the certifications are optimized, for example, by running components in parallel whenever possible. Also, it allows certifications made out of certifications themselves. In Fig. 5 we show an example of a certification, Certification$_2$ whose result is composed by Certification$_4$ and by Certification$_3$, which is actually fed by a component, Component$_1$.

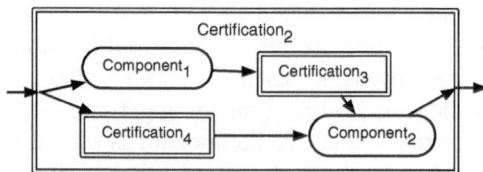

Fig. 5. A certification composed by both Components and other Certifications.

The definition of certifications based on components and other certifications allows our system to provide good testing and analysis for virtually any environment desirable, while also ensuring that the results are always on a standard format. In the next section we introduce the domain specific language in detail, together with practical and illustrative examples of its usage.

3 A Domain Specific Language for Creating Test Suites

The portal we present consists not only of an interface to analyze source code, but also as a repository of analysis tools, that we understand as Components. These tools can implement data handling and analysis or code slicing, for example, but a certification may not be constructed out of a tool if it is not able of producing a report in the required format. We could force users to upload a tool that, by itself, can analyze source code and produce a Report but this would mean forcing them to extend their solutions with features related to information input and Report generation. Also, the repository would never suit users that created a slicer, for example, since it is not an analysis technique by itself.

Figure 6 shows a context where a slicer (jSlicer) and an interface analyzer (iAnalysis) are used together to create a certification. In this figure we see that the certification implementer used a sub-certification that already existed on the system (Certification1).

In order to implement the sketched certification with the framework described so far, there exist (at least) two possible solutions: (i) to manually integrate the involved tools and to compile its results to obtain a single tool that implements all this flow of information; or, (ii), to run all the tools independently and to manually transfer the information among them. For reasons that we have previously discussed, both alternatives are tedious and cumbersome as they demand a significant programming/integration effort. The user would have to assume the responsibility of compiling and organizing all the code, which in the end would only solve a particular and specific problem.

In order to overcome this issue, we have created an interface, which was integrated in our portal, and that makes it simple to create new certifications, i.e., to organize components in a way that they provide the desired information from uploaded information. This interface is provided as a DSL embedded in Haskell as a combinator language. Before introducing our combinator DSL we present a little snippet of how it can be used to create the certification in Fig. 6:

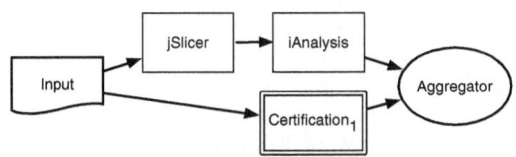

Fig. 6. An example of a user-defined certification.

```
Input >-  (jSlicer,"-j","-i") >-
          (iAnalysis,"-i","-csv")  >|
Input >- certification1             >|> (aggregator,"-r","-r")
```

From this code, our portal automatically creates an appropriate certification. What is more, it also statically analyzes the specification and checks it for type errors, as we explain in more detail later in this section. In this particular example, the user is specifying that he/she wants component JSlicer to be called with the arguments -java and -interface in order to slice the interface out of a program written in Java. This information is then channeled to the component iAnalysis, and this chain of components runs in parallel with Certification1 that takes the same Java input that jSlicer receives. The execution results of the two parallel processes are later aggregated, by component aggregator, to form a report.

The combinator language that we propose starts by defining data-types for certifications and components. These data-types are introduced as follows, as Certification and Component, respectively.

```
data Certification = Certification Name ProcessingTree data
Component = Component Name InputList OutputList BashCall
```

```
type Name     = String      type InputList  = [(Arg, Language)]
type Arg      = String      type OutputList = [(Arg, Language)]
type BashCall = String
```

```
data Language
  = Java | C_Source | C_Header | Cpp | Haskell | XML | Report
-- .java  .c          .h         .cpp  .hs        .xml  Report XML
```

A Certification has a name and defines a particular information flow, which is represented by data-type ProcessingTree, that we introduce and describe in detail later. A Component is represented by a name, the list of arguments it receives and the list of results it produces. These lists, that are represented by type synonyms InputList and OutputList, respectively, have similar definitions and consist of varying numbers of arguments and results. The arguments(results) that are defined(expected) for a particular component are then passed to concrete bash calls. This is the purpose of type BashCall, which consists of the name of the process to execute.

For a generic Java Slicer component that could be used in the context of the snippet previously shown, we may define the following Component.

```
Component "Java Slicer" [("-j", Java)]
          [("-i", Java), ("-s", Java)] "./jSlicer"
```

In order to represent the flow of information defined for a certification, we have defined the data-type ProcessingTree:

```
data ProcessingTree = RootTree ProcessingTree
                    | SequenceNode ProcessingTree ProcessingTree
                    | ParallelNode ProcessingList ProcessingTree
                    | ProcessCert  Certification
                    | ProcessComp  Component Arg Arg
                    | Input

data ProcessingList = ProcessingList ProcessingTree ProcessingList
                    | ProcessingListNode ProcessingTree
```

The simplest processing tree that we can construct is the one to define a certification with a single component. This is expressed by constructor ProcessComp, which also expects a name to be associated to the component and the specification of the options to run the component with. A certification can also be defined by a single sub-certification, here represented by ProcessCert. In addition to these, more complex certifications can be constructed by running processes in sequence, using SequenceNode, and in parallel, using ParallelNode. Constructor ParallelNode takes as arguments a processing list and a processing tree. The first argument represents a list of trees whose processes can run in parallel. The second argument is used to fulfill our requirement that all results of all parallel computations must be aggregated using a component. Therefore, this processing tree must always be a component that is capable of aggregating information into one uniform, combined output.

The ProcessingTree data-type can be used, for example, to describe the global information flow of a certification implementing a cyclomatic dependency analysis for Java programs while producing an information report.

```
RootTree
   ProcessComp
      Component "Cyclomatic Dependency"
               [("-j",Java)]
               [("-r",Report)]
               "./exec"
      "-j"
      "-r"
```

Having in hand the data-types that we have defined so far, we could already create, in a manual way, certifications with all the capabilities that we propose to offer. Nevertheless, manually expressing certifications would be of impractical use. This is precisely the main motivation to develop a language where simple and re-usable components can be combined into more complex ones, which themselves can grow as large as needed in order to implement extensive certifications.

With the addition of code becoming smaller, more elegant and easier to read and understand, the fact is that it will also be statically analyzed and type checked, and the script code that actually implements the certification it defines will be automatically generated. These features will be introduced in the remaining of this paper, together with the combinators that we use in our language, that we present in detail next.

The Sequence Processing Combinator. For sequencing operations, we define the combinator >-. This combinator defines processes that are to be executed in a chain, i.e., where the output of a process serves as input to the process that follows it. When sequencing processes, it is also the case that if one of process in the chain fails the entire chain will also fail.

The use of combinator >- must always be preceded by the use of constructor Input, which signals the beginning of an information flow. Then, as many components and certifications as needed can be used, as long as they again connected by >-. Next, we show an example of a chain of events defined using >-.

```
Input >- (jSlicer,"-j","-i") >- (iAnalysis,"-i","-csv") >- certif
```

Combinator >- can be used to sequence certifications, components and other processing trees that are defined using the remaining combinators of our language. When it encounters a certification, the combinator connects the processes before it to the processing tree of the certification, and ensures that the result of this processing tree is then channeled to the processes that follow it. This is the case of the sub-certification called `certif`. When sequencing components, users need to supply to >- both the component and its input/output parameters. In our particular example, `jSlicer` is to be called with input parameter -j to state that the process accepts Java code as input and with output argument -i to state that it slices the interfaces out of that code.

It is worthwhile to notice that the arguments that are specified within components are very important in that they allow checking the flow of information inter-processes for correctness, as the input and output types must match when the information is channeled. When using >- to channel certifications, the user is constrained by the input and output types that were associated to it, and this is an information that must be carefully observed to ensure that the involved types do match.

Finally, the result of a sequence defined using >- is a processing tree that implements the combination of processes.

The Parallel Processing Combinator. Now, we introduce the combinator that enables the parallel composition of processes, This type of composition is actually supported by two combinators, >| and >|>. The first one is responsible for launching a varying number of processes in parallel, while the second is mandatory after a sequence of >| uses and chains all outputs of all processes to a component that is capable of aggregating them. An example of how these combinators work together is as follows.

```
Input >- cert3                          >|
Input >- cert1 >- cert5                 >|
Input >- (jSlicer,"-j","-x") >- cert8 >|> (aggr,"-x","-r")
```

Combinator >| takes either a processing tree, a component, a certification or a set of processes constructed using the other combinators. The arguments of >| must always begin by constructor Input, to give a clear idea of the flow of information. In the case of this listing it is indeed easy to spot where the information enters a parallel distribution.

As for combinator >|>, it is mandatory for it to appear in the end of a parallelized set of processes. It is used to aggregate all the outputs of all the child processes into a single standard output, and it is able of combining varying numbers of parallel processes using an aggregation component.

It is worthwhile to explain further the relationship between the parallel combinators >| and >|>. In trivial cases, >|> can actually replace the use of >-. This is the case of the process Input >|> (aggr,"-x","-r"), which is equivalent to Input >- (aggr,"-x","-r"), as both processes channel the input to the aggregation component aggr. Finally, combinator >| can never appear alone in a certification, due to the constraint that all parallel processes must be aggregated.

A Combinator to Create Certifications. Our combinator language includes also a combinator to create certifications and to associate names to them. This is precisely the purpose of combinator +>, which always combines a processing tree, given as its left argument, with a String, given to its right. It then creates a certification associating the name with the processing tree.

As an illustration of the use of +>, consider again the process implementations that use our sequence and parallel combinators. In both cases, the result of running the implemented code is a processing tree (i.e., an element of type ProcessingTree), that needs to be given a name to become a certification (i.e., an element of type Certification). By simply appending, for example, +> "certification" to the end of both codes, we would precisely be creating certifications named certification with the respective trees of processes. For the first example, this would result in the code:

```
Input >- (jSlicer,"-j","-i") >- (iAnalysis,"-i","-csv") >- certif
    +> "certification"
```

An important remark about +> is that it analyzes the processing tree that it receives as argument and checks its correctness. This includes testing whether the implied types match, by analyzing all the parallelized and sequenced processes for their input and output types, and see whether or not they respect the flow of information. Also, it is ensured that the processing tree produces a report which is a mandatory feature for a certification in our system. Finally, if a certification is considered valid, a Perl script implementing its analysis is automatically generated. For the example certification just given, this overcomes the need to undergo the tedious and error-prone task of manually writing the script given in Appendix.

In the next section, we explain in detail the features that are implemented by our type analysis and how they are actually implemented under our framework.

The 'Finalize' Combinator. The last combinator of our language is #>>, that combines a processing tree with a flag instructing it to either produce a script implementing that tree or to simply check its types for correctness. The following examples show the two possible uses for this combinator.

```
Input >- (comp1,"-j","-x") >- (comp2,"-k","-o") #>> 't'
Input >- cert1 >- cert2 #>> 's'
```

In the first case, we are demanding a check on the types of running component comp1 after component comp2. This means that we are interested in knowing whether the return type of comp1 is the same as the input type of comp2. With the second case, we are asking for the script that implements chaining certification cert2 after certification cert1 and also checks if the types match.

4   Type Checking on Combinators

In the previous section, we have introduced our combinator language for the development of software certifications. In this section, we introduce a set of validations that are automatically guaranteed to the users of our system.

For once, we inherit the advanced features of Haskell compilers. In particular, the powerful type system of ghc helps us providing static guarantees on the certifications that are developed. Indeed, the order in which the combinators of our language are applied within a certification is not arbitrary, and the uses that do not respect it will statically be flagged. The simplest example of this is the attempt to construct a processing tree without explicitly using constructor Input, but more realistic examples are also detected, e.g., not wrapping up a set of parallel computations with >|> as well as the application of an aggregator.

Apart from static analyzes, we have also implemented some dynamic ones: we want to analyze if the types match in the flow of information for a certification, i.e., if the input type of a process matches the output type of the process feeding it. In our setting, we perform such tests on elements of type ProcessingTree, that we use our combinators to construct. These elements are then analyzed using validations that are expressed as attribute grammars (AGs) [9]: (i) for once, we are analyzing tree-based structures, for which the AG formalism is particularly suitable; (ii) secondly, because AGs have a declarative nature which in our context contributes to intuitive implementations that are easy to reason about and to further extend. In fact, we believe that it would be simple to integrate in our framework advanced AG-based and well studied techniques such as the detection of circular dependencies [10] and the use of higher-order attributes [11].

Our type checking structurally breaks down into analyzing the nodes of a processing tree which, in our case, correspond to the constructors of the ProcessingTree data type. The type checking is computed as the value of an attribute called typeCheck, of type Boolean, which indicates whether or not the analyzed types are correct. Apart from this attribute two other are involved: input and output, that support typeCheck. These attributes are of type Language and for each tree node give the input and the output types of that subtree. Next, we will explain how these three attribute are calculated in each tree node.

Type Checking Component *Nodes.* Components are the simplest units of our processing trees, and represent simple processes without any actual flow of information. This means that their type is always correct, and that the value produced for attribute typeCheck is always True.

As for the attributes input and output, they are computed analyzing the Component against the invocation that is made for it in a ProcessingTree. Indeed, whenever a component is associated to a certification, an element such as Process-Comp comp inp out is defined. But comp itself is an element of type Component, i.e., has the form Component name inplist outlist call. So, our validation starts by detecting whether or not inp (respectively out) is an option of inplist (respectively outlist). In case it is, attribute input (respectively output) returns the Language option associated with inp (out). Otherwise an error is raised.

Type Checking Certification *Nodes.* Certifications are, similarly to components, simple nodes of a processing tree, and in our setting, they must always be created using combinator +>. Therefore, everytime this combinator is employed, as in tree +> name, we automatically inspect the value of attribute typeCheck that is computed for tree. If this value is True, we create the certification Certification name tree; otherwise, no certification is constructed and an error is raised.

Actually, it is not only necessary that a processing tree type checks in order for us to be able of producing a certification out of it. Indeed, all certifications must always produce a report within our format, and we also check if the output attribute computed for tree is Report before actually creating a certification.

Finally, when we consider sub-certifications, again we use the fact that they are created using +>. Indeed, if the construction of a sub-certification succeeds, then the tests so far described have all also succeeded. Therefore, for certifications under ProcessCert nodes, we can always ensure that they type check. Also, attributes input and output are very simple to implement: we return the value of the same attribute that is synthesized at the sub-tree of ProcessCert nodes.

Type Checking Sequence *Nodes.* Sequence nodes are used to have a processing tree followed by another. They channel the information from the first processing tree into the second one and returns the result of the second.

The input and output attributes for this node are very simple to compute: input is the input type of the first processing tree, and output is the output type of the second. Similarly, typeCheck is also simple to determine: apart from checking if the output attribute of the first tree is equal to the input attribute of the second one, our AG-based implementation also demands the typeCheck attribute on each sub tree individually and checks whether both have value True.

Type Checking Parallel *Nodes.* Parallel nodes are the hardest to type check, in that all their sub processes must have the same input type and same output type, and this output type must be the same as the input type of the component that aggregates all the results that are computed in parallel.

Parallel nodes have two children: the second child, of type ProcessingTree, is a component that aggregates all the results of the processes that run in parallel, which are given as the first child, of type ProcessingList. The first validation we perform is to check whether the output value of the ProcessingList matches the input value of the ProcessingTree. If it does not, an error is raised; otherwise, the processes within the ProcessingList are type checked. Now, type checking processing lists is complex since it needs to analyze all the inputs of all the sub processes, which can be components, certifications or processing trees and see if they match, and to do this again for the outputs. We use the equality of the input and output attributes for the current element of the list and for the subsequent elements; by definition, a processing list must always contain at least one element so the attribute will always return a value.

The input and output attributes for parallel nodes are simple to compute: input is the input of one of the elements of the processing list, as they are all the same, and output is the output of the aggregator component. Finally, we have followed a safe approach when type checking processing lists: the input and output attributes for a processing list are given only after the type checking for the entire list is performed.

5   Implementation and Usage of the Portal

In this section, we present some implementation details about our portal and also a simple example of how it can be used in practice to create a sample Certification that outputs the number of lines of a source code file in C.

The portal has been constructed out of circa 320 lines of JavaScript and of circa 1500 lines of HTML+PHP code. In fact, from these 1500 lines, around 125 interface with a simple database for storing information related to the certifications of the portal, which itself includes 3 tables and 12 records. The DSL that the portal provides for re-arranging certifications and components was developed out of around 400 lines of Haskell code.

In order to use the portal to construct a certification that outputs the number of lines of a C program, we may rely on the existence of components readFile, that reads a file, input2Nlines, that takes an input and computes the number of its lines and int2Report, a component that takes an integer as input and produces a report. Since these components are already available in the portal, we express in our DSL a certification that arranges them as shown next:

```
Input
   >- (readFile,"-c","-string")     >- (cSlicer,"-string","-string")
      (input2Nlines,"-string","-int") >- (int2Report,"-int","-rep")
```

This certification starts with a component that reads a file in C (which is expressed by parameter -c) and returns a String (-string). A second component, executed in sequence, reads the string that is returned and filters the main procedure out of it, a text which is fed to a third component that counts the number of its lines. Then, a final component transforms that Integer into an information report. In the portal, after defining a certification, users must give it a name and describe the analysis it implements, so that it may be reused in the future.

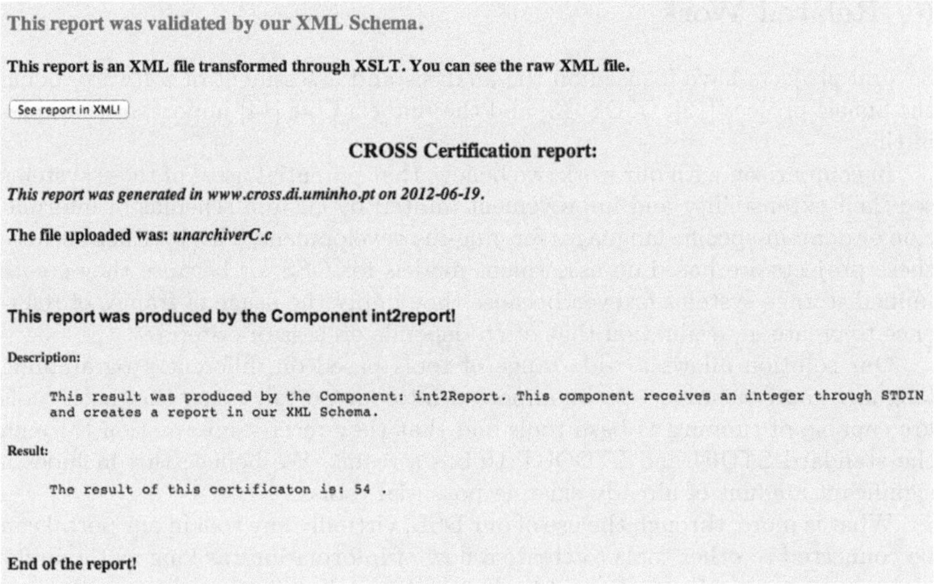

This report was validated by our XML Schema.

This report is an XML file transformed through XSLT. You can see the raw XML file.

[See report in XML!]

CROSS Certification report:

This report was generated in www.cross.di.uminho.pt on 2012-06-19.

The file uploaded was: *unarchiverC.c*

This report was produced by the Component int2report!

Description:

```
This result was produced by the Component: int2Report. This component receives an integer through STDIN
and creates a report in our XML Schema.
```

Result:

```
The result of this certificaton is: 54 .
```

End of the report!

Fig. 7. The result of a certification as it appears in our web portal.

Once a certification for a particular programming language is available, users just need to upload a file in that language to analyze it. Having done so, our portal only presents as certification options for it the ones that match its type. This means that, for example, having uploaded a Haskell file, users will only see the certifications that are available for Haskell. Then, by choosing one particular certification, e.g., the one we have just created, the web portal will produce a report similar to the one shown in Fig. 7.[2]

Our approach is modular, and even if a component with a given functionality is not available, users can create it in any programming language. Indeed, as long as that component is able of receiving information via STDIN and of outputting information to STDOUT, any program is a candidate for a component. Also, we expect the number of components and certifications available on the portal to grow, which will make creating new certifications increasingly simpler.

Although we have used simple examples to illustrate our framework, this does not compromise the range or the complexity of the analyses that we may perform. For example, component input2Nlines could be replaced by one that implements a powerful pointer analysis on C code. And it would be as easy to create a certification using it as it was to create the one above, without programmers of the new component needing to concern with file reading or output formats.

---

[2] In fact, the Fig. 7 shows the HTML that corresponds to the XML that is produced.

6 Related Work

Several projects have focused on the analysis and assessment of software, being the Squale project [12], QSOS [13] and the Alitheia Core [14] important examples of this.

In comparison with our work, we believe that potential users of these systems see their extensibility and improvement limited by custom schemas of information or domain-specific languages for plug-ins development. This is either because these projects are based on assessment models for OSS, or because they create unified storage systems or even because they imply the usage of frames of reference to create an evaluation that often depends on axis of criteria.

Our solution allows a wide range of tools based on different programming languages and techniques to be imported into our portal, taken that such tools are capable of running as bash tools and that they receive information through the standard STDIN and STDOUT Unix's streams. We believe this includes a significant amount of already existing potential tools.

What is more, through the use of our DSL, virtually any tool in our portal can be connected to other tools to create a flow of information (as long as the input and output types of two chained tools match), easily allowing the introduction of software assessments and the extension of such of assessments.

In [15] an implementation of the orchestration language Orc [16] is introduced as an embedded domain specific language in Haskell. In this work, Orc was realized as a combinator library using lightweight threads. Despite the similarities on the use of Haskell combinators, this approach differs from our DSL since we do not rely on any existing orchestration language. Rather, we generate low level Perl scripts from combinators whose inputs are direct references to system processes (Components). Also, the way we manage processes does not rely on Concurrent Haskell, but rather on the parallelization features of the target system. More information about our DSL, together with examples of the scripts that it is able of generating can be found in [17].

7 Conclusions and Future Work

In this paper we present a portal for analyzing source code artifacts and providing information reports about them. Our portal supports various analysis scenarios and is able of dealing with programs expressed in different programming languages.

We have also implemented a DSL that allows manually re-arranging the certifications and components that are built-in the portal. While several analyzes are already possible, we rely on inputs from the community to extend further the certification tools that our portal hosts, and by this to increase its impact.

Although our portal has been deployed and is fully-functional, we are still incorporating in it several features such as allowing for tool developers to configure themselves how their tools are constructed and executed on our portal.

References

1. Haigh, M.: Software quality, non-functional software requirements and it-business alignment. Softw. Qual. Control **18**(3), 361–385 (2010)
2. Stavrinoudis, D., Xenos, M., Peppas, P., Christodoulakis, D.: Early estimation of users' perception of software quality. Softw. Qual. Control **13**(2), 155–175 (2005)
3. Dromey, R.G.: Software quality prevention versus cure? Softw. Qual. Control **11**(3), 197–210 (2003)
4. Wilson, D.N., Hall, T.: Perceptions of software quality: a pilot study. Softw. Qual. Control **7**(1), 67–75 (1998)
5. Chulani, S., Boehm, B., Verner, J., Wong, B.: Workshop description of 4th workshop on software quality (wosq). In: Proceedings of the 2006 International Workshop on Software Quality, WoSQ '06, pp. 1–2. ACM, New York (2006)
6. Cunha, J., Fernandes, J., Ribeiro, H., Saraiva, J.: Towards a catalog of spreadsheet smells. In: Murgante, B., Gervasi, O., Misra, S., Nedjah, N., Rocha, A.M.A.C., Taniar, D., Apduhan, B.O. (eds.) ICCSA 2012, Part IV. LNCS, vol. 7336, pp. 202–216. Springer, Heidelberg (2012)
7. Cunha, J., Fernandes, J.P., Mendes, J., Martins, P., Saraiva, J.: Smellsheet detective: a tool for detecting bad smells in spreadsheets. In: Proceedings of the 2012 IEEE Symposium on Visual Languages and Human-Centric Computing, VLHCC'12. IEEE Computer Society, Washington (2012) (to appear)
8. Halstead, M.H.: Elements of Software Science (Operating and Programming Systems Series). Elsevier Science Inc., New York (1977)
9. Knuth, D.E.: Semantics of context-free languages. Math. Syst. Theor. **2**(2), 127–145 (1968). Correction. Mathematical Systems Theory **5**(1), 95–96 (1971)
10. Fernandes, J.P., Saraiva, J.: Tools and libraries to model and manipulate circular programs. In: PEPM'07: Proceedings of the ACM SIGPLAN 2007 Symposium on Partial Evaluation and Program Manipulation, pp. 102–111. ACM Press (2007)
11. Swierstra, D., Vogt, H.: Higher order attribute grammars. In: Alblas, H., Melichar, B. (eds.) SAGA School 1991. LNCS, vol. 545, pp. 256–296. Springer, Heidelberg (1991)
12. Squale: Front page. http://www.squale.org. Accessed August 2012
13. QSOS: Front page. http://www.qsos.org. Accessed August 2012
14. Alitheia Core: Front page. http://www.sqo-oss.org. Accessed August 2012
15. Campos, M.D., Barbosa, L.S.: Implementation of an orchestration language as a haskell domain specific language. Electron. Notes Theor. Comput. Sci. **255**, 45–64 (2009)
16. Kitchin, D., Quark, A., Cook, W., Misra, J.: The orc programming language. In: Lee, D., Lopes, A., Poetzsch-Heffter, A. (eds.) FMOODS/FORTE 2009. LNCS, vol. 5522, pp. 1–25. Springer, Heidelberg (2009)
17. Martins, P., Fernandes, J.P., Saraiva, J.: A purely functional combinator language for software quality assessment. In: Symposium on Languages, Applications and Technologies (SLATE '12). OASICS, vol. 21, pp. 51–69. Schloss Dagstuhl - Leibniz-Zentrum fuer Informatik (2012)

Open Source Software Process: A Potential Catalyst for Major Changes in Electronic Health Record Systems

Mirjan Merruko$^{(\boxtimes)}$, Eleni Berki, and Pirkko Nykänen

School of Information Sciences, University of Tampere, Kanslerinrinne 1,
Pinni B, 33 014 Tampere, Finland
{Mirjan.Merruko,Eleni.Berki,Pirkko.Nykanen}@uta.fi

Abstract. Electronic health records implementation has been a challenge for many governments worldwide, who have tried to realise a quality and cost-effective implementation through closed and/or open source software. The paper discusses the background and rationale for implementing health records through an open source software development process model. Whilst there are many benefits from the adoption of an open source software process model there are also many challenges. The paper discusses the ongoing research and outlines the position of the authors on why an open source software process would be a quality solution and a challenge for the implementation of electronic health records at national and potentially at European level.

1 Introduction

Some of the challenges that healthcare systems are facing are: increasing costs[1, 2], poor quality of service, lack of patient care integration, poor access to patient care information and a high number of medical errors [2].

The use of Health Information Technology (HIT) is expected to have a positive impact on cost reduction by reducing medical errors, increasing quality of care and [2] increasing patient mobility. Several countries such as Australia, Canada, the U.S. and many EU countries are currently investing in HIT initiatives [1, 3, 4].

In Canada for instance, the national infostructure project had received 1.2B Canadian dollars to advance Electronic Health Records (EHR) and tele-health systems [5], and the Obama administration has spent $19B in stimulus support for EHR systems [6], which aim at reducing the estimated number of 98,000 deaths and the number of injuries from medical errors [6].

The Electronic Health Records are at the centre of the HIT initiatives [1, 3, 7], a thing which becomes more apparent by the presence of an EHR project in most of the EU countries' strategic plan [4], and the fact that national implementations of EHR are internationally pursued [8].

Successful EHR implementations could lead to increased efficiency of the healthcare delivery process, improved patient information collection, speed up administrative processes, improve working conditions and, along with user acceptance, the outcomes will be improved safety, efficiency and quality of healthcare [9].

A. Cerone et al. (Eds.): SEFM 2012 Satellite Events, LNCS 7991, pp. 261–273, 2014.
DOI: 10.1007/978-3-642-54338-8_21, © Springer-Verlag Berlin Heidelberg 2014

However, EHR systems are a complex topic. There is no nationally interoperable system yet, or a standard approach to realise their benefits [8]. As [1] plays on words, he points out that EHR can also stand for "Exceptional Hidden Risks" as the cost of implementing those systems, which is quite high to begin with, rose higher than initially expected in some cases. Examples are Australia where it started from AU$500 M and rose to AU$2B, the UK where it started from £2.6B and rose to more than £15B, and the U.S. where the estimate was between $100B and $150B in implementation costs and a $50B/year in operation costs [1]. Those are 2006 figures.

The paper starts with a review of the EHR system literature. In doing so an overview of EHR systems is presented, aiming at examining if an open source software process would be suitable for the implementation of an EHR system at a large scale such as the national or, when applicable, the continental level. For instance, there has been an increased interest in European Union for the construction of a common European system of EHR and harmonisation of different countries EHR systems. Furthermore, we want to find out which problems, found in current EHR implementation efforts, could possibly be alleviated with the use of an open source software development process.

2   The Term EHR: Environment and Stakeholders

Before tackling the issue at hand, it is necessary to examine how our main topic of interest, the EHR, is defined.

According to the International Organization for Standardization (ISO) definition, the EHR is a repository of patient data in digital form which is stored and exchanged securely, and is accessible by multiple authorised users [10]. The term EHR covers a wide range of information systems from department specific to comprehensive medical records [10]. The term EHR has been used interchangeably with the term EMR to describe either local health record systems, or interoperable health record systems both in research and practice [11].

In [12] a compact taxonomy is given. The categories of EHR systems are classified as (i) local EHR systems; (ii) shared EHR systems; (iii) Personal Health Records (PHR), and (iv) Public Health EHR.

A local EHR system refers to a local system which has the detailed information for the local patients collected over the course of encounters with the patient [12].

A shared EHR system refers to a system whose purpose is to facilitate and record integrated and shared lifetime care to the patient in a group of diverse health service providers [12].

A PHR refers to systems allowing the patient to be in control of his/her record, and has some differences over the systems previously described [12].

A Public Health EHR refers to aggregated de-identified data which are used for public health, epidemiological purposes, research, policy development, health statistics and health service management and can be a obtained from an EHR or created from various sources [12].

The shared EHR systems are the ones that are pursued internationally and usually the prerequisite to such an implementation is the wide use of local EHR systems.

In this paper we will look at them in this combined fashion as two closely related parts. Different architectures may be used but both types of systems are necessary for exchanging medical records at the national or higher level. For more on those terms the reader can look in [12] and for examples of some architectures can look in [3] and [13].

3 EHR Implementations: The Current Impact

For nearly 20 years, EHR systems were expected to solve all the major problems of healthcare systems [14]. If the problems in healthcare were strictly technical issues, they might have been solved by introducing an EHR system. The expectations were certainly high but which has been the impact of EHR systems so far?

3.1 User Considerations

The physicians consider as important aspects of an EHR the following: improving quality of care, supporting direct contact with a patient, improving collaboration with colleagues, all of which will allow them to "just be good doctors" [14], as well as privacy [15] and security [5]. It is very important to mention that collaboration with colleagues also refers to colleagues working in a different organisation [14]. All these factors relate to allowing the physicians to improve their work process, the healthcare delivery process, and its outcomes.

A study mentioned in [14], which included other end-users besides physicians, found the next as the most important aspects: availability of the system, reduction of administrative work, providing information for research and management and allowing the uniformity of working processes. We would like at this point to note that availability as a term is confusing in the cited paper, as it is a term mentioned by physicians and not by software professionals. We take availability in this context to be the same as system reliability and information availability. Considering that, when asked whether they would prefer "reliability or availability" of the EHR, the physicians answered availability of the EHR. We base this assumption on the authors' statement "Reliability can sometimes be seen as the opposite of availability" [14], which would be correct if we are talking about information availability and reliability, where under circumstances a reduction of one side results in increase in the other; but as far as system quality is concerned, a reliable system is one which is available and performs as expected under certain conditions. Therefore, we cannot see how it can be that "Reliability can sometimes be seen as the opposite of availability" [14]. Our assumption on this factor is backed up by [16], where reliability was taken for granted as a case when the system was down for seven days is mentioned and the doctors had to input all the data gathered during the down period after the system was operating again.

Nonetheless, the improvement in the work process and its outcomes seems to be the fundamental requirement that the users have from an EHR system, which would explain why when users with different roles in the healthcare delivery process are included, different factors rank higher.

3.2 Usability: Beyond Human Computer Interaction

Existing EHR usability is rather poor [8, 14, 17] and a number of usability flaws have been reported [17] that back this up.

The importance of usability is mentioned in [15], as one of the studies reviewed there, found a strong correlation between user satisfaction from HIT and the ability of the system to do things in a simple way ('straightforward manner') and in [13] the user interface is mentioned as a critical factor for EHR success.

More specifically, in [14] it is mentioned that, while time and effort can be saved because the EHR makes searching for data and generating letters easier, it is argued that these effects are helpful for administrative personnel but the opposite holds true for physicians who experience a period of lowered consultation times while learning how to use the EHR. This period lasts from half to one year usually [14].

Usability though, goes beyond human computer interaction as it is carefully elaborated in [17]. The authors there argue that, applications have to be considered as integrated parts of a technological environment and usability should be described in the specific context while taking into account the use of the systems during the user's work process in order to complete tasks and achieve certain goals. In this approach they measure usability using three dimensions : (1) Compatibility between clinical ICT systems and physicians' tasks (2) ICT support for information exchange, communication and collaboration in clinical work, and (3) interoperability and reliability. The study was done in Finland and the findings were quite interesting.

The physicians gave relatively low ratings to the EHR systems. Half think that their EHR does not support decision-making and does not provide help with medical error prevention. About half expect better support for routine tasks, and 62 % think that the systems hinder their work by requiring a fixed sequence of steps, even though they had positive opinions on the interfaces of the system [17].

The physicians also consider information accessibility a problem. An 85 % disagrees with the statement that it is easy to access medical information from other healthcare organisations, as it takes too much time to exchange information. Collaboration between physicians in the same organisation is supported, but collaboration between them and the nurses, them and the patients, them and other physicians in distant locations is not supported. The collaboration with the patient not only is not supported, but is also hindered [17].

The findings of [17] that were also supported by other literature sources, as is mentioned there, are problems in data entry, inadequate integration between EHR and other systems. Hospital physicians were more critical towards the EHR systems, indicating the poor suitability of the current systems for hospital settings. On the other hand private providers, which in Finland are mostly clinics dealing with specialised areas, had a better opinion of their systems [17].

3.3 Interoperability

Interoperability between two systems exists when in regard to a certain task one can receive data from the other and perform that task in an appropriate and satisfactory manner without the need for another operators intervention [18].

Considering the central role of the EHR in HIT, as a system which all other HIT systems have to interact with, the importance of EHR system interoperability with other Health Information Systems (HIS) is increased. Interoperability between different EHR systems allows sharing of patient information, it therefore enables patient mobility. Interoperability is also an important property, which is necessary to increase collaboration between physicians from different healthcare organisations and, thus, increases the usability of the HIS as mentioned in the previous section. These two aspects make interoperability a very important quality property of EHR systems.

3.3.1   Interoperability and Standards

At this point health information is stored in different kinds of proprietary formats in different health information systems, which results in severe interoperability problems [18].

For this reason a number of standards have been proposed in order to provide a remedy solution to this problem. Some of the standards are XDS, HL7 version 3, openEHR and EHRcom. Most EHR standards are currently evolving and there is a trend of harmonising and unifying previous EHR developments [18].

Conformance to one of the standards or to a combination of them will not solve the interoperability problem according to [18] as the authors argue that it does not seem realistic that all the healthcare institutes will reach a consensus on using the same standards. If, however, a large number of organisations use the same data format and agree on an exchange protocol, there seems to be no reason why their systems cannot be interoperable. This seems to be the idea behind XDS where the communicating parties agree on document format, structure and content before exchange [18].

The issue of conformance to standards seems to be more related to the HIS development industry rather than healthcare organisations and this is backed by the opinion expressed in [13] where interoperability problems are attributed to a few systems complying with standards. The issue of interoperability came up quite often during this research work. The issue of achieving interoperability at a large scale seems feasible from a technical perspective, but is also affected by political and competitive issues [11].

3.3.2   Financial Impacts of Interoperability

An example of the financial importance of interoperability at a large-scale and for developed economies can be found in [11], where it is stated that the most cited study on EHR benefits was a RAND study in the U.S. which predicted that increased efficiency and safety will result in savings of an average of more than $77 billion per year when 90 % adoption rate was achieved with an average of $42 billion per year during the adoption period, figures which can be doubled if chronic diseases were managed and providers with consumers participated.

However it is also mentioned there that the study predicted those amounts by assuming a level of interoperability which highly exceeded the level of interoperability possible at the time.

3.3.3   Interoperability and Customisation for Local Needs

Standards have to be considered for large-scale interoperability but, there is also an issue of leaving room for customisation in order to fit the specific context [8]. The overall impression from the references used in this paper is that "room for customisation" is a somewhat vague term that has to be more specific in the sense that while intuitively a generic EHR system would not be suitable for the diversity of medical users and clinical practices, there could still be norms that would define the relationship between interoperability considerations and space for customisation in a more specific manner allowing some sort of classification of system characteristics.

4   Social Aspects of EHR Implementation

It should be evident by now that the implementation of an EHR system is by no means a strictly technical issue.

In different countries, healthcare delivery is organised in a different manner, it might be mainly public or mainly private. Typically, health services are divided in primary, secondary and tertiary care [10].

Primary care is provided in the community by general practitioners, secondary care is provided by a specialist facility after referral and tertiary care is provided by a team of specialists in a hospital [10].

In order to understand how beneficial the EHR is, we have to understand how it will affect the interactions that happen at multiple levels. The idea of understanding the information exchange interactions and the value they generate, at multiple levels is found in [11], where at the first level are the interactions within the same organisation, at the second are those between individual practitioners and hospitals, and at the third one are those between regional and competitive health networks. Either one agrees or not with the defined levels, it certainly touches an important aspect, that EHR systems have different effects, at different organisational levels.

Moreover, the work process of healthcare delivery is viewed as a complex system, which is a collection of people and tools interacting in a complicated manner [15] and the issue of implementation is connected to social and economic aspects [1]. The shortcomings of the current national EHR implementations are attributed to the negligence of those aspects, and the underlying organisational and human factors have to be taken into account [9].

As far as support for working processes goes, many EHR systems do not fit naturally in the work process [19]. Effects of EHR on quality of care are dependent on the characteristics of the EHR and its impact on the work process [9]. The opinion expressed in [11] is that realising the full value of HIT will require the creation of new work processes where technology is used naturally (the word embedded is used), it has shared acceptance, resulting in new capabilities, new structures and changes in relationships and culture. This is backed by the fact that benefits have been achieved in small scales where the systems were customised to fit the local context and the main challenges were embedding them in the clinical and organisational process [8].

The introduction of EHR into the workplace has the potential to change roles and processes, it also has the potential to have positive and negative effects on quality of working life [9]. The potential adverse effects may include usability deficiencies which increase frustration [9] or possibly increased intensity of work.

Understanding the dynamics of this change process becomes very important when examining things from this point of view. Without covering this in detail we will mention some factors.

We can say that the compatibility of the technology with the aims of the professionals is such a factor, as for example in [14] the physicians resorted to using paper, which offered a quicker working process thus allowing them to have more time, something they considered they were lacking. Without facing the underlying issue which is lack of time, the introduction of an EHR whose Usability was inferior to that of the paper record keeping, forced them in a certain sense to revert to the use of paper.

Financial and time saving incentives of the use of EHR may affect it positively [20] but this should also take into account different needs for the management and the healthcare personnel.

The management becomes crucial as it has the ability to empower the personnel by encouraging participation and involvement in the change process, which along with willingness to change are important adoption factors [20]. An important thing to note here is that participation is defined as the set of activities and behaviours performed by the users in the implementation process while involvement refers to a subjective norm [20].

However the process of adoption requires time and effort and some adverse effects are unavoidable, since the healthcare personnel will have to learn new skills and adapt to new processes [2] before being able to start optimising them.

In order for the EHR systems to have a transformative effect, those factors and many, which is not possible to cover here, have to be examined. The crucial aspects though are allowing information exchange in large areas in order to enable patient care integration, and supporting the working practices of the medical personnel [9].

5   Open Source Development as a Possible Change Catalyst

In this chapter we present some indications showing that considering and open source development model for large-scale EHR implementation could be beneficial.

5.1   Defining Open Source Software Development

First we have to start by defining open source. A software system can be said to be free and open source when a person has access to its source code, is free to use it, copy it and redistribute it, modify it and distribute the modified versions [21]. There is a variety of licenses (http://opensource.org/licenses/category), ranging from more permissive to more restrictive but they are considered open source as long as they conform to the freedoms mentioned [21].

The development follows a circular process and starts when the source code is made available online. When a contribution is made, a new version is produced, afterwards a testing period follows where bug reports are submitted by the users and fixed by the developers of the community, something which goes on until the version becomes stable. At that point the process starts again with a new contribution [21].

Besides this basic development pattern there is a lot of diversity among open source communities. There are differences to what motivates the community members to contribute, the way that project decisions are made and the main moving force in the project which may be a single person, a community, a company or members of the academia [22].

5.2 Motivational Factors in Open Source Software Development

Except users and sponsors, another stakeholders category that should be taken into consideration while adopting a software development process model is that of the various software developers [23]. Their knowledge, conditions of work and motivation are significant factors in the development of successful and socially acceptable software. EHR implementation, for instance, with or without open source software, leads to social software systems. This indicates the needs for high quality and shared conceptualization. These can lead to social acceptance of electronic health records. Social acceptance is considered an important part of any software system by the authors of this paper. Primarily, a systems development model is as strong as the user involvement it supports [24], in many phases of the development. For instance, this user involvement can clearly be evidenced by the system's use or avoidance, which, in turn, will also determine the degree of the system's maintainability. Thus, we must, next, examine motivational and other factors for software developers in open source software development methodology, with references to countries with developing or/and developed economies.

Open source can have an effect on developing economies because open source software can be used as a source of software knowledge that could be used by local companies and technology professionals, serving as a motivational factor for involvement [22].

A number of studies indicates that open source software developers are driven by peer recognition, the desire to be part of a community and internal motivation deriving from the creativity felt during the development.

However, there is an increasing number of developers who are paid to work on open source software. A survey mentioned in [22] states that "the majority" of developers involved in open source software are paid for it. Motivations are usually monetary gains, technical benefits, skill-acquisition and employment prospects especially for individual developers [22]. The increasing number of individual software application developers that are interested in this development shows that funding is necessary in some projects.

This is of great importance as it shows that open source projects can be funded directly by various organizations. The fact that they remain open can allow for the fruitful participation of different stakeholders from private companies to academic researchers and governments, while avoiding e.g. lock-ins and interoperability issues.

5.3 What Could an Open Source Software Process Offer?

The quality of open source was assessed in [21] using the ISO 9126 quality model and the authors concluded that while in some areas open source software, or more specifically free and open source software (FOSS), seems to do better than proprietary software there is room for improvement. For instance, FOSS tends to be more effective for projects where incremental change is rewarded, something that makes it more suitable for back-end development [21].

The open source movement has a commitment to implementing standards that promote functionality and interoperability, and are publicly available and royalty-free [21]. In fact open source seems to do better in projects with well defined requirements [21].

Implementation of functionality and interoperability standards has led to cases where useful feedback indicating errors in the standard was given by a project, something which helped improve the standard [21] and it is also supported that open source might lead to faster adoption of standards [21].

Open source software is reliable due to the quick rate of bug-fixing [21], something that comes as a consequence of having a high number of beta testers, who test the software in operational mode [21].

Availability of the source code allows peer review which, as results show, can lead to better security in the long term [21] although there is some controversy around that. It is stated that while availability of the source code allows it to be reviewed by contributors it also allows malicious users to find flaws which they can later exploit or they can redistribute their version of the software [25].

As far as Usability in open source is concerned the authors find that special attention is necessary at the point when the project idea is conceived [21].

Another aspect which is important is the philosophy of openness and community that is present in open source. By providing tools that facilitate communication in the medical community, this openness could potentially provide research materials about the shortcomings and strengths of the current HIT implementations, and allow professionals to share positive and negative experiences with HIT while at the same time empowering them to participate in the evolution of their HIT work tools.

5.4   Indications of Potential Benefits of Open Source

EHR implementation is considered an evolutionary process where professionals that don't use an EHR are not going to easily adopt an EHR with advanced functionality [14], something which falls in line with sophistication levels of HIT implementations presented by one of the studies reviewed in [15] where level 0 was no active electronic medical record. Also it is suggested that the process should start small and built from that [8, 13]. The early adopters with the most sophisticated systems or the HIT leaders as [15] calls them, have followed this process of developing their systems in-house over the years by local "champions" in an evolving process of evaluating the system and adapting it.

This would be the most effective way to develop such systems, if of course the benefits of this type of context based development, can be replicated at a larger scale by an open source development model, since open source follows this evolutionary process. This certainly isn't applicable for each and every one of the involved healthcare organisations but it would be applicable if healthcare organisations taking part in such an initiative would be grouped into organisations offering the same or very similar healthcare services. Open source development would then function as a platform for user involvement, which along with this evolutionary development process would allow the users to exchange experiences, suggest modifications to the EHR system and also be encouraged to suggest new work processes based on the capabilities enabled by the EHR.

In [13] the authors state that populating and using an EHR is very much the same, regardless the country which could enable possible funding of such an initiative by a number of countries that could benefit from this effort, or make the lessons from an effort like this generalisable.

Implementation of EHR standards in such a process could facilitate the harmonisation of the various standards, something that has already begun to some extent as previously described, and the openness could create an interesting interplay between standards development and the evolution of the system itself while enabling the achievement of a much higher degree of interoperability than the one possible now.

The availability of the code has other benefits as well. Some of these are building local capabilities in developing countries [22], building the capabilities of the health informatics workforce, it can allow the academic research from various related fields to influence implementation practice. At the same time, saving funding from licence fees while avoiding vendor lock-ins would be possible, but this has its risks if the project is not build around a community.

Another remarkable finding is in [14], where it is mentioned that 60 % of the market in the Netherlands at the time was in the hands of two suppliers, with systems that did not provide decision support and had a poor user interface. This high amount of concentration shows, at least to a certain extent, a high degree of shared conceptualization, which could be useful as a starting point in a transition to open source implementation, since open source software development has achieved much in applications with well-defined requirements [21] and the most robust community-based projects have a high degree of conceptualisation [22]. The poor results of those systems, are both an incentive to consider open source initiatives and the high degree of conceptualisation can be the starting point for the requirements, if the picture is the same in other countries as well.

Finally, by providing a high quality system for free would allow cost, one of the most frequent adoption barriers [15], to be overcome. A word of caution though is necessary at this point because even though the system could be free and wouldn't require licensing costs there is still the cost of support and training which should be examined.

5.5 Points to Consider

Although there are some interesting indications about some potential benefits of considering such a development model, its feasibility has to be closely examined. Issues such as licensing and transition strategies from closed source, involving compatibility with a number of legacy systems in use, and the community building process which would make this effort sustainable, would have to be considered.

A number of business models used in open source software would have to be examined in order to encourage companies to offer services and their expertise by becoming members of the community. The information found in [26] can be quite useful to finding some realistic possibilities. User training, installation, maintenance, establishment of backup and disaster recovery processes and procedures, on-site training tailored to users' needs are good candidates for business models [26]. Permissive license on the core of the system could be tricky as it could lead to replicating the current problem of the variety of proprietary formats being used.

The model has to be tailored to cater for Usability which is a crucial quality aspect as we presented in this paper.

A governance model has to be considered which should attempt to create the "local champion" effect and also take into account that there has to be a balance between user involvement and the core team making the decisions [15, 19] with the process itself having an evaluation framework built in [19] and at a large scale as the one we are considering, this is by no means a trivial task.

Another important consideration of the governance model is the quality assurance of new versions. Simply installing them frequently upon release, not only is not realistic in a healthcare organisation setting, but expecting it to be tested in operation to find the errors would be completely reckless and unacceptable in such safety-critical systems.

The final point to consider is the need for government funding in this effort and a strategic plan over a period of time. Government funding has been found necessary [5, 27]. If the various aspects of a source model suitable for this context are examined in more detail, clarified and shown to be potentially effective, the large amount of financial resources that countries have already spent or have offered as incentives to medical professionals to purchase proprietary software could be a reason to invest in developing high quality open source systems.

6   Closing Remarks and Future Work

In this work we provided some information about the necessity that drives HIT implementation, the central role of EHR systems in these efforts, we gave a definition of the term EHR and provided a picture of the current implementation landscape of EHR systems. The last part of this paper consisted of some indications of potential benefits of considering an open source software process model tailored to this context for large scale implementation, while also considering the challenges that such an endeavour would have.

Concluding, we can argue that healthcare software development is very complex by its nature and it involves technical, economical, social and political aspects. Further research is needed in order to identify and interconnect them and see how an open software development model that is holistic with respect to different stakeholders needs, realistic as to EHR requirements implementation and customisable for different healthcare application domains.

Future work has to develop a more complete understanding of EHR systems and build on the Sects. 5.4 and 5.5 and if possible provide an open source development process model for this case.

References

1. Charette, R.: EHRs: electronic health records or exceptional hidden risks. Commun. ACM **49**(6), 120 (2006)
2. Cherie, N., Sajda, Q.: Physician interaction with electronic health records: the influences on digital natives and digital immigrants. In: 2011 44th Hawaii International Conference on System Sciences (HICSS). IEEE (2011)
3. Jalal-Karim, A., Balachandran, W.: The national strategies for electronic health record in three developed countries: general status. In: IEEE International Multitopic Conference, 2008 (INMIC 2008). IEEE (2008)
4. European Commission: eHealth priorities and strategies in European countries. Office for Official Publications of the European Communities, Luxembourg (2007)
5. Noseworthy, T.: Advancing electronic health records in Canada: why, how and key learnings of potential value to China. In: Proceedings of the Fourth International Workshop on Design of Reliable Communication Networks, 2003 (DRCN 2003). IEEE (2004)
6. Shneiderman, B.: Tragic errors: usability and electronic health records. Interactions **18**(6), 60–63 (2011)
7. Karim, N.S.A., Ahmad, M., Mohamed, N.: A framework for electronic health record (EHR) implementation impact on system service quality and individual performance among healthcare practitioners. In: Proceedings of the 10th WSEAS International Conference on E-Activities. World Scientific and Engineering Academy and Society (WSEAS) (2011)
8. Cresswell, K.M., Ann, R., Sheikh, A.: Lessons learned from England's national electronic health record implementation: implications for the international community. In: Proceedings of the 2nd ACM SIGHIT International Health Informatics Symposium (IHI 12), pp. 685–690, (2012)
9. Carayon, P., et al.: Implementation of an electronic health records system in a small clinic: the viewpoint of clinic staff. Behav. Inf. Technol. **28**(1), 5–20 (2009)
10. Kristiina, H., Saranto, K., Nykänen, P.: Definition, structure, content, use and impacts of electronic health records: a review of the research literature. Int. J. Med. Inf. **77**(5), 291 (2008)
11. Sherer, S.A.: Value realization from adoption of integrated electronic health records. In: 2011 44th Hawaii International Conference on System Sciences (HICSS). IEEE (2011)
12. Kwak, Y.S.: International standards for building electronic health record (ehr). Enterprise networking and Computing in Healthcare Industry, 2005. In: Proceedings of 7th International Workshop on HEALTHCOM 2005. IEEE (2005)
13. Moller, J.E., Henrik, V.: Experiences with electronic health records. IT. prof. **10**(2), 19–23 (2008)
14. Spil, T.A.M., Christiaan, P.K.: Balancing supply and demand of an electronic health record in the netherlands; not too open systems for not too open users. In: 40th Annual Hawaii International Conference on System Sciences, 2007 (HICSS 2007). IEEE (2007)
15. Shekelle, P.G., Caroline L.G.: Costs and benefits of health information technology: an updated systematic review. Health Foundation, 2009

16. Karim, N.S.A., Ahmad, M. : An overview of electronic health record (EHR) implementation framework and impact on health care organizations in malaysia: a case study. In: 2010 IEEE International Conference on Management of Innovation and Technology (ICMIT). IEEE (2010)
17. Viitanen, J., et al.: National questionnaire study on clinical ICT systems proofs: physicians suffer from poor usability. Int. J. Med. Inform. **80**(10), 708–725 (2011)
18. Eichelberg, M., et al.: A survey and analysis of electronic healthcare record standards. ACM. Comput. Surv. (CSUR) **37**(40), 277–315 (2005)
19. Faber, M.G.: Design and introduction of an electronic patient record: how to involve users? Methods. Inf. Med. **42**(4), 371–375 (2003)
20. Spil, T.A.M., et al.: Value, participation and quality of electronic health records in the netherlands. In: 2010 43rd Hawaii International Conference on System Sciences (HICSS). IEEE (2010)
21. Samoladas, I., Stamelos, I.: Assessing Free/Open Source Software Quality. Aristotle University of Informatics, Greece(2003)
22. Camara, G., Fonseca, F.: Information policies and open source software in developing countries. J. Am. Soc. Inform. Sci. Technol. **58**(1), 121–132 (2007)
23. Siakas, K. et al.: The complete alphabet of quality software systems: conflicts and compromises. In: McGraw-Hill, A. (eds.) India 7th World Congress on Total Quality and Qualex 97, New Delhi, India, 17–19 February 1997, pp. 603–618 (1997)
24. Berki, E. et al.: A methodology is as strong as the user involvement it supports. In: ISSEU Conference March 97. Rovaniemi TAMK Press, Chicago (1997)
25. OSS Watch: Is open source software insecure? An introduction to the issues. http://www.oss-watch.ac.uk/resources/securityintro.xml (2012). Accessed 5 Sep 2012
26. Piliouras, T,. et al.: Selection of electronic health records software: challenges, considerations, and recommendations. In: 2011 IEEE Long Island Systems, Applications and Technology Conference (LISAT). IEEE (2011)
27. Edwards, J.: Case study: Denmark's achievements with healthcare information exchange. Gartner Industry Research (2006)

Using Open Source Projects in Higher Education: A Two-Way Certification Framework

Pantelis M. Papadopoulos[1(✉)], Ioannis G. Stamelos[2],
and Antonio Cerone[1]

[1] United Nations University, International Institute for Software Technology,
Macau SAR, People's Republic of China
pmpapad@iist.unu.edu, ceroneantonio@gmail.com
[2] Aristotle University of Thessaloniki, Thessaloniki, Greece
stamelos@csd.auth.gr

Abstract. The paper proposes a framework for the certification of free/libre open source software (FLOSS) projects. The process is two-fold and is based on our experience over the last four years of using FLOSS for teaching software engineering in Aristotle University of Thessaloniki. The premise of the paper is that students' engagement with real open source projects, and more specifically with the respective open source communities, can be an effective instructional method for skill development. We argue that through such a process, the students are able to get familiar with tools and technologies used in FLOSS and receive certification as FLOSS participants. On the other hand, the students can also review and evaluate the FLOSS project they use during the learning activity from different perspectives. In more advanced learning activities, this evaluation can be based on certification standards, providing in that way a valuable source of feedback to the open source community.

Keywords: Open source projects · FLOSS in education · Software certification · Communities of practice

1 Introduction

In this paper, we present a theoretical framework for a two-way certification process of Free/Libre Open Source Software (FLOSS) projects, involving students, both undergraduate and postgraduate, in Software Engineering courses. Our main argument is that university students have the potential to work on FLOSS projects in ways that would be beneficial for them, but also for the projects they work on. On one hand, students learn about software engineering by using appropriate tools and methods, and gain valuable experience through their participation in real FLOSS project communities. There is already evidence in the literature regarding the effective use of FLOSS in higher education (e.g., [1]). We suggest that the learning experience could be further extended engaging students even deeper in the analysis of a project, leading eventually to a *FLOSS Participant* certification that students could use in their later professional career.

A. Cerone et al. (Eds.): SEFM 2012 Satellite Events, LNCS 7991, pp. 274–280, 2014.
DOI: 10.1007/978-3-642-54338-8_22, © Springer-Verlag Berlin Heidelberg 2014

One of the many skills students can develop in this kind of activity is also the ability to apply certification-related techniques (e.g., testing) to evaluate and review different characteristics of the FLOSS projects. Hence, on the other hand, the body of students enrolled each year in a course can be a valuable source of information for the project team and also for the certification of FLOSS projects.

Since 2005, junior students in the "Introduction in Software Engineering" (ISE) and "Object-Oriented Analysis" (OOA) courses in Aristotle University of Thessaloniki have to participate in FLOSS projects as part of course assignments, playing the role of testers, developers, requirements engineers (for ISE), or analysts/designers (for OOA). Over the years, hundreds of students became participants of FLOSS projects, contributing as equal members of the open source community.

In the following, we present (a) the background of our approach (b) the instructional method we apply for teaching software engineering with FLOSS in Aristotle University (c) discussion for a two-way certification framework for students and for FLOSS projects/artifacts, and (d) concluding remarks.

2 Background

2.1 Open Source Certification

In this section, we explain what *certification* means in the context of our work. In the software world, certification is the assertion that a software product, organization, or person exhibits some significant characteristic. A typical example of organization certification framework is the CMMI model [2]. A software product may be certified for some quality aspect, such as safety or reliability [3, 4]. Software certification also stands for confirmation that a person possesses knowledge/skills in domains such as programming languages, computer network management or software project management. A common characteristic in existing certification frameworks is that of *certification levels*, i.e. ordered levels of maturity, knowledge etc. that provide further certification refinement. An example is the five CMMI levels (*initial, repeatable, defined, managed, improving*).

Our proposal covers all three types of certification (FLOSS related person, organization, artifact) and foresees different certification levels. In particular:

– A student is certified for his/her capability to participate successfully in a FLOSS project. In the context of the ISE course, the student can be certified as FLOSS requirements engineer, FLOSS tester or FLOSS coder. In the context of the OOA course the student is certified as FLOSS object-oriented analyst/designer. Certification is awarded after successful completion of one pre-specified task in a real FLOSS project. The results of the task and the overall experience (including communication and feedback from the project community) are reported in a predefined template (the *learning project*). Level ordering is as follows: Requirements, Testing or Analysis/Design, Coding, attributing higher importance to coding as the ultimate contribution to a FLOSS project.
– A FLOSS project/community is certified for its ability to sustain a community. The project is assigned a certification level according to a set of community-related

measurements including: speed of response to queries, speed of integration of artifacts, release frequency, number of postings per committers etc. A subset of such measurements, e.g. response speed is gathered during the students' endeavor with the project. For most of them, special tooling, such as data mining and web scrapping, is necessary.

- A FLOSS artifact is certified for achieving certain levels of quality attribute thresholds. Examples are the degree of coverage according to some pre-defined testing criterion, such as statement, path coverage, and linear code sequence and jump (LCSAJ). For project and artifact, certification is limited to specific project attributes, using a predefined set of tools, so students need to perform specific, well-defined tasks.

2.2 FLOSS as Instructional Tools

The use of FLOSS projects as instructional tools has already gained a significant audience in higher education [5]. Jaccheri and Osterlie [6] report on a course at the Norwegian University of Science and Technology that is based on the involvement of students in the NetBeans project and their interaction with its community. At the Athens University of Economics and Business (Greece), in the context of a master level course titled "Advanced Topics in Software Engineering", students are asked to participate and produce code in FLOSS projects [7]. Staring et al. [8, 9] also claim that "involving students in large scale, international open source projects has a potential for transformation of the relationship between students, educational institutions and society at large". Lundell et al. [10] report their experience from a practical assignment "designed to give students on an Open Source Masters course an insight into real involvement in Open Source projects" at the University of Skövde (Sweden). They also report on a reduced exercise for undergraduate students related to FLOSS. The authors found out that "the learning experience was both positive and valuable in that it gave real insight into Open Source participation". Finally they report that students were further encouraged to keep on participating in Open Source projects even after their course was completed.

Surprisingly, the underlying technology used by most FLOSS projects is relatively simple, yet mature, usually including versioning systems, mailing lists, chats, forums, wikis or similar knowledge bases. Additionally, free web based services such as Sourceforge provide each FLOSS project with an initial working and community environment therefore facilitating the take off of new projects [11].

3   Instructional Method

The core courses "Introduction in Software Engineering" and "Object-Oriented Analysis" are typically offered in the 3rd year of studies in the Informatics Department of Aristotle University of Thessaloniki. In the courses, we apply a hybrid approach combining formal, distance, exploratory and project-based learning. Theoretical concepts and models are taught in typical class lectures, until the students are ready to move from the book examples to real cases. At this point selected FLOSS projects are presented in class and students have the opportunity to see how theoretical principles are applied in real world contexts.

Students have to search and select one of the FLOSS projects readily available online, and actively participate in the project, choosing one of these roles: (a) tester (b) developer (c) requirements engineer (for ISE), or analyst/designer (for OOA). Students have to go through five steps according to their roles.

STEP 1: Find a Project. Students can search for a FLOSS project anywhere they want. To help them in their selection, we propose a list of criteria such as: compatibility with the operating system they use, highly active project community for timely feedback, and project maturity level. Regarding the latter, testers should look for beta versions (more bugs to be found), while requirements engineers should go for the mature/stable projects. Students are allowed to choose their project based on their personal interests and, possibly, feedback obtained by students of past years. Also, open source projects that wish to enroll students publish their calls on the OpenSE[1] platform we use for the courses in a separate place (called 'market').

STEP 2: Register the Project. Grant permission from the instructor to work on the selected project under the selected role. This is to avoid conflicts between students and evaluate the appropriateness of the selected project.

STEP 3: Preparation. Testers have to start using the project to understand its functionalities and check the appropriate way of reporting bugs. Most of the projects use a Bug Tracking System (BTS), while others use a dedicated sub-forum, or a mailing list. Developers have to grant approval from the project team on the proposed functionalities and gain access to the version control system (e.g., Subversion, Git, CVS, Mercurial) of the project. The proposed functionalities can be based on desired features or open bugs reported in the official project site. The requirements engineers have to grant approval from the project team to write a Software Requirements Specification (SRS) document and receive all the necessary information to write such a document. Finally, analysts have to grant approval from the project team to design UML diagrams for desired features.

STEP 4: Work on the Project. Testers have to apply multiple techniques taught in class for finding bugs (e.g., smoke, recovery), submit unreported bugs, and monitor them if case additional information is requested. Developers have to submit code gradually to the project and give time to the project community to respond with corrections and suggestions. Requirements engineers have to write the SRS document following a formal template, submit it to the project community, and revise according to comments and suggestions. Analysts have to submit UML diagrams along with their analysis, following the assumptions and vocabulary of the previous submissions.

STEP 5: Present the Project. Students have to submit a detailed report and give a slides presentation in class presenting the project. Information about the interaction between the project community and links to submitted work should also be included.

---

[1] http://opense.net

During the assignment, the students were able to use a learning environment. The main function of the environment was to be a digital library with all the necessary resources. Second, the environment was a hub for students, past and current. A basic set of communication tools were available (forum, blog, chat). Through them students could communicate with each other. Students also had personal blogs where they could upload information about their progress on the projects. After the first year, the environment served one more purpose; students were able to see what previous students had to deal with, by reading their reports and blogs. This helped students a lot, especially in selecting appropriate projects for them.

Regarding the assessment criteria, an obvious parameter was the quality of the work they produce. An equally important parameter was students' actual involvement in the open source community. Therefore, students had to elaborate in their reports on the collaboration they had with the project team. The volume and quality of collaboration could be estimated according to the number and importance of messages exchanged in forums, mailing lists, or project pages. Adoption of the submitted work from the community meant that the students were awarded the full grade for the activity. Since interaction with the project team was crucial for success, we allowed students to work on their assignments beyond the typical 12.5 weeks of the official lecturing period and submit it at a later time at 3 pre-defined dates per year – by the end of the course in February, or alternatively in June or September.

4   Discussion for a Certification Framework

Students' attitudes towards this new assignment format were very positive. Despite the expressed needs for more support in various steps (e.g., in finding a suitable project to work on), students' engagement was high. The success of the method is apparent on the fact that a lot of students continued their involvement with their FLOSS projects, even after the end of the assignment, while others returned on the learning environment and played the roles of mentors and advisors to new students.

The method, of course, can be expanded to cover more aspects of software engineering. Stamelos [12] has already proposed an analysis on the educational opportunities of FLOSS on the software engineering knowledge domains recognized by the IEEE Guide on Software Engineering Body of Knowledge [13]. We argue that students' involvement with FLOSS can be formalized and measured in a FLOSS Participant certification. We have already mentioned the different levels of such a certification in Sect. 2.1, with the ability to produce quality code that would be accepted by the community as the higher level of certification for participation in FLOSS.

In addition, we believe that the method holds many benefits for the FLOSS community. A lot of people are FLOSS users, but not many can effectively analyze and review a software project in a way that would be valuable for others. Through this assignment, it is possible to have a group of people each year, educated exactly on this task. Near future additions to the instructional method, already in place in Aristotle University, could be the roles of FLOSS project and FLOSS artifact certifier. The certification of a FLOSS project will be based on metrics such as the speed of response to queries, number of postings by participants, etc., while for a FLOSS artifact the certification process will be based on software quality metrics. A list of appropriate certification criteria found on literature can be provided to the students prior to the assignment. Eventually, through this process, the visibility of the project can be increased and opportunities for improvements can become clearer.

5 Conclusion

The paper presents a tested instructional method for teaching software engineering through FLOSS projects. We argue that this kind of activity can be further extended towards a certification process focusing both on FLOSS participants and FLOSS projects/artifacts. As we mentioned, a next step to materialize this framework would be the inclusion of the certifier role in the learning activity.

Acknowledgments. This work is funded partly by the European Commission in the context of (a) the OpenSE project under the grant agreement no. 503641-LLP-1-2009-1-PT-ERASMUS-ECUE (b) the Graduate Program of Studies of the Informatics Department at Aristotle University of Thessaloniki, and (c) UNU-IIST and Macao Science and Technology Development Fund, File No. 019/2011/A1, in the context of the PPAeL project.

References

1. Xing, G.: Teaching software engineering using open source software. In: Proceedings of the 48th Annual Southeast Regional Conference, p. 57 (2010)
2. Capability Maturity Model for Software, Version 1.1 (1993). Technical report CMU/SEI-93-TR-024 ESC-TR-93-177, February 1993
3. Denney, E., Fischer, B.: Software certification and software certificate management systems (position paper). In: Proceedings of the ASE Workshop on Software Certificate Management Systems (SoftCeMent '05), pp. 1–5 (2005)
4. Heck, P.M.: A software product certification model for dependable systems. CS-Report 06-20. Technische Universiteit Eindhoven, Eindhoven. http://alexandria.tue.nl/extra1/wskrap/publichtml/200620.pdf (2006). Accessed 6 June 2012
5. Cerone, A., Sowe, S.K.: Using free/libre open source software projects as learning tools. In: OpenCert 2010, vol. 33 of ECEASST (2010)
6. Jaccheri, L., Osterlie, T.: Open source software: a source of possibilities for software engineering education and empirical software engineering. In: First International Workshop on Emerging Trends in FLOSS Research and Development (2007)
7. Spinellis, D.: Future CS course already here. Commun. ACM **49**(8), 13 (2006)
8. Staring. K., Titlestad, O.H.: Networks of open source health care action. In: Damiani, E., Fitzgerald, B., Scacchi,W., Scotto, M., Succi, G.,(eds.) The Proceedings of the 2nd International Conference on Open Source Systems, pp. 135–141. Springer, Heidelberg (2006)
9. Staring. K., Titlestad, O.H., Gailis, J.: Educational transformation through open source approaches, IRIS'28 Meeting. http://wwwold.hia.no/iris28/Docs/IRIS2028-1106.pdf (2005)
10. Lundell, B., Persson, A., Lings, B.: Learning through practical involvement in the FLOSS ecosystem: experiences from a masters assignment. In: Proceedings of the Third International Conference on Open Source Systems, pp. 289–294 (2007)

11. Meiszner, A.: Communication tools in FLOSS communities: a look at FLOSS communities at large – beyond the development team. paper and presentation at the web based communities conference 2007, Salamanca – Spain (2007)
12. Stamelos, I.: Teaching software engineering with free/libre open source projects. Int. J. Open Source Softw. Process. (IJOSSP) **1**(1), 72–90 (2008)
13. SWEBOK: Guide to the Software Engineering Body of Knowledge. IEEE Computer Society Press, California (2004)

Guidelines for the Application of Data Envelopment Analysis to Assess Evolving Software

Alexander Chatzigeorgiou[(✉)]

Department of Applied Informatics, University of Macedonia, 54006 Thessaloniki, Greece
achat@uom.gr

Abstract. The assessment of software evolution in terms of quality poses significant challenges as different metrics have to be combined and normalized over the size of each examined version. Data Envelopment Analysis (DEA), a non-parametric technique from production economics, can offer a unified view of several design properties providing insight into global evolutionary trends. In this paper a set of practical guidelines for the application of DEA and the interpretation of the extracted results is proposed, with a focus on open source software, where limited information and documentation might be available.

Keywords: Software evolution · Software metrics · Data envelopment analysis

1 Introduction

Continuous metric tracking and change monitoring of evolving software is a key factor to ensure high quality [6] and to identify possible symptoms of software aging and degrading design. One of the most important challenges that quality assurance has to confront is the *combination* of several metrics that express different aspects of code and design quality into a single unified measure that captures the global trend in the evolution of software. In other words, even if a certain set of metrics (such as complexity and coupling) is agreed to serve as quantifiable properties expressing higher level qualitative properties (such as analyzability and changeability) [7] it is non-trivial to combine the different metric values into a single level or rank.

Data Envelopment Analysis (DEA) [2] is a non-parametric technique, usually employed in production economics to rank different companies based on their performance as captured by financial indicators. In the context of economics, the parameters for the analysis can be either outputs of the production process, such as profit and sales or inputs, such as personnel and raw materials. Beyond the ability to provide a single numerical value for the efficiency of each company, DEA offers the advantage of normalizing the extracted efficiency scores over the input variables.

We have previously shown that DEA can be effectively ported to the domain of software quality assessment and can be useful for comparing the design of open source libraries and application software [3] and for assessing multiple versions of the same project [4]. In this paper a number of guidelines are suggested, which according

A. Cerone et al. (Eds.): SEFM 2012 Satellite Events, LNCS 7991, pp. 281–287, 2014.
DOI: 10.1007/978-3-642-54338-8_23, © Springer-Verlag Berlin Heidelberg 2014

to our experience facilitate the application of DEA for software evolution analysis and investigate the impact of various decisions or missing data. The involved concepts are exemplified through the results on an open-source chart library, namely JFreeChart, of which 22 successive versions have been analyzed (from 0.9.0 to 0.9.21). It should be stressed that the results are indicative and emphasis is not placed on their interpretation for this particular project but rather on the advantages that DEA can offer. The proposed guidelines throughout the paper are marked in bold and italics.

2 Brief Introduction to DEA

Let us consider two companies A and B which are assessed by their annual profit (output of the process) and the personnel employed by each company (input). Assuming that the profit of B is larger than the profit of A, one cannot simply claim that B is more efficient than A. The reason is that, for example, the higher profits of B might have been achieved with ten times the number of employees of A. Efficiency could be trivially obtained in this case as the ratio of output over input. However, efficiency computation becomes a non-trivial issue when numerous factors should be considered simultaneously. DEA calculates a so-called "efficient frontier" which is a mathematical space formed by all efficient units. The degree of inefficiency of all other units is obtained by their distance from the efficient frontier [2].

In a software context, the goal is to compare and rank different software versions according to their design quality. Each version can be assessed by a number of metrics, serving as outputs of the design process under evaluation. In other words, design metrics are the outputs that the designers wish to maximize. However, the size properties (or the offered functionality) of each version should also be considered. The reason can be stated through an example: if we assume that two versions s_i and s_{i+1} achieve the same value for a particular metric (e.g. complexity), one would consider the larger one better-designed, in the sense that despite the larger code base or number of offered features, the designers still managed to keep complexity at the same level.

To summarize, we can employ DEA to rank successive software versions simply by providing as outputs the design metrics of interest and as input(s) the size characteristics of each version. Eventually, DEA extracts a single efficiency score for each version. An efficiency score equal to 1 indicates that a version is a good as it could be, according to the selected criteria. Efficiency scores less than 1 imply that there is room in improving metric values or that the version achieved certain levels for the design metrics but is rather small in size, compared to other versions. Results of the application of DEA on actual open-source and industrial systems can be found in [4].

3 Normal DEA Application

Let us assume that metric values characterizing the design qualities of interest are available for a number of consecutive software versions that we wish to analyze. For our example we have used as outputs, metric values concerning cohesion, fan-in and fan-out, retrieved without any modification from [5] in order to emphasize that DEA

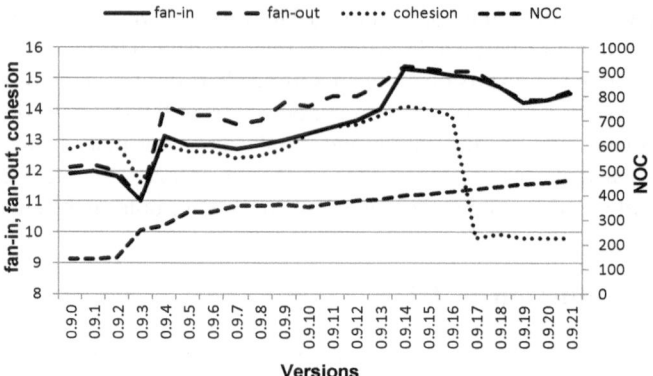

Fig. 1. Evolution of selected software metrics for JFreeChart

can be applied in any experimental setting. Since no information regarding quantitative measures of the implemented functionality in each version (such as Function Points) is available, we have used as substitute input metric the number of classes (NOC). The evolution of these metrics for the examined versions is shown in Fig. 1.

When the trends of individual metrics are not similar during periods of the software history it becomes difficult to derive a single representative trend. The problem is analogous to the extraction of a single trend of stock exchange progress when the trends of several individual stocks have to be considered. We have shown [4] that the added value of DEA depends on how much the series of metrics data are convoluted: *Guideline 1. DEA is suitable when the trends of individual metrics are convoluted*

To run DEA one should simply provide the metric values for each version, designating the inputs (I) or outputs (O). In the usual setting, DEA assumes that the goal is to maximize each output. However, for many metrics it is desirable to minimize their values (such as cohesion and fan-out). To allow for a proper handling of the corresponding variables by DEA, the simplest solution is to invert the metric values: *Guideline 2. When the goal is to minimize an output (metric) the corresponding values should be inverted before the application of DEA*

The application of DEA extracts an efficiency score for each version allowing a full characterization of software evolution. For JFreeChart the results are shown in Fig. 2.

The application of the simple DEA model might be not ideal in some cases when the approach extracts multiple efficient units (i.e. units with an efficiency score equal or very close to 1). In these cases it would be harder to discriminate among the examined versions. For example, in the evolution of DEA efficiency scores for JFreeChart shown in Fig. 2, it appears that several versions obtain a score that is very close to 1.

Under these circumstances an alternative is to use the super-efficiency DEA model [1] which is capable of providing a full ranking by differentiating between the efficient units. This is achieved by excluding the efficient unit under evaluation from the efficient frontier. The effect of this is to shrink the frontier, allowing the efficient unit

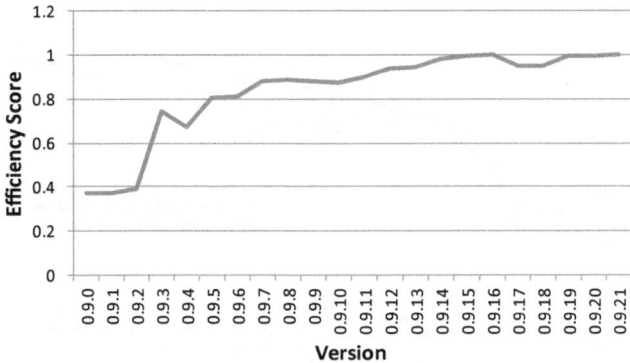

Fig. 2. Evolution of DEA efficiency score (basic model)

to become super-efficient since it now has a score greater than unity. The user simply has to select the corresponding model in the tool that he employs:

Guideline 3. When the application of the basic DEA model leads to multiple versions with an efficiency score equal or close to one, the super-efficiency DEA model should be used instead.

The application of the super-efficiency DEA model on the examined versions of JFreeChart leads to the efficiency scores shown in Fig. 3 (to illustrate the effect of selecting a different model the DEA results from the basic model are also shown).

4   Selection of Outputs

It is reasonable to assume that the selection of metrics plays an extremely important role in the assessment of software quality. The selection of output variables unavoidably impacts the extracted efficiency scores obtained by DEA and as a result the overall trend that is depicted as evolution of software quality. To illustrate this and

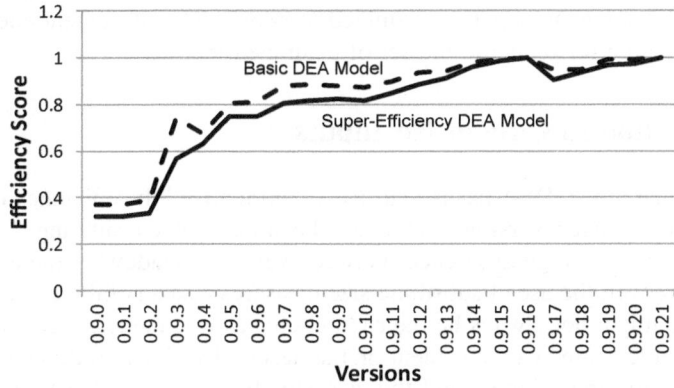

Fig. 3. Evolution of DEA efficiency score: Super-efficiency vs. basic model

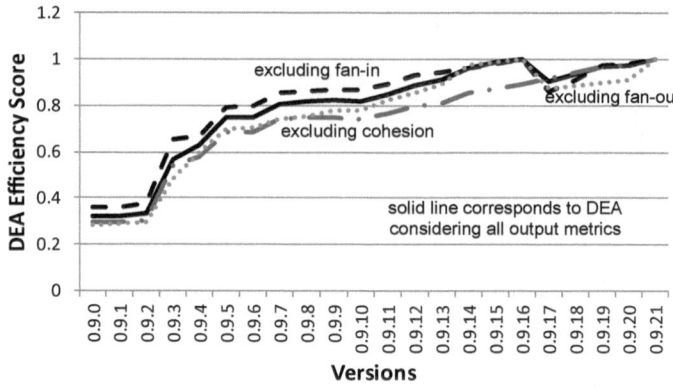

Fig. 4. Impact of excluding output metrics on the DEA efficiency scores

to emphasize the importance of selecting the most appropriate metrics, a 3-stage experiment has been performed, where one of the three output metrics is excluded from the set of outputs at each stage. The results are shown in Fig. 4 (the super-efficiency DEA model is employed). To allow a comparison to the results obtained when all output metrics are considered, the initial efficiency scores of Fig. 2 are also shown.

As it can be observed, the overall trend and ranking of the examined versions remains rather unaltered when excluding one out of the three considered output metrics from the evaluation. However, subtle differences can be observed and since the application of DEA is simple and effortless one should possibly investigate the various options by experimentation:

Guideline 4. The output variables can have varying impact on the extracted DEA scores. When not sure about the necessity to consider a metric, experimentation could highlight whether its impact is significant or not.

In general, DEA can handle any number of outputs. However, as the number of considered outputs increases, the discriminative power of the approach becomes weaker. Consequently, the consideration of a large set of metrics would not lead to a sharp discrimination among the examined versions. The aforementioned guideline might be valuable for reducing the set of examined metrics.

5 Application in Case of No Inputs

As already mentioned, DEA has the ability to "normalize" the efficiency over the size characteristics of each version. However, the impact of considering size might be large when there are large differences between versions, shadowing the effect of other metrics. Moreover, the use of substitute size measures instead of the amount of offered functionality might not always be the right choice as size metrics, such as number of classes or methods are also dependent on the design decisions. In these cases it might be preferable to ignore inputs and this can simply be done in DEA by providing a constant input to all examined versions, zeroing the effect of input variables to the

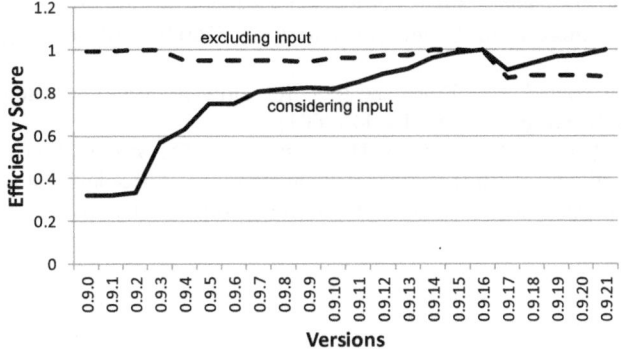

Fig. 5. Impact of excluding input on the DEA efficiency scores

model. In Fig. 5 the obtained DEA efficiency scores are shown when a constant input with value 1 is assumed for each version. To allow the comparison to the results obtained when input is considered, the initial DEA efficiency scores are also depicted.

The impact of the input on the obtained scores and the ranking of versions is significant, justifying the use of DEA as an approach for software evolution analysis: *Guideline 5. Inputs can be neglected from the application of DEA by setting a constant value to the input variables. However the exclusion of inputs might have a significant impact on the obtained evolutionary trends.*

6   Conclusions

Data Envelopment Analysis offers a promising alternative for the assessment of software evolution by combining several metrics that serve as quality indicators and by normalizing the obtained scores over the size characteristics of each examined version. In this paper the impact of several alternatives in the application of DEA is examined resulting to a set of practical guidelines.

Acknowledgements. This work has been partially funded by the Research Committee of the University of Macedonia, Greece.

References

1. Andersen, P., Petersen, N.C.: A procedure for ranking efficient units in data envelopment analysis. Manage. Sci. **39**, 1261–1264 (1993)
2. Charnes, A., Cooper, W.W., Rhodes, E.: Measuring the efficiency of decision making units. Eur. J. Oper. Res. **2**(6), 429–444 (1978)
3. Chatzigeorgiou, A., Stiakakis, E.: Benchmarking library and application software with Data Envelopment Analysis. Software Qual. J. **19**(3), 553–578 (2011)
4. Chatzigeorgiou, A., Stiakakis, E.: Combining metrics for software evolution assessment by means of data envelopment analysis. J. Software: Evol. Process. **25**(3), 303–324 (2013)

5. Lee, Y., Yang, J., Chang, KH.: Metrics and evolution in open source software. In: 7th International Conference on Quality Software (QSIC'2007), Portland, Oregon, pp. 191–197 (2007)
6. Lehman, M.M., Ramil, J.F.: Rules and tools for software evolution planning and management. Ann. Software Eng. **11**(1), 15–44 (2001)
7. Samoladas, I., Gousios, G., Spinellis, D., Stamelos, I.: The SQO-OSS quality model: measurement based open source software evaluation. In: Proceedings of 4th International Conference on Open Source Systems (OSS'2008), Milan, Italy, pp. 237–248 (2008)

A Certification Process for Android Applications

Harsha K. Kalutarage[1], Padmanabhan Krishnan[2],
and Siraj Ahmed Shaikh[1(✉)]

[1] Digital Security and Forensics (SaFe) Research Group, Department of Computing,
Faculty of Engineering and Computing, Coventry University, Coventry, UK
{kalutarh,s.shaikh}@coventry.ac.uk
[2] Centre for Software Assurance, Bond University, Gold Coast, QLD 4229, Australia
pkrishna@bond.edu.au

Abstract. The last decade has seen the emergence of mobile platform for software applications. An important factor in the remarkable growth in this area is the development of Android and a community of mobile application developers sharing open sourced and free software. While the emphasis for Android has been openness and user control, this brings with it challenges of validating and securing mobile apps. Development of dedicated tools and techniques to test mobile apps for functional and nonfunctional properties has been limited so far. Such an effort is made more difficult given frequent version updates for Android in its short history (over ten in ten years). The need for better security and assurance for mobile apps, on the other hand, is ever so more as apps providing important services such as banking, navigation, and identity management emerge. This paper attempts to converge on current concepts and practices of testing mobile apps. We provide a structured checklist approach to vulnerability assessment and permission mapping of mobile apps, which is underpinned by a set of available tools, and ultimately contribute to a framework for certification of mobile apps. The proposed certification process combines diverse sources and has a focus on automation.

1 Introduction

The last decade has seen the emergence of mobile platform for software applications. This has been helped by global telecommunication networks, offering ever increasing traffic capacity and coverage, along with remarkable developments in mobile processing performance in new generation smartphones and tablets. An equally important factor contributing to this growth is the development of open sourced operating systems, such as Android, and the support such platforms encouraging a community of mobile application ("app") developers sharing software and utilities for free public use. The Android initiative is led by Google and has a market share of over 50 % [5]. With nearly 5 million mobile apps available for worldwide distribution over the Android platform, estimates suggest that by the end of December 2011 over 10 billion apps have been downloaded [3]. Given the increase in mobile devices (including phones and tablets) software for the mobile platform will become a significant issue.

A. Cerone et al. (Eds.): SEFM 2012 Satellite Events, LNCS 7991, pp. 288–303, 2014.
DOI: 10.1007/978-3-642-54338-8_24, © Springer-Verlag Berlin Heidelberg 2014

The developer community welcomes the emphasis on openness and user control for development and distribution over the Android platform. While this is a factor in its growth and adoption, it brings with it the challenge of validating and securing apps [19]. Development of dedicated tools and techniques to test mobile apps for functional and nonfunctional properties has been limited. Such an effort is made more difficult given frequent version updates for Android in its short history (over ten in ten years) [5]. The need for better security and assurance for mobile apps, on the other hand, is ever so more as apps providing important services such as banking, navigation, and identity management emerge; the mobile application landscape is still young.

This paper is an attempt to converge on current concepts and practices of testing and certifying mobile apps. We provide a structured checklist approach to vulnerability assessment and permission mapping of mobile apps, which is underpinned by a set of available tools, and ultimately contribute to a framework for certification of mobile apps.

The rest of this paper is organised as follows. Section 2 identifies the main steps adopted in the certification process while Sect. 3 develops the details. Section 4 illustrates an application of the approach on a simple app. We have chosen a generic (not security specific) app to demonstrate the wide applicability of the certification process. Section 5 concludes the paper with a discussion for further steps to accomplish the goals set out by this paper.

2   Towards Certification for Android

Efforts to introduce security concerns at the early stages of development, as advocated by models such as SQUARE [20], CLASP [23] and PICOS [24] are not directly applicable in an environment where assurance needs to be established for mobile applications in the post-distribution phase; of interest here is only certification of the final product on delivery. The quality assurance processes used by such models [20,23,24] however could be adopted in a post-hoc certification process; of particular interest is

- *attack surface identification* to understand the access available to unauthorised users of the application,
- *threat assessment* processes to identify how vulnerabilities can be exploited.

Other information that supports the above, such as CWE, NIST and CAPEC could be adopted as part of this process. CWE (which stands for Common Weakness enumeration) is a collection of well known vulnerabilities in software. These vulnerabilities could be related to all aspects of software development including the design and implementation of a system. CAPEC (which stands for Common Attack Pattern Enumeration and Classification) identifies how such vulnerabilities could be exploited (or attacked). They are related to design patterns but focus specifically on exploiting well known vulnerabilities.

The key ideas in the process are similar to the quality assurance steps in any software development life cycle. We propose a structured process, consisting

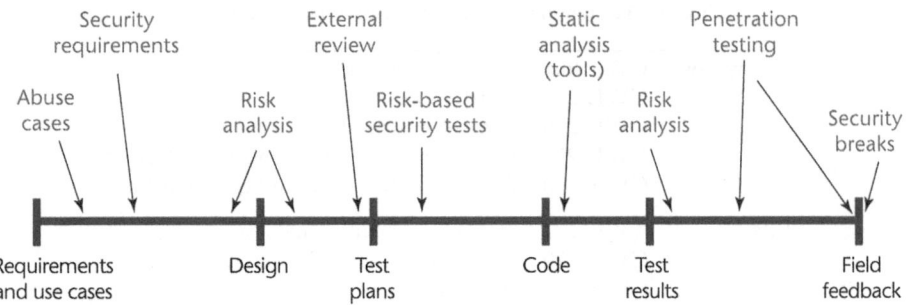

Fig. 1. Security activities as part of a software development lifecycle [7]

a series of three steps, selected from Bieber et al. [4] and the use of Common Criteria [22], to help towards certification as follows

1. *Identify the attack surface*
   We propose to use the CWE collection and NIST SP 800-70 Revision 2 standard for identifying access to application interface and resources that are accessible.
2. *Conduct threat assessment*
   We suggest using the CLASP process for these two steps. But it will use the classification scheme [1] to identify relevant descriptions. For instance, any use of confidentiality would imply that CWE descriptions 326, 261 and 287 are relevant. The attack pattern associated with confidentiality that would be derived from CWE 287 (to by pass authentication) would then be related to CAPEC 16 (dictionary based attacks).
3. *Link each precondition associated with the attack patterns to coding standards, verification conditions and test cases.*
   This process can be viewed as a specific instance of the process described in Fig. 1 by Chess and Arkin [7], reproduced below in Fig. 1, and using the classification [1] explicitly to link the patterns to specific steps in the mobile application development lifecycle.

The following section delves into further detail of the proposed process above.

3   Certification Process

In this section we describe the details of our certification process. The main step is to identify aspects of the attack surface. Towards this, we use relevant existing work. Section 3.1 is the main section describing the examination of the specification of security polices and their enforcement.

An analysis [14] has flagged 1.6 % (based on 311 size sample) applications in the Android market are potentially dangerous at the time they are installed. So about 1 in 50 applications require end user involvement to ensure security. The authors of the study claim manual certification through source code inspection

Table 1. Resources and relevant vulnerabilities

Passwords	CWE 251	Weak passwords
	CWE 259	Hard coded password
	CWE 256	Password stored in plain text
	CWE 257	Password stored in recoverable format
	CWE 260	Password stored in configuration file
File	CWE 732	Incorrect permissions
	CWE 379	Creation of temp file
	CWE 73	Path of filename
Encryption	CWE 326	Inadequate strength
	CWE 311	Missing encryption
	CWE 319	Transmission of data in clear text

is imperfect for mitigating malware and other software misuse. Instead they propose a lightweight certification service (Kirin) that can be performed at the time of install which decides whether security configuration of the Android application is safe using a set of predefined security rules. Kirin checks for a fixed number of security properties and is independent of the functionality of the application.

Enck et al. [13] conducted a study for better understanding the status of the Android application security using 1100 popular free Android applications. They have introduced a decompiler (ded) which recovers (re-engineers) Android application source code directly from its installation image. They report results on the analysis of 21 million lines of code recovered from 1100 application images, using automated tests and manual inspection. They use four different analysis criteria: control flow, data flow, structural and semantic. The ded and proposed analysis specifications can be used by third party Android application certifiers.

Based on the above observations and standard repositories such as CWE, we have identified some generic vulnerabilities and coding standards.

3.1   Policies and Enforcement

Felt et al. demonstrate, by launching attacks on Android applications, permission re-delegation is a widespread threat in modern platforms with per-application permissions and inter process communication (IPC) [17]. If an application with permission performs a privileged task on behalf of less privileged application then permission re-delegation is occurred. According to the authors permission re-delegation is a real threat. They found a third of the 872 Android applications surveyed are at a risk, especially of stealthy attacks that can be conducted in the background. The authors discuss potential ways (such as taint tracking, MAC systems, stack inspection) to address the matter. They present an implementation of IPC inspection mechanism which tracks information flows through inter application messages (not just within an application) at OS level. The IPC inspection mechanism maintains a list of current permissions granted by users for each application. Once an application receives a message from another, the privileges of recipient is reduced to the intersection of permissions of both

Table 2. Coding standards

CWE 798	Hard coding credentials	MSC03-J
CWE 732	Insecure Permissions	FIO01-J creating files
		FIO00-J no files in shared directories
		SEC03-J loading of trusted classes after
		untrusted code has loaded a class
		SEC00-J information leak across trust boundary
CWE 327	Broken Crypto	MSC02-J Generate strong random numbers
CWE 111	External Interface	Improper use of JNI
Android	Importing Classes	Android, third party and then Java

applications. But this requires changes to the Android system and is not directly relevant to our certification process. Reference [8] presents an analysis of inter application communication and identifies insecure developer practices. The authors report that most of vulnerabilities stem from the use of Intents (a message for a particular recipient) in Android for both inter and intra application communication. According to the authors a malicious application can intercept implicit Intents and can gain unauthorised access to all of the data in any matching Intent. Intent spoofing, sending Intent to an exported component that is not expecting Intents from that application, is another possible method that malicious application can use with success. Thus Intents are an integral part of the attack surface.

Reference [11] shows that Android's sandbox model is conceptually flawed and privilege escalation attack is actually possible. The Android system does not protect against a transitive permission usage which ultimately results in allowing an adversary to perform actions the application's sandbox is not authorised to do. They provide a detailed description of implementations of privilege escalation attack using the return-oriented programming attack technique.

Felt et al. [16] report that one third of investigated applications are over privileged and do not follow the least privileges policy. They identify the ten most common unnecessary permissions with ACCESS NETWORK STATE and READ PHONE STATE being the top two.

Conti et al. [10] claim granting permissions all at once and only at installation time is a coarse grained control as the user has no ability to govern how the permissions are exercised after the installation. Therefore authors propose an extension of the current security mechanism of Android which enforces fine grained security policies that depend on the context of the Smartphone. The certification process is only for standard Android and hence we only identify violation of permissions. This is related to the claims by Fuchs et al. [18] that enforcing permissions itself is not sufficient to prevent security violations in Android.

3.2   Android Specific Resources

In normal systems we need to worry about files. From our discussions, we can conclude that on Android based systems we need to be concerned about Intents, protected APIs etc. This is presented in Table 3. This is derived from Table 1 (inspired by CWE) and Android specific resources.

Table 3. Android specific details: derived from generic resources

Concept	Normal systems	Android specifics	Tool
Incorrect permissions	CWE 732	Android API	Stowaway
Phishing	CWE 601	Sniffing	ComDroid
Lack of input validation	CWE 20	Malicious action launching	ComDroid
SQL injection	CWE 89	Action misuse	
Cross-Side scripting	CWE 79	Activity Hijacking	
		Intent spoofing	
Covert channels	CWE 514, 515	Irrelevant broadcasting	ComDroid
		Broadcast theft	

3.3 Automation Support

For certification to be successful, support for automation is required. We describe three key tools that we have used.

The first is DroidBox [12] which performs a dynamic analysis of the target Android application. Information related to Hashes for the analysed package, Incoming/outgoing network data, File read and write operations, Started services and loaded classes through DexClassLoader, Information leaks via the network file and SMS, Circumvented permissions, Cryptography operations performed using Android API, Listing broadcast receivers, Sent SMS and phone calls is shown in a lengthy report generated at the end of analysis in addition to visualizing the behaviour of the package by means of two graphs: Behaviour and Tree map.

The second tool is ComDroid [8] which is a static analysis tool that detects application communication vulnerabilities. It emits warnings for both sending and receiving based Intent vulnerabilities and gives additional details on when the developer may be misusing Intents. ComDroid parses the disassembled .dex file of the application and logs potential component and Intent vulnerabilities through a static analysis. The tool identifies the location and type of vulnerabilities and possible data leakages/injections. However these warnings could be false positives and needs further manual investigation. A limitation of ComDroid is that it is not capable of detecting vulnerabilities like permission re-delegations discussed in [17].

The final key tool is Stowaway [16] which is also a static analysis tool that detects overprivilege in compiled Android applications. Stowaway determines the set of API calls that an application uses and maps those API calls to permissions to determine the overprivileges. Stowaway determines the maximum set of permissions an application may require. The tool detects over privileges in compiled Android applications determining the set of API calls an application uses and then maps those API calls to permissions to build the permission map which is a necessary for detecting over privilege in proposed approach.

ScanDroid [21] and Kirin [14] are another two miscellaneous tools we also used for this purpose. ScanDroid reverse engineers an Android application's installation image and then scans it through the code and detects possible vulnerabilities defined in an external rule file for application testing. The rule file should be defined by the application analyst as there is no pre-defined rule set available for ScanDroid. ScanDroid in [18] statically analyzes data flows through and across applications/components, while relying on an underlying abstract semantics for Android applications and makes security relevant decisions like whether it is safe to run the application with certain permissions automatically based on such analyses. It extracts security specifications from manifests file and checks the consistency of data flows with those specifications. The authors also note the current limitation of their approach where the Java source code or the compiled JVML byte code is required. Thus their approach cannot be applied directly to installation images. However authors suggest using de-compilers as plug-ins to the front end of the ScanDroid to avoid this issue. At the time of this analysis ScanDroid [18] was not available to us and only ScanDroid [21] was used for this work.

Kirin certifies apps at the time of install by looking at configuration meta data such as requested permissions. If the certification failed, the application is not installed.

In the next section we describe the use the features that we have identified earlier to a specific case study.

4   Case Study

In this section we demonstrate the application of our technique (i.e., the attack surface mentioned in Sect. 2 and concepts mentioned in Table 3) to FBReaderJ [15]. FBReaderJ is an e-book reader for the Android platform and hence written in Java. It performs various e-book functionalities such as searching books in network libraries, downloading books from free libraries, organizing libraries and supports a lot of e-book open formats such as epub, rtf, fb2, html, plain text and mobipocket. As FBReaderJ uses native code it is only compatible with Android ROMs starting from version 1.5.

Although Application's source code is available under the GPL, it should be noted that we did not use it for bulk of this analysis. We tested FBReaderJ using its APK. An APK file represents the code, resources and metadata packaged into a single file for an Android app, and is what is made available on the application market for distribution and download. The tools we use work on APKs and hence there was not need for the source code. We needed the source code only for some tasks such as the examination of the coding standards.

4.1   ApkAnalyser

AndroidManifest.xml and Classes.dex are the two most important items found inside an APK. AndroidManifest.xml contains essential information, including permissions required and other information about the application to the OS that is needed before any of the applications code can be run. Classes.dex contains all the Java code compiled to a bytecode format for the Dalvik Virtual Machine. ApkAnalyser [2] is an essential tool for looking at these files together with application source code as it helps unconditionally in both "threat assessment" and "linking each precondition associated with the attack patterns to coding standards, verification conditions and test cases" steps mentioned in Sect. 2. This tool is a powerful tool as it supports features like exploring code and xml, displaying architecture and dependency, facilitating injection and indexing and analysis resources. For instance, when FBReaderJ.apk is analyes, ApkAnalyser identifies various components including the source and the Android manifest. According to the decoded AndroidManifest.xml three permissions are requested by the application. There are many activities which are implemented by different classes that receive inputs and produce outputs (using Intent filters). See Fig. 2 for some of the relevant aspects of manifest file.

4.2   DroidBox

We use Droidbox for dynamic analysis of Android applications which collects the relevant information identified in Sect. 3.3. For the sake of brevity, we do not reproduce the full report generated by DroidBox for FBReaderJ. Only two graphs: Behaviour and Tree map are presented here in Figs. 3 and 4. Figure 3 shows the temporal order of activities performed by FBReaderJ which assists in the analysis to learn in which order operations are performed. For example, at time points 17.98760795593 and 23.6501660347 the application has performed "Read operations" (their "Path" and "Data" are logged in the detail report) and also at time points 26.0508430004 and 30.842184782 "AlertService" and "DownloadService" has started (their classes are also listed in the detailed report). The time stamp is relative to the analysis starting time and operation details can then be located in the analysis output.

Figure 4 is the treemap for the application that can be used to check similarities between analysed applications and hence for classifying malwares and their similarities. The treemap is a hierarchical (tree-structured) data presented as a set of nested rectangles. Each branch of the tree is given a rectangle, which is then tiled with smaller rectangles representing sub-branches. The most left rectangle of the given tree map represents the "SERVICE" operations performed by FBReaderJ during the monitoring period. The next (middle large) rectangle represents the "FILE" operations branch of the tree which has two leaf nodes "FILEREAD" and "FILEWRITE". It is tiled with two smaller rectangles representing these two leaf nodes as "FILEREAD" in the top and "FILEWRITE" in the bottom. The most right rectangle represents the "NET" operations branch of the tree. The same is tiled with three smaller rectangles to denote three

```
<uses-permission android:name="android.permission.INTERNET">
</uses-permission>
<uses-permission android:name="android.permission.WAKE_LOCK">
</uses-permission>
<uses-permission android:name="android.permission.WRITE_EXTERNAL_STORAGE">
</uses-permission>

<activity android:label="FBReader"
    android:icon="@drawable/fbreader"
    android:name="org.geometerplus.android.fbreader.FBReader"
    android:launchMode="2"
    android:configChanges="160">
    <intent-filter >
<action android:name="android.intent.action.MAIN"></action>
<category android:name="android.intent.category.LAUNCHER"></category>
    </intent-filter>
    <intent-filter >
<action android:name="android.fbreader.action.VIEW"></action>
<category android:name="android.intent.category.DEFAULT"></category>
<data android:scheme="file"></data>
    </intent-filter>
    <intent-filter >
<action android:name="android.intent.action.VIEW"></action>
<category android:name="android.intent.category.DEFAULT"></category>
<category android:name="android.intent.category.BROWSABLE"></category>
<data android:scheme="content" android:pathPattern=".*\\.fb2"></data>
    </intent-filter>
    <intent-filter >
<action android:name="android.intent.action.SEARCH"></action>
    </intent-filter>
```

Fig. 2. A part of AndroidManifest.xml of FBReaderJ

leaf nodes: "NETOPEN" (bottom), "NETWRITE" (middle) and "NETREAD" (top). It should be noted that, in a tree map, a leaf node's rectangle has an area proportional to a specified dimension on the data. Therefore tree maps can be used to check similarities between analysed applications and hence for classifying malwares and their similarities. However it should be noted that the classification is not automated in DroidBox. Certifying application using the information provided by this tool is the analyst's responsibility. In this particular application it seems all the activities (see Fig. 3) performed by the application is legitimate. However, for example, if this application is sending SMSs or phone calls to a particular phone number then it could be viewed as suspicious. This will warrant further investigations as that type of activities cannot be expected from an legitimate e-reader. From a certification view point, it flags the potential existence of covert channels.

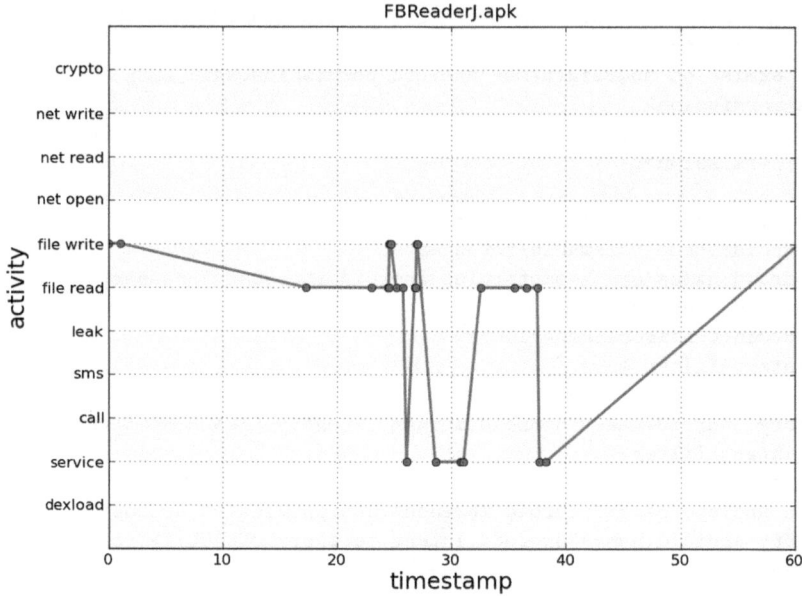

Fig. 3. Behaviour graph

4.3 ComDroid

Exposed communications found by ComDroid from FBReaderJ are given below. Repetitions of similar types of expositions have been removed and replaced by "..." to improve the readability and also due to space constraints.

```
Action Misuse:activity intent:org/geometerplus/android/fbreader/network/AddCatalogMenuActivity
/a(Lorg/geometerplus/android/fbreader /api/PluginApi$MenuActionInfo;) @16(at Source Line: )to
activity component:org.geometerplus.android.fbreader.network.AddCustomCatalogActivity with
android.fbreader.action.ADD_OPDS_CATALOG
... (3 more times similar types of expositions occurred here)
Possible Activity Hijacking: org/geometerplus/android/a/e/a(Landroid/app/Activity;Ljava/lang/
String;) @16, Source Line: , hasExtras=false, hasRead=false, hasWrite=false
... (14 more times similar types of expositions occurred here)
Possible Broadcast Theft (Sniffing): org/geometerplus/android/fbreader/FBReader/onResume()@17,
Source Line: , hasExtras=false, hasRead=false, hasWrite=false
... (3 more times similar types of expositions occurred here)
Possible Malicious Activity Launch: org.geometerplus.android.fbreader.BookmarksActivity, 1
... (12 more times similar types of expositions occurred here)
```

The tool covers communication vulnerabilities listed in Table 3 and logs each vulnerability with the details when the developer may be misusing Intents. For example, in above log, the first warning "Action Misuse" indicates the application is sending activity Intent with a unique action to the activity component.

Fig. 4. Tree map

Unless a component is purposely sending an broadcast Intent, this form of use is considered to be a vulnerability that unnecessarily exposes both the Intent and the receiving component. As explained by ComDroid developers this can be fixed making the Intent explicit and making the receiving component private. The second warning "Possible Activity Hijacking" is occurred in this particular application many times. This indicates that the application is starting an Activity implicitly and a malicious Activity could intercept the Intent and provide its own UI to the user. The data in this Intent can be leaked, and the attacker can also steal any data the user inputs in the UI (phishing attack). In most cases, when multiple Activities can handle an Intent, the user will be prompted to choose the appropriate Activity to launch. However, the user may select an application to be the default application to launch. Consider whether the information being sent in the Activity is sensitive and whether the information the user inputs into the receiving Activity is sensitive. This can be fixed by sending an explicit Intent to start the Activity [9]. (see [9] for more details and for details on other warnings).

4.4   Stowaway

The output produced by Stowaway for the target app FBReaderJ is given below.

```
Stowaway does not think your application is overprivileged.
Required Permissions
Stowaway thinks your application legitimately needs some permissions.
Here, we list the permission-protected API calls, Content Providers, and intents used by
your application.
android.app.NotificationManager.notify: [android.permission.VIBRATE or NONE]
android.os.Environment.getExternalStorageDirectory: [android.permission.WRITE_EXTERNAL_STORAGE]
android.os.PowerManager$WakeLock.acquire: [android.permission.WAKE_LOCK]
android.os.PowerManager$WakeLock.release: [android.permission.WAKE_LOCK]
org.apache.http.impl.client.DefaultHttpClient.: [android.permission.INTERNET]
org.apache.http.impl.client.DefaultHttpClient.execute: [android.permission.INTERNET]
```

In Android applications it is needed to request the appropriate permissions to access protected API calls in the applications' manifests. If an application request for more permissions than it needs, then the application is overprivileged. Preventing overprivilege is an important in conducting threat assessment during the certification process of the application. Stowaway lists the required permissions for the target application together with unnecessary permissions requested by the application. Here Stowaway reports FBReaderJ is not over privileged and all requested permissions (listed above) are legitimate. Security issues that can be covered by this tool are listed in Table 3.

4.5   ScanDroid

The output generated by ScanDroid is given below. However it should be noted that we used the prototype version of the proposed tool and a small rule set defined by us for the demonstration purpose only. We referred to CWE repository in defining the rule set.

```
Scanning files please wait...
Total Files Scanned: 900
Possible Vulnerabilities: 6
Output File generated at: ../ScanDroid/sca/output.txt

Permissions:
INTERNET
WAKE_LOCK
WRITE_EXTERNAL_STORAGE
```

```
Output.txt:
../ScanDroid/sca/src/org/amse/ys/zip/DeflatingDecompressor.java: Line: 73: private native void
endInflating(int k);
... (5 more similar types occurred here)
```

The tool lists the permission requested by the app FBReaderJ and detailed description of the vulnerabilities in a .txt file as shown above. As it is obvious three permissions requested by this application can be considered as completely legitimate according to the nature of the application. But, for example, as shown above using ScanDroid we found many times in this application "Direct Use of Java Native Interface (JNI)" to call code written in another programming language (CWE-111). It exposes the application to weaknesses in that code even if those weaknesses cannot occur in Java (e.g. buffer overflow). However the accuracy depends on the vulnerabilities listed for the analysis. A Sample rule file defined for ScanDroid is given below.

```
openFileOutput
openfileinput
Socket
Webview
[0-9]+[0-9]+[0-9]+[0-9]+
```

4.6   Kirin

Some of the Kirin policies are that an application should not have the permission combinations like

> "SET_DEBUG_APP", "PHONE_STATE, RECORD_AUDIO, and INTERNET"

and

> "PROCESS_OUTGOING_CALL, RECORD_AUDIO, and INTERNET"

at any time.

There are nine similar rules defined in Kirin and if the target application satisfies one or more of the rules, Kirin does not allow one to install the application. KirinManager is the Android application that manages these rules. It can be installed as either user application or system application. The authors used the prebuilt KirinManager which was run as any other user application on the target device. In this work, Kirin allowed us installing FBReaderJ on our Android virtual device which implies that FBReaderJ does not have any combination of permissions that can be act as malicious.

In summary, for FBReaderJ we have found vulnerabilities related to:

- Action misuse
- Malicious activity launch and activity hijacking
- Phishing attack
- Broadcast theft and
- Improper use of JNI.

Note that this is not to conclude that these flaws can be exploited. It is only to point out to the developer potential holes which need to be fixed to make the software more secure.

5 Discussion

The main contribution of this work is the development of a certification process that combines diverse sources. The focus is on automation and hence we use a variety of tools including ComDroid, DroidBox, ScanDroid, Stowaway, along with the Kirin service. This is also combined with vulnerability databases such as CWE. The main checklists are shown in Tables 2 and 3. These checklists include the tool that can be used in the automation of the assurance process. In this work we have not considered extensions to Android that improve security (e.g. IPC inspection) – the aim is to certify programs that run under the current Android model.

Our aspiration is to promote this certification process for wider adoption amongst the app developer community. Part of this adoption would be to release the original source code of the app for wider scrutiny, along with the output provided by the tools chosen for certification. This is to ensure that any gaps left unaddressed by an exiting set of tools and techniques is discovered and highlighted. In the true spirit of free and open source software, we hope that the above initiative will be community adopted and community led. The purpose here is to help transparency of the process, and any systematic enhancements would be supported by the academic community. Clearly, the process stands to be served better if various communities including the developers, academic and research, and users are all involved [6] as their interests converge. An alternative may be for distribution platforms, such as GooglePlay (the new name for Android Market), to mandate this process as part of app upload and distribution. However, it will be a challenge to achieve transparency, and an open framework for continual development as commercial priorities emerge.

An altogether different perspective is for the user community to actively participate in this process. As of now, the users are explicitly responsible for allowing app to be granted permissions to their devices (at the time of download); whether the wider user community carries the same perception is a different issue. A checklist-based process facilitates a structured step-by-step process, where outputs at each step could be recognised and ranked unambiguously. Widespread adoption of mobile platforms, and increasing media coverage of cyber attacks and privacy concerns mean that the user community is increasingly aware of the security challenges.

Acknowledgement. Harsha K. Kalutarage was supported by a grant from the Engineering and Physical Sciences Research Council (EPSRC) (TS/I000291/1).

References

1. Alvi, A.K., Zulkernine, M.: A natural classification scheme for software security patterns. In: Dependable, Autonomic and Secure Computing (DASC), pp. 113–120. IEEE (2011)
2. Apkanalyser. https://github.com/sonyericssondev/ApkAnalyser/wiki
3. BBC.: Google's android racks up its 10 billionth app download, 6 December 2011 (BBC)
4. Bieber, P., et al.: Security and safety assurance for aerospace embedded systems. In: Embedded Real-Time Software and Systems (2012)
5. Cellan-Jones, R.: Android and the economics of app, 7 December 2011. BBC
6. Cerone, A., Siraj, A.S.: Incorporating formal methods in the open source software development process. In: International Workshops on Foundations and Techniques bringing together Free/Libre Open Source Software and Formal Methods (FLOSS-FM 2008) and 2nd International Workshop on Foundations and Techniques for Open Source Software Certification (OpenCert 2008), UNU-IIST Research. Report 398, pp. 26–34 (2008)
7. Chess, B., Arkinm, B.: Software security in practice. IEEE Secu. Priv. **1**(1), 89–93 (2011)
8. Chin, E., Felt, A.P., Greenwood, K., Wagner, D.: Analyzing inter-application communication in android. In: Proceedings of the International Conference on Mobile Systems, Applications, and Services (MobiSys) (2011)
9. Comdroid. http://www.comdroid.org/
10. Conti, M., Nguyen, V.T.N., Crispo, B.: Crepe: context-related policy enforcement for android. In: Proceedings of the 13th international conference on Information, security (2011)
11. Davi, L., Dmitrienko, A., Sadeghi, A.R., Winandy, M.: Privilege escalation attacks on android. In: Proceedings of the 13th international conference on Information, security (2011)
12. Droidbox. http://code.google.com/p/droidbox/
13. Enck, W., Octeau, D., McDaniel, P., Chaudhuri, S.: A study of android application security. In: Proceedings of the 20th USENIX Security Symposium (2011)
14. Enck, W., Ongtang, M., McDaniel, P.D.: On lightweight mobile phone application certification. In: ACM Conference on Computer and Communications Security (2009)
15. Fbreaderj. http://www.fbreader.org/FBReaderJ/
16. Felt, A.P., Chin, E., Hanna, S., Song, D., Wagner, D.: Android permissions demystified. In: Proceedings of the ACM Conference on Computer and Communication Security (CCS) (2011)
17. Felt, A.P., Wang, H.J., Moshchuk, A., Hanna, S., Chin, E.: Permission re-delegation: attacks and defenses. In: Usenix Security 2011, (2011)
18. Fuchs, A.P., Chaudhuri, A., Foster, J.S.: Scandroid: Automated security certification of android applications, technical report cs-tr-4991. Department of Computer Science, University of Maryland, College Park, Maryland, Technical report (2009)
19. Hassell, R., Macaulay, S.: Hacking androids for profit. In: Black Hat USA, Caesars Place, Las Vegas, Nevada, USA, 3–4 August 2011

20. Mead, N.R., Stehney, T.: Security quality requirements engineering (square) methodology. In: SESS '05: Proceedings of the 2005 workshop on Software Engineering for Secure Systems - Building Trustworthy Applications, pp. 1–7. ACM Press, New York (2005)
21. Scandroid. http://www.net-security.org/article.php?id=1613
22. Taguchi, K., Yoshioka, N., Tobita, T., Kaneko, H.: Aligning security requirements and security assurance using the common criteria. In: Fourth International Conference on Secure Software Integration and Reliability Improvement (SSIRI), 2010, pp. 69–77, June 2010
23. Viega, J.: Building security requirements with CLASP. In: SESS '05: Proceedings of the 2005 Workshop on Software Engineering for Secure Systems - Building Trustworthy Applications, pp. 1–7. ACM Press, New York (2005)
24. Vivas, J.L., Agudo, I., López, J.: A methodology for security assurance-driven system development. Requir. Eng. **16**, 55–73 (2011)

Author Index